GEORGIA
DIARY

GEORGIA DIARY

A CHRONICLE OF WAR AND POLITICAL CHAOS IN THE POST-SOVIET CAUCASUS

EXPANDED EDITION

THOMAS GOLTZ

WITH A NEW EPILOGUE: THE OLYMPICS WAR

M.E.Sharpe
Armonk, New York
London, England

This expanded edition of *Georgia Diary* appends a new epilogue: The Olympics War is an account of the author's visit to Georgia during the Russian-Georgian war of August 2008. The epilogue to the 2006 edition is preserved here as Chapter 15.

Library of Congress Cataloging-in-Publication Data

Goltz, Thomas.
  Georgia diary : a chronicle of war and political chaos in the post-Soviet Caucasus / by Thomas Goltz — Expanded ed.
    p. cm.
  Includes index.
  ISBN 978-0-7656-2416-1 (cloth : alk. paper)—ISBN 978-0-7656-1711-8 (pbk. : alk. paper)
    1. Georgia (Republic)—History—1991– 2. Post-communism—Georgia (Republic)
    3. Goltz, Thomas—Travel—Georgia (Republic). Georgia (Republic)—Description and travel. I. Title.

DK678.G658 2009
947.5808′6—dc22   2008052422

Printed in the United States of America

The paper used in this publication meets the minimum requirements of American National Standard for Information Sciences Permanence of Paper for Printed Library Materials, ANSI Z 39.48-1984.

∞

IBT (c)	10	9	8	7	6	5	4	3	2	1
IBT (p)	10	9	8	7	6	5	4	3	2	1

For Alexis, who should have written his own,

and Nana, who was a far greater part of this project

than she ever imagined.

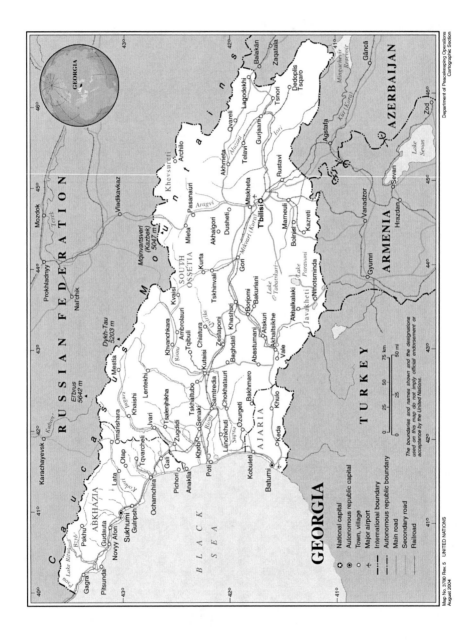

GEORGIA

National capital
Autonomous republic capital
Town, village
Major airport
International boundary
Autonomous republic boundary
Main road
Secondary road
Railroad

The boundaries and names shown and the designations
used on this map do not imply official endorsement or
acceptance by the United Nations.

Map No. 3780 Rev. 5   UNITED NATIONS
August 2004

Department of Peacekeeping Operations
Cartographic Section

vi

Contents

Photographic Essay follows page 191

Delegate: How long will the story take, Arkadi?
I've got to get back to Tbilisi tonight.
Story Teller: It's actually two stories. A few hours.
Tractorist: Couldn't you make it shorter?
Story Teller: No.

—from the Prologue to Bertolt Brecht's *The Caucasian Chalk Circle*

Preface

Mention the word "Georgia" in Montana where I live, and, with a few exceptions, folks will first think of the American state famous for peaches, Sherman's march, the corporate headquarters of Delta Airlines in Atlanta, and a certain song by Ray Charles.

Myself, I managed to get through the first thirty-eight years of my life quite oblivious to the existence of the Republic of Georgia, aside from a general idea that it was that part of the erstwhile USSR that gave birth to Joseph Stalin. The exception to this general ignorance was that I also had a vague awareness that "Georgia" was the backdrop for Bertolt Brecht's play *The Caucasian Chalk Circle*, thanks to my association with a production of that drama in Chicago more than thirty years ago. I have to confess that at the time I was less interested in the metaphysical questions of ownership, nature versus nurture, group belonging, and collective responsibility posed by the self-exiled German playwright than in the charms of a young actress playing the female lead role of the servant girl Grusha. It was only much later that I came to appreciate how central the leftist, philosophic content was to the drama, and, even later, how central that content was to an understanding of modern Georgia itself.

Written when Brecht was still in exile in California in the late 1940s, the piece is essentially a socialist educational play-within-a-play set in the context of the immediate aftermath of World War II, replete with an agitprop Prologue and Epilogue, both of which were rarely included in stage productions in the United States (at least while the Cold War raged). It opens with members of two collective farm villages of antifascist partisan fighters arguing about which has better claim to a stream-fed valley: the Galinsk Kolkhoz that specializes in dairy products or the Rosa Luxemburg Kolkhoz that specializes in the production of fruit and wine. The good Commissar arrives to settle the dispute, but before he decides on who deserves what, both groups of war-traumatized villagers are invited to watch the performance of a traditional storyteller, who warns those assembled that his story will be neither short nor easy to follow, and that no one should even think about leaving early: the subject matter is just too important to miss.

Following the post–World War II Prologue, the play opens with the story-poem of the governor, his wife, and Prince Kazbeki, set at the outbreak of a bloody revolution. The governor is killed and his evil wife runs away to save her own skin, insisting on taking her clothes but forgetting her child. The child ends up in the care of a maid named Grusha, our heroine, who raises the infant as her own.

Then the counterrevolution occurs, and the governor's wife returns to claim her abandoned son. All seems lost until the second (or third, if you count the Prologue) act begins with the entrance of Azdakh, one of the greatest deus ex machina characters in theatrical history (and the most convoluted bundle of contradictions ever invented by Brecht). A hermit and poacher of rabbits, Azdakh discovers he has inadvertently assisted in the escape of the Grand Duke, and thus, in a Bukharin-style self-denunciation, confesses to being an enemy of the people deserving execution. But for a joke, the two "Ironshirt" militiamen he demands arrest him instead decide to elevate him to the position of senior judge of the revolution. He rapidly turns his traveling court into a mockery of the law, trying two or three cases at once to save time, and openly demanding bribes from left, right, and center, with justice served to the highest bidder.

Of course, his is the bench before which Grusha's maternity case will be tried. After demanding bribes from the governor's wife and leering licentiously at Grusha to serve up sex in lieu of lucre, he draws the Circle of Solomon in chalk and invites both mothers to seize an arm of the disputed child and pull him out. Nature versus Nurture is the measure of the law. Grusha fails the test twice—at which point Azdakh awards her the child and beats it out of town before the counterrevolution finds him guilty of diverse (and largely well-deserved) capital crimes.

Curtain down, save for the Epilogue, where the now-edified post–World War II peasants of the Prologue agree to share their land and establish a mill on what will be their communal stream, from which will flow socialist solidarity, and not strife.

* * *

Whatever notional rebellion Brecht's classic play may have been based upon, there were quite a few real ones to draw on as sources. The early nineteenth century peasant revolt in the western Georgian region of Guria that was crushed by General Lermontov seems to be the most obvious candidate, but it is also possible that the playwright was referring to the chaotic career of the fifteenth-century Georgian antihero, Georgi Saakadze, whose life story had just been made into a patriotic mega-film at the height of World War II. Interestingly, Brecht's biographer Eric Bentley even suggests that the *Chalk Circle* was tacitly dedicated to that most (in)famous native son of Georgia and the Caucasus, Iosif Dzhugashvili, who had just defeated Hitler, liberated Brecht's future homeland of East Germany, and elevated the agrarian Russian empire to superpower status in the guise of the Soviet Union. History knows him as Uncle Joe Stalin.

Brecht praising *Stalin*?

Well, quite a few people in today's Georgia continue to praise Stalin, and look back on the bad old days of the USSR as the best times of their lives.

I knew none of this when associated with the *Chalk Circle* production in Chicago or when I first showed up in the newly independent, post-Soviet Republic of Georgia almost two decades later. In retrospect, a re-reading of the *Chalk Circle* might have served as a perfect introduction to the *real* state of Georgia in the post-Soviet Caucasus. Sadly, I walked in during the middle of the movie (or play, as it were), and have been playing intellectual catch-up on Georgian issues ever since.

The crisis list was and is long and almost constant, and certain Georgian friends have long complained to me that my understanding of their country was and is somewhat warped because I have never seen its beauties in normal times. This is not entirely true but close enough to make me respond with the rhetorical question: "What normal times are you talking about?"

There was the December 1991 military putsch against Zviad Gamsakhurdia by a troika of nasty warlords, followed by the return to power of Eduard Shevardnadze in March 1992. Next came the siege, encirclement, and fall of the city of Sukhumi and the rest of the province of Abkhazia in September 1993, with the attendant flood of refugees, social collapse, and yet another brief civil war that petered out in 1994. There was the energy crisis of 1995 and 1996 with blackouts of the capital city on New Year's Eve, as the newly wealthy frolicked on the slopes of an up-market ski resort and heated their private swimming pools while people froze to death only a mile away. Brigands controlled major highways in 1997, and the eightieth year celebration of national independence fizzled out in the face of renewed war in and over Abkhazia in 1998. This was followed by the Russian threat in 1999 and again in 2000 to invade part of the country in order to eradicate Chechen refugees whom Moscow was calling "terrorists." A tour through the country in 2001 revealed world-class corruption in high places and desperate gloom and pessimism in low ones, a state of affairs compounded in 2002 by the collapse of the power grid, and the attempt by Moscow to dominate the economy by leveling visa restrictions against "guest workers" from Georgia. These workers were trying to enter the Russian economy because there were no jobs at home, unless relatives pooled their savings to buy a position with the traffic police or in customs. Then, finally, in November 2003, people quite simply had had enough and rose to depose the man who had ruled Georgia, both Soviet and post-Soviet, for something like forty years: Eduard Shevardnadze.

I had been "following" Shevardnadze in the usually understood, journalistic sense of the word for thirteen years. Our first contact was at a press conference at the Moscow embassy of the Islamic Republic of Iran in early September 1991. He had briefly returned to his post as Soviet foreign minister in the waning days of Mikhail Gorbachev's government following the August 19 abortive putsch that signaled the end of the Soviet state. The last was at an oil conference in Istanbul in June 2002, when Shevy signed his autograph to an old black-and-white photograph showing a much younger and almost sinister version of himself standing next to his IMZ 650 cc, BMW knock-off motorcycle.[1] In between those dates I had met with Shevardnadze on numerous occasions, either in the form of formal interviews in Tbilisi, at state funerals and state birthdays in Turkey and Azerbaijan (those of Turgut Özal and Heydar Aliyev, respectively), or within the intense context of being under fire together in Sukhumi, when we had almost daily casual encounters, even if not a lot of words were spoken. And, throughout that decade of association, I believed I had gotten to know Shevardnadze to some degree—at least to the degree that a public figure allows a journalist and outsider to know him or her.

Cool to cold, the former Georgian president, former Soviet foreign minister, former Communist Party boss, former police general, and former motorcycle rider, Shevy was nothing if not a sly survivor who had managed to rise for more than forty years through the cut-throat Communist Party bureaucracy (starting more or less at the time of the demise of his fellow Georgian Lavrenti Beria) by being an astute reader of political tea leaves and high, intraparty intrigue. And yet, under his ten-year stewardship in post-Soviet Georgia, his native land had fallen from being one of the wealthiest and most pleasant of the fifteen republics to emerge from the rubble of the USSR to become one of the poorest and most chaotic of the lot.

To be fair, the collapse in status from that of a socialist-style industrialized economy to that of a third world agrarian state did not all happen on his watch. Georgia was already heading into free-fall in 1992, following the one-year failed experiment with populist nationalism (one is tempted to call it "lukewarm fascism") represented by Georgia's first post-Soviet leader, Zviad Gamsakhurdia. When Shevy returned "home" to Georgia from Moscow, the ship of state was already foundering on the shoals of social collapse and civil war. But the promise of years of administrative experience in the Kremlin, coupled with his international reputation based on his role in bringing the Cold War to an end, was never fulfilled: under Shevardnadze, things just got worse.

While lionized in the West as the personification of the "good" reformed communist, in Georgia, Shevardnadze was increasingly seen as the overbearing guest you could not get rid of. It was Shevardnadze who was blamed for losing Abkhazia due to incompetent command and for overseeing what even his closest aides called "the most corrupt government to emerge from the lands of the former USSR." Even if he had never directly indulged in graft and kickbacks himself, Shevardnadze had turned a blind eye when his immediate family sidled up to foreign investors interested in everything from luxury hotels to cell-phone systems and even bottled water, suggesting that having clan members on the corporate board as do-nothing associate directors might secure certain "competitive" advantages.

There was nothing new or particularly shocking about this sort of economic nepotism within the context of Georgia, the post-Soviet Caucasus, the former Soviet Union, or even countries and economies outside it. Relatives of prime ministers and presidents have been shamelessly abusing the names of high officeholders from Indonesia to Alaska since the dawn of time. The scandalous involvement of Baroness Margaret Thatcher's son, Mark, with coup-making mercenaries in Africa is well documented, as are the ridiculous efforts of Jimmy Carter's brother, Billy, to make a quick buck on the family name in Libya. George W. Bush milked the fact that he was his father's son in several (usually failed) oil deals when George the Elder served as vice president under Reagan and then as president. During Bill Clinton's first term, a brother (or brothers) of Hillary Rodham Clinton showed up in Batumi, banking on the family connection to turn a little coin in the local hazelnut bazaar. This story only came to light after a certain Lebanese-American dealmaker named Roger Tamras pitched up in Tbilisi pushing an oil pipeline deal with one hand and showing off a picture of himself with Bill Clinton in the other, acquired at the White House after Tamras had plunked down a cool quarter million bucks for the pleasure of a night's sleep in the Lincoln bedroom. To be sure, this is all chump change compared with the financial antics associated with the Bush White House idea of access a la Enron and Halliburton. The list goes on and on. . . .

What made the increased sleaze surrounding Shevardnadze so odious was not that it was so obvious and without any shame on the part of the gougers, but that it had the smell of permanence about it. Shevardnadze and his entourage just sort of assumed they could go on indefinitely, that his term of office would always be extended, that he would always remain in power, and that this state of affairs would be sanctioned in the West because the former Soviet Politburo member, former Soviet foreign minister, and former Communist Eduard Shevardnadze had pulled the Red Army out of Afghanistan, negotiated the end of the Cold War, allowed for the reunification of Germany, and let the Soviet client Saddam Hussein dangle during the first Gulf War.

The West owed Shevy a debt of thanks, said everyone from Maggie Thatcher to Helmut Kohl, Francois Mitterand, and certainly James Baker III. *Shevy was Georgia and Georgia was Shevy* in the eyes of anyone who had ever heard of the place.

In the West, at least.

The internal dynamic was quite different. While many Georgians truly welcomed Shevardnadze's return in 1992 as a promise of reestablishing some manner of stability, continued chaos and corruption associated with his government slowly but surely eviscerated his base support. This was true among both the late Soviet *nomenklatura* class to which Shevardnadze so thoroughly belonged, as well as the new, Western-oriented, American-educated class to whom the charade of democratic development as expressed in periodic rigged elections was both embarrassing and offensive. Western monitors, however, never did much more than slap Shevardnadze's wrist. It took three years for Shevardnadze to delegate a commission to investigate allegations of widespread voter fraud in the parliamentary elections of 1999, for example—and then only under pressure from the Parliamentary Assembly of the Council of Europe, which threatened to expel Georgia from that body unless such a commission was created. In any event, they could not do any meaningful work because all documents pertaining to the 1999 polls had been "lost." Shevardnadze's victory the following year for a second, five-year term as president was also marred by both uninvestigated irregularities and unseemly horse-trading with Adjarian strongman "Batono" (Lord Protector) Aslan Abashidze, who pulled out of the race at the last moment and cast his support to archrival Shevardnadze in exchange for unspecified (presumably economic) favors. Indeed, despite great personal animosity, Shevy had cut so many deals with Abashidze in Batumi that he was as implicated in grand larceny at the expense of the state as the Lord Protector himself.

The last straw for both the young idealists and the exhausted man-in-the-street was the attempt to rig parliamentary elections in 2003. This was not exactly because Georgians were uniquely attached to the concepts of democracy and the rule of law, but rather because so many people feared that the new parliament would somehow come up with a new law allowing Shevardnadze to run for president a third time, extend the presidential term from five years to ten, or create a new office loftier than that of president that would allow Shevy to continue to run the show because he always had run the show, because it was the only thing he knew how to do.

Georgians were sick of Shevardnadze, even if they had worked for him all their lives. President Mikheil "Misha" Saakashvili himself had served as minister for justice for a year before resigning in disgust and going into opposition. Zurab Zhvania, the late prime minister in Saakashvili's government, had served in that role under Shevardnadze, too. And if celebrated in the West as belonging to a "new generation of post-Soviet politicians," their service for and under Shevardnadze was not forgotten by many locals. Within three months of the Rose Revolution of November 2003, the atmosphere of liberation from the past was getting poisoned by the all-too-familiar Georgian habit of accusation by innuendo and malicious rumor mongering about who was really in the pay of Moscow, or America, or Israel, or Armenia, or the centuries-old Masonic conspiracy.

All that was standard Georgian political culture and hardly bodes well for the future of Saakashvili's regime of young reformers. Even as Misha stood beside George W. Bush on Freedom Square in Tbilisi in May 2005, mutterings of discontent were growing and continue to grow. As this book goes to press, the Georgian grapevine is rife with stories of Saakashvili's late-night philandering (not necessarily a political minus in the Caucasus, where many folks thought *better* of Bill Clinton for his indiscretions) as well as the concomitant egomania displayed by Georgia's most recent leader. By the autumn of 2005, former associates had even gone so far as to create an "anti-Soros Movement," in order to preserve traditional Georgian values, which they claimed were being swept away due to Saakashvili's willy-nilly embrace of globalization and the international rhetoric espoused by George W. Bush. Time, as they say, will tell.

In November 2003, however, there was a specific target—and that target was Eduard Shevardnadze. With roses in their hands and indignation in their throats, Saakashvili and his people putsched Shevardnadze from power, and, rather than stay and fight or flee the country to become a symbol *of something* in exile, he might be said to have fallen on his sword gracefully, retiring to his dacha outside Tbilisi, and wishing his successors good luck in governing the modern mess that is Georgia.

That story, of course, goes on.

As for the one related within the pages of this book, the focus is primarily on the Shevardnadze period, and especially on the unnecessary and tragic disaster of the war in Abkhazia, which continues to haunt Georgia to this day. Like Brecht's opus written some sixty years ago, it is a complex tale that will be neither short nor easy to follow, but hopefully edifying and even rewarding for those who make the effort to get through it.

Thomas Goltz
Preface to the 2006 Edition

Note

1. See page 83, below. The photograph was a private joke between us. In late August 2000, I had led a group of a dozen IMZ 650 cc sidecar-motorcycles and assorted support and salvage vehicles in a grand adventure down the two-thousand-kilometer-long Baku–Tbilisi–Ceyhan crude oil pipeline route that links Azerbaijani oil fields in the Caspian Sea to the main Turkish oil terminal on the eastern Mediterranean. Shevardnadze had deigned to receive us as we passed through the Georgian capital, and during our meeting, to the shock and dismay of his staff, he openly derided our idea of adventure travel. "Two thousand kilometers?" he said through his translator. "That's nothing. When I was a member of the Young Communist League, I rode *six thousand* kilometers across the length of the USSR and solo. . . ." Then he chuckled, ordered his staff to donate four cases of the best Georgian wine to our luggage, and invited us all to pose for a picture after shaking all our hands in his strange, almost clammy grip.

Acknowledgments and Special Thanks

There are many people to whom I am indebted for encouraging me to have the confidence to write this book. The reader will meet a number of these individuals within the context of the coming pages. Among them: Nunu, Nana (many Nanas, actually), Nino, Nata, diverse Zurabs, Vatangs, Gias, and Giorgis. The list is not only long, but made much longer by the anonymity of many angels who somehow found, saved, and/or nurtured me at odd and often awful moments during the course of the decade-long journey it has taken to start and finish this work. Some were taxi drivers who did not charge me; others were obscure homeowners in provincial towns who opened their doors after curfew. Shevardnadze's chief of staff Petr Mamradze and I somehow linked due to an intense interest in Hemingway; Alexander Rondeli and I bonded while marooned on a sailboat in an oil spill in the middle of Baku Bay in Azerbaijan; Gia Janjgava and I were nearly killed together in Sukhumi. Oktay Chitzia introduced me to the subject of the Abkhaz diaspora community in Turkey (and returnees to Abkhazia), and Tony Borden of the Institute of War and Peace Reporting managed to lure me out of self-exile in Montana with an invitation to a well-meaning (if ultimately useless) conference on peace and reconciliation in Tbilisi way back when in the summer of 1996, after I had become a burnout from the wars of the Caucasus, and had sworn that I would never return.

Among the outlanders associated with the early, nasty, tragic but also often ridiculously fun and funny post-Soviet Georgia that is the subject of this book, I feel particularly indebted to a handful of strangers who became lifelong friends: Alexis Rowell, Lawrence Sheets, Liam McDowell, and Steve LeVine. Without their generous sharing of crash-pad space, telephone time, and intellectual, emotional, and editorial support, my extended sojourns to Georgia would have been much more difficult and maybe even impossible. Thanks, guys. And, while the essence of this book is the attempt to create a literary version of the raw data that I collected as a journalist and observer between 1991 and 2006, there is no question about my intellectual debt to pioneering scholars on the Caucasus, either pre- or post-Soviet. Accordingly, I would like to issue a huge "Thank You" to Ron Suny, Stephen Jones, Paul Henze, Tamara Dragadze, and others for their insights; and special thanks to Giorgi Derluguian not only for his academic insights but also his wicked sense of Soviet-style, sociological humor.

The Divine Miss Margie Kidder has been a constant source of encouragement (and an occasional traveling companion to the region). Judith Gunderson Muncy has been an extraordinary critic of the manuscript through at least three permutations, as has Natalie ("the Jaguar") Sudman, who pointed out to me that multiple descriptions of intoxication are about as interesting to a nondrinker as stories of smoking yet another "last cigarette" are to former smokers. Thanks, too, to "J.K." Kimmel for her comments and corrections in the early stages of the manuscript. Particular editorial thanks, however, are due Jeffrey Werbock for his detailed efforts to align my various subjects with my various cases, as well as for his criticism of content within context. He has been indispensable in the elevation of this manuscript to book form.

Special knee-bending is due editorial director Patricia Kolb for having once again managed to convince M.E. Sharpe that producing another Goltz book is a good thing, to editorial coordinator Maki Parsons for tying together loose ends and making slash and burn decisions about the manuscript, copy editor Therese Malhame for polishing up the results, production editor Ana Erlić for dragging it all to the finish line, and my agent Diana Finch for having stuck with her client (me) in good times and bad. Lastly, thanks to Volkmar Sander who was the man who really introduced me to Bertolt Brecht and his peculiar, double-edged voice and vision.

> *Ach, was ist es fuer Zeiten*
> *Wann ein Gespraech um Baeume*
> *Fast ein Verbrechen ist . . .*

> *Ah, what times are these*
> *When a conversation about trees*
> *Is nearly a crime . . .*

And very special thanks to Tale Heydarov, Chairman of The European Azerbaijan Society TEAS) for his support to diverse Goltz Caucasus projects over the years, including the journey to Georgia during the dark days of August 2008.

Prologue: A (New) Caucasian Chalk Circle

It is May 26, 1998, the eightieth anniversary of Georgian independence from tsarist Russia and the date chosen as the equivalent of the Fourth of July by the citizens of the former Soviet Republic. They might have chosen April 9, the day in 1991 when the current generation declared themselves to be free and independent of the Soviet Union, but the 1918 date has wider resonance and gives more people reason to celebrate.

Rather than leading parades through the handsome capital, Tbilisi, or standing at the head of the receiving line at the gala reception set for the evening, however, Georgian President Eduard Shevardnadze is in virtual hiding, as are almost all senior members of his government.

No, "hiding" is too strong a word. "Shevy"—the nickname given by George Bush the Elder because he could not pronounce "Shevardnadze"—is not the type to duck trouble. When he returned to his chaotic, war-torn homeland in 1992, it was to face a series of coup attempts, bungled assassinations, and a civil war or two. "Balls of brass" is an accurate, if graphic way to describe the man who got the Soviet Army to withdraw from Afghanistan, who convinced Mikhail Gorbachev to allow the reunification of Germany, and who was the first to denounce the bungled "hard-liner" coup in Moscow on August 19, 1991, that signaled the end of the USSR. Another—and arguably more descriptive—moniker used by Shevardnadze's friends and enemies is "the Silver Fox," due both to his mane of shaggy white hair and his political cunning.

But Shevardnadze is not being sly, now. It would be more accurate to say that he and his entourage have entered a period of mourning, or maybe more charitably that they have conveniently removed themselves from the public eye due to acute political embarrassment. This is too bad, because I had been looking forward to seeing Shevy again. Actually, our last encounter had only been a few weeks before when we waved to each other as Shevardnadze sped out of Baku airport in the neighboring post-Soviet Republic of Azerbaijan in an armored Mercedes limousine. Shevy had just dropped in to wish Azerbaijani President Heydar Aliyev a very happy seventy-sixth birthday. The irony of the moment was delicious. During Soviet times, Shevardnadze and Aliyev were both heavy hitters in the Politburo and had devoted most of their professional lives to the spread of international (or at least, Kremlin-style) communism. Now both had recast themselves as local patriots, alleged democrats and believers in the free market economy, and were attempting to ally their small countries to the West, thus removing the Caucasus from continued Russian influence.

Given the tight security surrounding Aliyev's birthday, I was obliged to content myself with the waved greeting from Shevy as he sat in the back seat of the speeding Mercedes. It wasn't like the old days anymore, when you could just about drop in on the Silver Fox for a short chat about the nature of the changing world. And it certainly wasn't like the camaraderie of shared danger we had established during the siege and fall of Sukhumi, the capital of the breakaway Georgian region of Abkhazia. With bombs dropping and bullets flying, it would be a gross exaggeration to suggest that we indulged in extended philosophical conversation every day; a nod or wave of "glad to see you are still alive" said enough.

But now there wasn't even that thin rapport.

Shevardnadze was held behind a constant ring of security and if he had ever been interested in what real folks actually thought, dreamed, or hoped, the possibility of learning about it had been finally and irrevocably terminated with his self-imposition of the "gilded cage" sometime around the last assassination attempt against him the year before. In the years I had "known" him, I had never seen Shevy duck anything before, but he sure was ducking now.

* * *

It is renewed war in Abkhazia that forced Shevardnadze to cancel the festivities associated with the declaration of the first Georgian Republic eighty years ago. Although every one is blaming the Abkhaz (and thus the obscure forces in Russia that back them), the sad fact is that it is the Georgians themselves who have created the mess. It would seem that a number of nationalist guerrillas known as the Forest Brethren (others say it was the rival White Legion) decided to mark the anniversary of statehood by raising the Georgian flag atop the government building in the ghost-town city of Gali. The problem is that Gali lies on the far side of the Inguri River that divides Georgia proper from the breakaway (Autonomous) Republic of Abkhazia. From the Abkhaz perspective, the guerrilla infiltration is not only a serious violation of the existing cease-fire accords, but an open act of war. In addition to attempting to fly the national flag over the local Abkhaz administration building, the guerrillas also tried to kill the local Abkhaz administrator, an old pal of mine, Valeri Lomia.

A small, prematurely white-haired, former schoolteacher from the ugly coastal town of Ochamchira, Valeri is a man burdened with an almost impossible task. He is supposed to interface with the 250,000 Georgian/Mingrelian refugees who were flushed from Abkhazia in 1993, or at least the 30,000–60,000 (no one knows for sure) of them who have returned to their homes in Gali as part of a Moscow-brokered, Georgian/Abkhaz ceasefire and disengagement agreement, allegedly monitored by Blue Beret observers from the UN. Theoretically, Valeri is kind of like the returnees' mayor. But the reality is that he has little contact with the returnees because most of them are Georgians who hate and thus refuse to recognize the Abkhaz as the authorities of Gali (or the rest of Abkhazia). The returnees periodically express their antipathy by trying to kill him, and Valeri has narrowly escaped more than one assassination attempt. Other members of the Abkhaz administration in Gali have not been so lucky.

The same with the Russian "peacekeepers" who theoretically provide security in the Gali zone, who are themselves often targets of terrorist attacks, and thus limit their patrols to the main roads, or simply confine themselves to their barracks to drink themselves stupid and engage in acts of fratricide on a regular basis. Over the past five years or so, hundreds of these Russian grunts, collectively referred to as the CISPKF, or Commonwealth of Independent States Peace Keeping Force, have been killed or killed themselves along with a few of their friends unfortunate enough to be in the vicinity when the guy with a gun flips out.

Then there is the United Nations Observation Mission in Georgia, or UNOMIG, a 100-odd man contingent of unarmed military men drawn from some thirty member countries of the United Nations, who are stationed in the Gali region to keep an eye on Abkhaz militiamen, Georgian returnees (particularly the White Legion and Forest Brethren militiamen among them), and—although no one will admit this openly—the Russian peacekeepers. But no one is "observing" anything right now. Not only have the Abkhaz militia moved into the region in force and rooted out the Brethren and/or Legion, they have also forced most ethnic Georgians who had returned to the region under UN protection to flee back across the river. Over 200 guerrillas are said to have been killed and 50,000 civilians "ethnically cleansed." Add those figures to the 10,000–15,000 soldiers and civilians killed and 250,000 people flushed from their homes during the "hot" days of the conflict in 1992 and 1993, and you have the parameters of human misery in Abkhazia.

UNOMIG soldiers I have spoken with, some of whom are old friends from other travels to Abkhazia and whose word I trust, dispute the number of 50,000 ethnically cleansed Georgians announced by Tbilisi. The UN men say the number is probably closer to 20,000. The truth of the matter is that even the UN guys really do not know about numbers of refugees or anything else that is happening in Gali because their observation patrols have been shut down entirely on both sides of the Inguri River that delineates Georgia from Abkhazia. And their patrols were pretty limited before.

Still, as professionals, they were forced to admit that from a military point of view, the Abkhaz were doing what needed to be done: rooting out the guerrillas with overwhelming force and depriving them of their base of support. That meant destroying the rebuilt homes of suspected guerrilla supporters. That is what Israel does when it flattens the homes of radical Palestinians in the West Bank, what the Russians are doing in Chechnya, what Slobodan Milosevic tried to do in Kosovo, and what Saddam Hussein did to the Iraqi Kurds before he was flattened himself by the Americans, who are now doing in Iraq what they did in Vietnam.

"One man's ethnic cleansing is another man's overdue police action," said a cynical German captain, who asked to remain anonymous. That is the sort of remark over which a soldier might lose rank if attributed to him when promotion time comes around.

Meanwhile, all along the Inguri River the horizon is covered by a gray haze, the smoke belching from the flames consuming row after row of newly reconstructed village houses on the far bank. The crowd of women and men on our side of the river watch in stunned silence, only occasionally broken by the anguished howl of a homeowner who recognizes the most recent conflagration as emitting from his or her abode. I ask one weeping woman where she is from, and she points to one of the fires across the river and says one word.

"Taglioni," she whispers.

I am pretty sure I know what her house in Taglioni looks like. Maybe I have been there before, although if I had I would probably recognize the woman or she would recognize me. The problem with recognizing refugees is that they all seem to look the same after awhile, losing their individual appearances into the monotony of misery. The houses are more distinct, all built with a sense of rural grace and even style. The potholed roads around Zugdidi and all through western Georgia are lined with fine examples of this. The curious thing is that most houses were built during the Soviet period and reflect a prosperity that one does not associate with communism. More to the point, the tourism and citrus plantation-based prosperity they enjoyed during the bad old days of the Evil Empire are long gone, and if I were a resident of any of the many once prosperous but now poverty-infused towns of western Georgia, I would remember the nasty past as the Golden Days of tranquility and plenty, and I would probably follow to the ends of the earth any two-bit Pied Piper preaching the possibilities of returning to that fabled land. Actually, just being a voyeur observing the dichotomy between what was and what is or has become in Georgia, is enough to start turning me into a quasi-commie myself.

On the fringes of the crowd, a young man with a crazed look on his face sobs about his missing wife and two children, muttering darkly about "getting a Kalashnikov" and seeking his revenge if he cannot find them or if he finds them dead.

"*Tikho, tikho*," I say in Russian, and offer him a couple of cigarettes. "Calm down."

"Traitors, traitors . . . " he babbles. He is not talking about the Abkhaz or even the Russians whom almost all blame for this most recent catastrophe. He is maligning the government of Eduard Shevardnadze in Tbilisi.

The reason for his disdain and fury is obvious.

Although Shevardnadze has often delivered dark warnings about the "tragic results" of what might happen if the guerrillas continue to run out of control, there is good reason to believe that his government knew perfectly well what the Brethren and Legion members were up to when they crossed the river and started shooting up Abkhaz. The problem is finding hard evidence, because that is on the far side of the Inguri. Accordingly, there is only one thing to do. Go to Gali, on an unofficial inspection tour.

Happily, I am not alone. Joining me is my old pal and fellow crisis correspondent, Lawrence Sheets. Uncle Larry and I have gone through a lot of Caucasus craziness together over the years—Chechnya, Karabakh, and, of course, the siege and fall of Sukhumi, the Abkhaz capital. I guess that means that we are "war correspondents," although I hate that term. Still, it is a distinction that carries certain responsibilities, like going where others won't and don't think you should. Like right now. Everyone on the Georgian side, including the UNOMIG guys, thinks we are insane.

"Saddle up?" I ask Larry after we had grown tired of talking to UN troops who did not know anything and had grown bored with taking tear-jerk testimony from the mass of new refugees on the Georgian side of the lines.

"Git along, lil' doggies!" Sheets replies.

We jump into my gleaming, white Avis rental that I had acquired in Baku a few days before, flash the registration at the stunned border guards, and ease across the bridge.

"Good thing I've got Azeri plates on this thing," I joke, trying to stay cool. Quipping often helps control the queasy feeling in your gut. "Maybe they'll think we're diplomats."

"Avis learns you took this baby into Abkhazia, they'll never give you another car for any money," chortles Sheets.

An Avis rental car in Abkhazia, yeah . . . We figure the only thing that could happen to the car would be for it to hit a landmine, and then neither Sheets nor myself would really care what Avis had to say because we would be dead.

Haha, we laugh.

"What do you want?" asks one of the sullen soldiers at the Abkhaz check-point on the far side of the bridge, casually sticking the barrel of his gun in the window.

"Abzerus," I say in Abkhazian, probably saying "good-bye" instead of "hello." "Tell your *nachalnik* Sasha that his old drinking buddy Tomas is here," I add in Russian.

The kids look at each other and then back at me.

"Commander Sasha got killed at the post yesterday," says a baby-faced blonde boy. "I'm in charge now." He must be all of sixteen.

Abkhazia is not recognized by any country in the world and uses the Russian ruble as the national currency. But the government does like to issue its own entrance and exit permits out of general principle. The kid with the gun notices and likes the fact that I have one, although mine has long expired. I keep it in my second passport because if Georgian border guards saw it I might get arrested, shot, or declared persona non grata.

"Ah, my brother!" cries the youthful guard, my passport in hand. "Let us drink to Commander Sasha, while I call Sukhumi to get clearance!"

This is bad news, because it means we are about to fall into a so-called *chacha* ambush, and be forced to drink moonshine grappa here on the border while waiting to get through to the capital on the horribly antiquated Abkhaz telephone system.

"We have an appointment with Lomia," says Lawrence, referring to the diminutive schoolteacher who runs the Abkhaz administration in Gali. "Where is he?"

"Right here," says Valeri, coming out from behind the shattered security shack. "You don't have an appointment, but it is good to see you both again."

Bundling Lomia into the back seat of the Avis-mobile, we start down the ten-mile stretch of potholes that passes for a road linking the border to Gali town. Determining how much new destruction the new fighting has created is difficult because the old destruction is still in such ample supply. Both sides of the road are lined with the burnt-out shells of buildings, but that had been the case the last time I had driven down the road with Miss Kidder earlier that year, and the time before that, and the time before that, too.

"Nice car," Lomia remarks, patting the back seat.

"Avis," I say, as if that is the make of the car, which is actually a Turkish-made Fiat called a "Shahin," or hawk.

"What's that?" asks Lomia.

It is kind of hard to explain, given the lack of cultural context. Maybe they had some sort of car rental system back in Soviet times, when Abkhazia served as the Red Riviera, but even then the cars would have been something big and awful or small and broken. I remember hitchhiking a ride down the same road in 1997, and catching a lift from a state minister whose vehicle was literally held together with duct tape and kept breaking down due to the high water content in the gasoline.

We pull the Avis-mobile into Gali town. The place is thick with militiamen.

"We will exterminate every last pocket of resistance!" snarls a brick out-house of a man dressed in the standard, Soviet-era blue and white muscle shirt under his open battle fatigues. "We will crush them without mercy!"

As for the UNOMIG who were supposed to be in sector precisely to prevent this sort of crushing, well, they were nowhere to be seen—which is just as well, given the utter failure of their mission.

"Look at this!" says Lomia, in his booming baritone voice, waving a sheaf of official protests he had filed with the UN mission, documenting repeated Georgian violations of the spirit, letter, and substance of the ceasefire accord that theoretically bound both sides of the conflict to a number of peaceful pledges. "The United Nations mission here never investigated one complaint, never disarmed one guerrilla! We have found whole ammunition dumps!"

"Show us," we say.

Valeri tries to explain that it is too dangerous, that the situation is still not completely under control. What he really means is that he does not have any escort vehicle.

"Just give us a guide, and we'll use the Avis car," I suggest.

"You'll bring the soldiers back when you're through?"

"We promise."

"OK," says Valeri. "And try to tell the truth about what you see. We are getting really sick of the sob song about ethnic cleansing they sing all the time."

We are interrupted by the arrival of a large man with an extremely sad face and a shock of white hair. Valeri appears to be genuinely surprised to see him, but the timing of the man's arrival is almost too close to what we in the trade call "Central Casting," namely, a person or event staged for the benefit of appreciative journalists. In this case, the white-haired guy introduces himself. He says he is a Georgian and claims to have been taken hostage by the White Legion, thrown in prison across the river in Zugdidi, and tortured a bit before having been released to return to Abkhazia. In his hands he has a petition signed by some two dozen or so Georgian families who live (or lived) on a collective farm in the Gali region. They are all asking for permission to return to the farm and specifically asking for Abkhaz protection from the White Legion and Forest Brethren—that is, they are Georgians asking the Abkhaz for protection from other Georgians.

"We are so tired of this war," says the man, who identifies himself as the director of the collective farm. "All we want is peace and security, and we do not care what they call the place we live or who claims to control it."

Our next stop is the obligatory vodka-fueled lunch at Valeri's apartment, located on the third or fourth floor of a standard, Soviet-style slab-cement structure in some ugly part of Gali. If there is an elevator, it has not worked in ten years. The food consists of hominy grits with a chunk of goat cheese shoved in for salt and flavor, a variety of pickled vegetables, and *khatchapuri*—cheese melted inside a loaf of flat bread. Both Georgia and Abkhazia claim the above menu as their national cuisine. Both claim the same creation myth about God giving them the lands he had reserved for Himself because they were both out drunk when he was distributing the earth among the peoples. Both claim royal heritage from many of the same kings and queens, and both drink more homemade hard liquor than any other group of human beings on earth that I have ever encountered. So much for those ancient, unreconcilable, atavistic cultural differences that divide Georgians from Abkhaz, at least around the table.

Glug glug.

Down goes the first toast after a fifteen-minute oration by Valeri about peace, truth, fraternity, absent friends, and so on.

"How do you like this Abkhaz vodka?" asks Valeri, cracking open a new bottle. "It is a lot better than that Georgian poison they are trying to export to Russia. Do you drink it?"

"*Ya ne glupyi,*" says Larry, in Russian. "I'm not an idiot."

Everyone takes another shot of the most excellent Abkhaz vodka that tastes, of course, exactly the same as the much-maligned Georgian product across the Inguri. By the time our escort of two Abkhaz soldiers arrives, we are getting drunk, which is good because when we jump into the Avis car and turn off the main road to drive to our target village, our Abkhaz escort asks us to slow down because the road is mined. The vodka keeps that sick feeling in my stomach down to an acceptable level as I ease the car around water-filled potholes and creep it straight over scattered debris.

"Stay away from that one," says one of the militiamen in the back seat, pointing to a small pile of shattered blue bathroom tile scattered over a water pocket in the broken tarmac. I have already seen it and meant to avoid. If there isn't a mine under that chunk of rubble, I will eat the tiles for breakfast.

"Boom," I say, playfully jerking the steering wheel in the direction of the pile.

"Haha," says Larry, trying to control the urge to grab my hand.

The two Abkhaz militiamen sitting in the back seat have closed their eyes; their lips are moving as if in silent prayer.

Rounding a bend, we almost run into a jeep piled high with militiamen and their trophies—boxes and boxes of saucer-shaped mines. They had been collecting the killers from the divots and cracks and rubble on the road above, and the de-mining team was now working its way down the way we had come up. The militiamen also had another interesting trophy—a dark blue, riot-control helmet with a flip-down lid to protect your eyes, and made out of Kevlar. It is not standard issue anywhere in the lands of the former USSR, and the Abkhaz militiamen know it. As if further proof were needed, they bring our attention to the manufacturer's label inside the helmet.

"Look!" they shout. "The Georgians are receiving aid from the Arabs!"

This is an interesting charge, in that the Abkhaz are usually described as "Muslims" fighting against "Christian" Georgians even though they might be better described, collectively, as "Soviet-style animists." Anyway, I take the helmet from the tree-and-water worshipper holding it and take a look at the letters printed inside the head cover. The label is written in Hebrew.

We get back in the Avis-mobile and continue up the road, trying to keep our tire tracks in the dust-painted path made by the jeep until one of the guys in the backseat tells me to turn off the main road to a deeply rutted and very wet tractor path on the right.

"I think I'll take the field," I say, and move the car gently on to grass. At least you could see what was in front of you.

"You guys are real pros at mined roads," one of the Abkhaz remarks.

"Practice makes perfect," I say, lying. It is, in fact, my first time at the wheel while negotiating eternity. The beauty of it is that all you have to do is not die or have your legs blown off or bowels blown out, and you can claim expertise and demand profuse thanks from everyone else in the car.

"Well?" Larry asks everyone in general. "Where is the evidence of the regular Georgian army around here?"

"There," says the second Abkhaz, pointing at some exposed dirt on a crest overlooking the Inguri.

We get out to inspect what reveals itself to be a line of trenches. They could have been dug a day, a week, a month, or even a year before.

"Nothing here," I say to Larry, disappointed.

He isn't. Disappointed that is. Because he is standing in a pile of AK-47 rounds that have not been shot.

Bullets!

Our guides react as if they have found the mother lode of M&Ms, instantly forgetting us while they fill their pockets with precious shells. Ammo was and is in chronic short supply due to international sanctions. The pair could now not only reload their Kalashnikovs but also share the bounty with friends.

"And look at this," says Sheets. Behind a bush he has found a dark green wooden box packed with RPG-7 rocket-propelled grenades, the oilskin slips still in place. The tin serial number has been ripped off but the former owner seems to have forgotten to efface the country of origin: Ukraine. That is the main supplier of Soviet-style weaponry to Georgia. Then there is another box, and another, and another. We are indeed wandering around in an abandoned ammunition dump, and one not abandoned too long before.

"Ho!"

The sharp call is not from Larry, me, or our escort but from one of the company of ten armed men who have emerged from behind a shed back by the tractor path, their guns lowered at us. A quick exchange in Abkhaz follows, which is good, because had it been in Georgian we would have found ourselves in the middle of a firefight. It is also interesting because it suggests that the Georgian claim (and indeed, embedded belief) that the Abkhaz army was made up almost exclusively of Russian (or Chechen) mercenaries and not ethnic Abkhaz is just not true. For starters, the Russians and Chechens may have fought together on the side of the Abkhaz against the Georgians in 1992 and 1993, but since 1994 the Russians and Chechens have been fighting each other. Second, both Larry and I know enough Chechen (not to mention Russian) to understand that the language in use between our escort and the band of armed interlopers is neither of those tongues, but Abkhaz—a language that has something like seventy-six consonants and only one or two vowels, both of which sound like whistling to the uninitiated ear: *zEbza'ra Tsejm jEpsra 'gJE Tsejm*, which translates to something like "He who has a lousy life also has a lousy death," as the wise saying in Abkhaz has it.

No, the militiamen snapping up the explosive goodies scattered on the ground are not Russian or Chechen mercenaries but just local Abkhaz lads, coming to inspect the aftermath of a battle on which we had just stumbled. They are on their way to Taglioni to root out the remaining Forest Brethren, White Legionnaires, and, apparently, regular Georgian Army or police units who are still there.

Still there?

"I thought you guys were burning the houses of guerrilla supporters there," I suggest as delicately as possible.

"Why should we burn the houses?" asks one militiaman. "The Georgians are doing it themselves as they retreat across the river."

As they retreat?

That is when my cell phone rings. Here. In Abkhazia's Gali province, where no regular telephones work, and in an ammunition dump where the electronic tingle might . . . well, you know.

Time stands still as I push the "connect" button to at least get rid of the high-pitched squeal that might well blow us to kingdom come. It is my literary agent, calling from New York to congratulate me on placing a story in that day's *New York Times*, with a dateline from Zugdidi but no byline. This is because the bureau chief in Moscow had spoken with one of Shevardnadze's advisors by phone and added bits of that quoted conversation to the copy I filed, which somehow disqualifies my claim to be the author of the story. God knows what else the Moscow office or foreign desk back in New York struck out or stuck in—maybe even the crazy idea that the Abkhaz were threatening to blow up the BP/Amoco Caspian crude oil pipeline that transits Georgia from Azerbaijan to the Black Sea port of Supsa, just to add some geopolitical spice.

"I'm going to try and file a piece from this side of the lines today," I say.

The situation is completely inane. I am chatting with New York by cell phone while standing in the middle of an ammunition dump down the end of a mined road in an unrecognized country that is so far off the communications grid that regular telephones don't work.

This fact has been noticed by our Abkhaz escorts, who look at us with growing suspicion. They have never seen a cell phone before, at least not up close and working, especially with one party—me—speaking in a language they cannot understand while standing in an ammunition dump abandoned by the enemy.

"Speak Russian," they demand in order to understand what I am saying.

"But my agent doesn't understand that language," I try to explain.

"Speak Russian," they repeat, and so I say good-bye to my agent in New York in that language, turn off the phone so that no one else can call, and tell our suspicious guards that we have seen enough and that it is time to return to our good friend and their elder and better, Valeri Lomia. To reassure them further, we help our Abkhaz escort load the boxes of RPGs and assorted other evidence of direct Georgian military participation in the botched May 26 Independence Day debacle into the trunk of the Avis-mobile, grab a few nonlethal war trophies for ourselves, and then drive back to Gali to drop off our guards as promised.

"Thanks for returning the kids," says Valeri, referring to our escort. "Try to tell the truth."

"We will."

"And take these," he says, extending two bottles of Abkhazian vodka. "Give it to Shevardnadze when you get back to Kart."

"Kart" is shorthand for Sakartvelo, or "Georgia" in the Georgian language, as opposed to "Gruzi" in Russian, which we were speaking. When pronounced by an Abkhaz, the word has an almost nostalgic ring about it, a place name for a once familiar, but now impossibly distant, part of one's previous life. Valeri had studied in Tbilisi; botany, I believe.

We take the booze, get back in the car, and drive back down the empty main road toward the Inguri Bridge crossing, again passing the scores of once pretty but now shattered houses on either side that had been bombed yesterday, last year, the year before, or maybe even back in 1992 or 1993. The only way to estimate the date of destruction is by how much vegetation has grown up and through the burnt floors and roofs, if the house under inspection still has shingles.

Finally, the Inguri Bridge and the Georgian security post appear on the far side.

There, waiting for us, as she had been for many nervous hours, is Nino Ivanishvili, Reuters's television producer in the Caucasus, and her team, looking particularly relieved to see us come out. She could muscle herself through checkpoints manned by Spetsnaz goons in Chechnya like the best of them, but Abkhazia is special: her brother was killed there during the siege and fall of Sukhumi in 1993, dying aboard the same transport plane that fried *Wall Street Journal* troubleshooter Alexandra Tuttle. There were a couple of other members of the welcome-back-to-the-world committee there too, waiting for us on the far side of bridge and barrier, but not the ones I really wanted or thought should have been there: Professor Alexander Rondeli, the tall, dignified academic who now ran his own think tank consisting of his very best students on the third floor of the foreign ministry building in Tbilisi (of the five rooms on the floor, two were his and the other three were filled with refugees); Nunu Chachua, who had sheltered me back during the siege and fall of Sukhumi and whose whereabouts I currently did not know; Alexis Rowell, who had so burnt himself out chasing firefights in Georgia, Azerbaijan, and Chechnya that he had bailed out of journalism and was studying business—*business!*—in France. They were the ones to whom I wanted to explain what we had just seen on the other side and what it maybe meant. Sheets and I sit down at different tables in the delightful flower and citrus garden of the guesthouse we are staying at in Zugdidi to write up our reports. An hour later I call up an editor at the *New York Times* and say I have something to file, something that might add some balance to the report published in yesterday's paper along the lines of "the Georgians are not always the victims in this obscure little war on the shores of the Black Sea."

"I think we covered the story pretty well yesterday," comes the editorial reply.

I try to argue that much of yesterday's story was just more Georgian self-serving propaganda, but ultimately fail to convince the editor to take on something new. It has happened too many times before, this sort of *informanus interruptus*. Thank God Larry is filing for Reuters, although there is no telling what his editors in Moscow will do to his copy to make it politically correct and no guarantee that any newspaper anywhere in the world will ever use his story datelined "Outside Taglioni, Abkhazia." At least it would go into that great bank of information called the electronic archive. Otherwise there would be no chronicle record whatsoever of the Georgia/Abkhaz "story."

No, that is not entirely true. In addition to some papers written by a couple of post-Soviet scholars and the regular tendentious nonsense churned out by the local press, I had my notes and unpublished news stories and features dating back to the really bad old days. Bad old days like the siege and fall of Sukhumi; meetings with Mkhedrioni Mafia bandits at the Gudauri Ski Resort in the towering Caucasus mountains when the masses were freezing for lack of electricity and gas in the capital, Tbilisi; crazy plane rides aboard YAK-40s packed with corpses from the civil war; the killing of my old friend and CIA legend Freddie Woodruff; and even the funeral of Zviad Gamsakhurdia in Chechnya of all places.

Yes, I had my notes on Georgia over the past decade, notes taken long before the parachute journalism crowd started dropping in to stay in the fancy hotels with constant electricity and hot water, chatting with embassy-based Western diplomats who could not or would not leave their security compounds. I had my notes, and if they bounced around a bit it was because they were and are about rather bouncy times. I like to think of them as a literary rendition of one of those old mariners' maps that warns sailors to avoid certain uncharted seas because "dragons dwell there"; another possibility is to announce them to be a "reality-based" update on Brecht's *Caucasian Chalk Circle*.

Whichever way you want to view them, here they are, warts and all.

GEORGIA
DIARY

GEORGIENS

I

A COMPLEX HISTORY

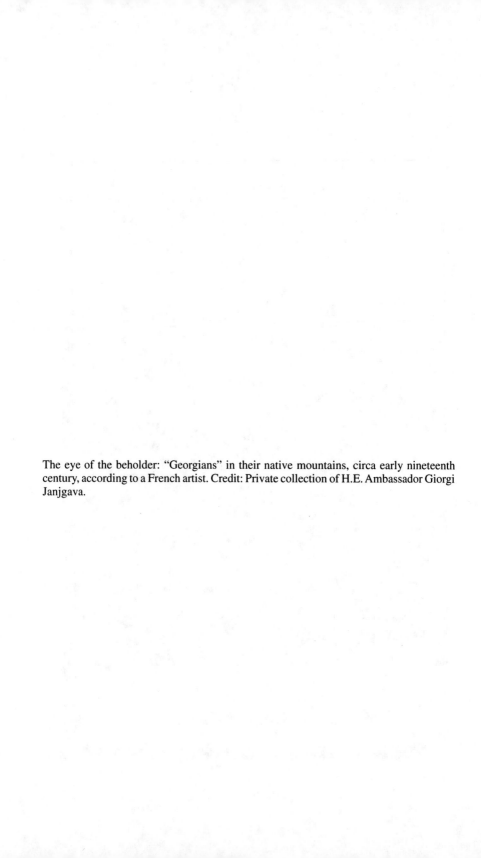

The eye of the beholder: "Georgians" in their native mountains, circa early nineteenth century, according to a French artist. Credit: Private collection of H.E. Ambassador Giorgi Janjgava.

1

The Quest for Gamsakhurdia

It all started in early January 1992, when the London *Sunday Times* called me at my office in Baku, Azerbaijan, and asked me to travel to western Georgia to conduct an exclusive interview with the almost former Georgian president, Zviad Gamsakhurdia, and to ask him about how he felt getting putsched from power.

"We want you to go find *whatshisname*," said Matthew Campbell from his editorial easy chair in London.

"Who?" I replied, just a tad nonplussed.

"You know, the Georgia fascist guy they just got rid of," said Matthew, illuminating the issue further. "You said he was in Azerbaijan. We heard you on the radio."

This was true. The day before, the BBC *News Hour* had called me concerning a rumor that the recently ousted president of Georgia, Zviad Gamsakhurdia, had arrived in neighboring northern Azerbaijan after fleeing Tbilisi with a trunk full of gold that he had allegedly heisted from the national treasury. As it turned out, the story about looting the till was nothing but disinformation, just like a very great deal of the media-take on the Tbilisi putsch and its aftermath later turned out to be based on not much more than well-placed lies. In any case, with a couple of strategic telephone calls, I had managed to confirm that Zviad Gamsakhurdia had indeed fled Georgia and had come to Azerbaijan, but that after a mere five hours he had gone to Armenia to seek asylum there, and reported this to the waiting world via a telephone interview with a reporter from the BBC's *News Hour* program. If this was thin soup, it was the best information about Gamsakhurdia anyone had offered in a while, and I thus became *News Hour*'s Man of the Moment, which is kind of like getting your Warholean fifteen minutes of fame, press-wise.

"That was Thomas Goltz, reporting from Baku . . ." said that stately British voice-in-the-box, referring to the world's newest "expert," on all things Georgian, namely, me.

The funny thing was that I knew next to nothing about Gamsakhurdia or the situation in Georgia. I had never met the man, never been to Georgia and my information about him and his country was limited to the Moscow evening news and the BBC. A true confession: aside from being able to confirm that he had set foot in Azerbaijan, I knew so little about Gamsakhurdia that I was obliged to cloak my new, putative expertise by avoiding the pitfall of mispronouncing his name. "Azerbaijani sources have confirmed that the Georgian leader . . ." was one way to get around the slurry of consonants. Variations on the same name-avoidance theme also included references to "the Georgian president," "the ousted mercurial headman," and perhaps even "the contentious chief of state." In other words, I did not know what the hell I was talking about but somehow managed to make it sound as if I did. Still, I had been on BBC *News Hour*, and thus by universal definition— or that feckless manner in which news is usually produced—had become an expert on Georgia, because what is reported on the BBC is the news all others have to carry, and what the BBC ignores is by definition not news. And now, as an expert, I was supposed to produce news on demand. That meant finding Gamsakhurdia, however you were supposed to pronounce his name.

"TASS reports that he has left Armenia and is back in Georgia," said Matthew helpfully, referring to the Soviet news agency regarded as a Communist Party lie-machine until the collapse of the USSR. Following that event, TASS had suddenly and miraculously been reborn—with exactly the same staff—as the Russian equivalent of the Associated Press. "He's in a place called—*hghmm*, let me look at my map—it's a place called Zugdidi. He has called for the start of civil war. File me 1,000 words with lots of color by Thursday afternoon."

"Matthew, today is Wednesday," I said. "And even if I find him in that place you just mentioned, how do I file from a country in the midst of civil war?"

"Okay, I get your point," said Matthew. "A Friday file would be fine."

"Matthew," I said. "This is impossible."

"I know. But if anyone can do it, it's you," said Matthew, booking the line space.

Friday, I said to myself and laughed. I had two days: one to prove the impossibility of finding Gamsakhurdia, and the second to write about whatever else I found. Parachute journalism at its superficial worst. But it was an excuse to get my feet wet in Georgia.

The Quest for Gamsakhurdia had been joined.

* * *

In the autumn of 1991, Zviad Gamsakhurdia had been in the news for months, and most information about him was pretty negative. "Authoritarian," "dictatorial," and "insane" were some of the terms employed to describe him. The most remarkable aspect about this appraisal was that it was a recent 180-degree turnaround in perception. Up until the breakup of the Soviet Union, Zviad Gamsakhurdia had been celebrated as the next best thing to Andrei Sakharov or Vaclav Havel. Gamsakhurdia was a committed dissident, with several stints in jail to prove it. Gamsakhurdia was an intellectual and had translated several important books from three or four European languages, including Shakespeare. Gamsakhurdia was the founder of the Georgia branch of the Helsinki Human Rights Committee and a hero of the April 9, 1989, massacre in Tbilisi, when the Soviet army rolled into the capital to put down a nationalist rally. Indeed, Zviad seemed to have done all the right things at the right time with one exception: he got himself elected and was thus obliged to make good on some of his campaign promises, like removing Georgia from the USSR.

Slowly, perceptions about Gamsakhurdia in Moscow and even in the West began to change. The pundits said power had gone to his head, that he had begun showing "undemocratic" tendencies. His reputation was further tarnished by his deep antipathy toward former foreign minister and fellow Georgian Eduard Shevardnadze, a man who, for many outsiders at least, typified the "new" Soviet man in the fading days of the empire.

But Gamsakhurdia apparently did not care what people outside Georgia thought of Shevardnadze. Nor did he care what they thought about the Soviet president, Mikhail Gorbachev, then regarded in the West as something close to a socialist saint. And neither did most of the people in Georgia care what the West thought about Soviet leaders. Their antipathy toward Gorbachev (and by extension, Shevardnadze) was less an indication of antidemocratic behavior than continued "anti-Centrism" pure and simple: both Gorbachev and his handmaid Shevardnadze represented the meddling hand of Moscow in the internal affairs of Georgia, and Gamsakhurdia promised to end that. But in the eyes of the world, Gorby was good (and thus Shevy, too), and anyone who opposed either of them was by definition bad. Accordingly, Zviad Gamsakhurdia was a bad guy, a supporter of bad guys, and deserved the fate of the other bad guys—like getting violently removed from power himself.

This process seemed to start rather quickly after the August 19, 1991, abortive putsch against Gorbachev that signaled the end of the USSR. While Moscow dissidents danced, and democracy reigned supreme in St. Petersburg, by early September, anti-Gamsakhurdia demonstrations began at the university in Tbilisi. These were led by well-meaning people with degrees and good English, and were consequently identified by foreign reporters as

"Western-oriented intellectuals." Opposing them were those who supported Gamsakhurdia. Most were country rubes and just folks with shotguns and pitchforks who spoke no English and often very bad Russian, and were therefore dismissed by visiting correspondents as "ultranationalist rabble."

In October, Gamsakhurdia was banging heads in South Ossetia, where the national minority that formed a local majority decided they wanted to secede, expelling the local minority (who happened to be part of the national majority) from the homes they had lived in for hundreds of years. As a result, in addition to having provoked the little matter of establishing a problematic DNA baseline of "ethnic purity" for both Georgians and Ossetians, Gamsakhurdia was faced with a rather thornier problem: many of the ethnic Ossetians living in Georgia happened to have kith and kin on the northern side of the mountainous border that divides the Caucasus into South and North, and that border was with post-Soviet Russia.

The mind grasps at comparisons in political stupidity. The main point is that almost as soon as he assumed office, Zviad Gamsakhurdia was biting off far more than he could chew, and while making his core *Georgia First!* ethnic entrepreneurs happy, he was alienating almost everyone else in the country and world—and in effect, entering into a proxy war with Russia.

In November, Gamsakhurdia was not only refusing to play ball with Gorbachev to save the dying Soviet Union, but also refusing to take part in the series of meetings that led to the formation of the Commonwealth of Independent States (CIS), the Moscow-dominated, rump USSR to be established by Gorbachev's archrival, Boris Yeltsin, in December 1991. Initially, Gamsakhurdia stayed away from the formative meetings because he had no intention of joining the CIS. Georgia, he said, was not and had never been a voluntary part of the USSR, nor would it be a part of any Russia-dominated clone of that organization. Then he stayed away because he couldn't go even if he had wanted to: the "Opposition" had begun a new series of strikes and demonstrations in Tbilisi, and the situation was rapidly spinning out of control. Zviad had a revolution on his hands. The much-oppressed Opposition had decided to save the country from his capricious, dictatorial rule and bring Georgia back into the international fold, which meant back into Moscow's orbit. Everyone applauded the idea. Everyone, that is, except for the citizens of Georgia who had voted Zviad into office.

Nightly news clips from the Georgian capital showed determined men in ski masks spraying automatic rifle fire down the main streets while army units aimed artillery pieces at the Presidential Palace at pointblank range. It was an incredible sight, terrifying and sad, and there was something not quite right about it all. As the death toll mounted it became pretty clear that it was the Gamsakhurdia loyalists who were doing most of the dying. Often they fell while holding signs of their beleaguered chief in their hands, trying to remind the world that the population had elected him, and that many still were willing to give him their final vote. The Opposition, meanwhile, were the guys doing most of the shooting, and from the looks of them on television and in newspaper photographs, they were not your usual professors emeritus leading al fresco seminars on political culture. They were putschists, pure and simple, and ones equipped with a pretty healthy arsenal of heavy weapons for being a bunch of college professors and poets. You didn't have to be a loony believer in Grand Conspiracy theories to understand what was going on. Someone else had supplied the weapons, so that one Georgian could kill other Georgians with greater ease. And that someone else was Russia, or its special and secret services, such as the military intelligence directorate called the GRU or that other organization once known as the KGB.

The end appeared to come on January 5, the day Gamsakhurdia managed to extricate himself from his palace, flee to Azerbaijan, and then Armenia, at which point he seemed to vanish into thin air. There were rumors he was in Turkey; that Gamsakhurdia was captured and in a KGB jail in Moscow (just as he had been as a youngish dissident in 1989); that Zviad was dead, martyred for the cause. Truly, in all my years as a journalist, I have never run into an individual that managed to put up such a smoke screen. Zviad was everywhere. But Matthew said that TASS reported that someone had said he was in Zugdidi, and having no better ideas myself, it was to Zugdidi that I planned to go.

There were several logistical problems involved in doing so. The first was that I didn't even have a visa for Georgia in good times, let alone bad ones—and a country in the midst of a civil war is pretty bad. The classic way around the visa business in the old Soviet Union was to travel by train. But the train from Baku, often attacked by robbers, ran only as far as Tbilisi, and that was on the wrong side of the lines. A telephone call to a pal with connections in the Azerbaijani air industry, however, managed to solve the problem. Because Russian journalists and those foreigners with Moscow accreditation could fly to newly independent Azerbaijan without problem, he reasoned, the reverse should also hold true, thus allowing Azerbaijani journalists or those foreigners with Azerbaijani press accreditation to fly to all other areas of the former USSR with equal ease. As it happened, I was the proud holder of foreign press pass 000001, the first such document in the young history of the Azerbaijan Republic born in the Soviet collapse of September/October 1991, and was thus uniquely qualified to make a principled challenge to the unilaterally imposed restrictions on press in the newly created Russian Federation. At least that is how I chose to look at my border-busting foray. And my path seemed clear. There was a semilegal flight the next morning to the Russian Black Sea town of Sochi, just north of Sukhumi, and thus Georgia at war. I bought the ticket that may have cost $25, boarded the still-seeming-internal Soviet flight, flew to Sochi, and walked through Russian customs without a visa, trying to act as natural as all the other illegal smugglers, carpetbaggers, and sundry international scum aboard my flight. Once in the airport apron, I flagged down a taxi and said I wanted to go to Zugdidi. Aside from the fact that it was across the border in Georgia, I had no idea where it was.

"Oh, no!" said every driver at the airport. "It is too dangerous!"

"What about Sukhumi?" I tried, looking at a map for something within striking distance of the Georgian civil war.

"Too dangerous, too!"

"I'm willing to pay," I offered and was soon ensconced in a big white Volga, roaring down the coastal road of the Black Sea.

My driver was a Russian bear by the name of Vlodi, and his assistant was a half-Georgian half-Russian character named Meri. They lectured me in Russian on subjects I could only vaguely understand even if I had possessed good Russian, although it is now much better for their effort to force communication on me. I said *Ia dumaiu chto ia ponimaiu* when I thought I understood and *Ia ne ponimaiu* when I knew I didn't. Then other verbs and nouns I had been learning started kicking in: *They Shot/They Killed/They Will Shoot/They Will Kill/They Are Crazy/You Are Crazy/We Are Crazy and Someday We Won't Tolerate It and Then We Will Revolt.* I was going through a crash language course—learning Russian on the Run.

"I can't take you beyond Sukhumi," Vlodi said, "It is dangerous. *Opasno.* There is war. *Voina.* There are bandits. *Khuligany.* They shoot. *Streliaiut.* They kill. *Ubivaiut.*"

Actually, the only bandit that I encountered was Vlodi because he overcharged me by several thousand percent for a journey that was, finally, no more *opasno* than driving from Livingston, Montana, to Gardiner at the head of Yellowstone Park during elk season. There were a lot of sullen, unshaven men with guns sulking alongside the road, but they weren't particularly dangerous unless you were a wapiti jumping out from behind a bush.

And the countryside was lovely, even exquisite: long stretches of beach pounded by the sea and trout-filled rivers cutting through pine-covered hills that begged exploration with a graphite rod and pocket full of flies. In between the rivers, wooded ravines and misty hills were small towns with quaint, two-story civil architecture, onion-domed Russian churches, and more ancient, conical-domed religious structures, all dwarfed or framed by snow-doffed peaks towering into the clouds. It was a fine drive.

By the time Vlodi dropped me at the Sukhumi railway station, evening had fallen and the rain was threatening to turn into snow. No amount of pleading would convince him that we should continue toward the civil war together.

"Come on, Vlodi," I tried to persuade the driver one more time. "Let's go see what's what in Zugdidi."

"I am a married man with children and the Georgians are crazy," he said.

He was kind enough to arrange a braver driver for the rest of the route and invited me back to Sochi sometime to hunt, fish, drink, and watch the patience of the Russian nation be stretched beyond the breaking point.

"Come in the summer," he said. "It is warm then and there will be a revolution."

Then he was gone and I was in another car, racing toward Zugdidi in the gathering night, skidding on ice-slicks formed on bridges over darkened rivers with checkpoints at both ends.

The new driver kept up a nonstop conversation in pidgin Russian. At first I thought the driver was distorting consonants, vowels, and grammar for my benefit, but eventually it became clear that his Russian really was not that much better than mine. He is probably the reason why people to this day say I speak Russian with a thick Caucasian accent, and why I still have problems understanding intellectuals in such cities as Moscow and St. Petersburg. It was also my first introduction to the social and demographic complexities of Georgia.

"You like Sukhumi?" the driver asked.

"I didn't see much of it," I replied.

"It is a fine town, especially in the summer—Russian girls, Ukrainian girls, Belorussian girls."

"Sounds dandy."

"Why are you going to Zugdidi when you could stay in Sukhumi?" the driver reasonably asked.

"I want to find Gamsakhurdia."

"*Serz* Shevardnadze!" crowed the driver in Georgian, apparently praising the former Georgian leader.

"Well I'd like to meet him, too."

"What?!"

"I just thought that—"

"The dog should die!"

"Who?"

"Shevardnadze! Long live Zviad!"

"Why do you like him and not Shevardnadze?"

"Because the dog is a Georgian and Zviad is Mingrelian."

"What is a Mingrelian?"

"It is a Georgian, too."

"And we are now in Mingrelia?"

"No, we are in Abkhazia."

"What's that?"

"Abkhazia is the part of Georgia where they live, and every one of us is Georgian except for the Abkhaz and the Adjars and the Ossetians and the Meskhits, but we got rid of them a long time ago."

"All of them?"

"No, just the Meskhits, and they want to come back but we won't let them."

"Why?"

"Because they aren't Georgians."

"But you said that Georgians were the same as Mingrelians."

"I was talking about the Meskhetians, not the Mingrelians."

"So who is the civil war between?"

"Civil war?"

"Yes."

"There is no civil war. At least not yet. That was last year. The problem today is between the Position and the Opposition."

"You mean Gamsakhurdia."

"No! The Opposition are traitors who love Shevardnadze and Moscow and who want to destroy the nation. We are the Position!"

It was going to be a challenge trying to define who was who around here. And by the time I got to Tbilisi several weeks later, the Opposition had embraced the concept of Position and had begun to call the Gamsakhurdia loyalists "opposition."

We moved on through the Sakartvelo night, or at least the Abkhazian part of it, until we crossed some darkened river and entered the Mingrelian part of it, after which we finally entered the outskirts of Zugdidi, which was still in the Mingrelian part of it, I think. Snow was everywhere, it was cold, and my feet were frozen. In preparation for embracing my new career as a war correspondent, I had decided to travel to Georgia in tennis shoes, in case I had to do any running, such as away from the war. Sadly, the shoes I had selected were a half-size too small, and were now chilled to ice.

"Well," I asked the driver. "Where can I find Gamsakhurdia?"

"You don't know?" asked the driver in amazement. "You mean we have come all this way and you don't know where he is?"

"No."

"Who told you he was here?"

"Nobody you know. The BBC, quoting TASS."

"Well, let's try the Prefektura. There's usually a crowd around there."

We drove through the slushy, snowy streets of Zugdidi until we came to the middle of town where several broad streets converged on a large *ploshchad*, or square, in which a huge bonfire was burning. Scores of people were warming themselves around it, coughing. Facing the square was a large, four-story building of an unprepossessing, centrally planned "commie" character, out of which people were hauling bits of broken desk and chair to stoke the fire. A huge Georgian flag hung from the third floor balcony overlooking the square, and a man was shouting into a microphone.

Gamsakhurdia himself?

I paid off the driver and began working my tennis shoes through the slush, ice, and snow of the parking lot toward the main door of the building.

"I am a foreign correspondent," I announced myself to the wild-looking bearded man with the Kalashnikov guarding the entrance. "And I wish to speak with your leader."

"Up there," growled the guard, pointing to darkened stairs leading to the floors above.

I paused on the third floor, crowded with people milling about in the half-light provided by candles and flashlights.

"Where is the leader?" I asked again, and was shoved into an even more crowded chamber packed with gunmen.

"Who are you?" demanded a suspicious, short, thickset man dressed in a ski cap and camouflage jacket. Sticks of dynamite stuck out of both pockets.

"A correspondent," I said. "I want to talk to your leader."

The man indicated that I should sit on a broken table while he went to inform his boss of my presence and request.

It was incredible. My impossible mission was really going to succeed! I had flown into Russian territory without a visa, taxied out and over the border into the eye of the Georgian civil-war tornado in one piece, and was about to meet the elusive big man—Gamsakhurdia himself! And, from all appearances, I was the first journalist to track down the peripatetic president for that much desired, dreamed-of "exclusive" interview.

I started preparing my questions.

Goltz: *Mister Ex-President, how does it feel to have been putsched from power?*

Gamsakhurdia: *Well, Mister Intrepid Journalist, it has not been very pleasant . . .*

It all seemed too easy.

It was.

* * *

As I waited for my interview with the deposed president, a crowd of scruffy-looking men ebbed and flowed through the smoke-filled foyer, jabbering away in Georgian, or its Mingrelian dialect. It was my first contact with either tongue, and it seemed to be a language with more Q, K, and X sounds than Arabic, German, and Xhosa combined. Writing down place names such as the Ztxenisztali River was a chore. Eventually a young man with a shotgun slung over his shoulder stumbled into the antechamber and started coughing out some news. The antechamber was silenced until the new arrival had said his piece, answered a few pointed questions, and then crashed through the door leading to the inner sanctum to deliver his report to the Position leadership.

"What was that all about?" I asked in bad Russian.

"Kutaisi," someone gasped. "The dogs have attacked again!"

At first I thought that Kutaisi was a person, but it was actually a city—the district capital of the next province over from Mingrelia, where a pro-Position meeting had been held earlier that day. Several busloads of Gamsakhurdia loyalists had driven up the road from Zugdidi in order to stage a nonviolent demonstration, but on the outskirts of town the protestors had been stopped by national guardsmen loyal to the Opposition, which meant the people in the new government who called themselves the Position, which is what the former (Gamsakhurdia) government still claimed to be.

"They terrorized us with airplanes," howled one man who had been there, describing how a MIG-29 fighter had buzzed the buses. "Moscow is on their side."

This was the first taste I had of the tendency to inflate the other side's warmaking capability. The MIG-29 is one of the most advanced (former) Soviet jet fighters, and the arrival of one with a defecting pilot at the controls flying from a Georgian base to NATO-member Turkey back in 1988 caused quite a stir among the defense and intelligence crew over at the American embassy, I recalled. It was likely that there was still a squadron of the aircraft stationed somewhere in Georgia, but the idea that the fighter could be leased to buzz a column of civilians in the mountains seemed rather farfetched. Clearly, however, the president would have to evaluate this most recent attack, and so I returned to my chair before someone took it to throw on the fire outside. I waited. And waited some more. Finally, after about an hour, I elbowed my way through the knot of men guarding or maybe just inadvertently blocking the door to the inner sanctum, and reiterated my request for the interview.

"I want to speak to your leader," I said.

"He's not here," came the reply.

"But you said he was an hour ago," I replied. "I must conduct an interview with him so I can tell the world about his views."

"He's not here. Take a look if you don't believe me."

"All right, I will."

The room was filled with smoke and smoking men, who looked up from their intense conversations to see who had entered. A couple of characters were chewing on pieces of bread ripped from two twenty-pound loaves.

"Sirs," I said, approaching the Position leadership collectively, but focused on a fellow sitting at the head of the table, who, although he didn't look like Gamsakhurdia, seemed to be the man in charge.

"What do you want?" he demanded.

"I want to speak with Gamsakhurdia," I told him.

Instantly everyone in the room was around me. *Where is he? You know where he is?*

I had, it now occurred to me, neglected to add the Russian verb "want" to my construction and used the past tense of the verb "to speak." Accordingly, the Position leadership had assumed I was a messenger from the leader. They were disappointed when they realized that this was not the case. So was I, because although I knew that I didn't know where he was, they were supposed to—and this, too, was not the case. It was rather clear that Gamsakhurdia had not, as reported by TASS, then the authoritative BBC, and finally multiple local and international media outlets, announced the commencement of civil war the day before on the balcony of the Prefektura building I was standing in. He had been nowhere near the balcony, building, square, neighborhood, or the very town of Zugdidi at all.

* * *

I was not the only person disappointed in not finding Gamsakhurdia in Zugdidi. Predictably, the TASS balloon report about his declaration of the start of civil war had set the world press into motion, and, within an hour of my interview with the Position leadership, the hack pack arrived. Their mission was the same as mine. *Find Zviad!*

There was Bridget Kendall of the BBC and her husband who represented some British television concern; there was a guy from Reuters I had once met but whose name I forget; an American I nicknamed Colorado Chris who was working for Agence France Press; there was a large CNN contingent led by some gray-haired guy who kept muttering that he was "too old to do this stuff"; and then correspondents from papers like *Figaro*, *El Pais*, and the *Guardian*. Additionally, there were those associated with (former) East bloc newspapers and magazines, as well as the odd representative of (former) USSR news organs such as TASS, the Russian News Agency, Moscow News, *Nezavisimaya Gazeta,* and even something called the Baltic News Service. I won't even begin listing the photographers. All had come down from Moscow to Sochi by chartered plane and then whizzed by car or bus to Zugdidi via Sukhumi, all questing to find Gamsakhurdia because the BBC quoting TASS had aired a report that he was there, or here, actually. Like me, the rest of the hack pack were sorely disappointed that this was not the case and suspicious that the Truth was being hidden from a waiting world.

Accordingly, to stave off disappointment lest it lead to anger and resentment, the Position HQ did the most reasonable thing in the circumstances. They held a press conference. The apparent leader, a guy by the name of Walter Shagua, spoke long and eloquently about the travesty that was the coup, the evils of Moscow, and what needed to be done to restore democracy in Georgia. There was, however, only one question anybody wanted to ask. *Where was Gamsakhurdia?* The answer, delivered in different ways according to the different ways of asking it, was always the same: *We don't know.*

So it was time to look elsewhere for him. I went to Poti to find him and failed. I went to a place called Abasha, where the Position had erected barricades on their side of the river in order to stop the Opposition from crossing, and failed to find him there, too. I went here and I went there, and so did other members of the hack pack during that cold January of 1992 in western Georgia. We were all looking for Gamsakhurdia, but only finding each other.

It started to look like a real-life version of *Scoop*, a novel by Evelyn Waugh about the hack pack descending on the faux nation of Ismailia, in which the leading lights of London letters simply made up leads in order to get space on the front page, while trying to avoid all the others in the area. From what I could see, none of the other real-life actors involved in the cold and dreary Quest for Gamsakhurdia could appreciate the moment, see the absurdity of it, or be amused or edified by it in any way. Obsessed with finding *the man*, they could not discern *the idea*. The point, I finally decided, was the search for the reality of what happened when one tried to establish even a distorted and warped version of democracy in a former Soviet Republic. But none of us wanted to see that. It was too painful. It ended in utter and complete disillusionment with the ideas that "we," as "Westerners," had long embodied for "them," the freedom-seeking ex-Soviets. They had believed in the dream, but all we had time for was the funeral.

The other journalists had somehow made arrangements to stay together at the only working hotel in town. It was a standard, cookie-cutter-designed lump of cement waiting to collapse like a house of cards in the first earthquake to rumble through the region. I am glad I did not stay there, not so much for fear of earthquakes or because it was cold and had no water or kitchen but because of the general news incest among the gathered reporters. They ran their satellite phones off the roof, sat around embellishing each other's stories about the different wars and coups that they had lived through, and shared apocryphal tales about fabulous expenses charged by one's distant colleagues to one's institution. The best one was the story told by a *Figaro* correspondent who always added a line item expense for whoring that he called a WANMOW— We Are Not Made of Wood.

Me, I stayed at a private home near the Prefektura—a normal sort of two-story Georgian house with a garden and a chicken coop out back, all guarded by a vicious dog. It was clean, pleasant, and owned by a woman named Little Lamara (because her neighbor was known as Big Lamara) who cooked for me and laughed when I came back from the market with a pair of oversized Soviet officer boots to replace the ridiculously thin sneakers I had selected as my war-footing footwear in Baku. Both Lamaras and all their neighbors were adamant on one point: they wanted their president back.

One day I decided to go to Sukhumi. Even though my deadline was long past, I was still infected by the news-angle bug and thought I might find Gamsakhurdia there. Actually, I was convinced of this because an alcoholic Georgian poet by the name of Rene had told me so. Rene, as a national poet, was of course an intimate friend of the ousted president and would set up the exclusive interview. So, we set off together over the nasty, icy roads back to the port city and then checked into his apartment on the outskirts of town. This was on the sixth floor of a standard Soviet high-rise, and the lift didn't work because there was no electricity. As in all such Soviet-style apartments, the WC was split into two tiny rooms—the toilet in one and the sink and shower in the other. This didn't matter too much, though, because without electricity there was no water to wash, and it was so cold that we never removed one article of clothing, even to sleep, and hence were more or less oblivious to our own odors.

Rene was a national poet of the Soviet school—that is, he had been pampered with grants and dachas all his professional life and was expected to think in terms of Big Cultural Ideas. As such, I was obliged to listen to a lot of cultural fare. Most concerned the courage, genius, and general merits of Gamsakhurdia and the intimate relationship between the poet and president. Whether this was true was hard to say. What was true was that Rene, like all good Mingrelian Georgians, drank like a fish, which meant that I felt obliged to drink a lot, too. We drank a bottle of brandy that first night while Rene extolled the merits of Gamsakhurdia. Then we continued drinking when we got up in the morning, starting in on the brandy we had not drunk the night before, and opening another bottle when it was done. Rene was determined to finish the second before leaving the apartment but I was insistent that we stop unless we wanted to fall to our deaths by tripping down the six flights of steps. It was not yet nine in the morning.

There was always plenty of drink to be had and time to drink it in Georgia, even if the land was war-torn and plagued by civil strife. It was an attitude I liked—up to a point. With Rene the National Poet that point came around noon the next day, when he insisted that we retire to yet another cafe for another meal of Georgian-style polenta grits and another two bottles of cognac before he led me to his personal friend, the president—or at least to some other personal friend who knew where the president was. By four in the afternoon, when we ended up at still someone else's house to eat more hominy, drink more wine, and make more endless toasts to eternal friendship among the peoples of the world, the indignant memory of the unlawfully ousted Zviad, and the day when Georgia might be free, I was not getting very drunk and sentimental anymore, only cold and angry. If the locals didn't want to produce their president for that all-important exclusive interview, then they might as well say it. I was getting tired of using the Quest for Gamsakhurdia as an excuse to open yet another bottle in another freezing household illuminated by candlelight and false hope. I finally ditched Rene the National Poet after he hauled me over to the Sukhumi train station, where his sources had told us the Position maintained its headquarters. There we learned that the Position had moved downtown, into the local branch of the Georgian National Theater, which just happened to be named after Gamsakhurdia's father, Konstantine, who was, or had been, a great nationalist and a poet to boot. Rene thought this was a good occasion to open up another bottle but I didn't quite see the connection. I told him I had to urinate, sought out a toilet as far away from where he was sitting as reasonable, and never came back.

I made my own way to the theater that served as the Position HQ without my National Poet as guide. There I found a bunch of people meeting in the dark, chain-smoking cheap cigarettes called Astaras, slurping cheap brandy, and conspiring.

"I am a foreign correspondent looking for Gamsakhurdia," I said at least fifteen times.

"Hmph," the conspiratorial smokers and slurpers responded, meaning "We suspect you are a spy."

But it was there that I met Nunu Chachua. She was the commercial director of the theater and had thrown open the doors of the building to use as the Gamsakhurdia HQ. She was also Medea, a raven-haired beauty with dark almonds for eyes, who was tough as nails, and possessed an absolutism that was both splendid and frightening.

"In America, the man you elect president serves four years," she noted. "And if you don't like him, you can vote him out, correct?"

"Yes . . ."

"And as the head of the state, he is entitled to defend his government from armed gangs who want to interfere in that process, correct?"

"Yes . . ."

"And in a general sense, America would like to promote that style of government, democracy, throughout the world, correct?"

"Yes . . ."

"Then why do you make an exception with Georgia? All we want is the return of the legitimate president of the country, whom we elected, and whom we can vote out of office if we no longer trust him!"

I tried to interject something but was overruled by Nunu.

"Shall I tell you why the situation here is different?"

"Yes . . ."

"Shevardnadze."

"But he's in Moscow," I tried to add.

"Today," she spat. "But tomorrow he will be here. All the chaos and suffering you have witnessed in your short time in Georgia is a direct result of your great democratic friend Shevardnadze's attempt to seize power and drive Georgia back into the USSR."

It was a bit rich as far as conspiracy theories went, and I tried to tell her so.

"Nunu," I said for starters. "There is no longer a USSR."

"You will see," she smiled. "First, Shevardnadze will return and create a national guard because he will say he is a Georgian Nationalist, which is a lie. Then the National Guard will destroy Sukhumi. Then the Abkhazians will revolt with the help of the Russians and bring chaos to the land. Then Shevardnadze will bring Georgia back into the USSR. Then he will beg for Russian soldiers to come and save him from the wrath of the people."

As I said, it all seemed a bit rich. The problem was that although it took a couple of years to germinate, almost all of it turned out to be true.

Nunu lived with her sister, Nana, and their mother, Lamara, in a pleasant two-story house just shy of the main bazaar and just a few blocks from the beach. There were a couple of lemon trees and rose bushes outside the iron gate, a small fountain and a framed faded black-and-white photograph attached to the outside wall. It was an image of Nunu's father, who had died some years before.

"What did he do?" I asked.

"He was an engineer," she answered, listing her father in that vast, curious category of technical "doers" that the USSR was famous for.

"He was purged by Stalin, but then he came back," chirped in Mama Lamara with a chuckle. I never got any further details.

* * *

Through Nunu, Nana, and Lamara I met a lot of other people who were equally disappointed in the world's response to the putsch against their president and increasingly irritated with journalists whose only concern was to track him down, bag that exclusive interview, and damn the (security) consequences.

"He is everywhere," said a man named Merab Kiknadze I met over at the theater. "He is in the East, in the West, he is here and there, and all around!"

At first I thought he was mad. Later, I learned that Merab was actually the chairman of Gamsakhurdia's parliament, and had seen his share of torture in Tbilisi before managing to escape, incognito, from the capital to join the resistance in Sukhumi. And after we had become friends, I began to understand what he was trying to say. Gamsakhurdia was not a ghost. He had become an idea. It didn't matter where he was physically, even if he were in the grave. He was the essence of Georgian independence that was being crushed, yet attempted to struggle on. I don't know where the other reporters were at this time. Probably hanging around airfields and ports, following up yet another rumor that Gamsakhurdia might be found in this or that village or town. And when Gamsakhurdia eventually did surface, it was not in western Georgia, Armenia, or Turkey, but in "Muslim-fundamentalist" Chechnya, and as the guest of the former (Soviet) Strategic Air Command wing-commander/bomber-pilot president of that blighted, breakaway state, General Djohar Dudayev. In January 1992, the only people in Georgia who really wanted to locate Gamsakhurdia were the press, and they failed. They failed to find him personally, and they failed to find what he stood for. And when the press realized they had failed in finding Gamsakhurdia, they got bored and listless, and then they left, and when they left I was alone.

But by then I had given up on finding the man.

I was looking for an idea.

I blush to say that I had Georgia on my mind.

2

A Far-Flung Piece of Paradise

As legend has it, when God was dividing up the world between the nations, the Georgians missed their chance of selecting a homeland because they were sleeping off a festive drunk. When they awoke, everything was gone with the exception of that part of the world that the Almighty had been reserving for himself, which was, of course, literally heaven on earth.

"Where can we go?" wailed the Georgians. "And we were late only because we were toasting to you and singing your praises!"

"Well," said a flattered God. "I guess I'll have to give you a piece of paradise."

Thus began, even in legend, the unique special-case client status of the inhabitants of the forested hills, towering, snowcapped mountains, fertile river valleys, and Black Sea orchards of Sakartvelo who have been flattering Friends in High Places to achieve their ends (or ensure their collective survival) since the theoretic beginning of time.

But being in possession of a little piece of paradise comes with costs, and "Georgia" has not only been coveted and conquered by outsiders since the dawn of time, but so beset by factional infighting among Georgians themselves, often in alliance with those same outside powers, that it has frequently disappeared from the map for decades or even centuries only to reemerge in a modified and often severely divided guise.

The saga of self-destruction might be said to start with the mythological story of Medea. Seduced by Jason of the Argonauts, the Cholchis princess first aided the outlander Greek against her xenophobic father, then killed her brother while helping Jason escape with the Golden Fleece, and finally poisoned her common children with Jason when he jilted her for the daughter of the King of Corinth.

A more solid historically based encounter was that of Xenephon, who, along with his 10,000 mercenaries retreating from their fourth century B.C. Mesopotamian quagmire, ran into groups of people he called the Tibal and

Mushki in the Pontic mountains overlooking the Black Sea in today's eastern Turkey. The indigenous groups fought tooth and nail against the outlander Greeks and then, facing certain defeat, committed collective suicide. In his *Anabasis*, Xenophon writes of how the desperate Tibal and Mushki women would first fling their children from the ramparts and then leap to their own death. No record remains about these events from a native perspective and, thus, no hard evidence that the Tibal and Mushki encountered by Xenophon were really even "Georgian." There was a great deal of ethnonational fluidity in Anatolia and the adjacent south Caucasus landmass before proper or even proto-history was written in cuneiform, and scholars and linguists continue to quibble over the issue.

What is clear is that by the time of chroniclers such as Herodotus, Georgia (usually called "Iberia" by the Greeks and then Romans, leading to a centuries long confusion and double-helix, faux co-ethnic solidarity between the Basques and Georgians), along with its neighbor Armenia to the south and Caucasian Albania (more or less today's Azerbaijan) to the east, had become the strategic transit land on the northern front of the age-old rivalry between East and West. This geographic position would be the curse the proto-Georgians would have to live with no matter who the great powers of the day might be: the Achaemenian Persians under Darius and Xerxes squaring off against the Greek city states; Alexander the Great rolling up those conquests in reverse; Alexander's Persianized Seleucid heirs losing the region to Roman legions under Pompey, then followed by the highly confusing, centuries-long showdown between the new Parthian/Sassanid Persian empire and the "New Roman" empire known as Byzantium, after the Emperor Constantine adopted Christianity and transferred the center of gravity of the "West" from the wicked "old" Rome on the Tiber to his new capital of Constantinople astride the Bosporus straits between the Black and Marmara seas.

The East–West standoff between "Zoroastrian Persia" and "Christian Rome" became even more complex over the following centuries, but arguably came to a head when the two adversaries delivered a double knockout punch to each other in the early seventh century following the conquest and counter-conquest of (surprise!) Jerusalem. Although difficult to prove precisely, one can assume that "Georgian" levies fought on both sides of the great East–West divide. Today, Georgians choose to revere the martyrs and monks associated with the Christian tradition, but the canvas of Georgian history suggests very clearly that the tendency toward apostasy (in this case, the instinct to survive) has always been part of the national character.

Constantinople managed to be the first to stagger to its feet following the hundred-year Perso-Byzantine war ending in the early seventh century. But then out of the deserts of Arabia rolled a tsunami wave of militant iconoclast

Christians, or possibly Jews. At least that was the first impression made by the armies of Islam on the icon-friendly Byzantine occupiers of the Holy Land, just recently freed of the Persian/Zoroastrian yoke. Before they realized what had hit them, it was over, and the entire Middle East, Persia, and a good half of Anatolia were suddenly under the control of a new and highly dynamic socioreligious polity: the Muslims.

The history of Islam exploding onto the world stage following the death of the Prophet Muhammad has been the subject of dissertations and books printed on a rainforest of trees turned into paper pulp and therefore will not be dealt with here. Suffice it to say that the advent of Islam, the Muslim Arab conquest of Zoroastrian Persia, and near conquest of the Orthodox Christian Byzantine empire had huge implications not only for proto-Georgia but also for the larger region we know as the Caucasus today. First overrunning eastern Anatolia in today's Turkey, the Muslims pushed east into today's Iran and then north into Medea (Azerbaijani Albania) and Armenia. "Georgia" (such as it was) succumbed in 645. With the exception of a few eras when Muslim Arab, Persian, or Turkish power waned, the fractured land known as Georgia (or more often, "eastern Iberia," "western Iberia" being today's Spain, on the far occidental edge of the Christian Europe) was slowly swallowed up by the greater Muslim Middle East. The process would continue until the first year of the nineteenth century, when core Georgia was absorbed piecemeal into the new great power on the scene, imperialist Russia.

Between those bracket years of 645 and 1801, the picture painted by historians remains devilishly complex. "Core" Georgia was almost always divided into two primary princely states (Kartli/Tbilisi in the east and Ergesi/Kutaisi in the west) that were as often at each other's throat over issues of royal succession as they were revolting against their feudal overlords (Arabs, Persians, Mongols, and first Seljuk and then Ottoman Turks). Apostasy was rife, with conversion to Islam a power card to be played again and again, even by individuals who have since gone down in Georgian history as great heroes.

Indeed, what collective consciousness there existed of "Georgianness" is open to question. The first time the word "Sakartvelo," or "place of the Georgians," appears in the chronicles is 1008, during a brief and almost co-incidental unification of western and eastern Georgia under Bagrat III and his mixed Armeno-Georgian-Abkhazian family line. That state's capital was at Kutaisi; Tbilisi remained a Muslim garrison town, as it had been for almost 400 years.

Nor were all of Georgia's trials and travails at the hands of Muslim over-lords. The attempt by Bagrat IV to reclaim traditional Georgian territories in Tao (in today's northeastern Turkey) from the revived Orthodox Christian Byzantine empire backfired badly, resulting in Emperor Basil II (the Bulgar

Slayer) laying waste to much of Georgia and subjugating the Armenian branch of the Bagratid clan at its capital, Ani.

Byzantium may have reached its apogee under Basil II, but the annexation of the Caucasus buffer states ultimately upset the balance of power in the region when a new geopolitical player emerged on the scene—the Seljuk Turks, whose signal victory over the Byzantine host at Manzikert in 1071 and capture of the emperor himself dealt a death blow to Byzantine pretensions in the east. Like Armenia, Georgian Iberia was to remain an obscure, mainly Christian outpost deep behind Muslim lines.

Paradoxically, this confused and fluid situation led directly to the brief flourishing of medieval Georgia under David the Builder (1089–1125), his grandson Giorgi III (1156–1184), and finally his great-granddaughter, Queen Tamar (1184–1212). With the Seljuks distracted by the Crusades, the Bagratids were able to lay siege to and capture the Muslim emirate of Tbilisi, which became the Bagratid capital. Other lands lost to the Muslims were also regained until, under Tamar, Georgia once again stretched from the central plains of today's Azerbaijan in the east to the high plateau of Armenia to the south, and as far west as the Turkish Seljuk emirates of Erzurum and Erzinjan in today's Turkey. Historians may quibble about Tamar's role in establishing the lesser Byzantine Kingdom of Trebizon on the south-central Black Sea coast, but there is little doubt about the Georgian character of the monasteries and churches in the Choruh river country around today's northeastern Turkish cities of Artvin, Ardahan, and arguably even Kars.

The era of Tamar also saw the expansion of literary, architectural, and material culture. Shota Rustaveli wrote his epic *The Knight in the Panther's Skin* under her patronage, and the grand cathedral at Mtskheta at the confluence of the Kura and Aragvi rivers was expanded to truly become the tomb of Georgian kings, as was the fabulous "hidden" monastery at Vardzia on the upper Kura River on today's Turkish frontier (although some scholars prefer to see this as a mark of insecurity rather than ostentation). The Gelati Monastery and academy built by David had become "a second Jerusalem of all the East for learning . . . a second Athens, far exceeding the first in divine law . . ." The perhaps overly enthusiastic Georgian historian Roin Metreveli also finds a substantial Georgian hand in the Iviron Monastery on Mount Athos, the Black Mountain Monastery in Syria, the Monastery of the Holy Cross in Jerusalem, and the Petritsoni Monastery in Bulgaria dating from this period. (A cross-cultural architectural historian might add a number of contemporary Seljuk Turkish mosque and *madrasa* complexes to the register, such as the phenomenally beautiful Ulu Camii in the little town of Divrigi in Sivas province of central Anatolia: it was built by Georgian Muslims under the guiding hand of a twelfth-century architect named "Al-Tbilisi.")

In 1189, Queen Tamar divorced her first husband, the Russian Prince Yuri, and selected an Ossetian named David Soslan as her new consort. Their son and heir, Giorgi IV, was known as "the Resplendent." Assuming the throne, he continued along his mother's path and was reportedly planning a Crusade to Jerusalem in 1220 when word came to court about the arrival of yet another group of strange, Asiatic horsemen on the scene: the Mongols. The conquerors from the East soon added Sakartvelo to the list of cities, countries, and empires to which they laid waste, and by the time the hordes melted away from the Caucasus a century later the glories of Queen Tamar and her unified Georgia state were a thing of distant memory. Petty nobles once again squabbled over meaningless titles, and Tamar's descendants feuded over who might control what bit of the ravaged and devastated countryside. Although he does not specify his milieu, my suspicion is that Bertolt Brecht cast his *Caucasian Chalk Circle* into the landscape of post-Tamarid Georgia. Or, as Ronald Suny writes, "by the end of the fifteenth century (Georgia) was divided into three kingdoms and numerous principalities . . . it was not again to be united until its annexation by Russia in the nineteenth century."[1]

The process of swallowing Georgia into the tsarist fold might be said to have begun with the marriage between Prince Yuri and Queen Tamar, and there is little question that religious affinity between the Orthodox Christian Georgians and Russians—especially after the fall of Constantinople in 1543 to the Ottoman sultans—was strong. In 1563, King Levan of Kakheti/Tbilisi asked the Russian state to take his kingdom under tsarist protection, but had to retract the offer under pressure from Muslim Persia. Levan's heir, Alexander II, repeated the offer and received a pledge of protection. His rival king, Simon I of Kartli/Kutaisi, meanwhile, attempted to make war on the Turks hoping for Russian aid. When none came, his forces were crushed and Simon was captured, leading to the slow Muslimification/Turkification of much of western Georgia. Then, in a replay of the great East–West rivalry between the Achamenian Persians and Hellenic Greeks and later the Sassanids and Byzantines, Georgia became one of the fields of battle for the two new heirs to that tradition, even if both were Muslim: Safavid Iran and Ottoman Turkey. A bizarre series of alliances ensued, pitting brother against brother, one seeking the aid of the distant Russian tsar, the second converting to Islam and courting the Persian shah or Ottoman sultan.

Then there is Giorgi Saakadze, the former *mouravi*, or "lord mayor" of Tbilisi who, in attempting to elevate his status to that of royalty by marriage to one of the two rival Georgian kingdoms of Kartli and Kakheti, overplayed his hand and was forced to flee to Iran. Converting to Islam, he led Persian armies on successful campaigns in Central Asia and Afghanistan, becoming an intimate of Shah Abbas. After ten years of loyal service, Saakadze was assigned the role of advisor to the commander and chief of another Persian expedition sent to Georgia to quell a revolt, a campaign that soon claimed tens of thousands of Georgian lives and the wholesale forced migration of thousands of other Georgian serf/slaves to northern Iran.[2]

Then something in Saakadze snapped, or perhaps he merely saw a traditional, Georgian-style opportunity. Luring the Persian commander into a dinner-party trap, Saakadze murdered him and, in a remarkable flip-flop, assumed a new role: that of the leader of Georgian revolt against the Persian overlord. A chaotic and brutal six-year guerrilla war ensued against Saakadze's former patron and dinner companion, the shah, which devastated and depopulated the country yet again, but ultimately led to the defeat of the Persians. National-hero status established, Saakadze once more attempted to elevate himself to royalty, but was rebuffed by Bagratid bluebloods again. Forced to flee once more, the Old Bull traveled west to offer his services to the Ottoman Porte, but was executed in 1629 because of the drunken conduct of the Georgian mercenaries whom he had brought with him into exile.

The sanguine saga of a man of such multiple allegiances (better known as treason) might be said to have a happy ending: in the darkest days of World War II, Stalin unleashed the ghost of Giorgi Saakadze on the Soviet masses as a blockbuster story to inspire them in the Great Patriotic War against the Nazi foe. The Soviet dictator even approved of the emotional climax of the film—the moment when Saakadze, drunk and feasting to victory over the Persians, opens a box containing the severed head of his eldest son Paata, who had been left at the court of Shah Abbas as a hostage. Stalin's own son, Yakov Dzhugashvili, had earlier been taken captive by the Germans, and died (or was killed) after Stalin refused to exchange him for Field Marshal Paulus of Stalingrad fame. "I will not trade a general for a private!" Stalin is said to have shouted.

Georgia's status continued to oscillate wildly through the mid- and late eighteenth century, with the two principal political entities, Kakheti and Kartli, appealing by turns to Catherine the Great for aid against the Persians, Turks, or often each other. The most serious plan for incorporating Georgia (or portions thereof) into the realm of the tsarist empire was expressed in the Treaty of Georgievsk of 1783, when Irakli II sought to place his fragile, multinational state under Catherine's protection. When war broke out with Ottoman Turkey in 1787, however, the tsarina pulled her troops out of the Caucasus to fight in the Balkans, leaving Georgia exposed not only to Turkish wrath in the west, but to a sudden lunge by the Qadjar Shah of Iran, who burned Tbilisi in 1795 and forced the aged Irakli to flee to the mountains, where he died in 1798. The last act of the 1,000-year Bagratid dynasty played out almost as farce in 1800, when Giorgi XII Batonishvili attempted to invite Russian aid against his rival brothers by willing his kingdom to Tsar Paul ("the Mad") on the condition that all titles, rights, and privileges of the Bagratid dynasty be retained. Paul accepted and then died. His son and successor, Tsar Alexander I, took one look at the contract and unilaterally abrogated the deal, abolishing the Bagratid throne.

Georgia—if there really had been such a state for 500 years—was no more.

* * *

Nations (or states) ebb and flow in history. What was an empire yesterday is now a colony, and what was a colony in history is today a registered member of the United Nations and World Trade Organization. Twenty years ago, who would have believed that Eritrea and East Timor would have achieved statehood, or that East Germany would disappear from the map? While the European Union continues to expand, with the ultimate goal of erasing the meaning of the concept of "frontier" between member states and blurring the concept of nationality down to a single, "European" essence, the constituent parts of the former USSR appear to be erecting ever greater barriers between themselves, even while ethnic atomization proceeds apace.

What does this have to do with Georgia?

Simply this: the geopolitical entity we think of today as "Georgia" has experienced the full spectrum of state existence over the millennia, from self-conscious mini-empire and overlord of others, to complete occlusion. And following its annexation by Russia in 1801, "Georgia" entered one of those long periods of time where it ceased to exist as anything other than an imaginative concept, and one that was often conflated with "Transcaucasia," a tsarist Russian territory defined by the Caucasus Mountains to the north, the Caspian Sea to the east, a fluctuating frontier with Persia/Iran to the south, and the Ottoman Empire and Black Sea to the west. In addition to "Georgia of the mind," also contained within this geographic concept was the fuzzy notion of "Armenia" (Yerevan was a mainly Muslim city until late in the nineteenth century; the main concentrations of ethnic Armenians were in the cities of Tbilisi and Baku) as well as the Muslim khanates formerly associated with northwestern Persia, which would eventually become known as "Azerbaijan."[3] Indeed, on an administrative and legal level, core nineteenth-century "Georgia" was further divided into two Russian-style provinces. Combined, they made up the Gruzinskaia guberniia, or Georgian Governorate, and covered perhaps half the territory eventually defined by twentieth-century geographers as being "Georgia." Curiously, the western province of Kutaisi was arguably far more "Georgian" than the eastern province of Tbilisi. This paradox was due to many factors ranging from the large number of Armenian merchants resident in the regional capital and the infusion of Russian (and German, Jewish, Polish, and other Slavic citizens of the empire) emigrants to the south Caucasus as soldiers and bureaucrats, as well as North and South Caucasus Muslims drawn to the "big town" to seek their fortunes.

The entire Black Sea coast, from today's Adjaria to Abkhazia (or Batumi to Sukhumi), was not even part of "Russian Georgia" at all, but dependant on Ottoman Turkey. Abkhazia only really became part of Russia in 1864, following the collapse of the so-called Murid Wars of Sheikh Shamil and the North Caucasus highlanders. The Georgian Muslim principality that today makes up Adjaria, meanwhile, was only ceded by the Ottomans to the tsar in 1877, more or less at the same time that U.S. federal forces were chasing the Nez Perce across Montana in the last chapter of the American Indian Wars.

Some scholars of colonial history like to compare the tsarist campaign in the Caucasus with the American conquest of the Old West in terms of both timing and style. While there certainly are a plethora of similarities, there is also one major difference: while virtually all the members of the newly conquered mini-nations of the American West were shunted off to reservations and utter poverty without respect to their social station, in the newly conquered Caucasus, the elite were almost always instantly assimilated into the ranks of the Russian ruling class. While peasants were turned into Russian-style serfs, aching under the burden of virtual slavery, the newly Russified Georgian nobility rushed off to the court in St. Petersburg, volunteering for officer service in the tsar's forces against Napoleon's march on Moscow in 1812 or to face the Charge of the Light Brigade in the Crimea in the 1850s.

In a word, Georgia (or at least much of the traditional Georgian aristocracy) did indeed become *Russian*—and with all the complexity that that word implies.[4] True, there was the odd, ugly peasant revolt against newly imposed tsarist-style serfdom, which often attracted other malcontents. The effort to replace Georgian with Russian as the language of liturgy in the Georgian church resulted in the most serious of such revolts and was centered near the western town of Lanchkhuti in the area known as Guria in 1820. The infamous Russian general Alexis Yermolov not only crushed the rebellion, but attempted to ensure that future generations of farmer/serfs would remember the trespasses of their elders with the maxim "extreme poverty will be their punishment!"

Guria, of course, remembered and became the deep base and cradle of Georgian national identity over the next 100 years, culminating in the so-called Gurian Republic of 1903–6, an agrarian "free-state" that at least one scholar maintains anticipated the anticolonial, peasant-based revolutions in the developing world in the second half of the twentieth century.[5]

* * *

Whether through forced or self-assimilation, the Russification of Georgia proceeded apace throughout the nineteenth century, with Tiflis (Tbilisi) serving as the growing cultural, commercial, and military center of all Russian realms south of the Caucasus Mountains. With the arrival of the steam locomotive, the city became a rail hub linking the booming new oil town of Baku on the Caspian Sea with the booming new oil terminal of Batumi on the Black Sea. The rail, wagon, and engine repair shops set up to keep the trains running soon attracted Russian workers from the north, creating an outlander proletariat class quite distinct from the local peasantry. From being a sleepy, Oriental backwater of some 50,000 souls to a bustling city of over half a million by the turn of the century, Tiflis was many things but a "Georgian" town it was not. As Stephen Jones points out, the bureaucracy was Russian (as were the majority of the resident industrial workers and soldiers), the merchants and bankers were Armenians, while the lower-class day laborers and fresh produce purveyors were Georgians, who only made up a quarter of the local population.[6] With the exception of the self-assimilated gentry class, to find "Georgians" in Georgia one had to travel into the countryside—and to increasingly self-consciously Georgian places such as Guria, which became the incubator of the leading figures in the social democratic/nationalist movement that was to culminate in the short-lived, quasi-Marxist Georgian Democratic Republic of 1918–21.

* * *

What distinguished the Georgian Russians (or Russified Georgians) from their co-citizens across the breadth of the tsarist empire was their response to the revolutionary movement known as the Russian Social Democratic Labor Party (RSDLP), which is often if incorrectly shorthanded to "the Bolsheviks."

The real Bolshevik's seizure of power in St. Petersburg in October 1917 was of course a momentous, historical event. But it was also part of a much longer process, dating back to the French Revolution, the industrialization of first England and then western Europe, and the 1848 "revolution that failed." That was the year that a certain Karl Marx penned his *Communist Manifesto*, which in turn resulted in the collected analysis of economics and society known as *Das Kapital*, which consequently spawned a vast number of interpretations and has served, ever since, as the theoretical basis for most of the socialist movements, revolts, and workers' parties throughout Europe, the United States, Russia, and eventually the entire world, of which the Bolsheviks were but one (albeit a very important) strain.[7]

The first contact young Russians of all ethnic persuasions (Russians, Tatars, Armenians, Georgians, Jews, etc.) had with the teachings of Marx and his colleague Friedrich Engels came in the universities and salon societies of Paris, Berlin, Zurich, and London. Like foreign exchange students today, the young "Russian" wannabe revolutionaries returned home imbued with hot new ideas, and fought fierce intellectual battles with one another over highly obscure points of theory, when not getting arrested for printing and distributing illegal pamphlets and newspapers or getting their heads beat in by roaming bands of Cossack enforcers of loyalty to the tsar, who cared little for the difference between Social Revolutionaries, Socialists Democrats, "Liquidationists," and "Vperedists," much less "Anarchists."

By the time of the failed revolution of December 1905 in St. Petersburg, the Marxist/Communist/Socialist movement in Russia had split into two basic groups, which for our purposes might be regarded as those who insisted on a top-down dictatorship of the working class masses controlled by a "knowing" revolutionary cadre in a unified, revolutionary state, and those who advocated the creation of a broad-based, working-class party from the bottom up, where revolutionary leadership emerged through the ballot box, and which allowed for elements of regional autonomy. The former policy became known as "Bolshevism," or the policy of the "majority," as that is what *Bolshevik* means in Russian. The leader of this faction was Vladimir I. Lenin, who needs no introduction. The "minority" view, in turn was known as "Menshevism," or the policy of the "minority," as that is what the word *Menshevik* means in Russian. The leader of this faction was Yuli Martov; his name does not even appear in the biographical entries of most comprehensive dictionaries.

In the Transcausus, the "majority" view was defended by a former seminarian from the Georgian town of Gori, who was named Iosif Dzhugashvili, but better known to history as Josef Stalin. His deep base in the region was the city of Baku, where he agitated among the thousands of oil-field workers who represented an ideal oppressed, "international" (multiethnic) industrialized proletariat ready to be radicalized. The "minority" view was defended by another Georgian, Noe Zhordania (Jordania), who hailed from the everproblematic western region of Guria, and whose primary base of support was the local Georgian peasantry and small craftsmen, whose consciousness had already been raised thanks to the establishment of Georgian-language newspapers, books, and discussion groups dating back to the late nineteenth century.

Today, it is tempting to speculate on how Caucasian history (and indeed, world Marxism) would read if the Menshevik strain of socialist democracy had survived as more than a footnote in history. That discussion, again, is outside the scope of this book, but for this footnote: from around 1906, when members of Jordania's Georgian Mensheviks decided to contest elections to the all-Russian Duma in St. Petersburg, they effectively entered into a coalition government with "bourgeois" elements in Tbilisi (and St. Petersburg) while establishing an agrarian-based, popular movement inspired by local (Georgian) "nationalism."[8] This was at odds not only with the theoretical Marxist revolutionary faction of Lenin's RSDLP Bolsheviks but also with the theoretical revolutionary framework of Martov's RSDLP Mensheviks. But unlike Polish, Ukrainian, and Jewish "national" communists associated with the Menshevik faction of the RSDLP who argued for a distinct national identity defined by territory, Jordania's Georgian agitators never declared themselves to be anything more than representing a particular region of "Russia" whose unique conditions demanded the inclusion of the peasantry (and good-thinking petty gentry) in the revolutionary movement on the fringes of the tsar's estate. Land reform was central to Jordania's program—but the keyword was "municipalification," as opposed to nationalization or collectivization. Free-holding peasants had the right to the title of their land.

Seen from an underground Bolshevik perspective (including that of Stalin), this was anathema. The Georgian social democrats/Mensheviks under Jordania were selling the larger Russian revolution down the river. Seen from a non-Bolshevik perspective, the evolving, compromising "Menshevik" shadow government of that part of the tsar's realm known generically as "Georgia" was at the vanguard of new ideas, such as the combination of social democracy with an explicitly "national" state.

Then came the cold, hard reality of World War I.

While the British and French faced off against the Germans in the fields of Flanders, and while the Anzac forces attempted to take Gallipoli in order to knock Ottoman Turkey out of the war, tsarist Russian forces faced off against the Austro-Hungarians and Germans across central Europe, as well as against Ottoman Turkey in the Caucasus and Black Sea.

The Transcaucasus front was arguably the most obscure theater of the Great War. This was due less to a lack of bloodshed and horror than to the sheer remoteness of the area. Whole armies froze to death in the frigid wilds of the high Anatolian Plateau in winter, or died of scurvy in the broiling summers. Meanwhile, both belligerents conducted campaigns of what we moderns might call "ethnic cleansing" of those elements of local society allied with the perceived enemy other.[9] But by the end of 1916, tsarist arms had managed to push the prewar frontier back some 250 miles, up to and beyond the Turkish city of Erzurum. Russia's traditional Turkish/Muslim great-power foe was supine, and the tsar's claim to be the heir to the Byzantine Empire (and thus Constantinople) appeared to be at hand. And then, seemingly from out of nowhere, came the February Revolution of 1917, the demise of the Romanovs and the establishment of the short-lived Provisional Government of Alexander Kerensky in St. Petersburg. While the Russian Mensheviks gave limited support to the post-tsarist government and its policies of continuing the war effort, the Bolsheviks under Lenin demanded an immediate end to Russian involvement in the conflict. Then came the Bolshevik putsch against Kerensky in October and the promised removal of Russian forces from the war.

On the Transcaucasus front, chaos ensued. Disgruntled soldiers were soon streaming to their homes across the breadth of what had been Russia, using "Georgia" as a transit zone. Facing the prospect of Ottoman invasion and occupation, a state of panic gripped Tbilisi as leaders of the sundry nationalist (Georgian, Armenian, and "Tatar"/Azerbaijani) and political factions (Menshevik, Social Democratic, Bolshevik, Social Revolutionary, among others) sought a means of avoiding both war with the Turks and a revolt by mainly "Bolshevized" Russian conscript soldiers garrisoned in and around the city. Thousands would gather at the Alexander Gardens in central Tbilisi to demand Soviet power and "peace at any price."

Even at this late date, remarkably, there was still little talk and less commitment to establish an independent "Georgian" state. Meeting at the Moorish-style State Treasury Theater (now the Opera and Ballet Theater on Rustaveli Avenue in central Tbilisi) on November 19, 1917, over 300 delegates drawn from all major ethnic Georgian (as opposed to Armenian, "Tatar," and Russian) political and social organizations gathered together to hammer out a mutually acceptable plan for the future. Addressing the congress, Noe Jordania continued to insist on Georgia and the rest of Transcaucasia remaining part of a unitary Russian state—albeit a new, democratic, and socialist Russia in which national minorities such as the Georgians (as well as the Abkhaz, Armenians, and Ossetians) would enjoy special cultural and political rights. The alternative to continued territorial association with Russia would be, in Jordania's words, "submission to the East," meaning that Christian Georgia would once again become a vassal to the Muslim Turkish empire.[10]

He also called for the creation of an army and militia separate from the command structure inherited from the tsars that was slipping into the hands of the Bolsheviks. The problem was the acquisition of arms from the local arsenal. On the night of November 29, on the secret orders of Jordania and his most intimate Menshevik/Social Democrat associates, a motley gang of some 300 Georgian peasant soldiers raided the armory. Not a shot was fired—and the nucleus of the first (and last) Transcaucasia Army was formed. Bolshevik forces in Tbilisi (and even Lenin in St. Petersburg) were taken by complete surprise, and soon decamped for their regional stronghold of Baku while legal power, now backed by guns, was delivered into the hands of the newly formed (and short-lived) Transcaucasus Commissariat. Although the Commissariat theoretically served all social groups in the south Caucasus, it in effect became the government of the forming state that would be known as the Georgian Democratic Republic, once shorn of the appendages that would become the future states of Armenia and Azerbaijan.[11]

Ottoman Turkish forces were on the move to take advantage of Russia's collapse and devolution into civil war. Under the provisions of the Brest-Litovsk Treaty, came the Ottoman occupation of the provinces of Kars, Ardahan, and Batumi that had been lost to Russia forty years earlier. Not satisfied with these gains, the Ottoman army (sometimes called the Army of Islam) under Nuri Pasha then began its long march across the Caucasus toward the greatest prize in the region—the oil fields around the city of Baku on the shores of the Caspian Sea. To legalize their eastward push, in early 1918 the triumvirate in power in Istanbul "helped" Caucasian Georgians, Armenians, and Azerbaijanis cobble together the ephemeral entity known as the Transcaucasus Democratic Republic, which served as the political vessel needed to "invite" the Turks in to crush the Baku Commune in Azerbaijan. This was a development that pleased neither the Bolshevik government now ensconced in Moscow, the government of Kaiser Wilhelm in Berlin that was allied with the Ottomans, or the British, who were still at war with both Germany and Ottoman Turkey. While the Germans negotiated percentage points of Baku petroleum production with Moscow if Berlin could keep the Turks away from Baku (for example, by denying them use of the railway lines crossing Georgia) and even considered the idea of recognizing Baku as a part of Georgia, the British launched the expeditionary unit known as the Dunster Force to save the day. The detachment, consisting of British officers and Sikh soldiers from British India, made its way to Baku from Mesopotamia via Iran with orders to secure or destroy oil production facilities lest they fall into the hands of the Turks, Germans, or Bolsheviks. Once in Baku, however, the Dunster Force ended up fighting on the side of the Bolsheviks and Right Social Democrats (Mensheviks) as well as the local Armenians. When the Army of Islam finally reached the city after having marched across Georgia (without use of the railway), a ninety-day siege ensued, ending in the collapse of the Commune in mid-September and the return of the government of independent Azerbaijan from self-exile in the city of Ganje, with the attendant massacre of Armenians by Azerbaijani Muslims intent on revenge for the slaughter of their kith and kin at the hands of Armenians the previous March, and the execution of the (Bolshevik) Baku Commissars after their evacuation to Turkmenistan on the far side of the Caspian Sea.[12] The Transcaucasus Democratic Republic meanwhile, had long been a dead letter, having self-dissolved when Noe Jordania's Georgian part of the troika declared its own independence under the secret sponsorship of Kaiser Germany.

The date was May 26, 1918, and is still celebrated as Georgia's "real" Independence Day. On May 28, the shocked and confused "national" governments of the Armenian and Azerbaijani parts of the defunct Transcaucasus Democratic Republic unenthusiastically announced their own independence and sovereignty; the Armenian declaration was made in Tbilisi, now the capital of a different country.[13]

It was a confusing time that was made more confusing by the multiple territorial claims asserted by each of the three principal Caucasus states against the other two, the spillover of the civil war raging in Russia between Reds and Whites, and then the sudden collapse of German arms in Europe in November 1918. Apparently convinced of a coming German victory, Jordania had chosen the wrong main-state sponsor for Georgian independence and received little sympathy from the victorious entente powers when the tide of battle turned in favor of Trotsky's Red Army against Denikin's Whites. Adding to the confusion was the newly created League of Nations, which required all new member states to define their borders by several criteria, the primary one being control of territory. One ugly result was the arming of less-than-perfectly controlled militias by the new nationalist governments, who then sent their "armies" forth to stake out a maximalist vision of "traditional" lands of the new/ancient nation state. State-sponsored "ethnic cleansing" is the modern term that comes to mind.[14]

* * *

By the spring of 1920, the Red Army under Trotsky had turned the tide against Denikin's Whites and secured Bolshevik power in Moscow and most of Russia. It was time to reclaim lands lost during the dark days of the revolution. High on the list were the Transcaucasus republics of Azerbaijan, Armenia, and Georgia, which had represented such an essential part of tsarist Russia for over a century, but which had fallen under the sway of the imperialist British following German and Turkish collapse in November 1918. The first push was against the Democratic Republic of Azerbaijan, which quickly led to the collapse of the "bourgeois" government of the Musavat Party. Next to go was the Armenian Dashnaksutyun government in Yerevan in early December of that same year. Surrounded and essentially friendless—the new British occupation forces that had replaced the Germans and Turks following the November Armistice would only guard the oil railway line from Baku to Batumi—the Menshevik government of Noe Jordania waited alone for the inevitable invasion of Bolshevik forces.

And when it came in early 1921, the Red Army was under the nominative control of a fellow Georgian, Josef Stalin. Jordania and his government fled the capital on February 25, 1921, and attempted to make a last stand in Batumi (which had simultaneously been declared the capital-in-exile of Chechnya, of all places). British aid was not forthcoming and three weeks later Jordania and his supporters boarded a ship and steamed across the Black Sea and into exile.

Georgia had just disappeared from history—again.

* * *

Following a ruthless purging of Mensheviks across the territory that had been independent Georgia, that entity was next subjected to the full weight of the Bolshevik interpretation of Marxism, as was the rest of former tsarist Russia under Bolshevik control. As such, it is not exactly honest to try to separate the Georgian experience from that of other national groups that would eventually make up the USSR, aside from this: while Stalin appears to have had little love lost for his native land (and even less for the deviationist Mensheviks) and aggressively pursued the policy of creating a centralized Communist state with its capital in Moscow, Lenin appears nearly to have had a soft spot for the country and came close to allowing Georgia to enter the USSR as a full, constituent member "Soviet Republic" along with Russia, Ukraine, and Belorussia at its creation in 1922, instead of merely as a part of the newly created Transcaucasus Federated Soviet Socialist Republic, or TcFSSR, which also included Armenia and Azerbaijan (and Abkhazia).

The TcFSSR itself was a compromise solution bitterly opposed by Stalin and his fellow Bolshevik Georgian, Sergo Ordzhonikidze. Both advocated the complete assimilation of all the small national groups (and large ones, too, such as Ukrainians) into the new, Russian-speaking *Homo Sovieticus*, or Soviet Man. But in keeping with Lenin's policy of "national self-determination" for all the peoples of the new Soviet state, the three primary south Caucasus Soviet entities that made up the TcFSSR were encouraged to preserve elements of "national" culture. Simultaneously, they were also subjected to various levels of atomization that theoretically reflected the communal needs and aspirations of national minorities living among the three, titular new nations.

In the case of Georgia, these subnational territories included the "autonomous district" of South Ossetia as well as the "autonomous republic" of Abkhazia (the Abkhaz insist that they were "federated" with Georgia as an equal partner) and the "autonomous republic" of Adjaria. The latter was unique in the lands of the USSR as being an autonomy designed to accommodate ethnic Georgian Muslims, who were not a nationality at all, but a religion-based community recognized by the officially atheistic state.

The standard Western interpretation of this Bolshevik or Leninist policy of creating subrepublic "reservations" within the larger Soviet states is that it was all part and parcel of a cynical policy of "divide and rule." The fact that all of these substates would become centers of communal confrontation and separatist strife when the house of cards known as the USSR collapsed in 1991 is seen, retroactively, as evidence of such an initial, nefarious scheme. But another reading of political developments in the Caucasus during the period 1918–22 is also possible. Essentially, it questions whether there ever was a monolithic Bolshevik position on the "nationality question," and posits that rather than being victims of a vast cynical plot, the majority of the 150-odd recognized ethnic entities that made up the peoples of the USSR actually benefited from Lenin's policies of ethnic particularism—or at least were allowed to survive in an atmosphere that would have otherwise led ineluctably to their total assimilation and disappearance. The prerogatives of the local majority might have been limited in favor of the local minority on a regional level (Ossetians within Georgia, for example), but within the larger context of the USSR, the "Great Russians" also saw their traditional status reduced in favor of smaller ethnic entities ranging from Ukrainians to Kazakhs, Koreans, and others.[15]

Georgia played a multifaceted role in this larger process, with Tbilisi serving as both the administrative center of the "Georgian" part of the TcFSSR as well as the capital of the entire TcFSSR from 1922 through 1936. That was the year of the next series of territorial and communal adjustments announced by Stalin and enshrined by the 1936 Soviet Constitution, which included provisions for Georgia, Armenia, and Azerbaijan to reemerge from the TcFSSR as separate and theoretically "independent" socialist states, but whose very first act of sovereignty was to ask to join the USSR. By that time, however, all three had been utterly transformed by the Soviet experience, and largely at the hands of yet another native son of Georgia: Lavrenti Beria.

History has been cruel to Beria, and few would argue with its verdict. His arrest and eventual execution in 1953 on the standard (if patently ridiculous) charge of treason against the Soviet state allowed Nikita Khrushchev to heap shame and opprobrium on Beria and blame him for all the excesses, exiles, purges, and indeed mass murders associated with the concept of "Stalinism" during the bloody 1930s and 1940s. Although Beria held many positions throughout his thirty-year career, from that of a Bolshevik spy posing as a young architect infiltrated into the Azerbaijani nationalist Musavat party in 1918, to that of chief of the NKVD (the future KGB) tasked with stealing the secrets needed to midwife the Soviet nuclear bomb program in the aftermath of World War II (the design center where captured German scientists labored was set up just outside his Beria's native village of Merkheuli, in the Sukhumi district of Abkhazia), his main purview of activity was as a "Chekist," or officer in the early Bolshevik Party security and ideology department, first in Azerbaijan, then Georgia, and finally Moscow, where he also served as *tamada*, or toastmaster, at Stalin's nightly table.

It had been a very long journey for Beria.

Born into a poor Mingrelian home in 1899, little is known about Lavrenti's youth. But even the official version of his adolescence and adult life is instructive about the contradictions and catapults of the life of a young Georgian in late tsarist Russian and early Soviet times. What is solid is Beria's decision to move from "Georgia" (there was none at the time) to Baku in 1915 to continue his studies at a technical school. Around this time, he joined the outlawed Communist Party (Bolshevik wing), was then drafted into a labor battalion of the tsar's army and sent to the Romanian front. God only knows what he saw, but the Georgian teenager from Sukhumi soon became a Bolshevik activist among disgruntled soldiers. Read from a certain aspect, the rest of his life was defined by extreme violence.

Following Tsar Nicholas II's abdication in 1917, Beria returned to Baku to witness the creation of the Baku Commune—and the slaughter of thousands of anticommunist Muslim Azerbaijanis. He was also witness to the Commune's subsequent collapse in September 1918, when Azerbaijani nationalists backed by the Ottoman Turkish army of Nuri Pasha stormed the city and slaughtered thousands of Armenians and Bolsheviks.[16]

Rather than go underground or flee, however, Beria started working as a Bolshevik spy within the Azerbaijani nationalist Musavat Party, and then as an informer and spy-runner in Tbilisi, where he was twice arrested by the Mensheviks. With the Bolshevik return to power in Baku in 1920, Beria returned to the Azerbaijani capital and embraced the life of an enforcer in the newly formed Azerbaijani branch of the Soviet *Cheka*, the acronym for the Extraordinary Commission for Fighting Counterterrorism and Sabotage.

Set up in 1917 by the notorious Felix Dzerzhinskii in Moscow to deal out summary justice to those opposing the Bolshevik revolution, the Cheka is a byword for Bolshevik terror to this day—and Lavrenti Beria was a Chekist nonpareil. So remorseless was the young Georgian that Beria came under criticism from fellow Bolsheviks for seeming to enjoy the torture he inflicted on his victims. Despite this, the young Chekist also displayed an uncanny ability to flatter and cajole superiors and rose quickly through the ranks. By 1921, he was reassigned to his native Georgia to assist in rooting out class enemies and Menshevik resistance to Bolshevik rule, to which he applied himself with vigor. This would seem to be the time that he attracted the attention of his future mentor and patron, Stalin.

The rest, as they say, is history. Beria soon worked his way first to the top of the Georgian Cheka and then the Transcaucasus Cheka (the former "national" and the latter "regional"; both forces were headquartered in the same building in Tbilisi, which was convenient, as Beria retained both posts). In 1931 he was appointed first secretary (chairman) of the Georgian Communist Party and then, in 1932, to the post of first secretary of the Transcaucasus Communist Party. Lavrenti Beria was the top ideological boss not only in his native Georgia but in Armenia and Azerbaijan as well—and just at the time that Stalin was gearing up to purge the USSR of so-called Old Bolsheviks unhappy with his increasingly dictatorial ways. The process began around 1934, reached its frenzied peak of terror in 1937, and slowly dissipated. The show trial, confession, and execution of Nikolai Bukharin in 1938 are generally regarded as the end of the bloodletting process.[17] By one estimate, of the 4.5 million people arrested during this period, 800,000 were executed.

The situation in Georgia under Beria mirrored the national trend across the USSR. Peasants, factory managers, writers, and musicians were scythed down. Long-standing members of the Party were tortured to death in prison or shot by the three-man judge–jury–execution squads known as *troikas*. Others, such as the Abkhaz Communist leader, Nestor Lakoba, simply died in mysterious circumstances and were posthumously accused of a wide variety of capital crimes. Party loyalty played little role in one's chances of survival. Even Eduard Bediia, the presumed ghostwriter of Beria's book praising the young Stalin (*On the History of Bolshevik Organizations in Transcaucasia*, which often placed Stalin at the center of events in extraordinarily imaginative ways) perished in the purge. By one estimate, of 4,000 full and candidate members of the Georgian Communist Party, at least 10 percent were eliminated. Among the mass of nonparty members in Georgia, tens of thousands are believed to have perished according to a quota system devised in Moscow. Beria himself barely escaped purging when his superior at the NKVD (Communist Secret Police) in Moscow, Nikolai Ezhov, instructed a subordinate to start collecting incriminating material on Beria. But fortuitously for Lavrenti, the subordinate in question turned out to be a Beria loyalist, and the Georgian top-cop turned the tables on his rival: Ezhov was soon arrested and executed for crimes against the Soviet state, and Beria assumed the chief police job in the USSR himself.

Ensconced in Moscow on the eve of World War II, Beria soon brought key elements of his so-called Georgian Gang of Caucasus enforcers to the Soviet capital, spending the rest of his life in the highest echelons of Soviet power, responsible for everything from running spies and partisans behind German lines, to moving Soviet industry from besieged Moscow to the far side of the Ural Mountains (and then back again, following the German collapse at Stalingrad). He also administered to the vast network of labor camps in Siberia designed for the politically incorrect that is known by its

Russian acronym GULAG (as opposed to the parallel network of slave-labor settlements designed to accommodate-until-death German and other Axis-connected prisoners of war). Beria's reputation as Soviet security boss nonpareil even made the cover of the March 1948 *Time* magazine, where he was erroneously described as the "cop at the keyhole (of the Kremlin)." In fact, Beria had left his post as top cop in 1946 and had become a Politburo member with responsibility, among other things, for developing the Soviet nuclear bomb. In the super-secretive postwar Soviet state, it was difficult for outsiders to know exactly who was responsible for what inside the Kremlin, with the best clues derived from the study of proximity to Stalin, as found in official photographs.

Following Stalin's death in 1953 (rumor and speculation still swirl around the question of whether he had a hand in Stalin's demise by neglecting to call doctors in a timely manner), Beria essentially took control of the Soviet government. But still he played coy. Intuiting that the idea of yet another Georgian assuming the mantle of absolute power in the USSR would create waves in rival power circles (particularly the military), the master manipulator ruled through several proxies—even though all indications are that Beria had an aggressive agenda for the future of the Soviet state, one tailor-made for his vision of the future.

First, he reversed the last of Stalin's purges aimed at leading cadres of his patronage network in the Transcaucasus republics, reinstating long-term subordinates who had just been thrown in jail. Next, he began pursuing a policy of de-Russification in western Ukraine, which would re-allow "Ukrainian national consciousness" to imbue the schoolroom and government offices in Kiev, decriminalize the Uniate (Catholic) Church, and allow the reestablishment of ties with the Vatican. Finally and most crucially, Beria embarked on what might be regarded as a truly radical "reform" package of pre-perestroika restructuring that ultimately envisaged the removal of hard-liner German communist boss Walter Ulbricht and the reunification of eastern and western Germany ("East Germany" or the German Democratic Republic was not established until 1954) as a demilitarized and neutral buffer state in Central Europe—concepts that were anathema to the top brass of the victorious Red Army and its (recently demoted) hero, General Georgi Zhukov, who had conquered Berlin in 1945 and meant to keep his tanks there.

Encouraged by the promise of reform and the prospect of ousting Ulbricht, however, the Eastern German workers soon pushed Beria's reform process over the precipice. Even as workers surrounded Brecht's Berliner Ensemble Theater on the banks of the Spree, demanding that the famed director come outside and help them "rehearse their revolution" (some say he was directing his *Caucasian Chalk Circle* at the time), Soviet tanks were rolling out of their barracks to crush the uprising. It was June 17, 1953, and the Soviet Union had never appeared so brutal—or so weak.

If Cold War analysts in Washington and the rest of the West were unprepared for East Berlin uprising and the Soviet reaction, they were taken by complete surprise by the next turn of the screw—the arrest of Beria in the Kremlin on charges of treason against the USSR and World Communism.

Officially, the day was June 26—but that was only announced weeks later—and Lavrenti Beria had gone to attend a hastily convened Presidium of the Council of Ministers in the Kremlin office of his long-serving ally, Georgi Malenkov. Perhaps lulled into a false sense of security by the fact the Kremlin and indeed the city of Moscow were theoretically under the control of elite internal troops called the MVD, who were loyal to Beria, the top cop left his personal guard outside the office, entered the familiar room dressed in casual clothes and did not suspect anything amiss until Malenkov began stuttering odd phrases that increasingly sounded like accusations against Beria. Any doubt about what was afoot ceased when Nikita Khrushchev stood up and made a "proper" denunciation. At that precise moment, other leading anti-Beria figures, including bitter rival General Zhukov, burst into the room, searched Beria for weapons, and spirited him away. It seems most likely that Beria was shot or throttled to death that same day to ensure that his vast network of supporters would not rally and rescue him; in any case, he was never provably seen again.

Still, the protocols of the Soviet legal system had to be observed.

In July, Beria was officially charged with the crimes of treason, terrorism, and participation in a counterrevolutionary group that was attempting to overturn the socialist society of workers and peasants set up by Lenin and return it to the evils of capitalism. Throughout the width and breadth of the USSR, Beria was denounced in the most scathing terms, particularly in the Russian heartland where Great Russian chauvinism was and remains a social and political factor. Even longtime associates from Beria's "Georgian Gang" of thirty years' standing, such as the Azerbaijani Communist Party boss, Mir Jafar Bagirov, got on the anti-Beria bandwagon, pleading blindness to Beria's manifest crimes, and asking for forgiveness in the spirit of self-criticism. Bagirov was begging in vain: he too, was shot. Others associates were sent into the GULAG system once run by Beria.

If still alive at the time, Beria must have had no illusions about what his fate would be. Throughout his long career as Chekist informer, enforcer, and then top cop in the Caucasus and finally throughout the USSR, he had been personally responsible for the deaths of tens of thousands and had extracted many a worthless confession from a former subordinate or perceived rival himself, all detailing political crimes against the state that everyone knew to be sheerest fiction. It was the system and one played along.

As Amy Knight cites in her excellent study on Beria,[18] when the good citizens of Tbilisi received word of Beria's arrest on the evening of July 10, 1953, they quickly removed all of Beria's pictures throughout the capital and immediately began the awkward process of renaming the streets and squares named after him during his long years of power. But they did so without enthusiasm. In less than a year, from Stalin's death on March 5 to the first official announcement of Beria's arrest in a tersely worded article in the Communist Party mouthpiece, *Pravda*, Georgia had lost the two individuals of power who many believed acted as their protectors and viceroys in Moscow. Although the cult of Stalin remained intact until Khrushchev's "secret speech" of 1957 began the process of de-Stalinization throughout the USSR, the cult of Beria came crashing down as soon as the official announcement of his removal from power was made. Lavrenti Beria had just been erased from history, save for the use of his name as that of the ultimate Soviet bogeyman, a state of affairs that continues until today.

But there is room to speculate that Beria's legacy in his native land was more haunting. Unlike Stalin, who occasionally vacationed on the Black Sea coast but seems to have had an active dislike for all things Georgian aside from food (he favored speaking Esperanto as a new "international" language and even scandalously missed his own mother's funeral, nominating Beria to be his plenipotentiary representative in this consummately "Georgian" theater of bereavement), from all appearances Beria reveled in his Caucasian roots. As head of the ideological police, then as chairman of the Georgian Communist Party, and after that as effective governor of all three Caucasian states, Beria was an implementer of Bolshevik policy in the region—and a believer in that task, whether it was increasing industrial production of oil or steel in accordance with the new Five Year Plan or rooting out *kulaks*, the farmers and former landlords grown too big for their own britches. While he personified the Bolshevik urge to crush any and all deviations from the party line, whether the petite bourgeois nationalism of the Georgian Mensheviks or perceived rivals along his rise to power, paradoxically he also evinced the urge to surround himself with kith and kin from his native region, indulging in the same sort of romantic localism that had been the cause for elimination of tens of thousands of his victims for their having resisted Sovietization.[19]

Thus, the question: just how "Georgian" was Beria, and what was and is his legacy in his native land?

As the head of ideology, he was responsible for inculcating the spirit of class struggle in the young. One technique of doing so was to create ideologues among teachers in secondary schools, particularly in rural areas. In addition to performing normal pedagogical tasks, the teachers were ideally placed to weed out ideological impurities among the parents of students. As elsewhere in the Soviet Union, children were rewarded for spying on and then denouncing their own parents as enemies of the people.

Not surprisingly, these rural or semirural functionaries lived better than the peasants and formed the bedrock of the system. Their offspring, too, enjoyed comparative advantages in the way of education and moved further up the party ladder than their fathers, often in the fast lane of the security services.

An example of this phenomenon was a young man born in 1928 in Noe Jordania's hometown of Lanchkhuti in the western Georgian region called Guria. His father was a schoolteacher and such a committed communist that it appears that his son was not even baptized. One report has it that an uncle was killed in the first communist revolt of 1905, making early communism almost a family affair; it remains unclear whether family sympathy gravitated to the Mensheviks or Bolsheviks, although the suggestion is the latter. A few daring scholars even go so far as to suggest that the entire family were Cheka—the notorious Bolshevik "security police" created in 1917 by Felix Dzerzhinskii, and the organization so intimately associated with Beria.

The young man in question is Eduard Shevardnadze.

Notes

1. Ronald Suny, *The Making of the Georgian Nation* (Bloomington: Indiana University Press, 1994), p. 46.

2. Speculation continues to this day about the ethnic origins of Shah Reza Pahlavi, whose family allegedly hails from the same area.

3. Although a detailed discussion of the differences in national development is outside the scope of this work, it is useful to point to a few seminal books on the subject. Cf. Ernest Gellner's *Nations and Nationalism* (Ithaca: Cornell University Press, 1983), as well as commentary on Gellner's theories, as found in *The State of the Nation*, ed. John Hall (New York: Cambridge University Press, 1998).

4. As the sociologist/historian Georgi Derluguian succinctly put it in an email to the author: "The upper class shifts of vassal allegiance and corresponding cultural conversions (have) had a long tradition in this part of the world." Translation: Georgia became Russia, and Georgians became Russians, whether it was the plebian response to Karl Marx's *Communist Manifesto* of 1848, or the elite response to the Treaty of Berlin of 1877, or the elite/plebian response to the call to arms in 1914, and the advent of World War I.

5. Cf. Stephen Jones's deliciously dense *Socialism in Georgian Colors (The European Road to Social Democracy, 1883–1917)* (Cambridge, MA: Harvard University Press, 2005), especially chapter 6, "The Gurian Republic." Standard Marxist–Leninist theory maintains that the urban proletariat is the vanguard class of social change and revolution; in "Georgia," the leading force was the peasantry.

6. This state of affairs has resulted in a sort of unspoken rivalry between Georgians and Armenians to this day. Ibid., p. 18.

7. I can think of no better overview of the period in question than Eric Hobsbawm's *The Age of Revolution (1789–1848)* and his *The Age of Capital (1848–1875)* (both London: Weidenfeld and Nicolson, 1962).

8. "Particularism" might be a better word; as a frontline province in the on-again/off-again conflict between Russia and the Ottoman and Persian empires, Georgians (and Armenians) regarded Russia as their ultimate protector, and there is little hard evidence to suggest anything akin to a national liberation or independence movement afoot among either group until *after* the collapse of tsarist power, and then only as the least worst choice given the circumstances.

9. That is where this writer will leave the issue of the alleged slaughter of Armenians at the hands of the Ottoman Turks and local Kurdish militias, as well as the slaughter of local Muslims by Armenians, Georgians, and other land-claiming Christians. The charge of "genocide" is a sword with two sharp edges.

10. Cf. Jones, *Socialism in Georgian Colors,* p. 261. Jordania also argued that an independent Georgia or even a Georgia federated with but technically outside of Russia would lead to (Georgian) "bourgeois domination" of the other national minorities inside a territorial Georgian state. Seventy-five years later, following the collapse of the USSR and the emergence of post-Soviet Georgia under the stewardship of Zviad Gamsakhurdia, this would be precisely the issue to bring so much misery to all parties concerned in the nationalist experiment.

11. Cf. ibid., p. 280.

12. For more on this fascinating and complex subject, see Ron Suny, *The Baku Commune* (Princeton: Princeton University Press, 1972), especially pp. 280–88.

13. To gain a flavor of the times, I would suggest two quite different books, not so much to read as an accurate history of the period, but to study as icons of the age: Kurban Said, *Ali and Nino* (New York: Random House, 2000) and P.D. Ouspensky, *In Search of the Miraculous* (New York: Harcourt Brace, 1949). The former is a Romeo and Juliet love story written in German that tells the tragic tale of an Azerbaijani noble youth and a lesser Georgian princess during the period 1914–20 as the old world of the tsarist empire collapses and the brave new world of independent Azerbaijan comes into being against the dark specter of the Bolshevik revolution and pending interethnic strife. No less an analyst than former CIA director Stansfield Turner once famously told a friend of mine that if one were to read only one book on the Caucasus to understand the basic dynamic, Ali and Nino is that book, although the issue of the identity of its author remains in dispute. The latter book consists of the memoirs of P.D. Ouspensky, a Russian Orientalist and chief disseminator of the teachings of Georges Gurdjieff, a mystic philosopher from the Caucasus of mixed Armenian/Pontic Greek descent, who cultivated an extraordinarily wide range of eastern traditions, ranging from esoteric Sufi literature written in Persian to Indian dance and even the musical theory of the mystery of the octave. Despite a weak command of Russian, Gurdjieff was nonetheless able to attract a substantial number of leading Russian intellectuals in Moscow and St. Petersburg to what some might today refer to as a cult; they then funded the opening of his Institute for the Harmonious Development of Man in Tbilisi in 1919. In his memoirs, Ouspensky relates how on their arrival to Tbilisi in 1918, the pair were obliged to spend the night on the train in Tbilisi station because it was simply too dangerous to go out on the streets, which were flooded with disgruntled soldiers returning from the Turko-Caucasus front, and quite a bit of action at the station, too. Ouspensky witnessed three executions on the platform that night: one of a soldier accused of theft, a second soldier mistaken for the first, and then the third mistaken for the second before the initial error in identification was discovered. The very idea that Gurdjieff was recruiting truth seekers in such an environment speaks volumes about the cross-cultural intellectual interaction/desperation of the times. With the arrival of the Bolsheviks, the guru and his followers next moved on to Istanbul, then London, Paris, and finally the United States, where the Institute for Harmonious Development of Man morphed into the well-respected Gurdjieff Society.

14. A meticulous map put together by the German scholars Robert Hewsen and Christian Randomer of Tübingen University's Near East Atlas department and published by the Dr. Ludwig Reichert Verlag (Weisbaden, 1991) graphically illustrates the territorial claims and counterclaims of some twenty-five different ethno/national entities in the Caucasus region circa 1918, and how these contested borders were finally resolved after 1921. The maze of color-coded vertical orange, horizontal yellow, diagonal azure, double-lined lime green, cross-hatched red, and quilted blue is a tough read, albeit a pretty good indication of not only what was going on in the maximalist minds of the leadership of Greater Georgia (or Armenia, Azerbaijan, Ossetia, Chechnya, etc.) of the time, but also the nasty confrontations between former neighbors on the ground. Most of those represented by colors or cross-hatch had probably never considered themselves "Georgians," "Armenians," "Ossetians," or "Abkhazians" before, and were most likely the genetic descendants of two or more of the newly declared nationalities, but were now forced to chose a single, ethnic tag—and then go and root out all others not belonging to the new national persuasion.

15. For more on this, see Terry Martin's *The Affirmative Action Empire* (Ithaca: Cornell University Press, 2001).

16. Cf. Suny, *The Baku Commune*, as well as Shevket Suereyya Aydemir's *Suyu Arayan Adam* [Man Seeking Water] (Remzi Kitabevi, Istanbul, 1930?), which are the memoirs of an Ottoman officer involved in Nuri Pasha's march on Baku and subsequent withdrawal.

17. To get an insider's sense of the insane brutality of the period, there is simply no better resource book than Simon Sebag Montefiore's *Stalin: The Court of the Red Tsar*, (New York: Random House, 2005). For those who prefer their history in the form of a novel, Arthur Koestler's brillant *Darkness at Noon* (New York: Macmillan 1941) is a barely fictional account of this most sordid chapter in Soviet history.

18. Amy Knight, *Beria: Stalin's First Lieutenant* (Princeton: Princeton University Press, 1993).

19. The theme of collective amnesia about the legacy of Beria, the Janus-faced cultured monster, is explored by (Soviet) Georgian film maker Tengiz Abuladze in his 1985 classic *Repentance* through the character named Varlam, the Georgian-chant singing, Shakespeare-sonnet reciting, psycho-killer "mayor" of Tbilisi. Upon his death and fancy burial, a dissenting voice emerges: the surviving, orphaned daughter of one of Varlam's many victims. She swears she will not allow the corpse to rest in its grave, and demands a reckoning with the unspeakable past. Finally, repentance is achieved after Varlam's son Abel unearths the rotting body from the ground and throws it to the crows.

What is curious about the film is that it was made in Soviet Georgia with state funds and starring State Artists, such as the legendary actress Variko (who also appeared in the 1943 epic *Giorgi Saakadze*) and thus was clearly sanctioned by the regime. To what end, however? Because the Soviet government thought the population needed to be reminded of Beria's crimes, thirty years after his execution and erasure from history?

3

The Silver Fox

For many in the West, the Cold War is symbolized by the crushing of the anticommunist uprisings in Berlin in 1953, Budapest in 1956, and Prague in 1968. But during those long years on multiple occasions, Georgians also flooded the streets of Tbilisi to demand that their small nation be allowed to leave the USSR and with the same result: Red Army tanks rolled out of the barracks and crushed the protestors claim to freedom. If the bloody crackdowns are known in the West at all, it is as distant events in a distant country deep behind the Iron Curtain, which, having given birth to Stalin, somehow deserved its fate.

It is not known what role the twenty-eight-year-old NKVD/MVD officer Eduard Shevardnadze played in the crushing of Georgian nationalism in 1956. But his rapid advancement through the ranks of the security services certainly suggests that his activities were politically correct. Indeed, young Eduard joined all the right organizations at the right time, starting in 1946 at age eighteen with that springboard for future party activity, the Komsomol (Communist Youth League), becoming a member of the Communist Party two years later, in 1948. Whether the twenty-year-old overachiever ever met or was cultivated by Beria is not known. Georgi Derluguian, for one, suggests that Shevardnadze was probably spared association because he was too young to have caught Lavrenti's attention. But given the circumstances of Beria's demise in 1953, including the dismantling of his extensive patronage network in the Caucasus (and the execution of many of his top lieutenants), a connection to the fallen Georgian was not something one would boast about. On the contrary, Shevardnadze's career may actually have taken a sudden jump upward after the elimination of the echelons above him in the security and Party apparatus. Thereafter, Eduard Shevardnadze not only survived but also thrived in his chosen role as regime loyalist during this crucial period in Soviet history, just as the Cold War was freezing over.

In 1957, he was appointed leader of the Komsomol organization throughout

Georgia (in the same year that Khrushchev announced the campaign to de-Stalinize the USSR). Appointed a member of the Georgian Supreme Soviet in 1959, he was next made minister of Maintaining Public Order in 1965, and then simultaneously elevated to police general and the post of minister of Internal Affairs (MVD) in 1968. His brief was to root out "economic enemies of the people," and he soon developed a reputation as an incorruptible ideologue. In one celebrated incident, Shevardnadze called together members of the local elite and asked them to vote with a show of hands on a law concerning corruption. He then demanded that all present keep their arms up while he inspected wrists—and made each man explain how he had obtained his Rolex.

By 1972, his pursuit of economic criminals in famously corrupt Soviet Georgia eventually led to the downfall of the first secretary of the Communist Party of Georgia, Vasily Mzhavanadze. In an echo of the reversal experienced by Comrade Ezhov at the hands of Comrade Beria in the late 1930s, Mzhavanadze discovered to his chagrin that his replacement was the young crime buster, Shevardnadze.

In 1976, Shevy was made a member of the Central Committee of the Communist Party of the USSR. He expressed his gratitude to his new mentor in Moscow, Leonid Brezhnev, by declaring that for Georgia, "the sun rises not in the east, but in the north, in Russia!"[1] By 1978, he had been made a nonvoting member of the Politburo and began juggling his time between Tbilisi and Moscow.

However revolting for Georgian nationalists, there are those who say that such kowtowing to the Russians was the only means of maintaining a modicum of independence and sovereignty for local communist bosses—and independence and sovereignty for their states.

"To understand Shevardnadze's behavior in the 1970s, one has to be able to understand the dynamics of both the micro- and macropolitics of the Communist Party," said Professor Tamara Dragadze of the London School of Economics tried to explain to me during a wide-ranging conversation about the land of her forefathers. "For Shevardnadze to openly espouse 'Georgianness' would have led to his immediate downfall and the destruction of Georgia itself."

But for many in Georgia, Shevardnadze's balancing act condemned him as at least a hypocrite—an ambivalence that came to a head in 1978 when Moscow announced that henceforth, the national language of Georgia would be Russian. The reaction of citizens was massive and visceral, and soon took on aspects of an anti-Russian riot. As in 1956, Soviet tanks ringed Tbilisi, ready to crush resistance. Two versions of the subsequent events exist. One has Shevardnadze bravely walking out into the middle of a soccer field under a hailstorm of stones, begging the crowd to disperse lest a bloodbath occur. The other version holds that Shevardnadze was himself deeply implicated in the Russification effort, but managed to finesse a victory out of a political disaster. When Moscow backed down and left Georgian as the official language of the country, Shevardnadze claimed the credit for having "saved" the cultural bedrock of the nation.

Less happy were events in November 1983, when Soviet Georgia was gearing up to celebrate a triple holiday: the 200th anniversary of the Georgievsk Treaty that established a Russian protectorate over Georgia, the sixty-sixth anniversary of the Bolshevik Revolution of 1917 and the sixtieth annual celebration of the creation of the USSR for good measure. On the eighteenth of the month a group of seven youths attempted to hijack an Aeroflot plane and fly to neighboring Turkey. Some say they were deliberately trying to humiliate Shevardnadze by ruining the celebrations; others say that they simply wanted to escape from the Soviet Union. At a crucial moment, the crew managed to lock themselves in the cabin and fly the plane back to Tbilisi. Waiting at the airport was Eduard Shevardnadze, his face ashen with rage.

The Silver Fox appealed to "his children" to come to their senses. The hijackers shouted back "we are not your children." Then the parents of the hijackers begged Shevardnadze to allow them to board the plane. But as the crowd stood by, a Soviet SWAT team went into action. Within eight minutes, it was over. Two of the hijackers were killed on board, the other five wounded and arrested. According to one eyewitness, as the stretchers passed in front of him, Shevardnadze lashed out at one. It was not until 1989 that friends and relatives were officially informed that the executions had been carried out five years before. No remains, not even bones, were offered to the bereaved families. The bodies, it seems, were destroyed by acid to erase all memory that they had ever existed.

In 1991, a commission of inquiry was formed in Tbilisi to investigate the hijacking episode and the subsequent executions. Members of the commission traveled to Moscow to interview Eduard Shevardnadze, who quickly and atypically lost all control. "I don't remember anything about it!" he shouted, and terminated the interview.

In an open letter to Shevardnadze that I acquired from the neglected archives of the U.S. Congressional Helsinki Commission, Professor Vaja Iveriely, whose two sons were among the hijackers executed in 1984, rhetorically asked Shevardnadze about this unusual memory lapse, as well as Shevardnadze's claim that he had no control over events in any case. "How can you say that you had no control when even a bird couldn't fly in Georgia without your knowledge?" Iveriely wrote. "The brilliant aspects of your career shouldn't deceive future generations. They should see the abominations and nastiness of your nature that you have attempted to mask."

* * *

The year 1983 is not remembered as being "the year of the abortive hijacking" in Tbilisi by anyone other than the Georgians. Rather, it is far more memorable as being the start of the process that began with the death of Leonid Brezhnev, continued with the elevation to Communist Party boss (and then sudden death) of KGB boss Yuri Andropov, and ended in 1985, when, following the death of Andropov's successor, Konstantin Chernenko, the old men of the Kremlin threw a political curve ball and elected a young agriculture specialist as the new chairman of the Communist Party. His name was Mikhail Gorbachev.

Almost immediately, Gorbachev was celebrated as a "different" kind of Soviet leader. Margaret Thatcher called him "a man we can do business with." A better description, perhaps, was provided by the standing foreign minister, Andrei Gromoyko (Mister *Nyet*), who characterized Gorbachev as a fellow with a "nice smile, but steel teeth." The world, of course, most intimately associated his name with the twin concepts of glasnost and perestroika instituted by Gorbachev with a certain Eduard Shevardnadze at his side.

In his book *The New Russians*, Hedrick Smith describes an initial meeting of the minds as the pair first became acquainted at a Black Sea resort in 1983, hashing out the problems of being local Communist Party bosses in the stagnating Soviet Union.

"It cannot continue," Shevardnadze told Gorbachev as their shoes crunched down the sand and gravel of the beach. The latter could only agree that their nation was being crushed by the weight of an antiquated, unworkable ideology.

Such notions leave some Sovietologists deeply disturbed. They argue that rather than springing Athena-like from the brain of Gorby, glasnost and perestroika were actually part of a program designed by Yuri Andropov, not so much to bring an end to the culture of fear and silence in the Soviet Union, but to rejuvenate the USSR in the face of American gains in the Cold War. In its most cynical interpretation, Andropov's plan was to let the Soviet Union fall apart and then, with the aid of a gullible West, to build it back together stronger than ever before.

One might quibble with the efficacy (or even accuracy) of this "grandest conspiracy of them all" theory, but the fact remains that events in Georgia over the past decade fit uncomfortably well into this putative scheme. Almost from the moment Eduard Shevardnadze left Tbilisi for Moscow in 1985 to become foreign minister of the USSR, dynamic change of a different sort began in Georgia. While Shevardnadze traveled the world with the message of peace and partnership between the West and the "new" USSR, including the espousal of the so-called Sinatra Doctrine for Eastern Europe (They Can Do It Their Way), the suppressed nationalist movement in Georgia grew and grew, coalescing around a long-time refusenik who had been twice jailed on charges of anti-Soviet thought crime. His name was Zviad Gamsakhurdia, and he was a man whose nationalist, dissident, and intellectual credentials were matched by his near-pathological hatred of Shevardnadze. In an interview in 1990, an American interlocutor asked Gamsakhurdia what he thought of his old jailer, Eduard Shevardnadze.

"He is an international spider and the man behind the conspiracy of glasnost and perestroika," Gamsakhurdia spat out.

When it was suggested that Mikhail Gorbachev might have had something to do with the process, Gamsakhurdia merely chuckled.

"He is a Russian," said Zviad. "And Russians cannot do anything without the help of Georgians, Armenians, or Jews."

Stranger than this logic, however, was Zviad's tone of voice and general demeanor when describing Shevardnadze.

"He looked like a mouse who has just been released from a cage containing a boa constrictor," the source related. "The mixture of fear, awe, hatred, horror, and fascination was almost overwhelming."[2]

There were strikes and demonstrations in the late 1980s focusing on one central goal: to restore the state of independence enjoyed in 1918–21 by freeing Georgia from the Soviet yoke. Then on April 9, 1989, yet another demonstration was held in Tbilisi demanding that Georgian independence be restored. This time, however, the local garrison of Soviet army conscripts usually called upon to maintain order was replaced by paratroopers, and when they moved against the sea of unarmed protestors, their weapons of choice and coercion were shovels. Nineteen protestors were bludgeoned to death, and many more seriously injured. Once again, the crackdown served only to harden the resolve of Gamsakhurdia and the nationalists. His anti-Soviet pronouncements might have been a little too shrill for foreign fans of Gorby and Shevy at the time, but not for most citizens of Georgia. In parliamentary elections held in October 1990, no fewer than 34 political parties (organized into 14 separate "blocs") contested the 250 seats of the "Supreme Soviet" of Georgia. All the parties, including even the Communists, were united on one subject: the need for Georgia's independence from the USSR. Gamsakhurdia's Roundtable/Free Georgia coalition won 155 seats. The Georgian "street" had just legally seized power through the ballot box.

> The high-status intellectual elite found themselves politically outflanked and ideologically disoriented. The old (Soviet) government that they were trying to make civilized, accountable, and rational had suddenly disappeared. Erupting from below was a social movement of epic devotion to national zeal whose icon was the former dissident Zviad Gamsakhurdia. To Soviet-style intellectuals, however, the "national movement" seemed more like an irrational mob. It is then that the stellar Georgian philosopher Merab

Mamardashvili, an all-Union celebrity, uttered his last famous aphorism: *If this is the choice of my people, then I am against the people!* Shortly afterwards, Mamardashvili died of a heart attack. In hindsight, this seems like the symbolic death of the Georgian intelligentsia and their mission to create a "civil society."[3]

While many independent monitors characterized the 1990 elections as "clean and fair," and the response from the public to the polls as "enthusiastic," other long-time observers of the Caucasus (and the Soviet Union) urged caution in accepting the event as the Georgian equivalent of, say, the Iowa caucus or the New Hampshire primary.

"Yes, the numbers were very impressive," admitted RAND Corporation analyst and former U.S. diplomat (and Caucasus expert) Paul Henze to me in a private conversation. "But no one really understood what elections were all about. They may have been free, but in the sense that one is free to cheer at a football game. Fundamental issues were glossed over or totally disregarded, starting with the reality that Georgia was still very much part of the Soviet Union and that its economy was totally dependent on that of Russia and the other Soviet Republics."

On April 9, 1991, evoking the theoretical right of secession granted by Lenin's constitution of 1922, the parliament of the Republic of Georgia declared itself free of the USSR. The world, however, was preoccupied with Saddam Hussein's invasion and eviction from Kuwait, and heard little of this seminal event. Or the next: on May 26, 1991, Zviad Gamsakhurdia was elected president of "independent" Georgia, receiving 86 percent of the vote on a platform of "Georgia for the Georgians."

It was sort of like Texas declaring itself to be independent again, with Spanish as the sole legal language of the land. In other words, the extraordinary had happened—*a constituent part of the USSR had just seceded.*

But there was scarcely an echo in the Western media, even if the implications were clear.

"We no longer have any communications with Georgia," a Soviet diplomat at the embassy of the USSR in Turkey admitted to me in June of that year, when I was attempting to get a visa. "Or rather, the only communications we have are all written in Georgian, and we have no idea what they are saying but suspect it is all rather vile."

If Russian-speaking diplomats abroad thought they were possibly being subjected to vile statements written in indecipherable Georgian, the national minorities living in Georgia who could read, write, and listen to Gamsakhurdia in the original understood all too well what he was saying to inflamed mobs throughout the country.

Georgia for the Georgians!

The problem, of course, was that throughout "Georgian" history, Georgia had never been a unitary or mono-ethnic state. In addition to the basic East–West split of "core" Georgia into Kakheti/Imareti by the great fold in the Lesser Caucasus mountain range that had played out over nearly two millennia and the further historical division represented by the sublanguage group areas of the (minority Georgian) Laz, Mingrels, and Svans as distinct from the (majority Georgian) Karts, as well as the Muslim Georgians of Adjaria, there were the Ossetians in the central-north, the Azeris in the southeastern area known as Marnauli, the Armenians of the south-central area known as Javakheti, and finally, the Abkhaz in the northeast—not to speak of the Mountain Jews known as Tats, Zoroastrian Kurds called Yezidis, or the sub-Georgian Khevsuretians, and local ethnic Chechens known as Kists living along the high mountain passes of the upper Argun River on the Chechen/Dagestani frontier. All had enjoyed some manner of state-sponsored, official status for the seventy years of the USSR, but were now watching it get stripped away by Gamsakhurdia's brand of glasnost-inspired street nationalism. Ironically, it was the grandest old Soviet dissident himself, Andrei Sakharov, who once famously described Georgia as "the little empire," in reference to the multiple ethnic and interest groups vying for power. Georgia, Sakharov implied, was but a microcosm of the moribund Soviet state itself: any attempt at top-down unification would only result in bottom-up fragmentation.

But no one was listening.

* * *

The easiest targets of the new Georgian nationalism were the Ossetians, paradoxically due to their dual connection with Stalin and "Russia."

A people of old Persian stock, the Ossetians had migrated to the mid-Caucasus mountains in the gray mists of time. Long before anyone had come up with the concept of "nationalism" as the basic building block of identity in the nineteenth and twentieth centuries, the Ossetians had married into all the communities with which they had come into contact—Georgian, Chechen, Circassian, and Russian. There were and are Orthodox Christian Ossetians, Animist Ossetians, and Muslim Ossetians. Some had shifted south and concentrated settlement around the town of Tskhinvali (some fifty miles outside Tbilisi). Others lived around the city of Gori, including the family of Josef Stalin, who was half Georgian and half Alan, which is what the Ossetians call themselves.

In high Soviet times, the Ossetians inside the Georgian SSR had received the status of living in an "autonomous district," one step down the sovereignty ladder from "autonomous-republic" status enjoyed by their more numerous cousins in the North Ossetian Autonomous Republic/Alania inside the Russian Federation SSR, who were so rewarded thanks to their prominent role in the tsarist Russian conquest of the Caucasus, and continued loyalty to Moscow under the communist regime even after the collapse of the USSR. The name of their capital city said it all: Vladikavkaz, a word that in Russian literally means "rule over the Caucasus."

Founded by the tsars as a garrison city equivalent to St. Louis or Fort Lincoln at approximately the same time as the American push into the Native American West, Vladikavkaz was the traditional push-off point across the Caucasus Mountains into the nineteenth-century unknown. A who's who of writers one associates with the classics of nineteenth century Russian literature all spent time there: Lermontov, Tolstoy, Turgenev, and Pushkin, to name a few. All then packed their kits and went up and over the mountains and down the Georgian Military Highway to the south, Tbilisi-bound. The Ossetians by that time had become the favored guides and trusted companions of the tsarist forces, sort of like "friendly" Indians like the Absaroka/Crow, who famously fought with Colonel Custer against Sitting Bull and the Sioux.

Cross-cultural analysis aside, tension between Georgia and the North and South Ossetians was already high when Gamsakhurdia announced the dissolution of South Ossetia's existing Soviet status. Not surprisingly, the leadership in Tskhinvali in turn declared independence from independent Tbilisi —and Georgia's first miniwar was joined. Scores were killed before the remnant Soviet military intervened on the side of the Ossetians, forcing a stalemate and thus de facto secession of South Ossetia from the Georgian state.[4]

A completely different situation presented itself along Georgia's south-western border with Turkey in the Autonomous Republic of Adjaria. Paradoxically, this was no ethnically based "autonomy" at all but a uniquely "religious" territorial entity set up to accommodate the communal aspirations of Muslim Georgians living along the borderlands of Turkey. Like virtually all other special communities in the theoretically atheist Soviet space, the Muslim Georgians of Adjaria became less Muslim and more Soviet by the decade. After enjoying seventy-odd years of autonomy, the only thing really left to them in the way of "specialness" was not that they were Muslim, but that they were . . . well, "autonomous," and thus enjoyed certain prerogatives such as having their own parliament and place in diverse Soviet-style affirmative-action quotas for university placement and Communist Party-style patronage. When Gamsakhurdia's people showed up in 1991 to inform the "Adjarians" that in the newly independent Georgia they were to be less special than before (*Adjarians! Remember—you are Georgian!*), the scion of a nineteenth century noble Georgian Muslim family, wearing the guise of being a Young Communist Youth leader, stepped forward in the spirit of protecting local traditions and shot dead the non-Adjarian Georgian representative. The specter of civil war loomed, then quickly abated when it was made known that the chameleon communist had sent flowers to all the wives of the local Russian garrison on International Women's Day (and, one presumes, slipped a little oil-industry-related revenue to the officers themselves . . .). Thus, the legend of "Batono" (Lord Protector) Aslan Abashidze was born. Almost immediately, autonomous Adjaria slid out of Tbilisi's control, with Batumi refusing to pay taxes to the central exchequer, to allow its youth to be drafted into the new national army, or to countenance any basic central governmental control in the region. Almost as quickly, Adjaria became famous as a black hole for dark dealings in the oil and arms industries across the Caucasus, a place where Armenian and Azerbaijani criminals toasted each other in true fraternity, and where the Rodham brothers (siblings of then first lady Hillary Clinton) rolled dice in the local hazelnut market.

Even more problematic was the case of the Abkhaz Autonomous Republic on the shores of the Black Sea. Unlike the Ossetians, who were at least a majority of the population in their autonomous district, and the Adjarians, who were (mainly nonpracticing) Muslim Georgians,[5] the Abkhaz were a non-Georgian people who were a minority in their autonomous republic. Conquered by the Russians with active Georgian participation in the mid-1800s, half or more of the native Abkhaz population had fled to Ottoman Turkey, opening up the lowlands to Georgian (and Russian and Armenian) settlers. Claimed as part of territorial Georgia by Noe Jordania's government in 1918, the native Abkhaz population sided with Lenin's Bolsheviks against the Mensheviks, and declared their own state in 1921. Abkhaz nationalists insist that their homeland was thus theoretically independent of both Soviet Russia and newly Sovietized Georgia for about a year, before being invited (or forced) into a federated union with Georgia when both were subsumed into the short-lived Transcaucasus Soviet Socialist Republic of 1922.[6] In the early 1930s, Lavrenti Beria, the new Communist Party boss of both the Georgian and the Transcaucasus SSRs, began applying increasing pressure to legally fold Abkhazia into Georgia proper and flood the area with western Georgian immigrants. The Abkhaz leader Nestor Lakoba applied to Stalin in an effort to resist but finally succumbed on the quid pro quo that Abkhazia would not be subjected to collectivization at the same rate as the rest of the USSR. Despite his acceptance of Abkhazia's demotion in legal status to that of an "autonomous" part of Georgia, pressure continued to open up the swampy, lowland territory along the Black Sea coast to Georgian/Mingrelian settlement as part of a larger agricultural plan to create citrus and tea plantations. Finally, in 1936, Lakoba accepted an invitation to travel to Tbilisi to meet

Beria to discuss the issue. He was discovered dead the next day, victim of a heart attack at the age of forty-one, and the floodgates to Georgian settlement in Abkhazia were opened. Although the Abkhaz were probably not a majority of the population in their autonomous republic at the time, by the end of the USSR in 1991 they had been reduced to a mere 17 percent of the population and were seething with resentment against seventy years of real and perceived wrongs. Curiously, that resentment was not so much directed against the Russians who had conquered their country in the nineteenth century, but against the two "Georgians"—Stalin and particularly Beria—who had stripped them of the quasi-independent homeland vouchsafed them by Lenin.

Whatever its legal status within the context of the Soviet Union, Abkhazia was *very* special in a different way. No less than thirty-three *sanatoriia*, or Soviet-style rest and relaxation resorts, dotted the coastal beaches and mountain valleys of the tiny republic, making it a playground for the *nomenklatura*, and wealthier than almost any other chunk of the Soviet Union.

"Abkhazia was a part of the leisure empire of the Soviet elite," explained Paul Henze. "Along with the wealth generated by recreation came special privileges and favoritism for those who ran the resorts and tended to the needs of that elite. Democracy—or at least the breakdown of the pecking order of the elite and the shift of power from Moscow to Tbilisi—was a direct threat to the interests of those who benefited most from the old system, and Gamsakhurdia and his supporters were the first to try and cash in."

* * *

Some argue that the roller-coaster ride toward state suicide in Georgia began with the parliamentary elections of 1990. Others say that event was signaled by Gamsakhurdia's election as president in April 1991. A more convenient date, however, is August 19 of that same year—the abortive putsch against Mikhail Gorbachev in Moscow. Alone among all leaders of the fifteen "titular" republics that theoretically made up the USSR (even though Georgia had previously declared itself no longer part of the fifteen), Zviad described the coup as "a fraud." This was interpreted as meaning Gamsakhurdia was either insane or—in the weirdest stretch of logic—pro-putsch.

"Oh, man!" George Bush the Elder winced when a CNN reporter asked him about Gamsakhurdia's insight during the three-day reign of the putschists in Moscow. "This guy better get his head examined!"

At the time, watching the pictures of Boris Yeltsin standing atop a tank in front of the Russian White House, defending Russia's fledgling democracy from the evil, "hard-line" communists, it was difficult to disagree with the notion that Gorby was good and anyone who questioned his goodness, bad.[7]

But if Zviad Gamsakhurdia thought the August 19 abortive putsch in Moscow was suspect, the real item soon began playing out in Georgia. By late September, the leader of the newly created Georgia National Guard, a former sculptor named Tengiz Kitovani, had removed himself from the government after a firefight that had left four dead, and anticipated many more over October and November of that year.[8] By December, the "opposition" was spraying the presidential palace with bullets and mortars, and the center of Tbilisi (or at least the most central 100 meters of Rustaveli Avenue) had been turned into a hellhole. On January 5, 1992, President Gamsakhurdia fled, leaving the capital in the hands of Kitovani and one Jaba Ioseliani, a "professor, playwright, and poet" who had spent seventeen years in Soviet jails on murder charges. Both were almost perfect prototypes for a personality type to emerge throughout the collapsing Soviet space: the warlord.

* * *

Meanwhile, from the vantage point of his think tank in Moscow, Eduard Shevardnadze took a benign view of events in his homeland. For example, he described the anti-Gamsakhurdia putsch as "not so much a violent take-over as a conflict between an authoritarian regime and democratic forces which were supported by armed formations" and consistently denied any involvement in the putsch or even any interest in returning to Georgia. At one point, he was on the famous people's lecture circuit and picking up serious coin for his efforts. One such event at Binghamton University in upstate New York was attended by then-graduate student Georgi Derluguian, who described it to me in a casual e-mail (I stress the "casual" aspect because Derluguian's prose is usually much more dense, if teasing):

> I actually saw Shevardnadze up close during those days. He came to Binghamton to give a talk—totally devoid of substance and lavishly paid (45 thousand dollars for a 45 minute speech) by the local business chamber [who were] astounded by the coming of such celebrity to their provincial town. I was first introduced to his wife in a sort of "Look, we have one of your compatriots here!" (That I am not a Georgian escaped the Binghamtonians.) She asked motherly: "Oh, dear, and what do you eat here? The bread is terrible and the fruits so artificial, aren't they?" Then she called her husband, and I was struck how out of his place Shevardnadze looked. He was out of power and didn't know what he was. I cannot relate in words what was his look when he said to me: "You know, I am retired now. . . ."

Shevardnadze was nothing unless in power, because he had been in power all his life. One might even describe it as his *habitus*. Fat-fee lecture gigs in the West were fine and dandy but not what he needed. That was power restored—and after the collapse of the USSR, there was only one place to go and get it: Sakartvelo, Georgia, the homeland.

Still, Shevy played coy.

When presented with a petition signed by 1,000 national guardsmen requesting his return to Tbilisi, Shevardnadze wept in gratitude but declined the mantle of leadership.

"He was sensitive to whether he would be accepted by the people," recalled Professor Dragadze. "He was afraid that most people only remembered him as an 'old communist,' and still hated for that."

But the petitions continued to arrive. And on March 8, 1992, announcing that "the fate of the nation" hung in the balance, a "reluctant" Eduard Shevardnadze boarded a plane in Moscow and flew south, to Tbilisi.

Meeting him at the airport were none other than Jaba Ioseliani and Tengiz Kitovani, who were soon to receive the portfolios of minister of the Interior and Defense, respectively, in the new, post-Gamsakhurdia "State Council."

The Silver Fox was home—and war was on its way.

Notes

1. Georgi Derluguian shared with me a joke from the period: Upon returning from a trip to the Caucasus, Comrade Brezhnev began experiencing extreme stomach pains, complaining to his doctors that he was unable to perform basic toilet-related functions. After examining the Kremlin boss, his doctors reluctantly felt obliged to inform Brezhnev that he did not have an anus. "Ah, those Caucasian flatterers!" sighed Brezhnev. "They must have licked it clean away!"

2. Conversation with Michael Ochs of the U.S. Congressional Helsinki Commission, circa November 1993.

3. Georgi Derluguian, *Bourdieu's Secret Admirer in the Caucasus* (Chicago: University of Chicago Press, 2005), p. 202.

4. James Brooke, "As Centralized Rule Wanes, Ethnic Tension Rises," *New York Times*, October 2, 1991, dateline Tskhinvali, USSR.

5. In his new book, Hugh Pope of the *Wall Street Journal* cites a surreal interview he conducted with Abashidze, during which the Adjarian Lord Protector, attempting to prove his devotion to religions of all sorts, showed Pope a miniature Statue of Liberty, which Abashidze insisted, was the Virgin Mary (*Sons of the Conquerors* [New York: Overlook, 2005], p. 256).

6. This structure was in effect ratified by the sub-USSR Abkhaz constitution of 1925 and the sub-USSR Georgian constitution of 1927. Both may have been mere paper documents when viewed through the prism of real power in the USSR but are seized upon today as forming the essential Abkhaz argument for resisting complete incorporation into Georgia.

7. There was, however, even then a hard core of Soviet specialists who agreed with Gamsakhurdia's unpopular analysis. "To all appearances, 70 years of KGB experience

were ignored in the tragicomic bumbling in Moscow that made the keystone cops look professional," wrote Professor Denis Papazian of the University of Michigan/Dearborn. "Rather than being a real attempt to unseat Gorbachev, there is room to imagine that the whole thing was a made for TV docudrama produced for a gullible West blinded by its hope to see a reconstituted Russia in its own image." Papazian also smells a rat in Shevardnadze's "suspicious foresight" of December 1990, when, in announcing his resignation as foreign minister of the Soviet Union, he intoned that "the dictatorship will not succeed" and that "the future belongs to democracy and freedom." The last line comes from the title of Shevardnadze's autobiography, *The Future Belongs to Freedom*, a work that Papazian describes as a "cornucopia of lofty aphorisms and pious platitudes" but not worth much in the way of information or insight into the Soviet Union. It only exists in English; there never was a Russian or Georgian original. (Draft copies of OpEd series in the Detroit Free Press, published August and September 1991, as provided by Papazian to the author.)

8. James Brooke, "Four Are Killed," *New York Times*, September 26, 1991, dateline Tbilisi.

4

An Abkhazian Interlude

As legend has it, when God was dividing up the world between the nations, the Abkhazians missed their chance to select a homeland because they were sleeping off a festive drunk. When they awoke, everything was gone with the exception of that part of the world that the Almighty had been reserving for himself, which was, of course, literally heaven on earth.

"Where can we go?" cry the Abkhazians. "We were late only because we were toasting you and singing your praises!"

"Well," says God, pleased with the flattery. "I guess I'll have to give you a piece of paradise."

Alas, no. This is not a typo or a cut-and-paste job gone awry.

The similarity between the homeland-acquisition legends of the Georgians and Abkhazians is almost exact, a sad fact that has led not to unity and fraternity but rather to belligerence and even denial of the very humanity of the other. Everything is in dispute here—contemporary history, language, and even the creationist myths about the very beginning of the world.

An easy example is the name of the two- or three-thousand-year-old principal city of the central-east Black Sea. The natives (others say they are not natives at all) call it *Aq"a,* the " marker being a whistle vowel in the local Abkhaz language.[1] The Romans and Byzantines called it *Dioscurias* until the Genoese renamed it *Sevastopolis.* Next came the Ottoman Turks who took a quick squint at the real estate involved and called the city *Sukum-Kale,* or "Water-Sand Fortress." That name remains enshrined in distorted form as the Russo-Soviet-style fun and sun and sand resort town set on the sweeping bay in the noncountry known as Abkhazia and its capital city: *Sukhumi* in Georgian and *Sukhum* in Abkhaz. In the eyes, hearts, and minds of the protagonists, the use of the final "i" (or its absence) is regarded as almost a capital crime, depending on what side of the argument one falls. Perhaps there are things worth fighting over and, for both Georgians and Abkhaz, Sukhumi/Sukhum is clearly one of them.

There is little question about the beauty of the Abkhazian hinterland, which somewhat resembles Florida merged with Montana or a combination of southern California and Alaska: a tropical hothouse along the coast that suddenly soars upward to the snowcapped, wildlife haven of the Caucasus mountains, its lower slopes sprinkled with dachas built for the likes of Stalin, Beria, and Brezhnev and other members of the Soviet elite. Then add the Soviet equivalent of Monterey or Boca Raton in the city of Sukhumi/Sukhum—the hustle and bustle of the citrus market, the quiet, verdant beauty of the botanical gardens boasting some 200 autarchic species of subtropical plants, flowers, and trees (including the tall, graceful, and rare Pitsunda pine), the ape, monkey, and primate zoo (some say experimental disease station) set in yet another unique preserve behind the city, the archeological museum with its collection of rare artifacts dating back to classical times, all framed by the toy-town architecture of cantilevered balconies and ornate onion domes made of only slightly oxidized copper, the faded-but-still-grand hotels facing the port, the Russian (or really, Soviet) military R&R resort down the beach, its huge stone mosaic portrait of Vladimir Illych Lenin smiling a welcome at the entrance to tourists from across the vast expanse of the Soviet Union. . . .

All this and more now belongs to a city and indeed "country" that can never be seen again, except in shattered, broken, and generally degenerate form, and then only by the most intrepid of travelers. The museums have been looted, the pleasant faux-Stalin-style buildings bombed and burned. The orchards and botanical gardens are largely overgrown with weeds; the monkeys, while kept alive by outlander alms, are nevertheless slowly dying of the various viruses and diseases injected into their mothers and fathers. The population of what was once a booming tourist city has been reduced by more than three-quarters. The detritus of war is everywhere, a decade and more after it was fought. A little paradise on the shores of the Black Sea has reverted to being a bleak backwater, forgotten by most of the world. It is a place where the tourist industry (such as it is) has become completely reliant on the dregs of Russian society, the sort of folks who don't mind an unrepaired shell-hole in the ceiling of their room because they don't have the money to demand better or to plan the now standard post-Soviet Russian vacation to Turkey, Cyprus, or Cannes.

* * *

At the time of my first arrival in the city, back in the Paleolithic period of early 1992, Sukhumi was still a tourist town, albeit one suffering from a long off-season: it was cold, overcast, and lacked heating fuel, urban services, and faith in the future. But, at the time, so did most cities and towns throughout the collapsing Soviet Union. Being cold and bleak was not unique; feeling like one was living on borrowed time before the hammer of war came smashing down on the town was.

Why did I choose to stay?

It is difficult to explain.

Having missed my deadline for my "exclusive" interview with Gamsakhurdia for the London *Sunday Times* by a week, perhaps I had nothing better to do than become ridiculously infatuated first with Nunu Chachua, then with her sister Nana, and then with Nunu again. Maybe I was trying to absorb as much about Georgia, Abkhazia, and the looming crisis as I could before getting back to Baku. I don't know. But I dawdled, working on my Russian (which improved by the day) and my even more limited Georgian:

Mi-vdivar/mi-dikhar/mi-dis/mi-dian . . .
I go/you go/she goes/they go . . .
v-ar/khar/ar-is/v-art . . .
I am/you are/he is/we are . . .
Bodishi . . .
Sorry . . .

One day among the many days, I ventured from Nunu's place to a palatial structure set in a huge garden behind a wrought-iron fence on the southern outskirts of town to see if Gamsakhurdia was there. He was not. But the palace (allegedly Joe Stalin's favorite Black Sea dacha; I have subsequently heard of several "favorite" dachas bearing this distinction) was next to a hotel/spa named the Aitar. The courtyard was a lush jungle of tropical and subtropical trees, shrubs, flowers, and ferns, all set up as a botanical garden through which fantailed peacocks free-roamed. The big birds bobbed like giant roosters or dwarf ostriches, crowing or howling the way peacocks apparently were designed to do, emitting a sound somewhere between that made by braying donkeys and stray dogs hit by speeding cars on wet roads. It was not clear if they were crowing for joy, sorrow, or anger, or just barking because they felt like it and were peacocks. The real attraction of the Aitar, however, was the prospect of sleeping in a heated room with scalding hot water gushing from the tap. Accordingly, I checked in and found myself ensconced in a basic room for about a dollar a night in prorated Russian rubles. The only other guests appeared to be a couple of Estonian correspondents whose main task seemed to be listening to Russian radio broadcasts on Moscow frequencies, then recycling what was said about Abkhazia as their own reporting, which would then be picked up by the same Moscow radio station they had heard it from for the very good reason that said radio station did not have a correspondent in the region. The Estonians were pretty thrilled at being able to identify themselves as being the source of all this news, even though they were only repeating what the very same broadcasters had announced a few hours before.

The essence of the exercise was this: the situation in Georgia didn't look good. The Opposition, or pro-Shevardnadze crowd of putschists, was slowly but surely closing the loop on the Position, or former government of Gamsakhurdia. A break in the weather—Georgia had just been hit with the worst blizzard in 100 years—had allowed an Opposition column of tanks and motorized guns to cross a pass in the mountains that divided Georgia down the middle. Having "conquered" Kutaisi, the column was now moving on the port city of Poti. Their next target would be Zugdidi, then Gali, and then finally Sukhumi.

If true, this was deeply disturbing. While Poti and Zugdidi were "Georgian" cities pure and simple, Sukhumi was different. In addition to being the last real redoubt of the Position, it was also the capital of the Autonomous Soviet Socialist Republic of Abkhazia. While legally part of Georgia, Abkhazia had unique rights within both Georgia and the greater Soviet Union, ranging from its own parliament (where half the seats were reserved for non-Georgians) to its own police force, where virtually all members were Abkhaz (or at least not ethnic Georgians, such as local Armenians and Russians). While things had been rocky between the Abkhaz and the government in Tbilisi during the brief tenure of Gamsakhurdia's regime, the prospect of allowing their "autonomous" republic to be the stage for an Alamo-like last stand by Gamsakhurdia's Position forces at the hands of the oncoming pro-putsch Opposition left the Abkhaz (and other non-Georgian citizens of the region) decidedly cold and looking at different options. One was secession. If Georgia could so famously break away from the Soviet Union and reclaim its heritage as an independent state that had been lost to the Bolsheviks in 1921, then why shouldn't the Abkhaz do the same and break away from Georgia, reclaiming their independence lost first to the Russian tsars in the nineteenth century and then to Stalin's whims in 1932?

Making the situation even more tense and complex were the schizophrenic politics being played by Moscow not only in Georgia and autonomous

Abkhazia, but also throughout the post-Soviet space. While Boris Yeltsin theoretically supported the leadership of the fourteen other post-Soviet republics that emerged from the collapsing Soviet Union and regarded them as (almost) equals, there were other elements in the New Russia that deeply regretted the dissolution of the Union and yearned for the old days of the unified Soviet state. Not surprisingly, at the head of this nonofficial, irredentist movement was the bruised and confused post-Soviet military. After having been flushed out of what had been East Germany and the rest of Eastern Europe with the collapse of the Warsaw Pact, the generals were less than enthusiastic about abandoning the scores of bases, airfields, and radar facilities that now lay scattered among the successor republics that had made up the Soviet Union, now on foreign soil. And in the case of Abkhazia, Georgian sovereignty represented not only a threat to the continued presence of Russian air, land, and sea force bases there (as well as experimental laboratories, dating back to Beria's nuclear bomb project of the late 1940s, that had allegedly become home to doomsday experiments on how to trigger earthquakes against the NATO foe) but also the much more alarming prospect of the loss of the Russian military's subsidized playground on the shores of the Black Sea—namely, the spas, sanitariums, and summer dachas sprinkled up and down the beaches of Abkhazia. Finally, there was even talk of Abkhazia joining with several of the "autonomous" republics in the Russian North Caucasus and creating some ill-defined Federated Republic of Independent Mountaineers, an entity to be independent of *both* Georgia and Russia, and with Sukhumi as its capital. As a working correspondent, I figured it was high time to find a couple of Abkhaz to talk to about all of this. The place to find them, I astutely guessed, would be the government building dominating the central square and botanical garden in the middle of downtown.

* * *

The Prefektura and parliament of the Abkhaz Autonomous Soviet Socialist Republic was a standard Soviet-style, lump-of-cement building with a statue of Lenin on a plinth dominating the parade ground square out front. My Georgian interlocutors over at the Position Headquarters had tried to impress upon me that this was because the Abkhaz leadership consisted of nothing but old-line Communists. It occurred to me that the real reason that the statue still stood was because the Abkhaz didn't want to remove it just because the Georgians said they should.

There was no one in the parliament that day, but poking around the back of the building I discovered that the local Abkhaz television station was right next door. I introduced myself to a stout young man by the name of Valeri, and he invited me over for dinner that night to discuss the nature of being an Abkhaz, which was rather trying due to the complexity of the subject and to my limited Russian. After the meal he taught me a few useful phrases of the language, which he assured me had no connection to Georgian whatsoever and was distantly related to such North Caucasian languages as Adyghe, Shapsug, and Ubukh (and more distantly Chechen and Ingush). Sadly, the last speaker of Ubukh had just passed away in a Turkish village some years before. . . .

"I lived in Turkey for years," I noted.

"*Türkce biliyormusun?*" he asked with growing hope that we had found a common tongue.

"*Gayette tabii,*" I replied.

"Well!" crowed Valeri, slipping into slightly fractured but fairly fluent Turkish. "Now we are talking!"

The dam had broken, and the words flooded out, albeit in Turkish. Valeri had relatives there, which is how he had learned some of the language. In Turkey, Syria, and Jordan, the Abkhaz were lumped together with other nineteenth-century North Caucasian refugee populations and generically known as Circassians, even though they were quite distinct, Valeri informed me. In fact Vladislav Ardzinba himself spoke fluent Turkish. The president of the Abkhaz Autonomous Republic was a noted Hittitologist who had spent years working in the archives at the Museum of Anatolian Civilizations in Ankara, and would I care to meet him?

"Sure," I said, and so Valeri picked up the phone, called the president, and informed him that there was a foreigner who wanted to talk with him about the nature of Abkhazia. The president said he would be delighted to meet the visiting foreigner who had expressed such a keen interest in understanding Abkhaz issues, and asked that I drop by the next day. Easy as that. Bidding my new friend Valeri goodnight, I returned to my heated digs at the Aitar, listened to the peacocks howl, and woke the next morning to make my way, in accordance with Valeri's directions, to the cold and unlit office of the most hated man in all of Georgia.

Vladislav Ardzinba, a young, handsome and likable man, was an anthropologist by profession. His candidate (PhD) thesis was entitled: "Hattic Sources of Social Organization of Ancient Hittite Society," and his last known scholarly paper before assuming the leadership of (Soviet) Abkhazia was "Towards the History of the Cult of Iron and the Blacksmith's Craft, or Worship of the Smithy Among the Abkhazians." But Ardzinba was no longer a scholar of early antiquity. He was the president of a noncountry lurching ineluctably toward war and he knew it. Still, he said he wanted peace with his neighbors, prosperity for his family, and independence for his country, Abkhazia, and told me so.

"But isn't Abkhazia part of Georgia," I asked, pointing out the uncomfortable fact, learned a day or two before, that the Abkhaz were a distinct minority within their own country—only 17 percent of the total.

Ardzinba scowled. This skewed ratio was the result of a deliberate process of colonization of the country by the Georgians such as Stalin, Beria, and more recently Shevardnadze, he said. These men had used the facade of the Soviet dictum "friendship among peoples" to advance their own ethnic claim to other people's territory. Even before Soviet times, the Georgians, in league with the tsarist Russians, had tried to culturally absorb the Christian Abkhaz while encouraging the majority Muslim Abkhaz to leave for Turkey and the other Middle Eastern states that once made up the Ottoman Empire. Did I know anything about this exodus? Did I know anything about the typhus and tuberculosis that had killed off up to half of the refugees who washed up in Turkish ports? Was I aware that many if not all of the Diaspora Abkhaz in the Middle East would not even eat sea fish due to the collective memory of having to throw the corpses of children and grandparents into the sea for burial? And as for the population statistics I was tossing around, they might be correct today but they were correctable. The descendants of the refugees and exiles now living in Turkey and the Middle East were likely to return to Abkhazia once it achieved independence from Georgia—that is, once it had reestablished the independence that it had enjoyed as recently as 1932. As leader of newly independent Abkhazia, Ardzinba was actively pursuing the policy of inviting immigrants from the far-flung Abkhaz Diaspora to return in order to rebuild the native population base.

I begged to differ. I explained that I had spent long years in Turkey and Syria, and that while I was aware that there was a so-called Circassian element among the Turks (and Arabs), these erstwhile natives of the Caucasus, of whom the Abkhaz were but one group, had long ago self-assimilated into Turkish (and Arab) society. They had lost their language and had no interest in returning to the ancestral homeland, where the main language spoken, as well as the dominant culture, was now Russian, the Soviet successor to the tsarist policies that had forced the Diaspora Abkhaz to flee more than a century earlier.

"You are wrong," said Ardzinba, specifying Abkhaz settlements in Turkey such as Duzce, Adapazar, and the Sapanci Lake district. He had been delighted to discover keen interest among the Diaspora Abkhaz, many of whom had preserved their language and culture in far better shape than the Soviet Abkhaz. They will return, he said.[2]

Was the president not concerned, I asked, that the religious differences between local Christian Abkhaz and returning Muslim Abkhaz might make for future problems?

"Not in the least," said Ardzinba. He, Valeri, and the young lady who served as the official translator (Russian to English) might all be nominally Christian Abkhaz, but they could all swear on the Bible that they were closer to the Muslim Abkhaz and other mainly Muslim "mountain" people of the northern Caucasus, such as the Adyghe, Ingush, Kabardins, Circassians, Chechens, and Dagestanis, than they were to the Georgians. In fact, it was Ardzinba's dream to join a free and independent North Caucasus Federation, a country that might also have room for Ossetia—the other autonomous region of Georgia that was also trying to break away and join the autonomous Ossetia that was part of the Russian Federation. The right of self-determination was the key.

This was beginning to sound like immediate absorption by Russia, the country that had destroyed Abkhazia in the nineteenth century. I wanted to take up that subject with the Abkhaz president, but Ardzinba had either run out of time or was fed up with wasting it on me, and the interview came to a rather abrupt end.

"*Abzerus!*" I said, in my best, newly acquired Abkhazian, probably saying "Hello."

"See you," said Ardzinba in English and in such a manner that I knew he spoke my native language perfectly.

On my way out the door, I noticed a brace of senior-ranking military men waiting in the foyer, a Slavic (or Russian) cast to their faces. I asked Valeri who they were, but he seemed oddly reluctant to talk about the new delegation, insisting that we retire to the abode of our translator to quaff down a couple of shots of local moonshine along with our breakfast, and celebrate the future.

* * *

Another of my truth-seeking stops was to the residence of a local man of religion, the Metropolitan David, bishop of the Georgian Orthodox Church. I had first heard of him at the wedding of my older brother in St. Paul, Minnesota, when my new sister-in-law introduced me to her pastor, a certain Very Reverend David Preuss, telling him that I was soon off to "Russia."

"If you ever get to Soviet Georgia, look up my friend Bishop David and say hello," the Very Reverend instructed me.

"Sure, sure," I had said, meaning "Fat chance."

My trip was to Uzbekistan in Soviet Central Asia; Georgia had not even been on the agenda at the time.

Then serendipity struck. That first night in Sukhumi town, guzzling down brandy with Rene the national poet, my host began bragging about his various friends in high places. One had even written two books in English, which Rene placed in my hands. One was entitled *To Deliver the Oppressed from Their Bonds;* the other *Live for the Sake of Peace and Justice.* The author, it seemed, was a priest or cleric who enjoyed the approval of the central authorities in Moscow to pontificate on antinuclear, antiapartheid, anticolonial, and proliferation theology themes—living proof that despite being officially an atheist state, the Soviet Union was really filled with religious and moral people. . . .

I was about to say something about how bored I was with such pious propaganda when I flipped the books over and was astounded to discover that the author was the same David whom the Very Reverend Preuss had suggested I seek out more than a year before. More to the point, the Metropolitan David was not, as I had assumed, in Tbilisi or Moscow, but bunkered down somewhere in the middle of Sukhumi. I got his telephone number and gave him a jingle to pass on Preuss's greetings. He asked me to stop by for tea. I brought Nunu along for kicks.

* * *

David looked exactly like his picture on the two books I had browsed through—and indeed, just as the books said he was supposed to look: an old testament figure with a great, gray beard and long white hair tucked under the big black skull-covering cap worn by Orthodox priests—Saint Nicolas in black pajamas, as it were. He also spoke just as the book jackets said he spoke: speech sprinkled with Biblical references and parables pertaining to local lore. He was actually pretty close to being a cliché of himself.

But the beard could not hide the tense, drawn lips and the cap could not conceal the furrows of worry on the Metropolitan's brow. David, bishop of the Georgian Orthodox Church diocese of Sukhumi and Abkhazia, was a man of religion faced with a very secular problem: his native land was being ripped apart by civil war, and the Church was still searching for a position.

"The Church has never been directly involved in local politics but has acted as a keenly interested observer of human affairs—especially as concerns the concept of justice," he told me, "But it is an indignation when a brother kills a brother—and that is the tragic situation that we are in."

The putsch had left the Metropolitan terribly confused. For the past decade, David had been one of the most conspicuous clerics of the former Eastern Bloc on the world stage, participating in so many international conferences on peace and disarmament that he had come under criticism for serving as a flunky for the former Communist regime.

"In my books, I have written about peaceful change in Africa and Central America, but I have also voiced my support for liberation theology—the active involvement of the Church in local politics in order to promote justice and liberate the oppressed. But taking an active side in a civil war is difficult. If your ten children are fighting, to whom do you give a stick to beat the others?"

David tried to duck the issue of talking about the official policy of the Georgian Orthodox Church in the current crisis. He said that he had been out of contact with the Patriarchy in Tbilisi since the troubles began. But when I pressed him on the subject, he admitted that while he didn't know the Church's position, he personally condemned the January 5 putsch against Gamsakhurdia. He described it as an "illegal act" that had brought sorrow and suffering to all in Georgia—a country that once regarded itself as a beacon of civilization and culture but was now acting more like "some place in Africa."

"I cry and pray every night and have not changed my clothes in weeks," said David, "I urge the people to remain calm and pray for an end of the bloodshed. But the main thing is that I do not support those who attacked the parliament and drove the president into hiding. I not only disapprove of this, I condemn it."

The Metropolitan said he suspected that the putschists were encouraged by "forces" in Moscow in order to reinclude the country in the Commonwealth of Independent States, which Gamsakhurdia had refused to join. He suspected this but declined to make a categorical comment until shown absolute proof that it was so. As a cleric, however, he preferred to locate the root cause of the troubles in Godlessness.

"In the beginning was the word and the word was God," the Metropolitan quoted Scripture. "The main point of Christianity is to struggle with words and not guns. And this, in the present situation, means dialogue—and that means democracy.

"We had elections. We had a parliament. We had a president. If you don't like him, elect another. But to effect change in the political structure of the country through force of arms is to invite the destruction of the nation. The events of January will be written on black paper."

But David felt almost powerless in stopping his flock from self-slaughter.

"If Georgia were attacked by Turkey or America, I would not hesitate to take up arms myself," he said, showing me a picture of a nineteenth-century Greek priest wearing a bandoleer over his robes and holding a rifle in one hand and a crucifix in the other. "But this situation is different. It is brother against brother. Still, I would not tell a fellow priest he had sinned if he were to take up arms to defend the president. Perhaps if I were a civilian, I would take up arms myself."

Then David abruptly changed the subject.

"Perhaps you would like to use the toilet?" he suggested. In fact, I did and followed him into a nearby room. It was the vestments room and there was no toilet to be seen. Then David shut the door and turned to me, his smile gone, and all the tension he was feeling showing on his face.

"Please try and tell the truth to the world!" he hissed. Then he reached in his robes and brought out several hundred rubles.

"Take these, as a gift! I have nothing else to give."

"Why?" I asked, trying to refuse the money.

"Please take it and tell the world," said the Metropolitan, "Something awful is happening in our country. Please!"

It was a strange and sad meeting with a strange and sad man: a priest, who after a Soviet-style career of preaching about imperialist evils, was discovering his real religious roots while coming to grips with the black hole of cynical Realpolitik in his native land. As for the strange token, I took it and did the only reasonable thing I could think of with it: buy several bottles of cognac and donate them to the thirsty folks over at the theater.

The next time I was back in Sukhumi I stopped in to see David again, but he had been recalled to Tbilisi. When I returned there, and sought him out at the Orthodox Patriarchy, I was told he was dead of heart failure.

Rumor suggested a darker end.

* * *

While Abkhaz President Ardzinba plotted and Metropolitan David prayed, the Georgians loyal to ousted Gamsakhurdia went on parade. There were rallies every day on the quayside in downtown Sukhumi. Sometimes my new friend "Mad" Merab Kiknadze would speak; sometimes it was others I knew from the theater HQ. Someone even helped an inebriated Rene the national poet climb aboard the truck that served as the stage and deliver a hoarse speech about something—maybe he was reciting one of his poems from memory. It was hard to tell, and I didn't bother to ask for a translation.

At yet another rally (the days merged with one another as they went by) a personal emissary from Gamsakhurdia read a message from the leader. He called on his people to take heart and not despair, to believe that democracy would triumph over fascism in the end, and that he, Zviad, was among them, that anyone who suggested otherwise lied. But when I went to take a look at the message, it became clear that it had been written about a week before—that is, there was no "news" in the announcement at all, even if it were Zviad's first communiqué in a fortnight.

The next day it was bitterly cold and snow was starting to fall over the city. A wind off the Black Sea sent huge breakers crashing into the sea wall, swamping several dinghies and even a small sailboat. Despite the weather, the crowds gathered for another rally along the quayside, where I ran into Merab and another parliamentarian named Nika. When the rally broke up I joined the boys at a seaside kiosk and ordered some coffee that was cold by the time we had walked it from the booth to our outside table.

"We have a request for you," said Merab.

"Anything you need," I replied.

"We want you to help us draft an appeal to the nations of the world."

In fact, writing appeals to the nations of the world from obscure governments in the post-Soviet Caucasus was rapidly becoming a new specialty of mine, I informed them. Why, just a month or so ago, I had churned out the English text for friends in the Azerbaijan Ministry of Foreign Affairs asking the kings, queens, monarchs, dictators, and democratically elected prime ministers, presidents, and parliaments of the world to recognize Azerbaijani independence from the defunct Soviet Union. The letter had been so effective that at last count forty-five countries had recognized the Republic of Azerbaijan, and I would be happy and honored to use my skills to help the Position cause.

"Great, great!" said Merab.

So with fingers turning blue and the ink almost freezing on the paper, we hammered out the following:

Appeal of Georgian Parliamentarians
   We, the duly elected representatives of the Georgian nation and members of the Supreme Council, or parliament,
   Noting that the legally elected president of the country has been compelled to leave the capital in the face of brute force,
   Condemning the state of terror in the land as the putschists continue to try and take control of the entire country,
   Declaring our support for a national strike and continued acts of peaceful

disobedience as the only means we intend to use to bring down the illegal regime now in power in Tbilisi,

Hereby request that the United Nations immediately send a delegation of qualified observers to assess the situation in the country and to oversee the peaceful restoration of the legitimate government and its freely elected president, Zviad Gamsakhurdia

Signed—

Nika and Merab were so delighted with the text (or so inured to gallows humor) that they immediately proposed that a statue to me be erected on the Sukhumi seafront, naked, with pen in one hand, and document modestly employed as a fig leaf over my private parts; they also assured me that the muscle tone expressed in brass or stone would be appropriately flattering. Then we all went back to Nunu Chachua's chilly theater building, where we waited for new reports about the imminent fall of Poti to the Opposition and the growing threat to Zugdidi, warming ourselves with another bottle of cognac, and illuminating the room with the aid of homemade candles— pieces of newspaper twisted for a slow burn. It was all pretty depressing, when I reflect on it.

"Do you still want to see Gamsakhurdia?" Merab asked me, teasing.

"In heaven," I replied sarcastically.

"We are friends now. I'm serious. Let's go!"

"Where?"

"To see Zviad!" crowed Merab, his mad grin plastered over his face. "You have proven yourself today!"

So, off we went in a caravan of three cars, careening through the icy dark streets of Sukhumi, eventually finding ourselves on the outskirts of town in front of a large house in a compound, facing a memorial to the Red Army. Someone within the compound responded to a password, the metal gate was flung open, and we quickly drove in.

"You excited?" asked Merab.

"Yeah."

"Got your tape recorder ready?" asked Nika.

"I hope the batteries will hold out."

At long last! My meeting with Zviad! . . .

We gathered in a large room along with maybe twenty others. One chair was left empty. Then a door opened, a man walked into the room, and a hush fell over the assembled. That it was not Zviad, I knew. But before I could say anything, the interloper took a tape out of his pocket, shoved it into the video cassette player, and sat down.

"I told you that you were going to see Gamsakhurdia," said Merab, poking me in the ribs. "I didn't say you were going to talk to him."

"Shut up," said Nika.

Like everyone else, his attention was on the VCR in the corner of the room. We were watching Zviad Gamsakhurdia on the TV.

The president was sitting behind a low wooden table in a room with yellow wallpaper, wearing a dark gray double-breasted suit. He looked just like his photographs—a smallish guy with gray hair, large, sad eyes, and a toothbrush mustache, which is maybe why some people compared him to Hitler. He seemed poised, or at least not overly nervous, but he didn't speak for long. Occasionally, there were murmurs of assent among the listeners in the room, but generally, aside from the president's voice, silence reigned supreme and I thought it best not to interrupt. I would ask for a translation later.

"What did he say?" I asked Merab when the three-minute address was over.

Merab asked the man who had brought the tape to rewind it so he could translate Gamsakhurdia's first public announcement since his removal from power. This is it:

On January 6th, in order to avoid further bloodshed, I, the legally elected president and the representative of legal government, left parliament in order to put an end to destruction and bloodshed. The change of place does not mean we have yielded. We represent the legal government of Georgia and I have not resigned! The new government tries to force deputies to call a new session of parliament to force it to illegal dissolution. I call to the deputies not to yield to blackmail and to not attend the session or meetings and not to shame themselves before the nation! And if the junta gathers them, it will be a false session. The Georgian people will not submit to the criminal junta and must denounce their criminal actions at meetings and gatherings and establish resistance committees. We will never submit! Georgia is One!

There was more. Gamsakhurdia called for a national strike and further acts of civil disobedience; he called the Russians an "army of occupation," and he condemned the "campaign of disinformation" that suggested he had fled Georgia, and then said that the current situation was simply a continuation of the day, February 25, 1921, when Bolshevik Russia invaded Menshevik Georgia and terminated the latter's independence.

"Tyranny and slavery are foreign to our national character," he said.

"Fighting for true independence is our history and our fate."

It was over, for the second time.

"Well," I asked. "Did he say where he was or when he made the tape?"

"He said he was in the country," Merab said.

"You forgot to translate that part," said Nika.

"Did he mention any dates?"

"No," said Merab. "But the junta's call for parliament to meet was only made last week, so the tape was made sometime after that."

"Could have been today," Nika tried.

"Or five or six days ago," I noted.

"Well it's better than nothing for you journalist types," snarled Merab, playfully.

There was only one thing to do: sit down at the table in the room next door and commence eating an immense feast, the centerpiece of which was a young suckling pig. We drank to Gamsakhurdia and we drank to kith and kin and we drank to democracy and freedom and we drank to all the usual things that people in Georgia toasted to. We drank to everyone in the room, especially the ladies who had prepared the fine meal. We had a very good time, and paid for it the next day with the worst collective hangover in history. We fixed that problem with more of the same in the morning.

By noon, I was ready to go. And that meant the road out of Abkhazia toward Zugdidi, then Tbilisi, and then, finally, back home, meaning Baku. I had flown out of that city for a weeklong journalistic romp through a country I had never set foot in before, one lurching toward civil war. I had stayed more than three weeks and had barely begun to scratch the surface but was starting to regard myself as an "expert" on Georgian affairs because no one else seemed to want to be.

"*Nakwandis*," said Merab, embracing me, speaking Georgian. "Next time."

"*Didi Madlopt*," I replied in the same tongue. "Thanks a lot."

The next time we would meet would be at Gamsakhurdia's funeral in Chechnya.

"*Poka*," said Nika, in Russian. "See you."

We would never meet again.

"*Jigiro Orda*," said Zurab, our host, speaking Mingrelian. "Until then."

We next met in Tbilisi, two years later, in front of the Hotel Iveria, when he saved me from an irate mob of refugees who were sick of foreign journalists taking their pictures and asking them if they believed they would ever be able to return to their homes in Sukhumi.

But all this was later.

Notes

1. Whether Abkhaz has always been the "native language" of Abkhazia, however, is also open to dispute: when the first-century B.C. Republican Roman General Pompey and his legions passed through the region while in "hot pursuit" of Mithraditis (the Osama bin Laden-like leader of the last, great anti-Roman revolt in Anatolia), Pompey was famously obliged to hire hundreds of translators in order to deal with the myriad tribal languages spoken by the clans populating the region around Sukhumi and the Abkhazian part of the eastern Black Sea coast.

2. It is a good thing I did not make a bet on this issue. Although no flood of Diaspora Abkhaz came pouring back into the country, a significant number did indeed return, both as volunteers during the coming war and as immigrants pure and simple. The most interesting of these was Adil Tokcan, father of Muhammad Tokcan, a Turkish citizen who famously hijacked the Avrasya Russian Black Sea ferry boat in 1996 in protest over the first Russian–Chechen war. To this day, the younger Tokcan is referred to as an "ethnic Chechen" from Turkey. Not so; he is Abkhaz.

5

The Fall of Zugdidi

It was a crisp, cold, January morning when I said good-bye to Nunu Chachua and her family in the Gamsakhurdia stronghold of Sukhumi, heading for Tbilisi and from there, back to my home sweet home in Baku. The general plan was to get to Zugdidi and then somehow to negotiate a way over the Position/Opposition lines (wherever they were) before crossing the intersection of the Greater and Lesser Caucasus mountains east of Kutaisi toward Stalin's hometown of Gori, proceeding from there via Gori and Mtekhi, more or less down the Mtkvari/ Kura River to the capital, where pro-Shevardnadze sentiment reigned supreme.

That is a mouthful, I know. But it was exactly what the *Tourist's Guide to Soviet Georgia* map I had picked up at the dysfunctional Sukhumi railway station suggested I had to do, less all the Position/Opposition jargon. The alternative was to try to talk my way back over the Russian frontier to the north, and then, if not jailed for spying, try to talk my way aboard a return illegal flight to Baku.

Fat chance.

So I headed south, then east—and straight into the civil war.

There was very little traffic going out of Sukhumi, and I was obliged to walk several miles before getting my first ride in a cream-colored, smoke-belching Volga sedan, the back seat of which was filled with bread. It was unclear to me whether the driver was hoarding or distributing the loaves, but we seemed to get ambushed in every town along the way, with no money changing hands. After the fourth apparent mugging in Gali, I got tired of the game and got another ride and then another in a series of cars and trucks, each of which seemed to be going only five or ten miles down the road. Some four hours later, I finally arrived in Zugdidi.

The situation looked pretty grim. The Prefektura building had been utterly trashed; the bonfire crowds had worked their way through the broken tables and chairs to the filing cabinets and bookshelves, then on to books and ledgers of records. And when these combustibles had run out, they had taken to burning tractor tires. The square in front of the Prefektura building was pockmarked with black rings and weird hula hoops of roasted wire—the guts of the big tires that would not completely incinerate.

I fought my way up to Walter Shagua's office, only to learn that he had already gone underground. People were yelling and screaming at me, grabbing me by the arms, and trying to lead me in five different directions at once. The Opposition demons were all junked high on dope and forcing their way into the northern suburbs, where they had already commenced a horrible campaign of looting and rape. No, they were advancing from the south, driving a wall of women and children in front of them; the Position could not shoot their own! No, the column was coming in from the east—could I not hear the gunfire in the distance?

I flipped a coin and went to the southern front to see this wall of captive women and children. I spied a local cop whom I had met during my earlier swing through town, grabbed him and made him hijack a car that ran. Instantly, there were eight people in it, all determined to show me the truth about the cowardly Opposition who would stoop so low as to use human shields rather than fight like men.

There was chaos all along the road. Groups of people were running this way and that. Some carried shotguns. Others had sticks of dynamite hanging out of their greatcoat pockets; there was even the odd Kalashnikov to be seen. Here was a semi-trailer truck, carrying a chunk of building block cement to use as a barricade; there a dump truck with one-inch thick metal walls welded on the sides, making it into a poor man's armored personnel carrier (APC), with shooting holes blow-torched through the armor.

"Georgian tank," chuckled the cop, whose name was Otori.

Then, as we clanked over some railway tracks, we found ourselves facing a wall of people moving our way.

"There, there they are, see!" screamed one of the guides from the backseat. "It's the human shield!"

It was no such thing. They may have been terrified women and children, but when we sliced right through them with the car, there was nothing behind them. But we were getting ever closer to the front, and after about ten minutes we started running into barricades. Most were unmanned. Then we were at the last one, and looking down a country road that crossed a small river via a small bridge that had not been blown. On the far side stood three APCs with their guns pointed in our direction. Closer inspection revealed that there were two machine gun nests on the near side, guarding the bridge from sabotage. The Opposition.

"Let's go say hello," I said to Otori.

"Why not?" he answered. "We'll say I am your translator."

It was crazy, but it happened so fast I couldn't really appreciate how crazy it was. To the amazement of everyone manning the last barricade, Otori and I put our hands on our heads and walked straight down the road to the enemy lines. Then I noticed that the driver of our car was walking with us.

"We can assess their positions!" he hissed.

"We need to assess our route of retreat," I suggested, looking at the collected firepower on the far side of the bridge and reflecting on the pathetic defenses on our side.

Once within earshot, Otori shouted to the guys in the machine gun nest that I was a foreign correspondent who wanted to talk with their commander. Word was passed back, and then someone walked across the bridge and signaled that we might approach. We did so, slowly. Meeting us on the bridge was a young lieutenant from Tbilisi. I asked him about the various allegations about his men being doped up and raping women and using children and old people as human shields. He denied them all. His men were patriots. It was the Opposition (meaning the Position) who were doped up and raping women and using children and old people as human shields. I was confused by this but not by his next statement. He said he hated the fucking war and just wanted to be back home, wherever that was. We then asked if we could see the commander, and our new friend brought us to a temporary command bunker/shack of some sort but the man inside it was drunk and said he did not want to talk to us.

"Thanks," we said, and took our leave before someone changed his mind about us poking around where we didn't belong, and started walking back across the bridge, hands over our heads in submission.

It was then that something occurred to me: while Otori was on my right, the driver who had accompanied us across the bridge was no longer with us. Logic suggested that he had been taken captive, or had been caught spying, or something. God only knew—perhaps he was planting a bomb on one of the APCs or placing a charge under the bridge. But there seemed only one decent thing to do in the circumstances: turn around and try to get him back. So we turned around and walked straight back toward the bridge with our hands over our heads. When we got within shouting range I demanded that my driver be given back to me. Baffled looks passed across the faces of the men in the Position/Opposition machine gun nest. In any case, I just kept on walking across the bridge and past the machine gun nest where the APCs were parked until we found some guy who looked like he might be in charge and demanded, on general international principle and respect for the press, that my driver be delivered back to me, posthaste, if he had not already been summarily executed. I didn't actually say anything about this last bit, but I was rather concerned about it. The stupid shit.

Then, amazingly, the driver appeared from behind a building, with an

Opposition soldier on either arm. They cuffed and shoved him toward us, as he gave a grateful yelp of joy and gratitude for his salvation. I felt pretty good about saving his ass myself, before another thought occurred to me: maybe the man had been less than lost or even interested in assessing the enemy's defenses than in telling them about our own, meaning of course the Position's. In any event, arms akimbo and hands above our heads, we returned to the Position's positions that had now been redefined as the Opposition's positions, and were met like heroes returned from the far side of the River Styx.

"What did they say! What did they say!" a dozen men demanded.

"They said they do not want to fight," I said.

"They lie! They lie!"

We got back in our car and returned to the Prefektura through ever larger and more agitated crowds. The object of everyone's interest was an exhausted and shell-shocked young man who had just brought in the latest news from the frontlines on the other side of town. The Opposition was massing to the east of the city and was about to march; there had already been a firefight out that way, with several Position defenders killed. The anticipated attack across the bridge had been a ruse.

"Let's go," I said to Otori, and we hijacked another car and started down the grand processional avenue that led from the city square to the eastern side of town, where the avenue turned into the main highway to Tbilisi.

It was here, literally at the place where the "Welcome to Zugdidi" sign had been erected, that we stopped at a pathetic cement block barrier. Behind it there was a bunch of people with shotguns, sticks of dynamite, and midnight special pistols.

"They're coming!" wailed two hundred people at once.

"I don't see anyone," I said to Otori.

"Neither do I," he replied. "Let's go."

So, like Clint Eastwood and Donald Sutherland in *Kelly's Heroes*, that Hollywood flick about World War II greed, gold, and mistaken heroism, we started walking down the road, now stretching empty off into the eastern distance. The difference between old steely-eyes and us was that once again we thought it prudent to put our hands above our heads as we walked down the middle of the road, lest the Position mistake us for Opposition, or vice versa.

boom . . .

There was a crack of something in the far distance.

boom boom . . .

Again the distant sound of someone else's battle.

Boom.

That one sounded a little bigger and a little closer, so I stopped walking. So did Otori.

BOOM! boom boom BOOM!

"I think we should go back," I said.

"Probably a good idea," he replied.

VREEEE . . . vBROOOM!

A light cannon round had exploded in the street 100 yards away and then all hell broke loose.

vBroom! vBRROOM! tRing, tRip, tRizz!

Bullets were ricocheting off the "Welcome to Zugdidi" sign and whistling past our ears. Otori and I were suddenly eating asphalt, if such a thing is possible, and watching the brave line of defenders behind us run screaming and shrieking away.

Vreee VBROOM! tRing, tRip, tRizz!

We were lying right in the middle of the road and suddenly I knew what it is to be a sitting duck—or maybe a bowling pin in an alley is a better metaphor. There must be several ways to describe the situation but none that really capture the moment. I was about to get killed. I had been in many sticky situations, and quite a few foolish ones, but I realized that I had never been shot at before, not really, and that there wasn't really much of anything special about it, aside from this: I was petrified.

"Afraid?" chuckled Otori from his prone position. "You should have been with me in Tbilisi."

tRing, tRip, tRizz! Ping Ping! Boom POW!

A few yards away stood a hopelessly thin tree, the decorative kind that municipal governments plant along boulevards. Otori made for it and I followed him. Though the tree trunk promised some protection, it also reinforced the bowling alley perspective of the situation. How many bullets could a trunk tolerate before it no longer acted as an effective shield? How many 72 mm slugs before it splintered into toothpicks? How many cannon rounds before it disappeared?

And then came a darker thought. The tree might give us marginal protection from the oncoming bullets and projectiles, but it gave us absolutely no protection from any return fire should the Position people actually decide to make a last stand.

Running parallel to the street was a shallow drainage ditch and beyond that a row of houses, partially hidden behind low walls. I liked the thought of those walls. So did Otori. He went first, splashing through the slush and crud of the drainage gutter and making it to the nearest gate, which he then opened. I went next, hunkered down as the bullets squealed above my head, and dove for whatever cover the inside of the gate and wall might provide. At least it wasn't the main street.

tRing, tRip, tRizz! Ping Pow Pong! BOOM!

The first house we broke into had a plate-glass window facing east. That wasn't quite what we were looking for, so we broke into the house next door, which had a brick or concrete wall between the advancing Opposition and us. We liked that better. Actually, we didn't exactly break in, because the people were home and not that surprised when we lurched into their kitchen. Maybe they thought we were Opposition about to occupy their house and that they had better be nice to us or we would kill them. We tried to make it as clear as possible that this was not the case. We stressed that Otori was proudly of the Position, and, that while I, the international journalist, had no positions as a matter of general press principle, my sympathies, to the extent that journalists are allowed to have any feelings, were clearly with the right group in this unfortunate conflict, namely, the Position. Relief washed over their faces, and suddenly we were being treated as honored guests. Out came a plate of hominy grits with a pork stew on the side to give it some taste, to be washed down with obligatory shots of *chacha.* Waiting there for the lines to pass actually turned into a bit of a party with the addition of some other folks, also seeking shelter and a bit of company. We ate and drank an amazing amount in a very short time. Nobody said this, but I think we all figured it might be our last supper.

tRing, tRip, tRizz! Ping Pow Pong! BOOM!

With a rumble, the first Opposition tank came rolling by. As we nervously peered out the door, the army of occupation anxiously swung their guns around at us, waiting for a wrong move. They were just as frightened as we were. Then the whole column came tearing down the road—two more rather antiquated battle tanks, a few half-track sort of mobile guns, an artillery piece towed by a fuel truck, and then, finally and pathetically, one of the armored dump trucks used by the Position as a poor man's APC, or as Otori was fond of saying, a "Georgian tank." A big black dent marked one side of the vehicle, where a bazooka round, or some other heavy shell, had hit but not pierced the one-inch thick metal. I didn't want to think about what that sounded like to anyone inside the device. Following the parade of Opposition armor were a couple of buses filled with heavily armed soldiers and, after them, a whole line of private cars, of all makes, packed with a motley crowd of Opposition volunteers, drinking warm champagne.

Zugdidi had just fallen.

The Opposition lines having passed us, we waited a reasonable period of time, then gingerly returned to the street, and followed the column to where it had parked in front of a house that had just been declared the new headquarters of the conquering army. I sought an interview with the commander.

"Ah, I remember you!" chuckled the guard at the door when he saw me approach. "I had you in my sights today but didn't blow your head off because I saw you were a foreigner."

"How did you know that?"

"Your stupid hat."

I have kept the lid to this day as a survivalist totem.

I interviewed the commander, a young man named Giorgi Karagashvili. He told me that he had lost seven men that day and wasn't sure yet how many the Position had lost. Of course, he used the word "Opposition" when talking about the Gamsakhurdia loyalist forces and "Position" when talking about his own. I made a private note to avoid both words henceforth, lest accidentally uttering the wrong one resulted in my facing someone's firing squad.

Following our conversation, I went down to the local telephone exchange and, amazingly, found someone still working there. She assured me that all the lines to everywhere in the city, country, and world were down. Evoking the name of Gamsakhurdia, I begged her to try to make a connection through the switchboard. With a click, a clack, and a shower of sparks I found I had a line through to Tbilisi, and from there to Moscow. I stretched my luck and tried to get two numbers: the BBC and the *Washington Post*. I got through to Bridgett Kendal first and told her that I was in Zugdidi and that the city had just fallen. I thought that she might appreciate the tip. Then I got the Moscow bureau of the *Washington Post* and managed to convince them that I had something to file. They had no time to take dictation but did offer to clip me into the automatic voice machine in DC. I talked into the ether, having no idea if the file went through because there was no one on the other end of the line—no "thanks, we got it," or "that's fine, goodnight," or even a beep back from the tape machine, telling me I had not been cut off halfway through. At least I tried, I thought bitterly. Later, tuning into the BBC, I heard Kendal telling her audience that "unconfirmed reports" from Zugdidi suggested that the city had fallen, signaling an end to the Position resistance to the putschists. About six months later, I saw my copy in the *Post*, which began with the same passive voice tone, although after the first prevaricating paragraph in which it was not clear where the news was coming from, they did run the piece at length, including reference to the "Georgian tank." Sadly, I had already quit writing for that newspaper in general disgust with what I perceived to be their ill treatment of me, the fall of Zugdidi story being a major element in the constellation of bad experience. Ah, well.

* * *

I stayed at Otori's that night. Despite the curfew, we left once to check out a huge blaze at a sports complex torched by unknowns, and then a second time to find his younger brother, who was wandering around town with a grenade in his pocket promising to start the partisan war. Otori asked for patience and took the grenade away.

The next morning it was time to push on toward Tbilisi, and there was no longer any problem about crossing the lines. The lines had crossed me. The first ride was with some putschist policemen, and they got me as far as Kutaisi, the ancient capital of western Georgia known for its thousand-year-old cathedrals and cultural legacy. I had time for none of it. Also, the city was digging itself out from under the worst blizzard of the century, making progress difficult for both man and beast, and certainly cars. I was obliged to walk the length of the town through snowdrifts up to my knees, happy to be wearing my pair of Soviet officer's boots—the ones I had picked up in the Zugdidi bazaar to replace the too-small tennis shoes—even if they were two sizes too large.

From Kutaisi, I caught a couple of short lifts down the road, one in a truck filled with Armenians bringing supplies down from Russia to their homeland. The two words I could understand from their conversation were *Tashnak* and *Arstach*—that is, the Armenian words for the ultranationalist Armenian party and Karabakh, respectively. I couldn't tell if they were praising or vilifying the party or what they had to say about Karabakh, so I thought it best to be prudent about revealing my destination—Baku, capital of enemy Azerbaijan. The truck overheated while climbing a mountain pass at dusk. So I abandoned the Armenians as they tried to melt snow with a blowtorch in order to refill the radiator and picked up a ride in a Niva four-wheel-drive jeep with a highway patrolman, who subsequently stopped a bus and put me on it. The kindness of strangers wearing badges of authority.

We arrived in Tbilisi around midnight, and I checked into a local hotel called the Adjaria. My room was fine—superb, given the circumstances. If it wasn't warm, neither was it freezing. There was hot water, and I bathed for the first time in more than a week. I washed my socks and underwear and then slid naked and clean into bed to sleep like the proverbial log. In the morning I ventured forth for a daylight look at the Georgian capital, feeling like a complete bum. My interior clothes might have been clean, but I was still dressed in the pants and jacket that I had slept in for two weeks. I was also stumbling down the avenue in the too-large military boots, which were fine for snow and slush but left something to be desired when used on pavement. The alternative was to wear my too-small sneakers. I reflected on this state of affairs for a moment, then decided that I had actually become used to life in the (post) USSR: I wore what I could find.

Well, not quite. Feeling like an utter bum in my filthy togs and too-big boots, I walked into a commercial shop, scanned the ill-stocked clothing shelves, and plunked down enough rubles for a new shirt and tie. If it wasn't a change of wardrobe, at least it was a start. The attendant adjusted the collar and tie and announced that I looked great.

"*Prekrasno!*" she said in Russian. "Excellent!"

She was lying just to make me feel good but the partial change of duds did change my attitude, until I proceeded down Rustaveli Avenue to take a look at the damage the brief civil war of January had visited on city center.

It was sobering. A swath of stately, turn-of-the-century buildings had been turned into the burned and busted brick one usually associates with Central European cities at the end of World War II. The centerpiece of the destruction was the parliament building. Not only was it riddled with bullet holes and scorch marks but whole segments of the columns decorating the facade had been shot through, leaving dangling pieces of wire and cement swaying in the breeze.

Parliament had taken the brunt of the attack but adjacent buildings had suffered, too: the main telephone and telegraph exchange, a school, the Georgian Museum, the National Museum, and behind it, the KGB center, which was totally gutted by a fire that reportedly destroyed a quarter of the documents inside. The stately old Intourist Hotel on a corner nearby had also been badly hit; another hotel project on Freedom Square still boasted doors bolted shut, although there were scarcely any walls left to hold up the frames.

Nor was all the action over. After circling the destruction zone, I was making my way down a back street cluttered with shattered air conditioning machines, when I saw a crowd of people in the main avenue below, marching under inflammatory banners. "Down with the Army of Occupation!" "We Demand Our President," and "Killers to Court," read some of the signs, helpfully written in English for the sake of international communication. Cynicism aside, these were some pretty brave people, marching around beneath the scar-marked reminders of what could happen to brick when the shooting starts. I followed the crowd around Freedom Square to their destination—the almost-unscathed Government House behind the presidential palace, where the military junta had its offices. The chanting continued and calls were familiar: *Zvi-a-de!* and *Serv Junta!* Then a window opened and the men inside the Government House turned on the fire hoses. It almost turned the crowd of angry demonstrators into a carnival circus.

"See! See!" laughed a young woman who recognized me as a foreigner, hence probably a journalist, "There are chemicals in the water! They sprayed me yesterday and I became giddy and had to sleep!"

Others soon gathered to tell me all about Saint Gamsakhurdia and the evil scourge of the junta, detailing its crimes, and sketching in exact detail the elements of the conspiracy started in Moscow that was designed to bring Eduard Shevardnadze back to power and Georgia back into the Moscow loop. It was a familiar litany, and one that was probably true, but one that had become impossible to listen to. Somebody else in the crowd was a journalist and said there was a press conference inside the building, so I flashed my Azerbaijani credentials that suggested I had something to do with the *Washington Post* and went inside, feeling vaguely criminal for having anything to do with anyone who worked there, doormen included. Once in, I discovered that the usual suspects had been rounded up for the function: Interfax, TASS, the Russian Information Agency (old Novosti), a stringer from CNN, VOA (I believe), and a number of local journalists representing the range of Georgian radio, television, and print media. They all seemed almost giddily anti-Gamsakhurdia. No sooner were we seated and treated to a general overview of the situation by the panel of Military Council members than the speechmaking began.

"Sir," a man from some magazine asked the minister of the interior, Tengiz Kitovani. "When are you going to start providing protection for journalists when they are attacked by irate and fanatical supporters of the Opposition?"

Say what? This was just the first portion of a large pile of other rhetorical, planted crap.

"Is it true, Mister Minister of the KGB, that Gamsakhurdia actually served as an informant for your agency for thirty years and was in fact placed by your agency as a national leader in order to dupe the people?"

"Well, I don't know about that," the spook replied. "Of course I had nothing to do with the old security system, and most of its records were burned by the fanatical followers of the fascist, but on the level, I think there is reasonable doubt about Gamsakhurdia's motivations. . . ."

"Is it true, Mister Chief of Police, that it was actually Gamsakhurdia's wicked and psychotic wife Manana who begged you to massacre the intellectuals last September, but that you refused?"

"Well, I didn't think this subject would come up here, but I was shocked when the witch called up my assistant and begged him to beg me to tell the troops to mow down the intellectual elite of our country! I refused, and it was at that moment that I realized that the time had come to topple the dictator and killer of his own people."

It was all pretty disgusting, sitting there in that conference room with the fat quislings on the dais and the somewhat thinner quislings in the chairs all around me.

* * *

The next day I went out to the airport to catch a plane to Baku, but it was not to be. There was no fuel for any transport, save for a plane bringing a bunch of Austrian skiers to their dream helicopter-ski vacation at a mountaintop resort called Gudauri near the Russian frontier. Ditto the next day, when I returned to the airport to find there were no flights anywhere, aside from another plane bringing a load of satisfied downhill enthusiasts back from

Georgia to Vienna. They confirmed that skiing conditions at the resort were "excellent." War-zone tourism at its worst.

I decided to proceed to Baku by road. This was regarded as exceedingly dangerous due to the large number of bandits, and I was warned against it. And the price, given the dangers, would be exorbitant: $10 prorated in rubles.

My driver turned out to be an ethnic Azeri. I discovered this when I suddenly couldn't think of the word for "food" in Russian and accidentally said *chorek*—the word for "bread" in Azeri.

"You speak Muslim!" he exclaimed.

We were soon on the road south toward the Red Bridge and Azerbaijan. And with every passing kilometer, the familiar wandering pigs of western Orthodox Christian Georgia disappeared from along the roadside to be replaced with flocks of sheep, even while the pleasant "typically" Georgian houses of Zugdidi, Sukhumi, and Kutaisi also underwent a not-too-subtle cultural transformation. Compound walls replaced open balconies, and the bare-shouldered women offering *chacha* were replaced by individuals wearing some manner of chador.

I was traveling through Marnauli, better known as Azerbaijani, or Muslim, Georgia.

After an hour of driving over exceedingly bad roads through an increasingly flat and denuded landscape, we reached the border, the so-called Red Bridge over the Algit River. At the customs post, a policeman stopped us, but it was to hitch a ride and not to search the car. No passports were demanded. Then the two Azeris—one from Georgia and one from Azerbaijan—began chatting away in a language I could eavesdrop on.

"Who is the infidel sleeping in the front seat?" asked the border cop.

"He's a Turk, I think," said the driver. "He has come from the war and is tired."

"Oh. Well, how are things in 'blisi?"

"Bad, bad, brother—bread is five manat (rubles) and gas one hundred for two liters."

"By God I didn't know . . ."

"Onions—twenty manat for the kilo now. No cucumbers."

"By God, we live in filthy times. It wasn't like this before."

"You could do everything, buy anything."

"Gorbachev."

"The dog."

"We lived well in the Brezhnev days."

"Yeah, we lived well then."

"Do you know what we need?"

"Stalin."

II
PAST AS PRELUDE

Eduard Shevardnadze. As a Young Communist (Komsomol) leader, Shevardnadze made a solo motorcycle trip of some 6,000 miles across the breadth of the USSR. Credit: Presidential archives, Tbilisi.

6

Along the Banks of the Mtkvari

It was not Stalin who returned to Georgia from his Kremlin-wall grave, but Eduard Shevardnadze from his office in Moscow.

The date was March 8, 1992, and it was his first visit to Georgia in eight years.

Meeting him at the airport were Mkhedrioni warlord leader Jaba Ioseliani, National Guard commander Tengiz Kitovani, and the third leg of the troika, Tengiz Segua, who had served as prime minister under Zviad Gamsakhurdia, and whose presence thus gave a fig leaf of legitimacy to the coup. Together, the three formed the "State Council," with Kitovani holding the defense portfolio and Ioseliani that of interior, the so-called power ministries that theoretically maintained a monopoly on organized violence in the country. Others referred to the group simply as "the junta."

"It was the moral equivalent of appointing John Gotti and Carlo Gambino as head of the FBI and the DEA," a longtime Georgia watcher told me. "Their portfolios seemed to sanctify any and all criminal acts carried out by their men as legal deeds."[1]

The one thing the troika lacked was legitimacy; the international statesman Eduard Shevardnadze was to provide them with exactly that. They, in turn, were to provide him what he now lacked: a job as "leader."

To prepare himself for that task in independent Georgia, the sixty-four-year-old former atheist received a belated baptism by the head of the Georgian Orthodox Church and was christened "Giorgi." A second benediction was the political baptism delivered by Shevardnadze's old political pal and fly-fishing buddy, American secretary of state, James Baker III, when he arrived in Tbilisi on May 25 to announce a package of aid to help nurture freedom and democracy in Georgia. It seemed oddly weighted in favor of security assistance, such as the training of Shevardnadze's bodyguards at Fort Bragg and high-level liaisons with the CIA. Local wags began referring to the higher caliber bullets used by masked Special Forces teams as "Bakers," while their German Shepherd police dogs became known as "Genschers," in honor of former (West) German Foreign Minister Hans Dietrich Genscher, who worked with Soviet Foreign Minister Shevardnadze at the time of the collapse of the Berlin Wall and repaid that political debt by gifting Shevy's security bulls dozens of snarling hounds to keep dissidents in line.[2]

The first major anti-Shevardnadze demonstration was held on National Independence Day, May 26. The following is quoted verbatim from a local human rights report, kinky English and all:

> Enormous quantities of people gathered (but) were not allowed to hold a meeting. The junta tried to put obstacles on their way, but in vain. 10,000 gathered. The meeting . . . lasted three hours. At last, the participants of the meeting came down the Rustaveli Avenue, singing and dancing. The sight was like a national festival. When the people reached the Rustaveli Monument, they were confronted by bands of Mkhedrioni and some other men in civilian clothes. Poor people were beaten, even women and children were beaten. Meanwhile, Eduard Shevardnadze with his "friend" [James Baker III] were attending the concert [marking Independence Day] in the [Philharmonic Hall] when in 50 meters distance was happening all this.[3]

None of the security assistance would have been possible without Washington's recognition of Georgia's status as a sovereign, recognized entity in the larger world, which DC had been loath to do so long as Gamsakhurdia was in power. Shevardnadze's return changed all that. And with Washington's recognition secured, in August of that year, Georgia claimed a seat at the United Nations. Membership in such clubs as the International Monetary Fund, World Bank, and Organization for Security and Cooperation in Europe were soon to follow, further legitimizing the State Council and its unelected leader as the legal government of Georgia and its people.

The problem of public perception was resolved on October 11, 1992. That was the day when Eduard ("Giorgi") Shevardnadze, "burning with desire" to participate in the democratic process for the first time in his life, was elected to the unique position of "head of state" of the Republic of Georgia by an overwhelming majority of the country's 5 million citizens, perhaps half of whom were eligible voters. Marring the moment was the fact that Shevardnadze ran unopposed. Worse, along with separatist groups such as the Abkhazians and Ossetians, the pro-Gamsakhurdia crowd in the country had boycotted the polls. Despite these objectively disconcerting elements and a general cry of "fraud," election monitors from groups as disparate (or similar) as the U.S. Congressional Helsinki Commission and the Organization for Security and Cooperation in Europe deemed the elections "free and fair."

The Silver Fox had come in from the cold.

* * *

American recognition of Shevardnadze and the State Council as the government of Georgia demanded some sort of American presence on the ground. Initially, this was minimalist and consisted mainly of running the occasional diplomat down from Moscow or up from Baku or Yerevan. Then, in early summer 1992, the American presence in Tbilisi was upgraded by the appointment of a real-life ambassador by the name of Kenneth Brown. It was one of the last diplomatic acts of George H.W. Bush before his electoral defeat by Bill Clinton in November of that year. For Georgia, it was a historic event, and almost immediately Brown (or the embassy that he represented) became the object of adulation, appeal, and eventually scorn and protest in the country.

I had seen the same phenomenon happen in newly independent Azerbaijan scant months before. A pair of seasoned American diplomats had shown up in Baku and checked into a set of shabby hotel rooms overlooking the gray Caspian Sea, where they ran up the Stars and Stripes to see if anyone would salute. Within a week, general salutations had turned into a friendship assault as the new embassy was subjected to a constant stream of late-Soviet dissidents still looking for asylum even though the USSR was no more, lines of now-former Soviet-state-supported artists looking for decent paying jobs as translators, drivers, or cleaning ladies, as well as the odd lunatic poet wishing the American people well out of general principle and the occasional drunken *biznesman* attempting to rendezvous with his favorite whore in the right room but on the wrong floor.[4]

Yes, these were wild times, replete with all-too-human, nontraditional diplomatic contact across the board. And, given the currently prevailing "Fortress America" notion that all embassies of the United States must attempt to achieve absolute security by moving from relatively reachable downtown locations to distant new offices, difficult to access, I suspect that those diplomats given such "hardship" assignments in the new republics of the former USSR remember the chaos of being sent into the thick of things with no security to speak of as the good old days of diplomacy. And, if they showed even a minimal interest in the process at play, they were treated like royalty.

Ditto for most of the other, nondiplomatic foreigners who arrived on the scene—and we were a decidedly eclectic lot: washed-up or wannabe war correspondents, fishy or fly-by- night businessmen interested in tea, tobacco, and titanium, oilmen looking for drilling rights and Caspian crude connections, and the odd entrepreneur looking to capitalize on the throw-the-dice rapacity of the others. One such was an American lady named Betsy who decided there was a market for a decent guest house at a quarter of the price of the gouging rates charged at the Metechi Palace; she made a killing by providing comfy beds and good, local food served by friendly local folks in a "traditional" Georgian setting. Another was some crack-pot character from

Tennessee (or was it Kentucky?) who was determined to acquire an abandoned collective farm and grow broccoli for the growing number of foreign oilmen in Baku. He failed.

It never made much difference what destiny brought us to the still-glowing (and sometimes burning) embers of the Evil Empire after its collapse. What was important was who you wanted people to think you were, *and then to become that.*

Rent a *nomenklatura* flat of five stately rooms for a hundred bucks a month from an out-of-work multilingual philologist who specialized in Brecht and keep her as your maid; take on an eminent Moscow-trained geologist/botanist who specialized in the medicinal properties of saffron culled from that unique crocus bud found only in that certain valley outside the mountain fortress town of Shatili, and hire him as your driver/guide/slave for pennies; place an ad in local Russian weekly newspapers that reads "thirty-five year old single European male seeks eighteen-year old female companion for fun and possible marriage, photograph in bathing suit required," and see how many mothers send pictures of their daughters looking for an exit strategy from a good life gone suddenly sour. . . .

Let us be frank: the collapse of the former Soviet Union may have resulted in trauma and poverty for most of the people living there, but it was a god-sent cornucopia of career-enhancing opportunity for others, including me.

While I shall refrain from the sort of excruciatingly painful self-criticism of the neo-Bukharinist crowd, the fact remains that so many of the Johnny-come-lately expert interpreters of events in the Caucasus were . . . well, *so many Johnny-come-latelies.* All were looking for some odd angle on a complex society collapsing on itself, a new wrinkle, a new angle, an intellectual niche on which to make a journalistic or academic career, usually based on someone else's misery. No collapse of the USSR meant no articles, no books, no invitations to conferences, no perceived expertise. . . .

It sounds a bit mercenary, but believe me, it is true.

In addition to the diverse, self-serving foreign types projecting themselves as truly interested parties and/or sudden experts on the scene, there were locals who regarded the collapse of the USSR as an opportunity for self-redefinition and aggrandizement that was not to be missed. If the career trajectory of a young Georgian graduate of the Moscow Institute of Foreign Languages might logically have led, say, a Spanish-language linguist to a posting at the Soviet embassy in Madrid, Mexico City, or Havana back in the late 1980s, that option ended with the collapse of the USSR in 1991, when the Russian Federation assumed all the debts and assets of the moribund mega-state and demanded that its diplomats be actual citizens of the New Russia and not "foreigners" from the former Soviet republics. But there was still a range of new and exciting possibilities to be explored in the brave new world of post-Soviet Tbilisi (or Baku, Yerevan, or Tashkent) for said young graduate: *retool yourself as a local area expert and go to work for the dollar-paying former adversary!* A rash of new European and American-funded nongovernmental organizations (NGOs) began to appear around Tbilisi, claiming specialization in "democracy-building," "security studies," "media transformation," "gender issues," and even "microfinance." All of these were donor targets for outside do-gooders, and the savvy creators of the entities making up the new NGO sector (or the best among them, meaning those who knew which buttons to push and how to most effectively write a winning grant proposal) soon found themselves winging off to international conference after conference, all expenses paid and pocketing per diems. Status, coupled with savings, soon conspired to create a virtual new class in post-Soviet society: the owner of the foreign-funded NGO. . . .[5]

* * *

During those early days of the Shevardnadze restoration, most of the foreigners I encountered worked in and around the media. The man at the center of the storm was the extraordinary force of nature that went by the name of Alexis Rowell.

A thirtyish Malaysia-born Brit, Alexis had done some work for the BBC in both the UK and eastern Europe (Prague, I believe) when Bush House had decided to open a limited bureau in Tbilisi. The logic of this was that doing so would allow its correspondent not only to track developments in Georgia in light of Shevardnadze's return but also to use Georgia as a neutral point to cover events in the other two South Caucasus republics, Azerbaijan and Armenia, which were even then locking horns over the disputed territory of Mountainous (Nagorno) Karabakh. Other conflict areas such as Chechnya were also but a relative stone's throw away.

Rowell and I first met during the course of a presidential fly-by visit made by Shevardnadze to Baku. What made this particular pit stop interesting was not that it focused on the meeting between Soviet insider Shevardnadze and Soviet dissident-cum-Azerbaijani president Abulfaz Elchibey, but that Shevardnadze's departure was delayed due to the sudden appearance of a third regional political player, namely, General Djohar Dudayev, leader of the self-described, breakaway Russian Autonomous Republic of Chechnya/Ingushetia, that now described itself as the independent Chechen Republic/Ichkeria. He was also the host of Shevardnadze's archrival, Zviad Gamsakhurdia. What was said between the three remains a mystery known only to Shevardnadze, because both Dudayev and Elchibey are dead. But the trilateral meeting gave Rowell the opportunity to track me down and initiate a professional and personal friendship that has lasted more than a dozen years and included many an adventure on the wild side. It was during Shevardnadze's delayed departure to Tbilisi that Rowell and I first met.

"Pack your bags," commanded *nachalnik* Alexis, who has been known to be a little bossy. "We are going to Armenia together to see whether they are really all freezing to death thanks to your Azerbaijani friends' blockade."

"Okay," I replied, docile as a lamb on its way to slaughter.

We drove south in a Lada packed with food and gasoline because of the horror stories we had heard. Allegedly, the Armenians were cutting down trees in city parks to burn for fuel and losing body mass at an alarming rate. "Welcome to Hell Frozen Over," was a typical newspaper headline at the time. Things were cold, nasty, and generally bad. But so were things in Georgia. The difference was that while the Armenians generally liked to advertise their pain, the Georgians remained mute. Pride vanquished the need for publicity.

Alexis and the BBC may have been the first to recognize Tbilisi's unique logistical advantages, but others were not far behind. In addition to Rowell's fiancée, Natalie Nougayrede of the French *Liberation*, the Tbilisi international hack-pack soon included Steve LeVine of *Newsweek*, Liam McDowell of the Associated Press, Lawrence Sheets of Reuters, and some guy named Gareth from the *London Daily Mail* scandal sheet who specialized in post-Soviet street sleaze. The BBC's Georgia specialist (and Rowell mentor), Rob Parsons, was also a frequent guest, as was that extraordinary war videographer, Rory Peck. The list would continue to expand through the years to accommodate a host of names now intimately associated with the post-Soviet Caucasus, but those just mentioned constituted the hard-core, resident press corps of the day; the rash of aid workers, consultants, parachute journalists, and democracy builders that would eventually descend on Tbilisi was still three or four years away.

Assisting Rowell and the other foreign informational shock-troopers in their newsgathering tasks was a parallel universe of fixers, translators, drivers, local intellectuals, drinking companions, and landlords (often all rolled into one person), most of whom were drawn from the small, English-speaking *nomenklatura* class. There were the devoted sisters, Nata and "Big" Nana Talakidze and their pal "Little" Nana Kiknadze who served as translators, office assistants, and rocks of stability for Rowell and LeVine and long-term visitors such as myself. Sheets's Reuters bureau soon brought in cameramen Big and Little Dato, who had both formerly worked for the Soviet-wide news agency TASS, as well as Nino Ivanishvili, whose job description started as being McDowell's AP translator (and Alexis's "mother superior") but then grew into being the tough-as-nails Reuters television producer for Georgia, then the entire Caucasus, and finally any war zone stamped "ethnic conflict" where regular Reuters staff feared to go, including Chechnya, Afghanistan, and Kosovo. Other members of the traveling circus eventually came to include professors Gia Nodia and Alexander Rondeli, who were initially encountered as sources of authority to issue the obligatory sound bites on the labyrinth that was Georgia, but who soon became constant companions and fast friends. And did I forget that extraordinarily oversexed dynamo named Lika, who eventually disappeared to London as a refugee-of-convenience, and her friend Katy who played a mean guitar? . . .

All were almost giddily pro-Shevardnadze and sang the praises of their native son's genius day and night, a mantra that was of course picked up and recited as gospel by the resident foreigners. I tended to keep my mouth shut about my "Position" friends who were now no longer even called "Opposition," but just "Zviadists," as if they were a criminal gang.

"My goal in life is to raise a second Shevardnadze," Professor Rondeli confided in me during one of our first meetings, referring to his stable of eager young students of international affairs over at the dark and cold campus of Tbilisi State University, where he taught (often by candlelight or at least in an overcoat). "Only a genius like him could possibly lead this nation of crazy poets and artists out of the catastrophe we have made for ourselves."

A large, teddy bear of a man with a shock of white hair and prominent nose that reminded me of a handsomer and more intelligent version of the American actor Leslie Nielsen, Rondeli seemed to personify all the contradictions of Georgia. Son of a prominent actor and lesser Georgian old family noble who had changed his name and a St. Petersburg/Leningrad-born Georgian mother, Rondeli spoke pristine Russian and immaculate Georgian as well as flawless Persian and almost perfect (and always very colorful) English. His manners were impeccable at all times, as were his clothes, even when he came down to Baku to visit me along with Rowell and the entire Tbilisi crowd to mark Azerbaijani Independence Day—and when the rest of the gang looked sore and sour from the ten-hour trip.

"You are a catastrophe," he announced, boarding a rickety sailboat I had hired to take a cruise of Baku's oil-slicked bay, using his favorite word in his sixth language. "You are a catastrophe—that is what you are!"

* * *

The train pulls into the station, and the conductor shakes me awake. It has been a long and nasty overnight ride from Baku in an overheated communal four-person cabin shared with a rotating series of brand new friends for life, all with their own bottles, and I am feeling so miserable and generally enfeebled that I am not even sure how I made it to this apartment somewhere off Lermontov Square.

"*Sad aris istancia otoboosi?*" I ask in what is probably a mixture of Georgian, Russian, and Azerbaijani, but the important thing is that my interlocutors get the "where is" part and piece together the rest because it is so obvious: *station (of the) autobus . . .*

Martskhniv moukhweit; Marjvniv moukhweit; pirdapir . . .

Turn left; turn right; straight ahead, or something like that.

Finally, I find my way to my temporary abode, collapse on the bed and wake to discover myself staring up at the ceiling of a strange, cold if familiar room trying to piece together the puzzle of where I really am, and why.

Georgia, that's right. Up from Bolshevik Baku to Menshevik Tbilisi like some modern-day John Reed exploring the opposite end of the *Ten Days That Shook the World* seventy-five years after the fact.

I put my feet on the cold floor of my guest bedroom and find a note about the dos and don'ts of the flat along with a set of keys. My hosts have left a note that they will be back in two weeks and I have the run of the place until then, but to please not bring in any street girls and always double-lock the outside door. Thieves are rife.

The flat is outfitted in a way typical of a certain class of late-Soviet elite. The living room is dark with no natural light whatsoever, and lit by a heavy chandelier that sort of matches the heavy dark furniture and grand piano, which is out of tune to the point that it is no fun tinkering around. Heavy oak bookcases line the walls, and are apparently organized into three sections: one crammed with the apartment owners collection of classic Russian literature and translations of foreign classics such as Ernest Hemingway, Jack London, and the like; the second containing what seems to be a proud assortment of classic Georgian literature and translations (I recognize several editions of *The Knight in the Panther's Skin*), while the third is a tumble of teach-yourself-English pamphlets.

The rest of the flat is also standard middle-class or lesser late-Soviet *nomenklatura*. The bed is big and sagging on broken springs; the kitchen counters are cracked Formica; the stove is gas fed and the tap water only runs very hot or only icy cold or not at all. Several large, plastic trashcans and a dozen bottles are strategically placed to fill with water and use as a depot in case of outage. The refrigerator is small and contains only a Spartan sampling of foods that could tolerate a day or two without being chilled (due to frequent electrical outages), such as a large jar of Georgian wine, a bottle of vodka, a bottle of *chacha*, a couple of chunks of cheese, and a bottle or two of *tkhemali* sauce to drizzle on bland food. There is a super abundance of pots and pans, cups and plates, mismatched sets of knives, forks, and spoons, and a fine set of crystal goblets and decanters, no doubt acquired in Prague when that city was the capital of Czechoslovakia and a favored tourist destination for "Russians" from places like Georgia. A reasonable tile bathroom opens off the kitchen. It contains a cracked sink and bathtub that is also filled with water for emergency use and flushing; a European-style electrical tank water heater has been added rather awkwardly to one wall and feeds a shower spigot that is also not part of the original design, sacrificing aesthetics for convenience and reliability. A Soviet-era washing machine is crammed in a corner; the device is a study in retrotechnology, requiring a bucket to load clean water through the top, and used suds flushed out a valve located at the back to drain through a hole in the middle of the floor.

A den or breakfast nook attached to the far side of the kitchen will serve as my office space. There is a black-and-white television there and a pulse-dial phone of an older sort. Beyond this is a tiny sunroom/atrium that is open to the sky and used to store wood for the fire and to dry clothes on a line, although hanging them there seems like an invitation to have to wash the laundry over and over again: the evaporating source of sky in question is a square of blue found straight up between two or three stories of gray, peeling walls that seem to be favored by pigeons, whose droppings are all over the atrium floor. I locate several emergency candles and matches, split the remaining stack of wood, light a fire, take a shot of *chacha*, and collapse back on my bed, waking in a pool of sweat some twelve hours later to the smell of trash fires and cat piss, mingling into a unique olfactory bouquet that crawls up the moldy stairway to the first floor from the street, and I know where I am again because there is no call to prayer.

Tbilisi.

Of course it was much more than that.

The town itself was a delicious mishmash of East and West, pre– and post– Russian Revolution, quietly quaint and utterly chaotic, stately urban beauty and ugly Soviet high-rise cement. The core of the city was the old town, and the core of the old town was the sulfur-bath complex from which the city took its name: *Warm Waters.*

Actually, the Soviet-era tour book I am using reminds me that Tbilisi is not really so old. Although founded in 452 c.e. as an alternative capital to Mtskheta some thirty miles to the west, the city has been razed to the ground repeatedly throughout history, most recently by the Persians in 1795, and is thus better regarded as a nineteenth-century Russian garrison town than an Oriental city gone to seed. But however defined, it was and is a delicious place. Nestled under the walls of the oft-rebuilt Narikala Castle on Mount Mtatsminda, and split and defined by the Mtkvari (Kura) River, "old" Tbilisi (or Kala) was a chaotic series of cobblestone streets filled with more churches, mosques, and synagogues than one could count or reasonably attempt to visit in a week. Mulberry trees dropped their sticky fruit underfoot, and straggling vines grew out of the cement, creeping up the red brick walls of once grand but now mainly long-neglected mansions. Old wooden balconies leaned dangerously over the narrow lanes, and many doors still boasted ornamental gargoyle brass knockers. Once regal, most of the older homes had been turned into communal apartments, entered through mysterious courtyards defined by a high density of draped laundry and illegal electrical lines, strung from window to spiral staircase and then the street.

If that sounds nasty, it was not. Old Town Tbilisi was actually very evocative and maybe even beautiful. The *Maidan*, once called "Tatar Square," downhill from the castle, was dominated by the turquoise tile facade of the old Persia bathhouse, much prettier on the inside than out. Next to them were the Turkish baths, less ornate but more functional, topped with a dozen, glass-inlaid miniature domes. Across the bridge on the right bank of the river loomed the Metekhi Church and adjacent prison, where most of the luminaries of the Social Democratic movement had spent time. But I was a left-bank kind of guy, and preferred a meander along the soft-curve of the stately if unused Yellow Arcade that served as part of the city-set for the film *Repentance*, and from there into the rabbit-warren of cobblestone streets which all seemed to merge around the handsome tsarist-era municipality building fronting Freedom Square. The "square" itself was a large traffic circle that had been called Yerevan Square during tsarist times, Lenin Square during the bad old days of the Soviet Union, but which had been renamed once again in 1991 when it served as the no-man's land between the Opposition and the Position during the so-called Hundred Meters War. A jag right and then left led to the Orthodox Theological Seminary, a religious institution once described by future Georgian Bolshevik leader Filip Makharadze as having produced more atheists than any other school in Georgia. One such student was the young Josef Stalin.

Behind the seminary was the central market, a wonderful, rambling, two-story warehouse surrounded by the fresh flower sellers, and teeming at all times with farmers, fishermen, and butchers (or their seconds) calling out the beauty of their wares to knots of finicky customers poking, jabbing, tasting, and haggling. The central space was filled with long tables sagging under the weight of a cornucopia of grains, greens, tubers, eggplant, apples, pears, citrus, twenty types of homemade cheese, green and purple *tkhemali* plum sauce in seventeen different size jars, pickled cucumbers, beets, cabbages, tomatoes, all the spices of the Orient, and dubious-looking bottles of homemade hooch, which proud distillers urged potential clients to sample from a communal plastic cup. Another section was devoted to the public display of live chickens, frozen broilers on the thaw, floppy fish, dead fish, and then an abattoir of blood-stained butcher blocks and meat hooks from which dangled diverse chunks of animal flesh, guts, trotters, whole heads, raw legs and loins of pig, cow, and lamb, mounds of different types of sausage and buckets of bone to be turned into *khashi,* or early morning "glue soup" to be washed down with early morning shots of vodka.

Yummy.

Yes, indeed. The bazaar was a most lovely, unsanitary place, and it was difficult not to amass two armfuls of groceries before realizing that you were not on your way home, but going over to a meeting at some ministry or other.[6]

The main drag through "modern" Tbilisi was Rustaveli Avenue, originally built by Count Vorontsov in the mid-nineteenth century when it was called Golovinskii Prospekt before being renamed in honor of the national poet by the communists. By any name, it was a handsome thoroughfare lined by block-stone buildings of various vintage and in varying stages of decay or repair, especially right around parliament, which had been the center of the so-called Hundred Meters War of late 1991.

At the far end of the avenue was the National Museum of Georgia, which, like many of the monumental structures in Tbilisi, had gone through several name changes and additions. First opened as the Caucasus Museum in 1852, it was renamed the Dzhanashia Museum by the Bolsheviks in 1923, and finally the National Museum of Georgia in 1991. There may have been a shift of exhibit emphasis with every renaming (for example, the rooms devoted to the subject of Soviet Georgia on the third floor were closed for what seemed to be almost permanent renovation), but the basic thrust of the dark and brooding interior space was archaeology, including fragments of the first mandible jaw and skull of earliest man in Europe as discovered in the southeastern Georgian region of Dmanisi. How this might impact on the debate about the ascension of man from ape to humanoid to human is a subject I thought best left to the experts; what did intrigue me was the museum's impressive collection of bronze-age daggers, swords, and other such tools of war, iron-age ax head and needle molds, and other works of ancient metallurgical martial arts. How could these naked apes, my putative forefathers, figure this stuff out, when much-more-modern-me trips over a Costco ladder to screw in a light bulb? The most amazing exhibit, however, were the Alexandrian, Roman, Mythic, Byzantine, Ottoman, and of course Georgian gold and silver coins that had somehow managed to elude looting hands at the time of the collapse of the USSR, when anything "owned" by the state was regarded as fair game to steal and then resell. Ditto with the Russian-era icons, triptychs, and other sacred art: someone had cared for the stuff and kept it under lock and key for the sake of future generations, and the odd, appreciative "tourist" as the likes of me.[7]

Across the street was the parliament, formerly known as the *Dom Sovetov* or House of the Soviets, the Government House of the Georgian Soviet Socialist

Republic. It was actually two, Stalinist-style, monolithic structures made of handsome blonde blocks and columns built around a central courtyard and constructed between 1938 and 1953. As such, it served as the centerpiece of Soviet rule in Tbilisi until it became ground zero of the putsch against Zviad Gamsakhurdia, after which it had required massive repair (from the Shevard-nadze Fund) to make it functional again. I remember Alexis Rowell wondering with almost mock amazement about what he assumed were my journalistic exaggerations when I told him what the stately building had looked like in February 1992: smashed.

"You can't be serious," said Doubting Lex, circa February 1993. "There is no water, gas, or electricity now, but you are trying to tell me they patched up the RPG-destroyed columns of the parliament that they still don't use with money they do not have out of general principle so that it might look nice?"

"Well, yes," I truthfully replied.

Next to the restored parliament was the Viceroy's Palace. Here, Prince Mikhail Vorontsov once held court during the glory days of Georgia's absorption into the tsarist fold in the mid-nineteenth century, and where Count Illarion Vorontsov-Dashkov sat almost helplessly during the "troubles" of 1903–6 as that same Georgia began its slow slide out of tsarist control. The handsome structure (or several rooms in it) next served as the abode of Stalin's mother in the 1920s and '30s, after which it once again reverted into some house of high Soviet-style protocol. Next door was the Alexander Nevsky Cathedral (how many Nevsky cathedrals are there in the Slavic world?) and next to that, the Number One Classical Gymnasium for Boys, now an innocent vignette of moms and dads picking up uniformed children from school, but once the site of an infamous massacre of students on October 22, 1905, when the youths declined to tip their hats in respect to a nasty crowd of psalm-singing, pro-tsarist soldiers and railway workers, who were counterprotesting an earlier demonstration of tens of thousand s of red flag-waving Georgians demanding social justice and the release of political prisoners. It was burnt to the ground in 1991, but rebuilt with Russian money.

Pogo-sticking between cars lurching down Rustaveli, Lex and I crossed again to the National Museum side of the street, and the Kashveti Church, an early twentieth-century quasi-replica of a tenth-century cathedral at Samtavi, some fifty miles outside of Tbilisi. The irony here was that virtually all pedestrians and many car drivers actually believed it to be the original, ancient structure and felt suddenly seized with the need to stop on the pavement (or the street) to cross themselves when passing, making it a rather dangerously congested zone of instant worshippers.

"*Bodoshi*," I (or we) would say, bumping into such sudden-stoppers on the street outside the church. "Excuse me." There was rumor of a certain

Scottish bridge builder buried in a crypt below, but I never checked it out.

Then there was the building I always referred to as the "Blue" art gallery, but never found open to the public when I had time for a glimpse. They said it contained the very best examples of all the plastic arts of the Georgian nation, from Pirosmani to August Rodin's disciple Nikolashvili to contemporary guys and gals called—well, I don't know, because I was never allowed in when it suited me, which one might argue is a massive failure on my part. So be it. Whatever it contained within, the Blue Gallery was flanked by an extraordinarily pleasant sculpture park dedicated to the memory of Tsar Alexander (II). Set beneath plane trees and among fountains, the Alexander Gardens had once served as a place of horseracing and wrestling for the nineteenth-century elite, and then the rallying point for disgruntled soldiers and other malcontents during the twilight of the Romanovs, and then the chaotic period bookended by Lenin's October Revolution in St. Petersburg and Noe Jordania's seizure of the arsenal for his Georgian Menshevik Guard in late 1917. Following the collapse of Jordania's Georgian Democratic Republic in February 1921, the park was renamed "Communards Gardens," in memory of the Bolsheviks shot down there by the Mensheviks, but then reverted to the tsarist era name of Alexander with the collapse of the USSR in 1991. The worm turns, and former heroes become contemporary dupes, and have their once glorious names erased from history, while former dupes find themselves re-installed to glory they might not rightly claim.

A different fate awaited the nearby Georgian Society for Friendship and Cultural Links With Other Countries, known during Soviet Times by its Russian acronym, GODIKS, but today known as nothing at all. A pamphlet I picked up spoke of a lively, Soviet-style intercultural past that had no reflection in present reality. Perhaps it was only lies.

> GODIKS links the 30 sections of Soviet Friendship societies now functioning in and near Tbilisi. Among its 500 collective members are factories and plants, agricultural and building enterprises, printing presses and research institutes . . . and each section is headed by a leading figure in science, literature or art. GODIKS . . . takes an important part in festivals of the Soviet Union which are held abroad and feature Georgia in any way—for example, in Belgium, Hungary, the German Democratic Republic, Greece, Italy, Poland, France and Sweden . . . GODIKS welcomes 50,000 foreign guests every year.

Even allowing for Soviet-style, *friendship of the peoples* sort of exaggeration, this one ministry's claim of attracting 50,000 (presumed) non-Soviet foreign visitors to the GODIKS offices every year to celebrate multiethnic art and culture is impressive, even if one clips off a zero. Not everything was bad about the good ol' Evil Empire all the time, even if I had once been taught to think so.

Across the street from the nameless park/hippodrome/never-open "Blue Gallery" were the ruins of the Hotel Tbilisi, a stately edifice dating to 1915 boasting a rounded (as opposed to square) street corner that might (or should) serve to teach today's architects about the subtle elegance of curvature and line in brick and cement. Alas, the lobby and all balconies served as snipers' nests (and thus also targets) during the Hundred Meters War, and the grand hotel on the unfortunate corner of Rustaveli and Giorgiashvili streets had been turned into so much rubble.[8]

Next down the line came the quietly elegant, baroque Rustaveli Georgian Drama Theater, the preferred venue for Shakespeare, Ibsen, Chekhov, and notably Brecht's *Caucasian Chalk Circle*. I saw an advertisement for a showing once but decided not to attend due less to the fact that the performance was in Georgian than because of a power outage that meant I would have to imagine the staging while sitting in the dark. We had attended an experimental performance of some original Georgian-language play a month or so previously out of a sense of obligation to the gods of High Culture. It had been seriously claustrophobic when the stage lights had dimmed to nothing and remained so while the cast scurried around lighting candles. Therefore my enthusiasm to see Brecht's masterpiece in situ, as it were, was not high enough to subject myself to the same experience for the sake of theatrical history. I regret that decision still.

Nor can I extol the cultural delights of attending performances at the Tbilisi Opera and Ballet. The house itself should have lured me in: a neo-Moorish study in horizontal yellow and brown striped stone, the building was once known as the State Treasury Theater, and served not only as the Lincoln Center of the cultural Caucasus during tsarist times, but also as the most popular venue for public politics, a place where Noe Jordania and his cohorts made the momentous decisions that molded "Georgia" into what it is today. Alas, the sad fact remains that during all my time in Georgia I did not attend one single cultural event in the building that so preeminently defines Tiflis. That is the name that Tbilisi is still known by in much of the world, because that was the name by which it was known at the zenith of Russian influence in Georgia, when opera was extremely trendy. This was the time that Beethoven was writing his "prison" opera, *Fidelio*, when Verdi was spiking tunes for the Egyptian Khedive, and when in post-Decembrist Russia, seemingly every poet, novelist, musician, or composer of note in the tsar's realms spent time in Tiflis.

Pushkin, Tolstoy, Lermontov, Gorky, Tchaikovsky, and others—the list is extraordinarily long. Some arrived as soldiers and others as dissidents, sent into exile on the fringes of the tsar's realms. All were enamored of the "Kavkaz," or Caucasus, which was the Wild West of the tsarist empire, a half-Oriental half-Occidental land of mountains, instant fraternity, and lurking Islam. The ill-fated Alexander Griboedov remains perhaps the most symbolic example of this Georgian/Russian/East/West synthesis. Betrothed to the great Georgian writer Ilya Chachavadze's daughter Nino, the thirty-four-year-old Russian poet and diplomat was torn apart by an irate Muslim mob while on a "Great Game" diplomatic mission to Persia in 1829 but was later re-interred in Tbilisi with a parallel street above Rustaveli named after him.

Political figures from the Soviet period have not been so fortunately regarded by posterity either, in the way of buildings, street names, or squares. Just down the street from the opera house was the monumental Stalin-style Georgian Affiliate of the Institute of Marxism-Leninism of the Communist Party of the Soviet Union's Central Committee.

> Founded in 1933, the Institute researches into the history of the communist organizations and the revolutionary movement in Georgia and Transcaucasia, studies and popularizes the biographies of famous revolutionaries who were active in the Caucasus, and produces Georgian translations of the Marxist-Leninist classics. . . .

Stripped of every last vestige of its original function after the collapse of the Soviet state, the building served as a cold, smoke-filled alternative parliament when the post-Gamsakhurdia putsch Government House was under repair and eventually as a series of offices for lesser parliamentarians, who lacked the tenure or stature to be someplace warmer. During communist times, the offices associated with the state media, information, and publishing entity run by the Georgian Writers Union, known as Gruzinform and Merani/Pegasus were across the street at Number 42 Rustaveli. For wandering Western hacks like me, however, the entire gray building was known as Reuters because Lawrence Sheets and his staff of mad cameramen, translators, and drivers had taken over the fourth floor and stuck a generator up on the roof so that the Reuters office almost always had electricity, even if the elevator did not always work.

Ah, Rustaveli!

The grand avenue sort of split in two across from the "classical" Khrushchev-era cement-block Grand Post and Telegraph Office, with the right spur diving down a cobblestone street past an equestrian statue of Herekle II, the eyesore Brezhnev-era Hotel Iveria[9] and toward the pleasant, pedestrian strolling zone and embankment restaurants of the Mtkvari River, and the several bridges leading to a part of Tbilisi that I never got to know well at all, save for the horrors of the train station. The left spur continued on by the handsome Academy of Sciences building until eventually turning into Chachavadze Avenue near the university that was once named after Lavrenti Beria, but is now known simply as Tbilisi State. Monster though he certainly was, there is no question that Beria's tenure as Stalin's viceroy in Georgia in the late 1920s and early 1930s and his continued connection to his ancestral homeland in the Caucasus until his arrest and execution in 1953 resulted in much of the urban allure of contemporary Tbilisi, and it seemed almost churlish that, in a city where seemingly every third building, no matter how humble, had a bas-relief of a famous poet, scientist, journalist, or war hero embossed in cement or steel on an outside wall of their erstwhile residence ("Here Lived the Thinker Sultan Papba, 1888–1999"), there was not a street or park or square named after Beria. If the shack in which Stalin was born in the town of Gori could become a museum, was it too much to expect a little historical recognition of Beria, a man secretly admired by many, including Shevardnadze? The most appropriate place, in my humble opinion, would be a plaque in the cozy little garden in front of his handsome, two-story residence and office at Machabeli Street, Number 11, saying something like "Lavrenti once lived here." Alas, no. After his arrest, the house became the headquarters of the Central Committee of the Communist Youth organization Komsomol, once headed by Shevardnadze, and then, following the collapse of the Communist Party of Georgia, the house on Machabeli Street became, ironically or appropriately enough, the Office of the Public Defender. The decorative bust in the garden is dedicated to the memory of Galaction Tabidze, the suicidal romantic poet known simply as Galaction by all Georgians, but of whom few people outside of Georgian literary circles have ever heard.

If the history of Rustaveli was rich and layered, commercial life was patchy to nonexistent. The exception to this general, post-Soviet dearth were the growing number of former state-run shops that had been turned into privatized *Komision* shops, which specialized in everything from Korean playing cards, Malaysian school supplies, fake Camel cigarettes, vodka of dubious origin, Iranian shoes, and the occasional made-in-Turkey leather jacket. Oddly, perhaps, the only state ventures that remained open were bookstores, which somehow managed to maintain a constant supply of Soviet-era engineering textbooks, as well as multilingual, lavishly illustrated translations of Rustaveli's eleventh-century epic, *The Knight in the Panther's Skin*. It may have been a masterpiece, but it certainly was a tough slog to get through. The text consisted mainly of the manly adventures of a knight errant from Georgia who befriends a mysterious Indian warrior intent on revenge, all cast within the context of a convoluted triple love story.

However, from the checkerboard brick mayoral offices on Freedom Square at one end to Chavchavadze Avenue at the other, the most notable thing about Rustaveli were the people. Strutting up and down in their Sunday best or huddled in front of braziers and wearing greatcoats against the cold, the grand avenue always seemed filled with folks on promenade, rattling away in that multiconsonant jabber that was Georgian. It remained an unanswered question whether most of the strollers were there for a purpose, just out of habit, or simply because they had nothing better to do than sit shivering at home remembering the good old days. Adding color and content to the mix were scores of highly cultured street vendors, most bearing aquiline noses of prodigious proportions, who hawked all manner of artistic output and Soviet and religious kitsch. There were icons new and guaranteed old, *matreshki* (nesting dolls) in various thematic designs drawn from the immediate Soviet past (Yeltsin inside Gorbachev inside Andropov inside Brezhnev inside Khrushchev inside Stalin inside Lenin), traditional Caucasus drinking horns and *kinjali* daggers, paintings large and small and good and bad on a thousand different themes, and then what were clearly hand-me-down heirlooms and other personal possessions placed on the street for painful sale: sets of silver, glassware, rugs, musical instruments, doll collections, and even prescription glasses that no longer seemed needed on someone's nose. With the infusion of aid money, Rustaveli would boast buffed-up boutiques specializing in Bata shoes, jewelry, cell phones and accessories, Armani togs, high-end eyeglasses, art galleries, pubs serving Guinness beer, and eventually, inevitably and sadly, a three story McDonald's all run by a world-class collection of diesel generators, humming and thumping away on the sidewalks and supplying electricity to the better shops. In 1992, it was all rather bleak, a good place that had somehow gone bad, or at least seen much better days.

* * *

Diplomats, advisors, and even the local filthy rich generally preferred the Metechi Palace Hotel as their idea of the "new" Georgian. This was sad, because the hotel was a garish island of Western-style "comfort" in the midst of a sea of seething instability. Access to the gleaming glass and marble high-rise structure was affected via dodging seemingly suicidal pedestrians meandering among smoke-belching cars careening down convoluted traffic lanes on the main city–airport road. A taxi ride from the airport to town cost around $5 if you got off on the street; once inside the hotel grounds, however, the rate would suddenly jump to twenty or at least occasion a furious argument and renegotiation of the fare to around ten bucks. The charge for a hotel-appointed drive to the airport cost something along the lines of fifty greenbacks. Of course, there was the issue of the style and status of one's hired car. The "city" taxis could be anything from broken down Ladas wheezing steam out of broken radiators, and driven by university professors trying to augment their ridiculously low salaries to off-duty cops behind the wheel of a semiprivatized black, government Volga with a *TAKSI* sign slapped in the window. The Metechi-approved fleet, in contrast, were sparkling new, red and white Turkish-made Opels on long-term buyback leases to the drivers, who most often turned out to be younger brothers of Mkhedrioni and National Guard commanders in need of a "class" job.

Once dropped at the hotel's oval driveway, the dreary, cold, and generally nasty world of Tbilisi circa 1992 evaporated. The atrium revealed internal balconies soaring upward a dozen floors, accessed via three glass and steel exposed-elevators running up the far wall like so many gigantic metal yoyos. First-time guests from the city would excuse themselves from meetings and ride the lifts like children might ride a Ferris wheel for the first time, grinning like idiots and waving to friends waiting below on the deep-cushioned, real leather-upholstered couches in the multilevel, spacious reception area, tearoom, and bar. Pretty waitresses dressed in natty traditional costumes flitted among the tables while a former employee of the state music conservatory tinkled the ivories of the grand piano set off in a corner, creating the perfect acoustical ambience for discrete conversations between dealmakers and diplomats under the watchful gaze of thick-necked security guards (and, one imagines, the eyes and ears of spies from a dozen nations). True, the cult of the loose gun had become so extreme that the management had gone so far as to post a sign at the entrance asking patrons to check their weapons with the concierge. Not all did so, and the atrium became an occasional venue for shootouts that sent guests diving for cover. From his sixth-floor internal balcony, my fellow reporter Hugh Pope witnessed one bang-bang altercation that left folks sprawled and hiding behind the chairs and tables scattered on the marble floor below.

Guns and gangs were everywhere in Tbilisi, and as a foreigner you never quite knew with whom you were dealing until someone raised a weapon to your head and demanded your money or hoisted a toast in your honor and declared you an eternal friend. The latter experience was much more common than the former, and what sometimes appeared to be a kidnapping was merely an invitation to some rank stranger's home for an instant feast celebrating the fact that the taxi driver with the Kalashnikov had never met an American before and wanted to show off the rare prize to his wife and kids.

Not all chance encounters were so rosy. In June, Alexis decided to throw himself an alfresco birthday party in Lermontov Park and issued invitations with the request that all weapons be left at home. When advised that not only was this unlikely but also that the "block-party" atmosphere would attract undesirables, Alexis changed the birthday-bash venue to the spacious and seemingly secure new abode of Reuters correspondent Lawrence Sheets, situated kitty-corner from the High Court building. Fifty or sixty guests were drinking and dancing the night away, when an uninvited Mkhedrioni guardsman, bearing a machine pistol and looking for his girlfriend (who quickly exited via a window), broke up the party. The dance floor emptied and sudden sobriety reigned supreme.

"Let's talk about this," said Alexis Rowell.

As soon as the gunman began his *I-have-been-abandoned* whine, Lex snatched the magazine clip out of the gun and thus disarmed the interloper, who then broke down in tears. We called the police. They advised us to give the man his gun, with magazine clip, lest his gang come back and kill us all. We did so, and the show went on as people laughed and danced in the face of, or perhaps because of, the fact that they were living in a real-life *Cabaret*, a society that was singing while spinning downward into doom.

Banditry on the roads had also become endemic. Returning at dusk from a trip to Yerevan, Alexis, and I discovered several armed men standing around a likely looking ambush point. Happily, we were left alone—possibly due to the fact that we were traveling in a beat-up Niva with Georgia plates, and thus did not represent a choice target for a shakedown. (That I stuck my camera tripod half out the window, which made it look like an over/under AK-47, probably helped, too.) Several days after we had run the gauntlet, a Landcruiser with American plates and filled with U.S. diplomats came up the same road; the passengers were robbed at gunpoint and all official traffic down the road was banned for the next year. Lawrence Sheets was luckier. Traveling out west near Zugdidi, brigands grabbed his Niva jeep, which was packed with expensive television cameras and a satellite phone. He complained to the local Zviadist commander, and everything was returned the next day, with apologies and an invitation to dinner.

Yes, the parties. They were almost endless, and almost all with delicious food prepared by people who no longer had the money or means to pay for entertainment but still *had to* provide, out of general principle and disposition. Whether held in one of the few cold, candlelit basement restaurants such as the Pir Osmani (or "Three Men and a Dog," as we called it after the signature painting by the Georgian artist the establishment was in fact named for) or in an eighth-floor flat in a high-rise with no electricity to run the elevator or in one of the newly "privatized" shacks down by the river, the idea of feasting was a basic pillar of the Georgian identity, no matter how expensive such pretensions of nobility were to maintain. As Rustaveli once wrote: "Everything you give away remains yours, and everything you keep is lost forever." Tables sagged under the weight of the diverse dishes that never seemed to change: *khatchapuri*, or flat bread stuffed with goat cheese, *khingali*, or steaming hot dumplings that must be doused with black pepper and eaten with the fingers, the juice splashing down your chin, *kharcho*, or spicy meatball soup, *lobio*, or bean soup, and of course *mtswadi*, or *shashlik* kebabs made of pork and doused with *tkhemali*. Pickles, greens, eggplants rolled in crushed walnuts, explosively spicy tripe sausage and other offal-based sweetmeats, all washed down with a chaotic mixture of the overly salty mineral water famed throughout the former USSR called Borjomi, carafes of (usually) delicious wine and then, of course, plastic bottles of the Georgian-homebrew fruit vodka known as *chacha* if strong and *chachacha* if stronger, each toast led by the *tamada*, or toastmaster, raising his shot glass to *Life, Georgia, Present Company, the Ladies, Future Generations, Missing Friends,* and of course *Life* once again, however ridiculous celebrating such notions seemed in a country suffering from a declining birthrate, eroding identity, increasing whoredom, collapsing currency, and the most insanely suicidal highway culture in the world.

"*Gaumarjos!*" Professor Rondeli would intone, and then begin to extol the "catastrophe" of individuals gathered around the table.

We were over at Nino Ivanishvili's brother's apartment, a gang of at least a dozen souls, performing a cacophonic symphony on plates, pots, pans, glasses, ashtrays, spoons and forks, half-filled bottles, and a slightly out-of-tune piano used more as a percussion piece than melody-producing instrument, and feeling fine.

"*Gaumarjos!*"

In Georgian, that meant "Cheers!"

* * *

Notes

1. Personal interview with member of the U.S. Congressional Helsinki Commission.

2. I did not know it at the time, but the man selected to spearhead this delicate operation designed to protect Shevardnadze while weaning Georgia away from the Russian sphere of influence was none other than my old tennis partner from Ankara, Turkey, in the mid-1980s, CIA "super-spook" Freddie Woodruff.

3. Report of May 26, 1992, acquired from Georgia folder of the U.S. Congressional Helsinki Commission files.

4. One guest was Heydar Aliyev, the Azerbaijani strongman then out of office but plotting his return to power, who showed up on his way from his domicile in Naxjivan to a medical checkup in Moscow and literally took over the two-room embassy to hold a "spontaneous" antigovernment press conference.

5. The United States of America is hardly exempt from this sort of slackers' economy. The city of Bozeman, Montana, now boasts the highest percentage per capita of nonprofit

environmentalist organizations in the country, far in excess of any rational need. How many were set up by trust-fund recipients in order to create status jobs for themselves is open to question; but imagine that half of the 500-odd enviro-NGOs were actually funded by foreign coin and thus open to foreign influence. That was and is the case in Georgia and much of the rest of the former USSR, as witnessed by the "popular" revolts in Georgia, Ukraine, and Kyrgyzstan in 2003, 2004, and 2005.

6. The market was moved to the other side of the river in 2005, and the "traditional" market described above converted into a sort of shopping arcade for perfumes and knick-knacks.

7. The utterly fabulous collection of Colchis treasures, discovered at Vani in western Georgia, that make up the Golden Fleece exhibit was not mounted until 2005, but now appears to be a permanent show and serves as proof-positive that the story of Jason and the Golden Fleece was not mere fantasy.

8. It remained so for nearly a decade, until international investors lovingly restored the Tbilisi to its former eminence, but as a member of the Marriott chain, charging for a night's nuptial stay an amount that it takes the average Georgian a month to earn.

9. The Iveria was doomed to become the eyesore and emblem of political disaster in the country when all twenty-two floors were turned into "temporary" refugee housing following the siege and fall of first Gagra, then Pitsunda, and finally the city of Sukhumi in September 1993. As this book goes to press in 2006, the Iveria refugee residents have all been bought out for a reported $7,000 per room and sent on their way to make do how they might. Rumor now has it that the gutted and emptied hotel will be restored along the lines of the Hotel Tbilisi (now the Marriott) or that it will be razed and an entirely new structure built upon the awful ruins of the old, which everyone wants to forget.

7

(Muslim) Georgia on My Mind

Alexander Rondeli was not only an excellent *tamada*, or toastmaster. He was also a primary guide to lead greenhorn Georgia specialists like me (and Rowell, Sheets, and other members of the post-Soviet hack-pack) through the minefield of post-Soviet Georgian politics in general and specifically in regards to Georgia's increasingly strained geostrategic relationship with Russia.

But an exploration of the complex and often bitterly contentious problem of Georgia's multiethnic and multidenominational heritage required time outside of Tbilisi to appreciate, which meant solo journeys of discovery.

The list of distinctive Georgian subregions (and thus subpeoples) was long. In addition to the main east–west split among Georgians themselves and the dual, breakaway entities of Abkhazia and South Ossetia, there were the Armenian borderlands called Javakheti to the south, the almost insanely rugged mountain region along the Russian frontier known as Svanetia, as well as the self-styled neo-Crusader mountain-men known as Khevsurs living around the extraordinary mountain fortress called Shatili on the upper Argun River, the latter two being sub-Georgian groups. And did I forget the Turkish-speaking Greeks dwelling in the mainly Armenian zone of Tsalka, just south of Tbilisi, or the Azerbaijani-speaking Zoroastrian Kurds of Marnauli, or the ethnic Chechens called "Kists" who lived in and around the Pankiski Gorge on the Chechen/Dagestani frontier?

While delightful on an intellectual level, Georgia increasingly seemed to epitomize the concept of ethnoconfusion and consequently potential conflict in the post-Soviet space, a place where the detached foreign observer could not only *sense* a troubling nationality-based dynamic at play but also actually *see* it unfold. Eastern Georgians against Western Georgians; Georgians against Abkhaz; Georgians against Ossetians; Georgians against Armenians; Georgians against Adjarians . . .

Oops!

Weren't Adjarians merely Georgian Muslims, not "Adjarians" at all?

Objectively, only a minority continued to practice the "imposed" Islamic faith. And yet, subjectively, Islam was part and parcel of the identity of Georgian Adjaria, even if no one (or very few people) believed in it per se. And if the Georgian-speaking Muslims of Adjaria were reluctant to shake off their 500-year-old "difference" between themselves and their co-ethnic, same-language kinsmen, then what about the differences between the Georgians and the Catholic, Apostolic, or even Orthodox but still mainly Turkish-speaking Armenians of the region?

* * *

I had long planned a trip to Adjaria—for over a decade, in fact.

Back in the 1980s, when I was a resident correspondent in NATO-member Turkey for various U.S. and U.K. publications, I was told to keep an ear cocked to what was happening in the Balkans, the Middle East, and the Soviet Union. The communist giant abutted Turkey along the straggling and highly militarized Caucasus frontier, from the Azerbaijani exclave of Naxjivan on the Iranian border on the south, Armenia facing Mount Ararat in the middle to the divided village of Sarp/Sarpi on the Turco-Georgian Black Sea coast to the north.

In the mid-1980s, this was all terra incognita, the ends of the known earth beyond which (at least from the perspective of NATO-member Turkey) Soviet dragons dwelled. And while I had no particular interest in Soviet Azerbaijan or Soviet Armenia at the time, Soviet Georgia held an almost mystical allure. The reason was fairly simple: the Eastern Black Sea region included some of the most beautiful territory in Turkey and, although it was remote and difficult to travel in due to its high security profile, for those like myself who managed to penetrate the region, the rewards were astounding. "Georgian" Turkey was a vertical world of ancient churches tucked away in hidden valleys, roaring rivers crossed by swaying, wooden footbridges, teahouses visited by wandering bards called "Ashiks," spontaneous knife- and knee-dancing theatrics, and springtime fertility festivals in high meadows, often marked by "bull wrestling" events pitting one testosterone-crazed bovine boy against another. Although few of the local "Turks" would admit it, these were the lands of the modern descendants of the Tibal and Mushki, the Turkish "Gurjular," or "Georgian Turks," the upland cousins of the Laz, who shared (and share) the southern shore of the Black Sea and the slopes of the Pontic/Kachkar Mountain range behind it with the Muslimized Greeks and Armenians (the latter known as Hemshins) as well as other marginal members of the ethnic kaleidoscope of peoples that make up the highly diverse bloodline of the modern, Black Sea "Turk."

Nor was history a thing of the distant past in these parts. After having lost the east bank of the Choruh River to tsarist forces in the 1870s (along with the port city of Batumi), as well as the canyon-land region along the upper Kura River (along with the notorious slave-market city of Akhaltsikhe, or "Old Castle"), the Ottoman Turks reclaimed the entire area in 1918, only to have to cede it to the USSR in exchange for various guarantees hammered out between Soviet leader Lenin and Turkish generalissimo Mustafa Kemal Atatürk and summed up in the still-contentious Treaty of Kars in 1921. Twenty-five years later, Stalin demanded the "return" of the Turkish provinces of Artvin, Ardahan, and Kars as the price Turkey was to pay for its neutrality in World War II. The bellicose behavior might be regarded as one of the first acts of the Cold War and it resulted in Harry Truman sending the battleship *Missouri* up the Bosporus and into the Black Sea on maneuvers and Turkey's application to and acceptance in the anti-Soviet collective security treaty known as NATO. For the next forty years, the gorgeous roaring rivers and pine and walnut-covered slopes of the Shavshat Mountains along the Turco-Georgian frontier would be a long and heavily patrolled "zero-point" line between NATO and the Warsaw Pact. This was particularly true at the little town of Sarp/Sarpi, where the Choruh River tumbled into the Black Sea in a brown torrent of water. Families were split in two by systemic political enmity, and foreigners evincing too much curiosity about local customs and family connections were inviting arrest on charges of spying. One suspects, but cannot prove, that the long frontier starting at Sarp/Sarpi and ending on the northern flank of Mount Ararat where Turkey ends and Iran begins, was a favorite place of infiltration of the other by both sides in the Cold War that never got hot.

Then came the East–West thaw associated with the rise of Mikhail Gorbachev in the late 1980s, the concomitant easing of travel restrictions on Soviet citizens in 1990, and the sudden collapse of the USSR in 1991. Instantly, Sarp/Sarpi and (thus the larger towns of Batumi in Georgia and Hopa in Turkey) became the favored legal crossing point for the hordes of so-called "suitcase" merchants from the newly independent republics of the now former Soviet Caucasus. They brought in state-subsidized merchandise (caviar, vodka, bicycles, tools, cameras, etc.) to sell in relatively prosperous Turkey in exchange for Turkish goods: textiles, tennis shoes, and better-quality light industrial products for the kitchen and office, as well as tons of supermarket fare ranging from nicely packaged spaghetti and canned goods to literal busloads of eggs and pop-top beer.

At its peak, the mainly open-air "Russian Bazaars" along the Turkish side of the frontier had an estimated turnover of $40 million a month, and provided jobs or at least some manner of economic lifeline for tens of thousands of un- or underemployed citizens from Georgia to southern Russia and beyond. The most visible of these economic migrants were the "Natashas," or prostitutes, whose scandalous presence in brothels and hotels up and down the coast resulted in a veritable sexual revolution. Conservative Muslim Turkish men, who were loath to let their wives work let alone hang around clubs in skimpy halter tops, were suddenly confronted with the reality of extraordinarily beautiful blondes (and brunettes) with professional degrees in law, medicine, and nuclear physics, who were offering sexual services as a temporary financial fix to the economic straits they had been thrown into due to the collapse of the USSR. This in turn led to a reaction among local Turkish women, who started demanding a much more public voice about just about everything than heretofore. Hit songs were even written about the phenomenon, including one ditty called "Natasha." The chorus went:

> *Natasha, Natasha*
> *Verdin, bize, atesha . . .*

> (Natasha, Natasha
> You have thrown us into the flames . . .)

Meanwhile, and as might be expected, the sex circus spawned all manner of "protection" activity on both sides of the border, often very ugly. The owner of my favorite hotel in the town of Artvin, who had formerly been singularly devoted to promoting the touristy charms of the area and whose clientele had previously consisted exclusively of kayakers, trekkers, wild boar and bear hunters, and seekers of obscure medieval Georgian churches hidden away in the vertical world of the Choruh River basin, suddenly found himself nominated by local authorities to be the proprietor of a major brothel, whether he wanted that title or not.

"What can I do?" he wailed, a clutch of painted strumpets sauntering by, babbling away in Russian although from their looks they were girls from somewhere in the Caucasus, not "Natashas," or Slavic women at all. "The mayor, the chief of police, the second-in-command of the *jandarma*—they all want a place to fuck!"

It was wild and stayed that way until marginally better economic activity at home, coupled with cheap charter flights from larger population hubs in Russia, Ukraine, and Moldova (the putative main sources of the ladies-for-hire) direct to larger population or proper "tourist" centers in Turkey (Istanbul, Antalya, and Bodrum) eventually conspired to reduce the Sarp/Sarpi Batumi/Hopa markets in wares and women to a shadow of their former selves during the salad days of 1991–94.

During one of my first trips to Adjaria, legal and illegal traffic was thick. So was the atmosphere, literally. Arriving in Batumi, I was met by increasingly acrid coal smoke while entering a darkened town that had seen much better days, and not so very long ago. My transport dropped me at the back door of the once stately but now just cold and empty Intourist Hotel on the quay, I swam through the smog to the reception area, lit by candle, and checked in to room 326. As a matter of course, or mere idle thought, I wondered if the room was equipped with secret cameras. Call it mild paranoia—but a rational paranoia, based on proven experience. Once in my room, however, I quickly dismissed the thought: there were no electricity or batteries to run a spy cam in the dark.

I awoke the next morning and started to explore, commencing with my room. It had seen better days. The bathroom tiles were cracked, the water fixtures leaked (when the water ran), the parquet floor was curling at the seams, the floral wallpaper detaching from the walls, and the paint peeling from the ceiling. The chandelier lacked five of its eight obligatory bulbs, and the bed springs sagged on both single beds (which had been shoved together to create the impression of a king or double). And this was one of the special "for foreigners" rooms.

The view from the balcony, onto which I pulled one of the rickety wooden chairs to enjoy my coffee in the morning sun and to study my Georgian grammar, was a mixture of the faded elegance and creeping squalor of the city. Most of the seafront apartment buildings, probably built in the 1950s and 1960s for the local *nomenklatura* of the day, had not seen whitewash for a decade. The public buildings of obscure function (schools?) were in worse repair, sporting missing chunks of masonry and roof tile and soot-blackened and broken windows. Only several newer one- and two-story buildings seemed to enjoy anything approaching external maintenance. I assumed that these were built by and for the Adjarian leader and Lord Protector Aslan Abashidze's cronies, but I could not be sure.

Descending the marble staircase to the reception area, the impression of a once grand structure gone to seed increased with every step. The phones no longer worked, the gift shop was empty, and the receptionist surly in a way only made possible if said receptionist truly understands that his or her monthly salary is half what the demanding guest is paying for a single night's rest. Happily, the hotel still boasted a small but tasty restaurant serving standard Georgian fare, albeit with an alleged local twist: the *khatchapuri* was left open in a sort of boat-like form with egg and butter lathered on top, and called "Adjarian pizza." For anyone familiar with Turkish fast food, it was identical to the cholesterol bomb known as *Karadeniz pidesi*, or Black Sea pizza.

After a snack, I emerged from the hotel and walked toward a seaside park via a large, oval entrance garden. I imagined that the management once had maintained an al fresco restaurant or café here, but the space was now empty save for the occasional stray dog. The park was attractive enough, if you were a connoisseur of dilapidated swings and slides and broken bumper-car rides, but eerily deserted of human beings.

Moving away from the ocean and back into town, my eye caught the more familiar gray, cement-slab, three- and four-story structures one usually associates with mass housing in the lands of the former USSR. Square and almost identical down to the conversion of balconies into extra rooms overhanging street and courtyard, the buildings were graced with absolutely no charm whatsoever.

Happily, however, there was more to Batumi than Soviet-style cement. Scattered here and there among the neighborhoods stood Protestant church spires, Orthodox onion domes, and the minarets of quite a few mosques. The godly spires rebelled against the communist-ordinary and, in a queer and inexplicable way, made Batumi city almost attractive. All streets seemed to converge at the main, downtown market across from the railway station. As might have been expected, the rambling, two-story warehouse was a culinary emporium packed with the familiar cornucopia of Georgian farm products within and Turkish supermarket delights without. The people of Adjaria would never starve.

Whether they would ever collectively get rich was another question. Although Batumi was the end station of a growing number of oil-tanker cars bearing the liquid black gold of Azerbaijan and Kazakhstan to a fleet of tankers anchored in Batumi Bay, very little of the revenues accruing from transit fees and oil storage trickled much further down than the immediate family of "Batono" Aslan Abashidze. On a lark, I decided to explore and inspect the oldest surviving oil terminal in the Caucasus—a creaking, rusting assemblage of tanks, ladders, and wandering cows that so heavily reeked of diesel and gas fumes that I was afraid to light a cigarette lest the very air explode. Built as a state-of-the-art facility by an American company in the 1920s, it was a sobering reminder that what was once new always gets old, and that Georgia has long been a strategic transit point for Caspian crude to world markets, with all that that implies: ridiculous levels of corruption.

After touring the semi-abandoned tanker farm with an engineer named Avtandil (who apparently assumed I was a member of yet another delegation of shady Western oil traders looking for a score), I moseyed over to the end station of the Baku-Batumi oil tanker train line, talked my way inside, and toured a surreal landscape of spigots, ramps, wheels, and scarred tanker wagons being drained of their precious, liquid black gold cargo. Huge metal hoses were slung around like giant worms by an army of workers, all stripped to their waists, stained black, and oblivious to even the barest minimum of safety precaution. Nearby was the open, swimming pool-size sump, where boiling hot crude oil bubbled away like a vast witches' cauldron from hell. Presumably, this was the bottom of the barrel and part of the 1 or 2 percent assumed loss of freight weight between the point of loading (Baku) and shipping (Batumi) that reverted to the shipper after the tanker wagons were flushed since they were still good for making lubricants and other subgasoline products. Rumor in the Baku oil patch strongly suggested that "Batono" Abashidze made very sure that the flushed product was closer to 10 percent, that the product belonged to him, and that the central government in Tbilisi never learned exactly how much oil was actually being moved in and out of Batumi. The spot market in places like Israel and Armenia reportedly paid nice premiums for discretely delivered Azerbaijani "ice cream," as oil is called in the trade.

One thing, however, was absolutely clear: the Lord Protector of Autonomous Adjaria, "Batono" Aslan Abashidze, was less interested in sustaining the traditions of the Muslim Georgian people of the area from the predations of Tbilisi than he was in maintaining an iron grip on the oil tanks and train wagon facility that fed the port. Money, lots of it, was flowing through Batumi, and "Batono" Abashidze wanted to continue getting his fair share. To deflect criticism, "Batono" had even appointed a fellow with the family name of Shevardnadze to the lucrative post of chief customs inspector on the Sarp/ Sarpi frontier. In conspiracy-obsessed Georgia, the appointment cut like a double-edged sword: the customs inspector named Shevardnadze had been appointed because he was indeed a relative of the leader or he was not but sounded like he was.

* * *

Behind Batumi unfurled green hills of tea, hazelnut, and citrus groves, rising to the south, east, and north, and all dotted with single-family farmhouses nestled in what certain international political analysts might call "communist"-imposed clusters, but which I saw as traditional communities set among distant snowcapped mountains.

I determined to go there. But where?

On a chance meeting with a Turkish-speaking Georgian journalist (and recently reborn Orthodox Christian) working for the quasi-fundamentalist Istanbul news agency (go figure), I found my direction. Our conversation went something like this:

"You're not Turkish, are you?" asked the journalist.

"No," I confessed. "Yourself?"

"Georgian."

"Adjarian?"

"There is no such thing as Adjarians, only Muslim Georgians," said the reporter with a hint of irritation. "And I am Orthodox and from Tbilisi."

"So, what is the news?"

"There is a mid-level delegation of Turks in town come to express their active concern with the situation in Adjaria and to urge a peaceful resolution to all conflicts."

"What does that mean?"

"I don't know. But it is what they said before they went in to meet with Abashidze."

We waited around about an hour or so, until the security door to "Batono" Abashidze's residence finally opened, the Turkish delegation emerged, and crossed the street to the awaiting cameras. The group was led by a gentleman who once served as Turkish foreign minister but was now serving in the role of "special consultant to the government on marginal affairs that no minister or deputy minister could be bothered with," or something like that. The number two in the delegation was a Turkish parliamentarian of royal (if Muslim) Georgian descent from the province of Artvin who spoke an archaic form of Georgian passed down through his family. The ex-minister and ex-prince then issued a joint, jejune statement of their reason for being in Batumi. It had something to do with Turkey's expression of neighborly concern, expressions of solidarity, and ultimate goal of urging peace and tranquility on all parties involved in the most recent wrinkle in the ongoing Georgian–Adjarian dispute of the day.

"Mister Foreign Minister," I said, addressing the head of the delegation with an honorific he no longer owned, and in Turkish. "Does the Turkish Republic regard the Republic of Georgia as an outside power in Adjaria?"

"Let's not discuss deep history on the street," the former minister snarled, knowing precisely what I was driving at. In 1921, Soviet boss V.I. Lenin and Turkish nationalist leader M.K. Atatürk stitched together several desperate diplomatic deals that have resonance to this day. One was the Treaty of Kars, which granted Turkey the right of intervention into the Azerbaijani exclave of Naxjivan as well as Adjaria should their autonomous status be violated by any outside power.

"But it is the essential question," I persist. "Does Turkey reserve the right to intervene in Adjaria in the event of—"

"The Republic of Turkey regards the brotherly and fraternal neighboring Republic of Georgia as a sovereign and unitary state," says the former minister diplomatically, but with a new coldness in his eye. "As there are no further questions, and in that we have a long road of return ahead of us, let me issue my regards, and bid you members of the international media farewell."

And then they are gone. The brief exchange, however, had piqued interest among the other journalists left standing on the street with their tidbit of non-news.

"Interesting question," remarked the Turkish-speaking Orthodox Christian Georgian from Tbilisi. "Do you think the Turks would really intervene to preserve the autonomous status of Abkhazia?"

"No, but it is fun to ask them about it," I replied.

"My parents were Muslim but I'm not," interjected an attractive young lady holding a TV microphone, and thus identifying herself as a journalist. "All my friends have embraced the Orthodox faith and now go to church."

"Why?" I asked. It was the first time I have heard of this sort of mass apostasy, meaning a conversion of Muslim Georgians to Orthodox Christianity from Minimal Islam.

"To be Orthodox Christian is more Georgian, and we are all Georgian," she replied.

"God bless you," said the Turkish-speaking Georgian Orthodox reporter from the conservative Turkish news agency.

"Well," I asked. "Where can I find some of these traditionalist Muslims from whom you descend but whom you now reject?"

"Khulo," said the Orthodox reporter guy from Tbilisi.

A place.

A name.

A new destination.

Saying farewell to my new friends, I prowled through the descending blanket of nasty, coal-fired fog, stopped into a cold but clean and totally empty version of someone's notion of a fancy Istanbul-style *kebabhane*, and ordered up a portion of pork *shashlik* and a half carafe of local red wine. Following the perfunctory meal, I continued meandering through the almost chewy, smog-choked, darkened streets of Batumi until I eventually landed at a café (called *Venice*, I believe) with a disco bar in the basement that was favored by Russian soldiers from the local garrison. This in itself was odd, because everywhere else in Georgia everyone was sort of officially anti-Russian out of general habit, although maybe they expressed such sentiments only when meeting Americans. The main point was that the "Batono" (Lord Protector) Abashidze had not only allowed the Russian military to maintain bases in Adjaria in direct contravention of bilateral and multilateral treaties signed by the central government in Tbilisi concerning their removal, but had cultivated the image among the citizens of Adjaria that the Russian troops were the ultimate protectors of Adjarian semi-independence. In other words, the Russian troops were there to protect Adjaria from Georgia itself.

After a last double shot of *chacha* at the Venice, I returned to the candlelit lobby of the Intourist Hotel where four men were singing traditional Georgian chant in one corner, and the staff watching an MTV-like program on a fuzzy TV powered by an outdoor generator in the other. The cacophony was too much, and I ascended the once-grand but now long-tattered staircase to room 326. There was a knock on the door but I correctly assumed that I already knew who it was: the persistent floor lady, offering to provide certain services for a certain fee.

"A nuclear scientist this time?" I asked, playfully.

She didn't get the joke, and I waved her away with a smile and goodnight.

* * *

Morning and Khulo.

My map suggests it is a town of about 10,000 located about fifty miles straight up from the sea, which probably means three or four hours of travel by bad road in a taxi that will gouge me for about a hundred bucks that I don't have or at least do not want to spend on an up-mountain meander.

Happily, there are other options.

Leaving my bags at the reception desk for what I hope is safekeeping, I hit the streets in the direction of the bazaar, insisting on using Georgian to ask directions to the minibus station that serves the Khulo area.

After a couple of false steps (no matter; this is an ambulatory language lesson), I finally arrive at the chaotic bus station and identify a minibus with the curlicue Georgian letters X U L O taped across a slightly shattered windshield. I ask how much the fare is in Georgian and am very glad to be informed that it is less than 10 lari, not so much because that is cheap but because I have not yet mastered the complex words for the odd-numbered double digits (thirty, fifty, seventy, and ninety) in the Georgian tongue, such as *twotwentiesandtenplusnine*, which is the way you say "fifty-nine," for example. I pay the fare, receive change, and squeeze in next to three other passengers in the front seat of the minibus. With the driver, we make four. The three back seats are filled just as completely, but apparently the driver wants to wait for one more fare to really make it all worthwhile.

"*Tzavadit!*" says the man wedged in next to me, using the collective suggestive command of the verb "to go," or whatever that form is called. *Let's go!*

That is exactly what he said, and I understood it as such! I am happy for actually having applied myself to this strange tongue.

Everyone else on board the minibus apparently assumes I am Georgian because that is the only language anyone addresses me in until I run out of one word sentences of avoidance or just patient silence and am obliged to use Russian to ask the man next to me to please not flick his watermelon seed shells on my lap.

"You're Russian!" beams my new best friend, introducing himself as a retired captain from some branch of the Soviet military, and offering me some seeds.

"No," I reply, not wanting to get myself trapped in a web of lies. "I am not Russian."

"Ukrainian?"

"No," I say, and we start to play the guess-my-nationality game. I guess I have some sort of generic post-Soviet look about me, with most folks assuming I come from the country (or ethnic group) next door or often their own.

"Armenian? Turkish? Bulgarian? Azerbaijani?"

"American," I finally tell him, knowing exactly what he will say next, which he does.

"There is no such thing," my interlocutor informs me. "What is your nation?"

"American," I repeat.

"There is no such thing as an American," he says emphatically. "Aside from the Red Indians, and you are clearly not one of their number."

It is an old argument, based on Soviet nationalities policy as announced by Lenin and then implemented by Stalin. It is not so much a denial of my existence, as a demand that I choose between various forefathers and establish a national identity for myself.

"American," I say again.

"That is a place; what are you?"

"Well, what is 'Adjarian'?"

"That is a place, our place; we are Georgians."

"But Muslim Georgians."

"Praise be to God," says my companion, in Arabic prayer form, albeit with the hint of a sly, mocking smile. "Praise God!"

The minibus pulls over at a shoddy canteen and bakery set up on a bank overlooking the roaring Acharistskali River, a tributary or perhaps even twin source of the Choruh River in "Georgian" Turkey, which they call the Chorokhi here. Everyone piles out for a smoke, stretch, piss, or piece of fresh bread from the bakery, as well as a slurp of the ice cold and fantastically pure-tasting water from a communal spigot/spring. The snowcapped Meskheti Mountains rise to 8,000 feet to the north and the Shavshat range in Turkey to an equal or greater height just a valley or two away to the south. We are less than fifty miles as the crow flies from the sea and in the midst of a vertical world.

I have spent a lot of time in the valleys and gorges of Artvin and Yusufeli on the far side of the frontier, in Turkey, and remember when this was the end or edge of the known world, seen from "Western" or "NATO" eyes. I have fighter-bomber flight plan maps in my house in Montana today, designating "first strike" opportunities.

Right now, such thoughts seem utterly ridiculous.

This is Gurdjieff country. I can see the sage walking over the rickety footbridge beneath us, from one terraced plot of land to the next on the far side of the frothing stream, dwelling on his most recent meeting with remarkable men, or reflecting on the nature of the octave in music and life.

"You're here for the elections, aren't you?"

It is my new friend, the former officer in the Russian army, who denies my right to call myself an American. He introduces himself as Memed but says his friends and family call him Misha, which is the diminutive of the Russian "Mikhail, as in the angel."

"Like Gorbachev," I note, referring to the now former Soviet leader.

"Yes, kind of like him," says Memed/Misha.

"So, who are you going to vote for?" I ask Memed/Misha.

"Doesn't really matter much, now does it?" he answers cryptically, while sort of glancing around gauging audio distance between us and everyone else at the rest stop.

"What do you mean?"

"You know what I mean," he says, lowering his voice.

"But who do you want to vote for, even if you can't?"

The driver is honking the horn and the rest of the gang are half loaded, so Memed/Misha and I return to the bus and board, chatting about the beauties of Montana and the hunt and the delights of Baku for the next hour or so, while the overloaded minibus claws its way ever upward through the vertical world, finally pulling to a stop in front of an ugly power station or some other public utility structure set on a slab of concrete pilings overlooking a 1,000-foot drop into the river below.

"*Khulo ak aris!*" cries the driver. "This is Khulo."

Memed/Misha is bidding me farewell, and I am suddenly alone on a wide spot of the mountain road, wondering why I have come here.

* * *

They say that Khulo is a town of 10,000 souls but it might be helpful if someone were to define the meaning of the word "town" first, and proceed from there. My wide spot in the mountain road seems more like an extended village, or villages, spread out over agricultural terraces above and below. As a trained observer, however, I am able to discern a footpath winding up from the highway to a sort of bluff, and following it, discover a cluster of graceless Soviet-style administration buildings, a hospital, and a school. As for public facilities, there is one restaurant, which is essentially a wooden shack set on stilts over a gully. It sports three small tables and perhaps five chairs in the main hall and what seems to be an "exclusive" banquet or maybe "family hall" consisting of a couple more tables and perhaps six more chairs set up one step from the public sector and discretely curtained off from the rest of the place by some plastic shower curtains bearing a worn if vaguely familiar floral design. At the far end of the establishment is the open kitchen where several vats of *kharcho* soup bubble away. Vodka bottles and shot glasses list at a precarious angle on a sloping shelf over the sink.

It is not prepossessing.

I enter, sit down, and order bread, soup, and fifty grams of vodka, not because I really want to drink that much but because I know I do not want 100 grams, and ordering the smaller amount will give me cause to use the number "fifty" for practice, which in Georgian is expressed as "two twenties and ten."

Two young men sitting at one of the tables listlessly look up for a moment, then go back to talking about something in intense, low tones that I cannot understand: "he" and "him" are several words I managed to capture on an audio level, but whether they are references to me I cannot tell. It doesn't make any difference whether I am American, Azerbaijani, Armenian, Ukrainian, Russian, Turkish, or even Georgian. In Khulo, I am an utter stranger, and the town has got that ineffable air of being a place suspicious of folks like me. I eat in silence, down the booze, and ask for the bill. It comes to 6 lari, meaning about $3, once more allowing me to avoid the tricky numerical -teens.

Back out on the one paved street, I make the existential decision to walk up, as opposed to back down, on the logic that I know there is only the empty highway below, but there may be someone or something more above.

Turning a corner after about twenty paces, I encounter two young men, both perhaps in their thirties, and both wearing the standard Caucasus tough-guy uniform of dark slacks, dark turtle necks, black leather jackets, and dark blue or black, brimless, woolen pullover ski caps. The three of us sort of shuffle our feet in silence for a moment or two.

"You here for the elections?" asks Skinnier.

"Not really, just sort of a tourist."

"A tourist?" scoffs Skinnier. "Here? There's not even a hotel!"

More shuffling of feet, and then Skinnier flaps his hand at me in a clear signal that I should follow him.

"Let's go drink some tea," he says.

"Great!" I say.

A teashop; a public place where experience has shown me my new host will either show off his newfound foreign friend, someone else will adopt me, or at least I will be able to engage in some manner of superficial conversation before the cops come and arrest me out of general principle. But no.

Skinnier (who has now introduced himself by the good Muslim name of Suleyman) has decided to take me home—and "home" is a tiny, airless, two-room apartment on the ground floor of an extraordinarily ugly and cramped cement block building that seems about to collapse under its own weight. The windows, which do not open, look out at a filthy courtyard cluttered with bits and chunks of discarded metal and the remains of what appears to be a radio tower.

"Fatosh!" Skinnier/Suleyman barks at his wife, whose name would appear to be Fatimah. "We have a guest! Prepare the tea!"

Fatosh emerges from the tiny bedroom beyond the tiny kitchen and sitting room, and instantly begins tidying things up for the unexpected guest, me.

It is an awkward moment, or perhaps it's better expressed as an awkward first half-hour. I am seated in the place of honor, meaning on one side of a springy couch facing a wobbly table with some fake flowers on it while Fatosh rummages around a glass cupboard for some cups, fetches, and fills a kettle with water from a tiny sink attached to about six inches of cracked Formica countertop, and places it atop a potbellied stove in the far corner, stoking the fire with a couple of chunks of green wood. Mr. Suleyman/Skinnier, meanwhile, has somehow produced a box of very special chocolates for me, an ashtray for himself, and a jug of the foulest tasting sweet wine ever bottled. Subscribing to the general Georgian principle that NO TELEVISION SET SHOULD BE LEFT OFF WHEN PEOPLE ARE IN THE SAME ROOM, he turns on the house entertainment set—a small, fuzzy black-and-white museum piece that apparently picks up only one channel, the Adjarian state channel at that.

I look at the TV with keen interest. The alternative point of visual reference is to stare at Suleyman's WC—a seatless toilet set in what looks like an upright coffin between the tiny kitchen and the entrance door. Once again relying on my powers of observation, I realize that it only appears to be a coffin because the walls and door to the WC are so narrow that they make it resemble a box designed to tuck cadavers into the earth. On second thought or consideration, a coffin would probably have had a lid that fit more snugly than the door to the WC does to its frame, and thus not force guests of honor like me to stare at it, meaning the seatless toilet inside the upright coffin-like WC.

"Cheers!" cries Sasha/Suleyman, my host, lifting his glass of horrible wine, indicating that I should do the same. "To our new friendship and the friendship of all peoples, everywhere! Now tell me why you are really in Khulo . . ."

* * *

For my part, I am not sure where the conversation ended and where the interrogation began. I am pretty sure that it was all rather confusing for my host and interrogator, too. My Russian, while functional, is not great; his was much worse than mine. Through this lingual haze we quickly established that Suleyman was a member of "Batono" Abashidze's personal militia, but not a policeman per se, and that because I was a foreigner interested in information, by definition, I was most likely a spy.

These were not the details Suleyman was interested in, however.

"What is your salary?"

"I don't have one unless I am working and I am not working right now, so I do not have one," I reply. "What is yours?"

Silence.

"Well," I say at last. "Perhaps it is best for me to be moving along . . ."

"Go?" cries my host. "That is impossible! And where would you go to at this hour, anyway? It is too dangerous . . ."

"What is so dangerous out there?"

"The bad ones, the provocateurs . . ."

"Which 'bad ones,' which 'provocateurs'?" I ask.

"Those who wish to take away our autonomy!"

"Who are they and what autonomy do they mean to steal?"

"You cannot know . . ." slurs Suleyman. "It is too dangerous."

"You are talking dangerous?" I counter. "I have been to Abkhazia . . ."

"Abkhazia?" babbles Suleyman after a moment.

The name of the benighted country was a byword for misery in Georgia. It never fails to impress.

"Yes, Abkhazia," I say, seizing the moment. "And you have kept me here for the past six hours, talking around in circles. Am I under arrest?"

"No!"

"Then I am going out and back to the restaurant to have a drink."

"No!"

"Why not?"

"Because—"

"BECAUSE HE DOESN'T HAVE MONEY AND HE OWES THEM!"

It is Fatosh, bursting into tears across the tiny room, speaking in decent Russian and confessing the horribly obvious truth: I am being kept under virtual house arrest because Suleyman does not have the means to host me in style at the pathetic restaurant on stilts in downtown Khulo because he is already in debt to that establishment.

I had just committed the unconscionable: I have exposed a Georgian man to semipublic mortification.

* * *

My new friend Suleyman was a Georgian Muslim, which might seem like a contradiction in terms, unless one reflected on the arch of Georgian history, where a few centuries of subscribing to a different religion or national identity for the sake of convenience was and is quite normal.

But then there was the question about the Ahiska, folks who might be best described as "Georgians of the Mind."

My first encounter with the Ahiska occurred on the day I returned to Azerbaijan from Uzbekistan in September 1991, some two weeks after the abortive putsch against Mikhail Gorbachev that signaled the end to the Soviet Union. The Tashkent–Moscow–Baku flight landed around three o'clock in the morning, and I was hurling insults at some surly internal border guard with a bad attitude when a slight gentleman approached and asked if I needed any help.

"*Yardim istiyormusunuz?*"

He was not speaking Russian or Azerbaijani, but rather a fluent if curiously antiquated form of Turkish. He also had atrociously bad breath.

"My name is Ibrahim," the stranger replied, showing his Soviet passport. "And I am a Turk." Sure enough, right there in the "Nationality" column of his obligatory Soviet-style documentation, my interlocutor was identified as exactly that: *a Turk.*

Ibrahim was clearly proud of this distinction. But in the hierarchy of officially recognized ethnicities in the USSR, being "Turkish" registered somewhere near the bottom of the totem pole. "Nations" were theoretically *countries*, and even such synthetic, Soviet-created "nationalities" as the "Turkic" Kazakhs, Uzbeks, or Turkmens had defined homelands such as Kazakhstan, Uzbekistan, or Turkmenistan to fall back upon when called to answer any and all questions about what they kept near and dear as an officially recognized "people." It was three o'clock in the morning, and time to find somewhere to sleep. Throwing caution to the wind, I agreed to spend the night, thus opening up a strange world: that of the nonpeople—the Ahiska Turks.

* * *

The Ahiska first lost contact with their western, Ottoman Turkish kin in 1878, when tsarist Russia overran the eastern Black Sea provinces of the Ottoman Empire and made the highland theirs. A more permanent division occurred in 1921, when Lenin and Turkey's founder Mustafa Kemal (Atatürk) drew up a new frontier between the nascent republics of Turkey and the southwestern tier of the Soviet Union. Local residents were given six months to choose on which side of the frontier they wished to live. The majority chose to stay where they were—not out of any love of Leninism or Kemalism, but simply because their homes were their homes and their land was their land. A border was needed, and if it did not split the Ahiska here it would have split them there.

The result was that, in accordance with the Treaty of Kars, half of the transborder Turks called the Ahiska ended up as citizens of the new entity called "Turkey," and the other half citizens of the to-be "Georgian" portion of the newly created USSR.

Unlike their co-religionist Georgian Muslims in Batumi/Adjaria, who had converted to Islam over the centuries and spoke Turkish as a second language but still retained Georgian as their primary tongue, the Ahiska regarded (and regard) themselves as Turkish-speaking Muslims who ended up in Georgia by a fluke of history and only speak Georgian (or Russian) as a second tongue. Living in tightly knit communities in the mountains in and around the town of Akhaltsikhe (Old Castle) on the upper Kura River, before it tames itself into the brown stream defining "core" Georgia between the eleventh-century cliff-face monastery of Vardzia and the famed mineral water resort spa of Borjomi, the Ahiska were famed as the most efficient farmers of the region. Whether they were "Turks" is an open question: in the eighteenth and nineteenth centuries, Akhaltsikhe was known for being one of the most notorious Circassian slave-export depots of its time, and claims to any sort of ethnic purity by anyone associated with the area over the past 300–400 hundred years are by definition suspect. The nation-slicing knife has never had a very clean or sharp blade.

What happened to the Ahiska Turks on November 14, 1944, however, was both clean and sharp. That was the day that Josef Stalin deported all 125,000 Ahiska Turks from their mountain villages around Akhaltsikhe and sent them to collective farms in Central Asia. Stalin's rationale was that the Ahiska Turks, along with fellow Muslims such as the Crimean Tatars, Chechens, Ingush, and Balkars, had made common cause with the Nazi foe, and therefore needed to be removed from the zone of conflict lest they collectively aid Hitler in his attempt to conquer the Caucasus. Like the other small, mainly Muslim peoples just mentioned, the Ahiska deny the charge. If they were guilty of treason, they say, Stalin should have moved them out in 1941, instead of waiting until 1944 when the war was almost over, and most young Ahiska men were serving the Soviet Army at the front.

Perhaps one day, when the Kremlin archives pertaining to the period are opened up to scholarly inspection, the real motivation for the gratuitous, mass deportations of hundreds of thousands of people down a Soviet-style "Trail of Tears" from the Caucasus to Central Asia will come to light. Certainly, in the case of the Chechens, the trauma of dislocation from their ancestral homeland has conspired into an unholy mix of criminality-cum-rabid nationalism-cum-Islamic extremism. Among the Ahiska, however, a similar extreme social psychosis resulting from having been ripped from their traditional villages in Georgia has so far not occurred. Although one might well ask why: here is yet another group of people of totally insignificant numbers that was declared a "nonpeople" in Soviet terms and times, who remain in legal limbo and obsessed with the vindication of alleged historic sins. And, like the Chechens, Ingush, Balkars, and other Caucasian Muslims similarly deported throughout 1944, the Ahiska remain determined not to assimilate into any larger whole until they are restored to the status enjoyed half a century ago.

* * *

"I didn't learn about the deportation until the day of my demobilization in 1947, after spending four years in the Soviet Army," recalled Ramiz Rahimov, born in the Georgian village of Adigun in 1926. Like all other seventeen-year-olds of the time, Ramiz was drafted into the Great War against Hitler and spent two years on the front in the most violent conditions, ending his war in Königsberg (today's Kaliningrad) on the Baltic Sea. That was where he learned that there was nothing but defeat in victory.

"Another Turk came up and told me there was no point in going to Georgia because there were no Ahiska there anymore," he said. "After all I had been through, I did not want to believe him. But then he gave me an address in Uzbekistan and told me to go there, and I found out the truth."

Ramiz spent two months on trains, buses, horse carts, and foot, bouncing from one collective farm to the next, looking for his exiled family. When he finally arrived, their joy in seeing him alive—he was thought dead, as no word had come from him since he entered the war—was intense, but mitigated by the fact that the family had buried his younger brother the day before. The official report said that the cause of death was "mental distress." Among the Ahiska, this was known as the curiously fatal disease they called "pining for the homeland."

Thus began the long years of exile, the long years of resisting assimilation, and the dogged preservation of a separate identity predicated on the idea of the eventual return. Even as the Soviet authorities disallowed the term "Turk" on identity papers and forbade the teaching of Turkish in schools and its publication in books, children were taught to retain their language at home as well as to identify themselves by the names of their native villages in the region of Akhaltsikhe. Adigun, Ahalkelec, Akhunda, Aspirza, and Bogdanoka—these are but a few of the names of the 198 subregions of the emotional Akhaltsikhe area—the responses in answering the question "where are you from?" when encountering an Ahiska Turk. It is a singular, psychological place-devotion, as oblivious to the new, distorted, or obliterating names of towns and villages in Israel, Gaza, and the West Bank as are displaced Palestinians of the pre-1947 period.

When the identity of "Turk" was reallowed in the 1988 Soviet Union census, exactly 207,562 Ahiska emerged from the woodwork, scattered throughout the fifteen Union Republics of the day.

The majority found themselves in Uzbekistan, and despite more than forty years of exile, most were still dreaming of *The Return.*

Then came the summer of 1989 in the Fergana Valley in Soviet Uzbekistan, a country (or idea) that was a byword for nastiness then as it is today.

The causes of the ugly events of that time, like many things in the bad old Soviet Union, remain shrouded in an official silence that gives easy birth to theories of manipulation and conspiracy. For years, the thrifty, industrious Ahiska Turkish farmers had been suing for their right to return to the Georgia they had been illegally evicted from almost fifty years before. But Moscow remained deaf to their pleas or, perhaps more to the point, had its own ideas of how best to use the rural energy of the Ahiska. Like many events that played out during the fading days of the USSR, speculation about grand, centrally planned, and deeply nefarious designs remains rife, even if difficult to prove.

The essence is this: sometime in 1985, Moscow issued a proposal to the Ahiska inviting them to move to villages in southern Russia that had been or soon would be abandoned by ethnic Russians intent on moving from the country to the cities. The Ahiska responded with the answer that they had no problem with the idea of leaving their collective farms in Uzbekistan and elsewhere—but only if the move were to be to their homeland, Akhaltsikhe, in distant Georgia. Official consultations continued, with the "Center" pushing for a collective move from Soviet Uzbekistan to southern Russia. The Ahiska remained interested but adamant: either the homeland, or we stay where we are.

Then, as if from nowhere, ethnic Uzbeks began a series of actions against the Ahiska that can only be termed pogroms—despite the two ethnic groups being linked by being both "Turkic" and "Muslim." Houses were torched and looted, pregnant women butchered, and a general atmosphere of hatred reigned supreme—all for reasons no one has yet been able to fathom, save for an alleged native lunacy among the Uzbeks (and more sober whispers of KGB instigation thereto). Thousands reportedly died, and, virtually overnight, the Ahiska of Uzbekistan found themselves living in squalid tent cities, and under the protection of forces of the Soviet internal ministry while Moscow tried to figure out what to do with its most recent interethnic disaster.

The Ahiska leadership maintains that Moscow knew very well what it planned to do with them all along.

"At the height of the crisis, the Russian television program *Vremya* conducted a thirty-minute interview with one of our elders in a temporary tent camp, and asked him where the people wanted to go," related Ismael Hamidov, the eldest son of Ramiz Vezirov and a key man in the Ahiska movement. "Our man repeatedly said that the refugees all wanted to return "home"—to Georgia."

But the interviewer pressed the elder, asking him again and again the theoretical question of whether the Ahiska would accept (re)patriation to Russia as an alternative choice.

"Given the desperate circumstances prevailing in Uzbekistan, our man finally responded that yes, if Georgia were impossible, the refugees would go to Russia," Ismael Hamidov told me, shaking his head. "In the editing process, only the request to go to Russia came out, and as a plea."

Within days, Decision 503 was announced. It "invited" the refugee Ahiska Turks from Uzbekistan to occupy the empty farms in southern Russia that they had resisted moving to for four years. It also provided air transport—and television and press coverage—to get them there.

"Live in tents in Uzbekistan or cultivate abandoned Russian farms?" Ismael asked me bitterly. "Tell me what you would do."

Not all of the refugees went to Russia, however.

Large numbers accepted the invitation of the government of Soviet Azerbaijan to settle in houses and regions vacated by Armenians in 1989 and 1990. If they were not "home" in Georgia, at least they were swimming in a Caucasus environment that was friendly and familiar: the Azeris were almost Turks, too. More to the point, the Ahiska Turks who settled in Azerbaijan were closer to the homeland than ever before. The smell of the valleys of Akhaltsikhe was nearly palpable in the air, the promise of return a simple agreement away. . . .

"Less than 60,000 Georgians now live in the area once inhabited by 125,000 Turks," said my new friend Ibrahim, trotting out what seemed like familiar statistics. "And of 120 villages in the Ahiska area when we were deported,

80 are now completely deserted. We are not asking Georgians to move. We say "Let the Georgians remain in every house they occupy, even if that house belonged to my father." We only want unused land. I will build half my house and my son the other, but we will be home."

We were sitting in the village of Adigun. But rather than that ancestral hearth once found in the rolling forests along the raging, whitewaters of the Kura River in western Georgia, it was the "new" Adigun, located on a wide, mosquito-breeding irrigation canal in the cotton-growing lowland of south-central Azerbaijan.

"Do you speak Georgian?" I asked, as delicately as possible.

"A few words that I learned from my dad," said Ibrahim, lying.

"Why should the Georgians let you back after fifty years of exile?" I asked, pushing the envelope. "You insist you are Turkish and not Georgian or even Azeri and want to project yourselves back into a country known for its anti-Muslim, anti-Turkish, anti-other, militant ethnic chauvinism. Why?"

"Because it is our home," said Ibrahim.

* * *

One day, Ibrahim came over with a very special invitation: to attend the annual meeting of the "All Union Society for the Meskhetian Turks." The gathering was to be held the next day at a place called Medrese, a former Armenian town in the lesser Caucasus range of central Azerbaijan, which had become "home" to a number of those in this curious community of exiles who had bounced across the width and breadth of the USSR with no nation of their own.

We arrived late, but still found a meeting in progress in the Medrese town hall, a nondescript, rural-Soviet, cinderblock structure where the president of the All Union Society for the Meskhetian Turks was still holding forth, spewing spit and vinegar from his pulpit, as it were. His name was Yusuf Sarvarov, a short, round, balding man who waved his bowler hat in the air with one hand while stabbing the other at his audience, making questionable points while refusing to answer pointed questions.

"Do not shoot at your parent with a pistol for their . . . *um, err, ah* . . . failings," bellowed Sarvarov, imperfectly quoting a Dagestani poet of a martial turn of mind. "Lest your children . . . *um, er, ah* . . . fire a canon at you for yours!"

He had a remarkably loud voice for a man of such short stature, I thought.

A murmur of qualified approval passed among the graybeards in the audience, while the youth looked at their shoes. If the meaning was not perfectly clear, Sarvarov proceeded to elucidate it for the ignorant and hard of hearing or doubters.

"Yes, we have . . . *um, err, ah* . . . failed to achieve our aims," he shouted. "But we are trying and failing as our forefathers . . . *um, err, ah* . . . tried and failed, and if you are not careful, your sons . . . *um, err, ah* . . . will accuse you of failure, too!"

"The Vatan . . ." grumbled the assembled, on cue.

That meant "the Homeland."

Ahiska . . . They had heard it all before.

Then came the recital of a different message, sad but well learned. The essence was this: after years of appealing in vain to Moscow to listen to their pleas, in early August 1991, the Ahiska had finally found a sponsor in the inner corridors of the Kremlin, a man who swore on his honor that he would process their application to return to Georgia. His name was Gennady Yanayev, and he was chairman of the sixty-hour putschist government that temporarily ran the Soviet Union during Mikhail Gorbachev's curious "illness" of August 19 of that year, the date that hailed the collapse of the USSR. Not surprisingly, with the fall of the short-lived Yanayev regime, the Ahiska cause not only seemed to have been stymied, but appeared to have been brought all the way back to square one, meaning zero.

"God only knows! God knows!" cried Sarvarov, waving his hat above his head at the Medrese meeting. "Perhaps it was a sign! Who knows what would have awaited us if . . . *um, err, ah* . . . Yanayev had managed to send us back then! What disaster might we have been spared? Look at Georgia today, when one can't tell who is who? It was a sign, a . . . *um, err, ah* . . . sign! 'Let us not be water on the . . . *um, err, ah* . . . the enemy's mill!' It is time to believe and praise God and believe! . . . *um, err, ah* . . . We will return!"

"The Vatan," everyone gathered duly grumbles. "The Homeland!"

"Amen," stutters Sarvarov. "AMEN!!"

The assembled have heard the prayer a thousand times before.

Finally, the session was over, and Ibrahim and I walk out into the penumbral darkness of Medrese, a town situated in a perfect valley in the lesser Caucasus range of the Republic of Azerbaijan, trying to digest what we have just heard. The reality is that there is no place to go—not a bar or restaurant or teashop—save for the natural center of the town: a small, intimate, two-domed church structure built in the traditional geometric mode of the Armenians and dating to 1864. Elsewhere it might have been converted to a civic center, but here it has been given over to public use as a silo. A single, leafless tree grows out of the roof, planted long before the church was built, but now contained by it.

"They will be yearning for this place just like we yearn for ours," said Ibrahim, speaking of the vanished Armenians. "This was their home and it is not ours—only Ahiska is."

"Hmm," I respond, in noncommittal think-buzz.

What I am asking myself is this: When does it end? When the end of this insane irredentist obsession, of Freedom as confused with Self-Determination? When every people or part thereof feel rooted in this world and can then proceed to be *not* themselves?

Or then again, maybe never.

8

Storm Clouds over Sukhumi

I may have been taking my measure of the ethnic complexities of Georgia, but taking my measure of Eduard Shevardnadze was a lot more difficult. Although I had applied for and been promised an exclusive interview via new friends working in his administration or members of the National Security Council, months passed.

Part of the problem, of course, was that while I was "Caucasus" based, my home turf was Azerbaijan, and while I spent a lot of time in Georgia, it was episodic: a week here, a fortnight there. The flip side of this journalistic frustration was that even when I was in Tbilisi, Shevy seemed to be constantly on the run. For example, during one week that I waited for him to beckon, Shevardnadze had held negotiations with the Adjarian strongman, "Batono" Aslan Abashidze, to try to prevent the creation of a new Abkhazian-like crisis in the mainly Muslim province on the Turkish frontier, evicted Kitovani and Ioseliani from their government posts in a parliamentary showdown, traveled to Sukhumi by plane to try to reassure the army, and returned to Tbilisi only to be called down to the Armenian border to snuff out a brewing conflict between rival Svanetian gangs. A Svani had reportedly pulled a grenade and waved it in front of Shevardnadze; Shevy allegedly disarmed him with words, before dashing off to the western city of Kutaisi where "unknowns" (later revealed as Mkhedrioni) had raided a Russian army base for weapons—and just days before a "crucial" summit between Shevardnadze and Boris Yeltsin in Moscow.

It seemed that big-ticket political summitry would trump my journalistic desire when the call came from Shevy's press office. I had been granted an audience of ten minutes, starting in about ten minutes. I rushed over to the temporary parliament building next to the post office, went through a security check, galloped up to Shevardnadze's office—and then, apparently typically, sat around for over an hour until I was finally ushered into a drab conference room.

The room was so ordinary that I cannot for the life of me remember any details, aside from the fact that at the far end sat Eduard Shevardnaze, all hound-dog eyes and a shock of white hair. He rose from behind his desk to greet me and extended his hand, and grinning a professional politician's grin.

Shorter and stockier than I had imagined him (recollection is too strong a word for our brief encounter in Moscow back in 1991) Shevy was still an impressive presence, a man who carried himself in the aura of "leader."

Quite frankly, I was intimidated, awed—I don't know.

So, I apologized for taking his valuable time and promised to keep within the allotted ten minutes, all this said through a translator.

"Take your time," said Shevardnadze in his deep, soothing voice. "Take as much time as you want."

My first question was whether he thought he resembled a "fireman."

"If I act like a fireman, it is because Georgia is on fire," cooed Eduard Shevardnadze, staring at me.

I picked a point on the bridge of his nose and stared back.

We spoke about many things—the situation in Abkhazia ("tragic"), his trip that day up to Kutaisi to inspect the shootout at the Russian arms depot ("a provocation"), his relations with Kitovani and Ioseliani ("the nation owes them a debt of gratitude"), and even the business about the Svanetian with grenade who had threatened to immolate both himself and Shevardnadze ("It is no fiction," the Silver Fox said). Then I asked him about putative Russian involvement in the growing problem of Abkhazia, and he preferred to blame all such incidents on an unidentified "third force."

Finally, I asked him the obligatory cliché question that all Western journalists asked him because we all knew our editors would want it in the story: What motivated Eduard Shevardnadze, high-ranking communist and foreign minister of the USSR, to become a cheerleader of the West? I phrased it somewhat differently, but that was what I meant and he knew it.

"I changed," said Shevardnadze. "I realized the error of our ways."

We bantered back and forth for some more minutes, and then the interview was over. I thanked him again profusely for having shared his thoughts with me during such a hectic time.

"Not at all," said Shevardnadze. "Anytime!"

I nearly bounded down the steps and back to Alexis Rowell's BBC office over on Lermontov Square.

"How'd it go?" he asked.

"It was great!" I crowed.

An exclusive interview with Eduard Shevardnadze!

But as I went back over my notes of the interview, I was left with a queer impression: Shevardnadze hadn't said very much that was concrete about himself, the thugs who had brought him to power, or anything else about the real state of affairs in Georgia. And about Russian involvement in Abkhazia, he had said nothing at all.

* * *

Yes, while we were out cavorting and exploring ancient cathedrals and extolling the genius of Shevardnadze, there were other dynamics at play. And, while it was advised to tread softly around local political issues, lest a conversation with a disgruntled taxi-driving professor of philology who was unenthusiastic about Shevy's return lead to said individual's arrest, it was also unforgivable how little interest the crowd of pro-Shevardnadze boosters among the newly arrived foreigners paid to such stories.

I have in my possession a stack of letters sent to newly elected President Bill Clinton in the spring of 1993, all decrying the deteriorating human rights situation in the country. The main focus expressed in the letters, however, is the utter indifference to this sad state of affairs evinced by the American envoy to Georgia, Ambassador Ken Brown.

Here are a few samples; I have left all errors in the original unless they defy comprehension.

To the President of the USA, Mr. Clinton

Dear Mr. President,
    The person who lives in Georgia Republic in the condition of dictatorial regime of Shevardnadze writes you this letter. The fact of the opening of the Embassy of the U.S.A. in Georgian Republic with Mr. Brown as ambassador, was like a light beam of hope in our unbearable life. We began to hope that the ambassador of the country that we always regarded as a pillar of world's justice and real democracy. But we were bitterly deceived. Mr. Brown quickly became in unison with the fascistic junta of Shevardnadze. The shooting of the peaceful demonstrators, rughly [sic] breaking of Human Rights,—these are usual things, that occurred very often in front of him. Mr. President! If this is the democracy, I personally refuse the democracy like this, because it is worse than fascism.

Sincerely Yours (signed)
Lia Enukhidze
Flat #8, Vazha Pshavela 20
Tbilisi, Republic of Georgia

Or:

To the president of the USA, Mr Clinton:

Dear President,

I, the citizen of Georgia, Greek by nationality, am violated with the horror that makes Shevardnadze's Junta in Georgia: the rushing and shooting of peaceful manifestants and meetings, beating, killing and often different fascistic dealings. But what makes me upset most of all (is) that the Ambassador of U.S.A. Mr Brown has appeared in the role of faithful companion in this shameful business. The olimpic calmness, how he regards to the events in Georgia, speaking with nice smile on his face in the TV screen, surrounded with juntists creates the opinion that he is not the official representative of the country that we always regarded as a pillar of democracy in the world . . . (etc.)

> Gela Djigauri
> Micro District 2, Bld 5
> Tsotne Dadiani Ave
> Tbilisi, Republic of Georgia

Or:

Dear Mr Clinton

To be sincere, we began to hate the word "democracy." You ask why? All Lenin-Stalinist communists, all thieves and robbers, narcomans and bandits in Georgia are wearing the name "democrat." That's why! And all that happened in Georgia under the bless of ambassadors of U.S.A. and Germany. We assure you dear Mr. President, that no "big politics" can excuse the doing the things together with murderers, criminals, neocommunists. This criminals that named himself "the democrats" poured the rivers of blood in Georgia . . . the leader of this is the "great democrat" Shevardnadze, who could not stay in Georgia even for one day without his machineguns. We are fighting for real democracy and we will continue the fight until victory, but please, don't disappoint us in the democracy of West and America.

> With great respect,
> Khethevan Kiphiani

To my knowledge, none of these epistles or the stack of similar appeals I have in my files were ever answered or acknowledged.

* * *

The biggest change wrought by the Shevardnadze "restoration" was that there was now a very real war in the country—and no longer of the half-baked variety that had marked the putsch against Gamsakhurdia or its aftermath in the spring of 1992.

Just as my friend Nunu Chachua predicted, war had washed over Abkhazia.

Who started the killing remains a subject of bitter dispute. There is evidence to suggest that Vladislav Ardzinba had been preparing for the showdown with Tbilisi for several years, stocking up weapons and importing gunmen seconded from the Russian GRU, or military intelligence agency and state security KGB in anticipation of Abkhazia's secession from Georgia and accession to Russia.[1] While Tengiz Kitovani managed to secure the immediate objective of saving railroad transportation from the depredations of kidnappers and criminals, it can also be easily said that due to the Georgian tendency toward self-aggrandizing stupidity (or more cynically, the Georgian tendency toward complicity in conspiracy), he went too far.

"We were warned by the Abkhaz opposition to Ardzinba not to do anything foolish, because the Russian military was just waiting for us to do so," Shevardnadze's chief of staff, Petr Mamradze told me years later. "'They are ready to send us guns, men, heavy weapons—even aviation!' one of them told us. 'Please don't do anything provocative!' But we did exactly that, and walked into the trap."

If indeed a trap, it was sprung with precision. On July 23, 1992, the parliament of the Autonomous Republic of Abkhazia, meeting without a quorum and skewed heavily in favor of the Abkhaz minority (thanks to one of the final acts of Zviad Gamsakhurdia to ameliorate the titular population of the region by overrepresentation of the Abkhaz population), passed a resolution repealing the late Soviet-era constitution of 1978 and replacing it with an early Soviet constitution of 1925, in effect declaring independence from the rest of Georgia. The flag of the "Republic of Abkhazia" was then hoisted over the government house. The parliament in Tbilisi met in emergency session on July 25 and declared the voting in Sukhumi to be null and void. They then prepared for celebrations on August 7 marking *all* of independent Georgia's admission to the United Nations, which included lifting emergency rule throughout the country and offering a general amnesty for "Zviadisti" who would lay down their arms and disavow devotion to Gamsakhurdia. Significantly, the leader of the (restored) Autonomous Republic of Abkhazia (within Georgia), Vladislav Ardzinba, was also invited to attend the Tbilisi ceremonies, but somehow managed to miss the plane.

Events moved rapidly thereafter. A spate of train robberies and hostage-takings were mounted in the Zugdidi (Georgian) and Gali (Abkhazian) districts along the Inguri River by what appeared to be Georgian and Abkhaz "bandits" working in tandem. In a national radio address on the night of August 11, Shevardnadze declared, "I believed that evil has its limits, but now I am convinced that it has no bounds . . . we have demonstrated mercy and pardoned all our enemies, but now there will be no forgiveness."

On the night of August 13, a railway bridge across the Inguri River was blown up, presumably to prevent the Georgian National Guard from mounting a punitive action to free hostages held in the Gali district of Abkhazia. The Georgian National Council decided to move fast before the last road link between western Georgia and Abkhazia (and as a result Gali) was also destroyed. Shevardnadze called Ardzinba to explain that Georgian troops under Tengiz Kitovani would be entering Abkhazia to secure the roads and railways, and assure him that the operation was directed at the bandits, and not the Abkhaz. He even suggested that a joint Georgia–Abkhaz security operation would be ideal.

On the morning of August 14, Kitovani's forces crossed the bridge into Abkhazia, prompting Ardzinba to sign a decree of mobilization for the adult population of Abkhazia to defend the homeland.[2] Resistance was bitter and brief: Ardzinba and his forces withdrew across the Gumista River to the town of Gudauta, which just happened to serve as a Russian air-base and thus offered protection from other Georgian forces, who were also landing at the tourist town of Gagra, burning and looting the villas that the Mikhedrioni officers did not privatize for themselves. On August 17, after a three-day orgy of violence, Tengiz Kitovani returned to Tbilisi with the flag of Abkhazia stripped from atop the parliament building in Sukhumi as a trophy of war, slapping it down on the table of the National Council. That same day, in the Chechen capital of Grozny, the "parliament" of the Confederation of Mountain Peoples of the Caucasus passed a resolution calling for volunteers from among the Chechens, Ingush, Kabardins, Adyghe, and other Circassians to join the good fight against the Georgian "occupiers."[3] Cossacks and additional volunteers from other parts of the Russian Federation were not far behind. The war over the "Soviet Riviera" had just been joined. Within six months, the conflict would spawn over 100,000 refugees and result in some 5,000 dead, after the two rag-tag armies settled into slogging it out with artillery duels and commando forays across the Gumista River five miles from Sukhumi's city center.

In March and then again in April, the "Abkhaz" launched major offensives across the Gumista to try to take Sukhumi but were beaten back with huge losses on both sides. I put the word "Abkhaz" in quotations because it was becoming an open secret that Ardzinba's forces of the "Gudauta Republic" (named after the tourist town turned temporary Abkhaz capital sufficiently north of Sukhumi and the Georgian lines to be outside artillery range) were less Abkhaz and more of a crazy patchwork quilt of former and future allies and enemies, motivated by everything from pristine idealism to the prospect of looting, booty, and future rights to vacation real estate. Some were drawn from the smaller minority groups of Abkhazia such as the Armenians, Greeks, and ethnic Russians who also wanted to resist Georgian rule or to take revenge for the atrocities and excesses committed by the Jaba Ioseliani's Mkhedrioni "Knight Horsemen" militia and other criminal gangs posing as patriotic "nationalist" armed groups. Others came from the "Circassian" diaspora in Turkey, Syria, and Jordan, men and women who had "returned" to refight a war of liberation against the Russians that their forefathers had lost 100 years before—only this time they were fighting with the Russians against the Georgians.

The most effective frontline unit, however, was something called the "Abkhaz Battalion," which had very few Abkhaz fighters in it. Rather, it was composed almost wholly of volunteers from Chechnya and led by a man who would gain great notoriety in the coming war in that country: Shamil Basayev. His motivation in taking part in the battle for Abkhazia seemed partially based on the theoretical notion of creating a Federation of (mainly Muslim) Mountain Peoples stretching from the Black to the Caspian seas (more or less coinciding with the territory associated with the North Caucasus "Emirate" set up by the nineteenth-century Imam Shamil during his decades-long resistance to Russian rule) and literally as a training ground for the looming war between Chechnya and Russia. In Abkhazia, ironically enough, the Chechen volunteers were allied with freebooter Cossacks from southern Russia, a group whose historic role was to expand Russia's borders while allowing Moscow the ability to deny responsibility and control. The Cossacks had little or no ideological motivation whatsoever, save for a general interest in martial adventure for tradition's sake, and the promise of collecting whatever televisions, refrigerators, and cars were to be gleaned from Sukhumi once it fell. Little more than a year later, the Chechens and Cossacks would be slugging it out among themselves in Grozny.

Then there were the real Russians—the men in the Ministry of Defense in Moscow. They were more often felt than seen, limiting their activities to assisting the Abkhaz forces to acquire weapons, or purveying electronic information that would allow those forces to use that weaponry with greater effect. The favorite rationale for this Russian behavior as deduced by old-style Cold Warriors in the West went something like this: that amorphous, irredentist thing known as "the Center" (meaning "Moscow" or perhaps better, "the Kremlin") meant to have its revenge against Eduard Shevardnadze, the "CIA-stooge" who had helped dismantle the Soviet Union by negotiating the Soviet pullout from Afghanistan, allowing the peaceful unification of the two

Germanys, and acting as midwife to the hated and self-destructive policy of glasnost and perestroika imposed on the USSR by the "traitor-dog," Mikhail Gorbachev. Others, such as Nunu Chachua, saw everything being played out in Abkhazia (and indeed, the rest of Georgia) as part and parcel of a deep, dark plot aimed at restoring the Soviet Union to its former power and grandeur, and Eduard Shevardnadze as in fact a Russian agent and an active participant in this long-term, nefarious project.

The reality of Russian involvement in the Abkhaz–Georgian conflict was and is probably based somewhere in between those two extremes, and might be best summed up as a vague if bloody play of intermittent interests involving everything from naval ports and coastline for potential use against theoretical enemies as diverse as Turkey, Bulgaria, Romania, and Ukraine, to the use of the dozens of health resorts by noncommissioned officers and their kopek-counting families and the enjoyment of the luxurious dachas built for and by Stalin, Beria, Khrushchev, and even Gorbachev for the three- and four-star brass. Moving away from the realm of the needs and interests of the Russian military, the use of a nonrecognized, nontaxable black-hole economy for semi- and fully illegal purposes also suited the vast underworld structure that arose with the collapse of central authority in Moscow. The problem for Georgian policy makers was in trying to establish just what Russia perceived her "strategic interests" in Abkhazia to be and then how to possibly address them.

"We have repeatedly asked the Russians what they mean when they talk about their 'legitimate strategic interests' in Georgia but have yet to receive a clear reply," complained professor Alexander Rondeli. "Then we asked the Americans if they could define what the Russians mean. The Americans, too, were unable to give us any clear definition—not even what America thinks Russia's interests should be. We are victims of a willful lack of clarity."

We were sitting in our overcoats at his new "Foreign Policy Institute," which consisted of two cold rooms on the third floor of the cold and moldy building that had been declared the Foreign Ministry of the Republic of Georgia; all of the other four or six rooms on Rondeli's floor were inhabited by refugees from Abkhazia, and you had to be careful not to garret yourself on the laundry lines strung across the corridor when coming or going in general, low-light gloom.

There was, clearly, only one thing to do.

Go to Abkhazia, and check out details on the ground.

9

Pending War and the Death of a Friend

The train ride from Tbilisi to Zugdidi and then Sukhumi took sixty hours. In the bad old days of the USSR, it might have taken ten hours, maybe fifteen, maximum. But this was post-Soviet Georgia, and things were different. For starters, there were power outages all the way down the tracks, and west of Kutaisi, the so-called Zviadisti brigands also interfered with our passage, although their activities seemed limited to preventing men of military age (or aspect) from reaching Sukhumi and the front. Certain youths got the shit beat out of them in public, but the rest of us were left alone.

Yes, it was a tedious and cold ride, spiked by sudden nastiness, and when the train lurched to a halt some miles outside of Sukhumi on the night of the third day, we passengers were obliged to sleep in the carriages again lest we be shot by soldiers casually enforcing curfew. In the morning, cold, hungry, and filthy, I walked the rest of the distance into town and started looking for Nunu Chachua, wondering if she was dead, alive, or had fled along with half the population. I found her working as an accountant in a local bank that had no money, either for credit or for salaries to be paid employees.

"It is something to do," said Nunu, throwing down her ledger and inviting me home for a lunch of tomato pickles and Slim-Fast noodles. This was apparently some American charity's idea of giving aid to starving Armenians in Yerevan—but the noodles had accidentally fallen off a truck and been "privatized" for sale in the local bazaar in Sukhumi instead. Nunu chuckled when I told her about the low-cal diet she was on and laughed out loud when I told her I had gone looking for her among the refugees in Tbilisi.

"Run away? No, I am here until the end."

There was no electricity to power pumps, and the black-market gas was so expensive that she used it only for cooking, never to heat the water she hand-pumped for bathing. She told me about other indecencies, too—like how the Mkhedrioni and Guardsmen had arrived in Sukhumi that August, had driven her Abkhaz neighbors away, stolen their possessions, and then started preying on the local Greeks, Armenians, and Russians.

"Animals," she said about her own countrymen. We did not talk about personal violation. "The Abkhaz civilians were our protective umbrella, even after Ardzinba and his people ran away. But then the Guard decided they were suspect, or maybe the Guard was just greedy and started looting and killing normal, civilian people, and so all the Abkhaz left. Now that they are gone, the Abkhaz soldiers have no compunction about lobbing shells into civilian areas and doing whatever else they want because that is exactly what our so-called Georgian government forces are doing to them."

We walked over to the bazaar near her house. An incoming GRAD surface-to-surface missile had hit it two weeks before, and forty people had died. But it was crowded again, mainly with people trying to hawk family heirlooms just to raise the scratch to pay for potatoes or boat fare out of town. Armed men in a variety of uniforms prowled the streets, some marching in formation, others obviously drunk or doped up; the hospitals were regularly looted of anything vaguely resembling narcotics or even painkillers. Small machinegun fire was almost constant although it was unclear what anyone was shooting at, and the *whowump-boom!* of artillery from someone's backyard sent me scurrying for cover.

"Outgoing," she chuckled. "You'll get used to the difference."

Leaving Nunu for a few hours, I went over to the military command in the city to ask about an assessment of the situation. The press officer, a small, knotty man named Sasha, told me the only way to understand the lay of the land was to go to the front, represented by the Gumista River, less than five kilometers north of city center. I thanked him, but declined the invitation. Then a knot of militiamen/National Guards saw the camera dangling from my neck and insisted I join them in the back of their truck.

"Ha, foreign journalist—you are coming with us to witness reality!" they said, or something to the effect that they were demanding I become "embedded" with them.

How could I say no?

The dozen or so men were members of something called the Rustavi Battalion, as all were residents of the horrible industrial city by that name located about halfway between Tbilisi and the Azerbaijani frontier. In Soviet times, Rustavi was a huge steel mill. With the collapse of the USSR and the severing of economic ties between the various republics, the factory city was deprived of everything from pig iron to power, but not people. The result was massive unemployment, which translated nicely into a pool of eager men seeking to supplement their nonincomes with war-related plunder, ranging from refrigerators and furniture to tangerines.

"This is ours," said the unit's commander, referring to a vast citrus orchard extending from the group's farmhouse headquarters down to the river, perhaps 200 meters away. The real owner, I later learned, was an Armenian, who had fled with his family in August.

There was plenty of food to eat and *chacha* to drink, and the excursion to the Gumista seemed more like a picnic with a bunch of heavily armed men until the sun began to set.

"Well, I think I'd better be on my way," I suggested.

"Suit yourself, but I would settle in for the night if I were you," chortled a huge Azeri Georgian named Muzaffer, who had once been a boxer. "We shoot anything after dark."

Sporadic sniper fire began at dusk, slowly swelling into a constant snare-drum roll of heavy and light machinegun fire as both sides put up a withering barrage designed to ensure that the other did not cross the river under cover of darkness. I was petrified, and the men laughed at my nervous twitching and futile efforts to conceal the fact I was trying to duck whenever a mortar exploded somewhere outside the house. Then, around midnight, there came another sound: a monotonous drone, coming toward us from the north. The sneer on my new friend Muzaffer's face disappeared, as did the smirks and smiles of the other members of the Rustavi Battalion holed up in the shattered farmhouse.

"*Aviazia!*" someone breathed, "aviation."

Instantly, all candles were extinguished, and the commander insisted that I put out the cigarette I had just lit. The droning sound of the jet engine came closer and closer, now directly overhead, then behind us, seeking out its target in the otherwise dead-silent night.

Time stood still as the hunter wove a pattern of noisy, invisible circles in the night sky. Sometimes it seemed that we were included in the aerial loop, but the main focus appeared to be something about halfway back to city center, in the residential area of town called Novyi Raion (the New District). I snuck out the back door to watch, and caught the plane as it began a long and almost languid swoop, wings slowly humming and then screaming out a two-second warning to whatever and whomever were below as it delivered its payload about one kilometer behind our position. After maybe five or six seconds that seemed like an eternity, a ball of fire erupted, illuminating an entire neighborhood. It was followed an instant later by first the sound and then the concussion of a tremendous blast that shook the earth under my feet.

The phantom aircraft had just dropped a so-called vacuum bomb, a device that is technically known as an air-fuel explosive: 500 kilograms of liquid death and destruction explodes above the ground, thus maximizing the air-to-ground explosive impact. It makes multiple missile launchers and artillery shells look like toys.

"God in heaven!" whispered Muzaffer in Azeri.

But the phantom's mission was not over. The plane continued to circle the site of the blast, now easily marked by flames on the ground as fires spread. Then it dove again, screaming down on the same area, strafing the streets with rocket and machinegun fire before climbing back into the sky and banking west over the Black Sea. And as the droning of the jet engine receded, the devilish drumbeat sniping over the Gumista slowly resumed and continued until dawn, when it finally, mercifully sputtered to an end.

I dodged my way away from the Rustavis at around eight or nine in the morning, making a zigzag pattern down the exposed lane that led back up from the river to the main road through town and Novyi Raion. It didn't take long to find the area hit by the phantom fighter-bomber the night before. The 500-kilogram "vacuum" bomb had vaporized a two-story residential house and torn off the back half of four other houses surrounding it, with collateral damage spreading several hundred meters further. Miraculously, only one man—a local doctor—was killed outright, although his wife was said to have later died in a local hospital after she was brought in for treatment. Traces of the strafing attack were equally easy to find. Football-sized divots defined the path of the rockets and cannon, while the accompanying machinegun fire had ripped apart cars and fences along the street leading to the destroyed house, as if the pilot had intended to catch survivors or rescuers out of doors as they dug through the rubble of their friends' homes. That no one was killed in the strafing run was a miracle, although over a dozen people had been wounded. One man by the name of Serge Tromidova told me how he had been lying in a bedroom on the ground floor when a rocket blasted through the top story of his house and penetrated two walls before exploding, sending a piece of shrapnel through the floor that dropped hot, but no longer deadly, on his chest.

"The Russian pigs," he cursed. "The only way they fight is bombing civilians."

His charge could not be proved, although logical extrapolation seemed to suggest the veracity of his claim. The Abkhaz had no air force; the plane had flown in from the north through Russian Black Sea air defense space and returned more or less the same way. They were Russian planes, possibly piloted by freelance aviators or more likely by Russian air force men on "loan" to terror-bomb civilians in Sukhumi. But nobody wanted to know about it, at least nobody at the foreign news desks of the papers I worked for.

"Why would Yeltsin bomb Shevardnadze?" demanded an editor. "They are both democrats! And how can you prove that the planes were Russian?"

The "mystery plane above the Gumista" story was never published, apparently because it was not news fit to print. Perhaps there was an upsurge in violence in Bosnia at the time, and the digest of obscure foreign wars had been filled for that day or week.

The government in Tbilisi was having a hard time convincing anyone outside the country about Russian involvement, too. Even when the Georgians managed to shoot down a MIG-29 and recover the body of the dead Russian pilot with all his papers, the Kremlin refused to admit any involvement. Confronted with the evidence, the Russian minister of defense, Pavel Grachev, denied that any Russian aircraft were operating anywhere near the theater— and then charged Georgia with terror-bombing its own citizens. When it was pointed out that the markings on the aircraft were distinctly Russian, Grachev blithely replied that the Georgians had painted his country's insignia on the plane in order to disguise it.

When the Georgians brought down a second "mystery" aircraft, they invited a United Nations military observer to inspect both it and the papers of the dead pilot. The observer later told me that although he was convinced that the dead man was indeed a professional Russian pilot flying a Russian MIG-29, he was unable to categorically state that the pilot was operating under orders from somewhere inside the Russian defense ministry.

"We need to see orders, written orders, and we need to see the pilots receive them, get in their planes, take off, bomb, and then return to fill out mission completion forms," the frustrated observer said. "We are never going to get all that."

* * *

What seemed to be a closed case about at least some element of the Russian military aiding the Abkhaz separatists for whatever romantic or Realpolitik reasons was also rejected or adapted to local circumstance by certain Georgians, including Nunu Chachua.

"You see?" she almost laughed when I described my night with the Rustavi Battalion. "He will stop at nothing to destroy us."

"Who?" I demanded. "Boris Yeltsin?"

Nunu looked at me with incredulity.

"Yeltsin? I mean your democratic friend, Eduard Shevardnadze."

This was too much, and I told her so.

"Look, you might not like the man, but how can you blame him for this? The bombs were dropped from Russian planes. What does Shevardnadze have to do with that?"

"I keep telling you but you do not seem to listen," she said like an indulgent teacher. "There is no difference between Shevardnadze and the Russians.

They are working together to make life so unbearable that Georgia will beg to have the Russians back."

"Well, if you're right, they are sure doing a good job," I said.

"I want to introduce you to some friends," she said. "Then you will understand."

She led me over to a neighborhood school that served as the headquarters of group of men who called themselves the "White Eagles."

"They are our protectors," Nunu explained as we walked up the steps past a knot of men sporting ten-day beards. "They might look like rabble, but in fact they are Position."

In other words, the Eagles were loyal to Gamsakhurdia, and not Shevardnadze. The commander confirmed this, saying that his task was to ensure that the Guard soldiers, such as my new pals in the Rustavi Battalion, refrain from looting civilians again.

"We will not take part in any operation we regard as offensive in nature," the commander informed me. "We will only shoot at the Abkhaz if they attack us."

This sounded like the Eagles were awfully close to being a fifth-column in the Georgian ranks. But the government forces could not afford to excise them, lest they alienate whatever remnant of pan-Georgian feeling there was in Sukhumi and find themselves facing not only the Abkhaz in the trenches across the Gumista, but the "Zviadists" behind their backs. That this was no idle threat was underlined by a meeting arranged by Nunu in Zugdidi with the overall leader of Zviadist forces, a gentleman by the name of Vakhtang Kubalia, better known as Commander Loti ("the Drunk").

"Our task is to prevent the putschists from further looting and plundering," slurred the commander over a bottle of noontime vodka at his headquarters. "Our aim is to get rid of Shevardnadze, the Russian slave, and to recreate a unitary state of Georgia ruled by law."

Kubalia was a local hero for having driven the hated Opposition from the town, where seemingly every wall was plastered with posters either celebrating Zviad as a savior sent by God, or heaping calumny on Shevardnadze as the Devil incarnate.

* * *

It was another cold and dirty, midwinter hitchhike across Georgia. The best ride was the shortest—a ten-minute cruise over some twenty miles of pavement at roller-coaster speed in someone's stolen Mercedes; the worst one was the longest—a ten-hour slog over 100 hundred kilometers, with yours truly cramped in the freezing back of a World War II–era jeep driven by two utterly stoned and drunk Mkhedrioni militiamen. When we ran out of gas somewhere around Gori, my new pals expedited a post-midnight refill by banging their guns on a local innkeeper's door until he woke and filled up our tank for free. We pulled into the driveway of a mansion on the outskirts of Tbilisi near dawn and were invited into the kitchen to drink tea and eat *khatchapuri* while my Mkhedrioni pals were debriefed by their boss about their recent spree of raping and looting in Abkhazia. Or so it seemed to me. *Babble babble babble*, cackled one Knight, swinging his Kalashnikov around the kitchen. *HarHarHar*, chortled the well-manicured boss, peeling out a thick roll of rubles for distribution.

Filthy and exhausted but on an expense account for the first time in ages, I left the Knights at noon and checked into the luxurious Metechi Palace Hotel, that island of Western-style comfort and luxury in a sea of poverty and despair. I showered and slept until six, then got up and showered again. To get my money's worth I invited friends from the tiny Tbilisi foreign press corps over to bathe. The response to the offer was commensurate with the situation in the capital: Lawrence Sheets, Alexis Rowell, and the new AP correspondent Liam McDowell brought over their diverse assistants, girlfriends, and even drivers. By day's end, some twenty people had used my shower, including Professor Rondeli, if I am not mistaken.

The revolving-door shower party was winding down and I was sitting with a few folks at a table in the pastry shop/mezzanine bar drinking overpriced beer when I noticed the man at the table next to ours signal the waiter that he wanted his bill. Some dim glow of recognition lit up in the back of my brain. Then the man at the table began jabbing his index finger into the air in what can only be described as a muscle-bound exaggeration of the moment. There was only one person I had ever met who owned such a distinctive way of calling for service. It was Freddie Woodruff, the last of the cowboy spooks.

I waited a moment for discretion's sake, then excused myself on some pretext from the small group, and went out to the atrium.

"Excuse me," I said to the fellow. "Are you—?"

The question never left my lips.

"*Abi*," said Freddie, using the Turkish word for "elder brother" that really means "friend," embracing me, and kissing me on both cheeks. "It has been a long time."

Six or seven years, in fact—and the past washed over us both with that un-American male embrace. We had met at a New Year's Day polar bear party at a frozen lake outside the Turkish capital, Ankara, in 1986. It was a curious interim period when journalists, diplomats, businessmen, and bureaucrats were able to cross invisible lines and do unconventional things outside their job descriptions, and establish unconventional friendships. I remember seeing Freddie in a Superman costume in what I recall as being a Tom Stoppard play put on by the Anatolian Players; he was to have played the ambassador in Woody Allen's *Don't Drink the Water*, but was forced to quit when the American ambassador to Turkey complained that it was taking too much of Freddie's time. He wanted to join the Persona Non Grata blues band I played in (the replacement lead singer went on to become British Foreign Secretary Malcolm Rifkin's private secretary and then governor of Gibraltar, I believe, while the Dutch bass player was last seen installed as the deputy chief of mission at the Royal Dutch Embassy in Washington while waiting for a juicy ambassadorship somewhere), but we had to turn him down because he could not hold a tune: an Oklahoma boy given to C&W music, he wanted me to teach him how to sing and play a song called *Let's Fall to Pieces Together*, but despite my best efforts, I failed because he just did not have an ear.

Meanwhile, I got to know a great deal about Freddie. There was, for example, the first wife who tried to imbue their daughter with the precepts of a certain antimusic chapter of the Baptist Church; when the daughter came for a visit, Freddie asked me to show her the Ankara disco scene. There were dinners with his second wife, Meredith, and their kids, football and poker games, and even a bizarre Halloween party over at the Canadian Embassy, when Freddie showed up as the perfect clown. There were long, late-night conversations about his days in Berlin as a young draftee, and more obscure references to time spent as a diplomat to what was then the Soviet Union.

At a certain point, I guess, it became clear that Freddie Woodruff was more than just a regular State Department employee. But that knowledge never interfered with anyone's liking or loving the man. Unlike other individuals who I knew were spooks, Freddie Woodruff was capable of friendship, warmth, and generosity. Perhaps this was part of his cover. If so, it was one that suited his personality to a tee.

Freddie's popularity was reflected in the full month of going-away parties, receptions, dinners, and dances given in his honor when the Woodruffs moved on from Ankara, culminating in a wild jamboree for 1,000 guests held at the usually stately State Guest House. Guests were invited to attend in either Freddie's preferred black tie or, in deference to his new assignment in Ethiopia, "safari." The aforementioned Persona Non Grata blues band, with tin-ear Freddie as guest soloist, provided entertainment. Between numbers, guests were treated to a surprise farewell video designed to prove to posterity that Freddie Woodruff was indeed the most popular guy in Turkey, presidents and prime ministers included. Some friends had gone around with a life-size cardboard likeness of Woodruff, rather along the lines of those portraying the president outside the White House for tourists to pose with, inserting it in the hands of friends, strangers, taxicab drivers, tea-stand proprietors, and general folks on the street of all ages and inclinations, and asking them to explain on camera why Freddie Woodruff was their best friend. For those who spoke no English, cue cards were at hand.

"Thank you, *abi!*" Woodruff had almost tearfully said as the grand soiree wore down to a close. "This is the best party of my life—the only thing better would be to top my career with a coup!"

That was said in humor and was the closest Freddie ever came to suggesting his real responsibilities.

And then the Woodruffs were gone. I received a Christmas circular (in 1987, I believe) that detailed their new life in Ethiopia. Occasional messages or bits of gossip were passed through mutual friends. Freddie was back in Washington; Freddie was on temporary duty in Kazakhstan; he was here or there in the lands of the former USSR following its collapse. As a Russian language specialist, it was natural that he be assigned some task of importance in the brave, new world of post-Soviet diplomacy in the newly independent states. The only question was just what that role might be, a subject that only Freddie could address if he chose to: you never ask a spook to tell you anything, because they will only dress up a lie out of old habit.

"*Abi*," said Freddie, discreetly jerking his head toward my company in the Metechi atrium pub. "Ditch your friends and hang with me. The rooftop."

I did as instructed. Claiming exhaustion, I informed my hack-pack friends that I was going to bed, but really joined Freddie at the Metechi's rooftop bar. I found him eyeballing a tall, brunette bartender, while simultaneously watching the steady stream of mafia types with whores on their arms wander in and out of the establishment after dropping a hundred bucks for a bottle of Scotch and $10 for each beer.

"What can I getcha," said the brunette barmaid, who introduced herself as Marina, in perfect American English. She was almost stunningly beautiful, and, with a jolt of self-protective instinct, I knew that her looks and eavesdropping-capable language skills were probably only part of the talent package she brought to her duties as barkeep among wealthy foreigners and mafia types.

"A beer," I said, wondering if Freddie had picked up on the odd vibe that I had. His was professional paranoia; mine the amateur variety.

You don't ask your spook friends embarrassing questions like what they are really up to. I let Freddie tell me as much as he wanted and didn't ask much. Those were the unspoken rules.

So we jawed about Ankara and the old days, mutual friends last heard of working here or there, smirked at Marina, and generally treaded water until we were the only ones left in the bar.

"Shevardnadze's in trouble," said Freddie after we ordered another round of drinks. "He doesn't have the friends in Washington he once had, and the Zviadists. . . ."

I listened, took a long hit of my booze, and then leveled with him.

"Freddie," I said. "Shevardnadze came to power as a result of a putsch, and the putschists are the guys who are still in power and destroying this country."

Freddie gritted his teeth.

"There are problems," he admitted after a pause. "I have seen more stretch limousines pull up in front of this hotel than in front of the White House. I am just glad that Shevardnadze still drives a Volga."

The limousines he was referring to belonged to Defense Minister Kitovani, who had recently expanded his portfolio to include a lucrative export/import business to bring in bananas from Ecuador. The suspicion was that a more precious Andean product was packed in the same cases to supplement the prescription highs and lows afforded by drugs looted from the nation's hospitals.

I told Freddie about the "mystery" bombing raid on Sukhumi, and trotted out my circumstantial, if massive, evidence that it was a Russian plane that was responsible.

"Vacuum bombs," said Freddie softly and explained the nature of the beast.

We closed the bar with a final wink at Marina, retired to Freddie's room, and drank some more while wading into the past, present, and future. Some subjects of interest were never brought up due to tacit, mutual agreement, such as that day back in 1988 when several of Freddie's presumed professional colleagues slapped me to a polygraph machine to determine whether I was a double agent, and the subsequent hell I lived through while trying to clear my name after my pulse, sweat, and heartbeat had so horribly let me down.

"*Abi*," said Freddie at four o'clock in the morning. "It is so good to see you. It is so good to be with . . . friends."

"Likewise," I said.

"I am . . . *err* . . . one of the highest paid . . . *uh* . . . civil servants in the United States government. I can afford it. Why don't you stay here a few more days as my guest?"

Feeling lonely, super-spook or not? Don't we all have the need to be human and relax with old friends? But I couldn't stay—I had to get back to Baku.

"*Abi*," said Freddie, raising his signature fist-with-extended-index-finger over his head. "I am going to call Meredith right now and tell her you are here. It has been so good to see you."

It was the last time I saw him.

On August 8, 1993, Freddie Woodruff was shot in the head while riding in the back of a car driven by Shevardnadze's security chief, Eldar Gogoladze. The barmaid named Marina was at his side when a twenty-year-old soldier named Anzor Sharmaidze took a pot shot at Gogoladze's vehicle because the latter refused to give him a ride. But the killing was so weird and seemingly senseless that many wanted to imbue it with nefarious meaning—such as the notion that Moscow was drawing a line in the sand about where spheres of influence started and stopped, and engineered a hit on Freddie specifically to underline the point that Georgia would remain in Moscow's orbit, no matter what Washington thought or Georgia wanted. The fact that CIA turncoat Aldrich Ames had pitched up in Tbilisi on an inspection tour scant weeks before Freddie's death added ominous spice to this theory, although to my knowledge, in his confessions, Ames never indicated that the visit had anything to do with "the Woodruff case."

Myself, I chose to accept the judgment of Freddie's widow, Meredith, who told me it was all "just a stupid accident," and resist the temptation to listen to those promoting the idea of a grand conspiracy, namely, that my old pal Freddie had been targeted with assassination.

The older we get, of course, the more people we know who die. Knowing people who were killed is something else. I try not to think of my dead, killed friends too often because to think of them all together makes me wonder about how I managed to stay alive. You might say that I am filled to the brim with survivor's guilt, "There but for the grace of God go I," and all that.

* * *

Shevardnadze may have avoided saying anything derogatory about Russian involvement in the conflict in Abkhazia because of his imminent summit meeting with Boris Yeltsin. He traveled to Moscow on May 14, and, according to all the press generated from the trip, recorded a great success: a ceasefire was signed on May 20. If the moment was soured by the fact that Russia, as an "interested" third party had played such a major role in the negotiations, at least the Silver Fox had managed to effect a first: in addition to having to stomach Russian troops as peacekeepers on the ground, the ceasefire would be monitored by United Nations peace observers.

As in Bosnia, their presence did not seem to make any difference, and possibly made it even worse. By late June, war was raging again after an Abkhaz attack that seemed timed to coincide with Shevardnadze's visit to the headquarters of NATO in Brussels. A massive missile attack on Sukhumi on July 2 left 39 dead and over 150 wounded, and anticipated an assault on the city from across the Gumista that ended with the literal decimation of the combined Abkhaz/North Caucasus volunteer formations. Some described it as being the late twentieth-century equivalent of the hecatomb slaughter of the British, French, and AnZac (Australian and New Zealand) forces at Gallipoli in 1915. The massed assault was only repulsed when the "Zviadist" commander Loti Kubalia joined forces with the regular Georgian National Guard, breaking the siege of the city and resulting in new ceasefire negotiations.

On July 27, the guns again fell silent. Heavy weapons like tanks and cannons were either removed from the theater or disabled by having parts of the breaches and firing mechanisms removed. The United Nations vehicles and personnel arrived in the southern Russian port city of Sochi on September 15, ready to deploy southward and monitor the process of reconciliation, and some of the 150,000 refugees flushed from the region began returning home.

But the blue berets were never deployed. On September 16, an Abkhaz commander launched an assault south of Sukhumi along the Kodori River, effectively severing the overland lifeline to the city. On September 17, Eduard Shevardnadze flew to Sochi to restart the peace process. He was rebuffed. Rather than return to Tbilisi, he flew to Sukhumi as the city slid back into the maw of siege warfare.

On September 18, I joined him there.

III

THE WRETCHED RIVIERA

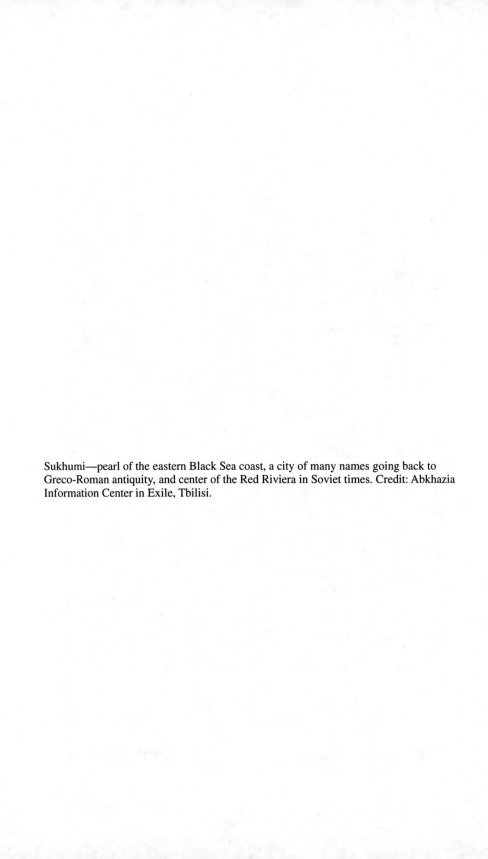

Sukhumi—pearl of the eastern Black Sea coast, a city of many names going back to Greco-Roman antiquity, and center of the Red Riviera in Soviet times. Credit: Abkhazia Information Center in Exile, Tbilisi.

10

Sarajevo by the Sea

We took fire as we washed out deep over the Black Sea to avoid detection, and we took fire coming back in to make our approach to Sukhumi field.

KrrooOOMP! went the air, and the YAK-40 would shudder and drop ten feet in the air pocket created by the explosion. *Flak*—the sort of stuff my uncle flew through during World War II. *What am I doing on this plane*, I asked myself, numb with fear.

I knew the answer all too well. After more than two years in the Caucasus, chasing chaos and war and living on journalistic hand-outs, I needed a break. A very long break, in fact. My wife and I were on the verge of divorce, my finances in shambles and the only out seemed to be a return to Montana to lick my psychological wounds and do something else with my one and only, dear and precious life. Accordingly, I had decided to fly up to Tbilisi from Baku, bid my Georgian friends farewell, probably during the course of a sustained drunk at a table with an appropriate toastmaster, then return to Azerbaijan on the train before packing my bags and leaving the Caucasus, probably forever. That was the general plan, anyway. Then the fates intervened. Deboarding my plane at Tbilisi airport that late September morning, I had literally run into Shevardnadze's press secretary as he walked across the airfield toward a different aircraft.

"Where's Shevy?" I had asked, more out of habit than anything. I had not even thought of seeking a last interview with the Georgian leader as part of my farewell visit.

"Sukhumi," he replied. "Let's go."

I followed him to an awaiting Yak-40 jet idling on the runaway, and boarded the aircraft without bothering to pass through customs. I had joined the presidential party, and was thus exempt from normal legal procedures. Perhaps the *New York Times* might even take a story: Shevardnadze's presence in Sukhumi to negotiate a peace deal with the rebellious Abkhaz might add just the sort of journalistic color and spice that would get my proposal over the editorial bar; an interview seemed almost self-assured, given the fact that I was to be delivered into the lair of the Silver Fox aboard his own airplane!

I sat back in one of the many empty chairs aboard the forty-seater, but changed often to enjoy the view. The first half-hour of the flight was through crystal clear sky and all of Georgia was visible from the portals. To the left we could see the great river valleys of Kartli, Imeritia, and Mingrelia; to the right we could see the highlands of Svanetia leading up to the towering peak of Elbrus, standing like a sentinel to all events in the northern and southern Caucasus. One was tempted to reflect on the novels and poetry of Tolstoy, Turgenev, and Lermontov or even the role the mountains played in classical mythology: Prometheus the Titan, bound to a rock up there, for having had the temerity to teach humankind how to build a fire . . .

A minute or so later, Shevardnadze's press man got up from his seat, where he had been engaged in intense conversation with a colleague, and wandered over to where I was sitting to hand me a news bulletin that had been written in English, but signed by Shevardnadze. The title contained the words "an appeal to the world," and the first paragraph devoted itself to begging world leaders to demand an immediate end to renewed hostilities in Abkhazia.

"But this is old news," I pointed out to the press secretary. "Isn't Shevardnadze in Sukhumi to sign a peace agreement?"

The press man looked at me with incredulity.

"You don't know?" he asked.

"Know what?" I replied, a sick feeling rising in my gut.

"The Abkhaz terrorists have surrounded the city, and we are fighting for our lives."

As if to underline that fact, a deep shudder rocked the aircraft, followed by a barely audible boom outside the fuselage, sort of like flying through a thunderstorm on the way in to Gallatin Field outside of Bozeman, Montana.

"Put your seat belt on," advised the press man. "We have just entered Abkhaz airspace, and they think we are fair game."

Wroom! Another explosion rocked the plane and then the Yak-40's engines went silent and the plane was dropping like a stone from the sky. I suppressed a scream and started making a life-list of once done wrongs and rights, now all undoable.

Then, with a shudder and roar, the jet engines started again. The pilot had apparently just turned them off to avoid attracting a heat-seeking missile . . .

1,000 feet . . . 500 feet . . . 100 feet . . . less . . .

I could see flashes on the ground out the windows of the plane, followed by a shudder-*wallop!* as the explosives opened in the air around us.

BOOM! BANG! and the plane lurched to one side as something big connected. We were hit and about to die. . . . But it was only the wheels touching the runway.

We were down safely in Sukhumi, a place I would soon start regarding as a little Sarajevo by the sea.

Someone opened the air-compression door for us to disembark, but actually setting foot on terra firma was up to us: a thousand wailing would-be refugees surged toward the portable staircase we had to descend, all clamoring and claiming the need to be evacuated from the besieged city before it fell. The reason for this was soon apparent: ours was the only functioning aircraft on the field. Within 100 yards lay three Tupolev-154 passenger jets, their right-side engines uniformly shredded as if someone had taken a giant can opener to the plating: heat-seeking missiles had hit home but too late to bring the aircraft down. Troops may have arrived aboard the aircraft, but no one was going to depart in them again, ever.

"I think I'll stay on board," said a Spanish photojournalist who had flown in with me from Tbilisi, taking a few frames of clawing, would-be refugees desperately trying to get aboard the Yak-40, before he ducked back into the cabin to re-secure his seat. I thought about doing the same for about one nano-second, and then it was too late to think about anything other than being pitched to the tarmac below by the animal that was the crowd, members of whom had managed to wedge themselves between me and the door. It was all I could do to cling to the metal banister of the rolling staircase punched up against the side of the aircraft.

I fought my way down through the melee and eventually managed to clear the crowd surrounding the plane. When I turned around, soldiers were beating off the last few insistent folks so they could close the compression door again. The plane taxied back out to the runway while people begged for it to return, fired up its engines, and left. As it rose in the sky, I wondered about the Spanish photographer. Was he a coward for making the journalistic decision to get his pix and then cut and run, or just so much wiser than I appeared to be? If not shot down, he was out. Myself, I was stuck—with no one to blame but myself.

Idiot, I said to myself, watching my airplane disappear into the misty skies above the Black Sea.

I poked around the airport for a few minutes, vaguely looking for Nunu Chachua. I couldn't see her, and I was pretty sure she wouldn't be out at the field among the would-be refugees, anyway. Satisfied (or completely confused; at the moment there was not much difference), I jumped into a jeep crammed with ammunition and rode into town.

Lawrence Sheets was standing in front of the Abkhaz parliament building that served as the Georgian headquarters. It was good to see a friend.

"What's the book on this place?" I asked.

"It is bad and getting worse," Larry replied jauntily.

"How so?"

"Well, it is like this," Larry began, but the smile was suddenly wiped off his face and he was dragging me to the ground.

ttTREEE-WROOM!

The air was screaming but the GRAD missile had already slammed into a nearby apartment block.

"Been like that all morning," said Sheets, smiling. "Got a smoke?"

"Sure," I said, pulling a pack of cigarettes out of my shirt with shaking fingers, then giving him matches to light his own because I could not.

"Larry," I said, once I remembered. "You don't smoke."

"Do now," he replied and inhaled deeply.

A two-car procession pulled up in front of the parliament building: a black Volga sedan bearing Shevardnadze in the backseat, followed by a flatbed truck with wooden sides carrying about two dozen enormous men dressed in black flak jackets and wearing black ski masks. If there remained any doubt about their identities, the assortment of American-made hardware in their possession gave them away: in the place of Makarov pistols they wore Smith & Wesson revolvers at their hips, and instead of Kalashnikovs they had M-16s slung from their brawny shoulders. They were Shevardnadze's personal guard, trained at Fort Bragg, North Carolina. The difference between the elite troops and the motley crew of other fighters hanging around the parliament building to greet their leader could not have been more striking.

Shevardnadze emerged, and I caught his eye and waved to him. The guard tensed, but Shevy threw them a signal and beckoned me over.

"Hello," he said in Russian. "What are you doing here?"

"I flew in with your press secretary today," I replied. "How are things?"

"Oh, not too bad," he replied, with a weak smile.

"Is it possible to sit down and talk at some time?"

"An interview? Sure, why not? But later, later, when things settle down a bit. . . ."

Then he was off, joining Tamaz Nadareishvili, the ill-fated governor of Abkhazia in the Volga, and followed by the truck filled with his elite guard.

"What did he have to say?" asked Lawrence.

"Not much," I replied. "An interview today or tomorrow, when things cool down."

"Fat chance," said Larry. "The Abkhaz aren't playing around. They are going for it."

He was going to elaborate when we noticed most of the people standing in front of the plate-glass windows on the ground floor of the parliament building start diving for cover, and we instinctively did the same.

VvrooOMM—BAMMM! It was another GRAD missile, slamming into a building north of where we lay, in the direction of Nunu's house near the bazaar.

We found Nunu sitting with her mother Lamara and a neighbor in the grape arbor in front of the house. As always, she greeted me almost as if she expected me.

"Ah, *Tomas*, you're back for the last act, I see," said Nunu.

We were soon ensconced at the family table, drinking *chacha*, listening to Nunu excoriate Eduard Shevardnadze and praise Zviad Gamsakhurdia. Some things never seemed to change.

"Zviad Gamsakhurdia is the legitimate president of this country and would never, ever make common cause with the putschists!" she said when Larry and I mentioned the hopeful rumor circulating that Gamsakhurdia was making plans to return to Georgia, raise his forces around Zugdidi, and march north to the Kodori River to break the siege of the city. "Zviad may lead them to believe that is his plan, but we now have the traitor, Eduard Shevardnadze, in our hands—and it is time draw the noose shut!"

"But that will mean the destruction of the city," I said.

"What is the destruction of a city compared with the destruction of a country?" Nunu spat back. "After all this time, you still do not seem to understand. . . ."

During a lull in the shelling and heavy machinegun fire, we made our way back to the parliament building to see about the interview with Shevardnadze.

"I am sorry," said Shevy's press counselor. "But the head of state has asked me to give members of the press this statement that you may pass on to your diverse newspapers."

We grumbled, but accepted the statement, which was written in English. In it, Shevardnadze described the resumption of hostilities as a "well-coordinated, highly synchronized joint blow" delivered by the Abkhazian leadership and "the highest echelons of the Russian military." Although highly quotable, the text was strange for one very special reason: no one in the Shevardnadze entourage in Sukhumi spoke English well enough to translate the document. Perhaps someone faxed it in from Tbilisi.

I went up to the ninth floor of the parliament building, fought for the use of the single outside telephone line, and booked a call to the *New York Times* bureau in Moscow via Tbilisi. Miraculously, I was punched through—only to have the line redirected to dictation in New York because the Moscow bureau had no time to take down a word. I had been through this same "too busy to take your copy" business when I had worked for the *Washington Post* a year or two before, when I had made my miracle-file from occupied Zugdidi. While that had been ridiculous, this was almost criminal.

"We'll see if we can squeeze something in, but your story is a little . . . ah . . . histrionic," said the foreign editor from 5,000 miles of safety away. "Whadja got there, a ceasefire or something?"

"No," I replied. "Just a little lull in the action."

The words were scarcely out of my mouth before the sky was on fire and the building shaking. One of Shevardnadze's guards was waving a pistol in my face and screaming at me to dictate my story in Russian so he could understand and assure himself that I was not a spy. I attempted to comply.

"What are you jabbering?!" shouted the distant foreign editor. "I don't have all day!"

Then the line went dead.

My next file would be a recording of my voice picked up via Ham Radio, which let the *Times* know I was still alive after various news sources had reported me missing and presumed killed.

* * *

It had been ten days of hell, and just when you thought you were getting used to it, it got worse. The Abkhaz artillery had been clearing swaths out of neighborhoods while heavy machineguns planted on the top floors of the ugly, Soviet-style high-rises or on the hills in back of the city sprayed rounds down the wide avenues, cutting the Georgian defenders to pieces. No one really knew how many soldiers and civilians had been killed. The shrinking perimeter prevented an accurate count of bodies because most were left on what became the wrong side of the lines during the course of yet another tactical retreat. A week before, the front had been along the banks of the Gumista River; it was now just outside the train station in city center, near Nunu Chachua's house. Getting there had become rather tricky. You had to rabbit-run across the intersections and alleys and hope that making a zigzag pattern would prevent the snipers from drawing a bead on you. Then you had to hope the front had stayed where it had been half an hour before. That is, you hoped you didn't accidentally run beyond it or that it would not overrun you while you remained where you were.

That had nearly happened to Eduard Shevardnadze during one of his forays to the forward lines.

"Once more into the breach, dear friends!" Shevardnadze was alleged to have cried, or something along those Shakespearean lines, as he waved a machine pistol and rallied his men near the railway station. His valor had managed to staunch the threatened breakthrough that night. But the railway station fell in the morning, and the defenders lost control of the main road that cut across town from the sea to the hills behind it—and thus lost control of the northern half of the city to the Abkhaz onslaught.

The Abkhaz were good. Too good, in fact, to be only Abkhaz. Shevardnadze told me that 80 or 90 percent of the separatist forces were "mercenaries," that is, citizens of Russia, like the Chechens and the Cossacks, who theoretically had no reason to fight in Georgia aside from the lust for looting and cash for killing. Then there were the "others," men who just happened to have very good connections to the Russian defense establishment and enjoyed access to everything from fighter-bombers to satellite photography.

"It is a fight to the death, but not with the Abkhaz—with Russia!" intoned my old friend, Nodar Notadze, the sixty-four-year-old leader of the National Front who toted a Kalashnikov on his stooped shoulders as naturally as he might carry, say, a log. "Shevardnadze will never submit. We may die here, but Georgia will rise again!"

Brave words from a brave man. But, like most of the commanders and volunteer soldiers, he seemed to forget what happened when you mistake élan for organization: you die. The bravest—and most foolish—were the first ones killed as they threw themselves at the enemy guns blazing, Audie Murphy-style. One company I got to know had tried to retake "television hill," a strategic knoll dominating the center of the city that someone had forgotten to defend and, as a consequence, had to be retaken. They used a tourist map of the city for orientation and wore white sashes to identify friend from foe.

"Here," said an eighteen- or nineteen-year-old-looking kid named Gia, signing some message to posterity on the bill of his puke-green army cap before flipping it to me. "If I come back, give me my hat; if not, keep it!"

Then he was gone, laughing and smiling, all courage. The hat remains with me.

No, Georgia was fighting Russia, and while the latter were pros, the former were not. Aside from a few really mean men from the Mkhedrioni militia group, most of whom were more interested in looting than fighting anyway, the Georgian troops were farm boys, mechanics, teachers, lawyers, and doctors. Men who responded to Shevardnadze's call to arms even though they didn't know how to hold a gun and were led by commanders who didn't have the first idea of how to command. One was a locally famous theater director, who came ready for his new role as Rambo dressed in a spiffy uniform showing off a factory-new, over-and-under Romanian-made AK-47, which had yet to fire a shot. Another captain was the head of the Green Movement. Still another was the leader of the Georgian Royalist Party.

And when they were not getting killed by the Abkhaz (or Russians), the Georgians were killing themselves. And I do not mean "friendly fire." They were just killing each other. One night, while we were sitting in the cafeteria of the parliament building that served as Shevardnadze's downtown headquarters, chowing down on the bizarre diet of Slim-Fast noodles washed down with the Georgian equivalent of Beaujolais wine, a doped-up, drunken, and crazed Mkhedrioni burst into the mess hall. His friend had just been killed and he wanted revenge. He got it by blowing away another comrade with a fork halfway to his mouth. Then someone else killed him. Everyone went on eating the Slim-Fast diet noodles and drinking the new wine. They knew the new harvest would never be allowed to ripen or mellow into the Georgian viticulture equivalent of Burgundy, so it was best to drink it *now.*

Yes, play soldiers all, following a play commander-in-chief, Eduard Shevardnadze. Gone were the famous smile and the deep, throaty chuckle that only a week before seemed to promise that everything would be all right.

"Do you want me to build you a bunker?" Shevardnadze had jokingly asked as we stood in the corridor of the ninth floor of the parliament building, waiting for a camera team to check levels for an interview. Shells were bursting outside and tracer fire lit up the night sky. I was new to the siege and maybe looked like I wanted a safer place to stay.

"This is as good a place as any," said Shevardnadze with a smile. "My men are here. I am here. Why not you, too?"

Then, as the cameras whirred, Shevardnadze purred, almost jauntily repeating his pledge to "stay in Sukhumi until the end."

"I feel obliged to be here at this critical moment in the destiny of our small country," he dramatically intoned. "It would appear that my personal destiny and that of Georgia are bound up together. I will remain until the last drop of my blood."

He had said a lot of quotable, poetic, and even prescient things then, even if some sound bites seemed a little theatrical: "I am here in betrayed Sukhumi not knowing whether this message will ever reach you . . . the fighting is only blocks away. . . ."

Or, prophesying the shootout in Moscow on October 4, when Boris Yeltsin "restored" constitutional authority by having his tanks blow up the Russian White House and mow down scores of protesters outside the Ostankino Television center, my friend Rory Peck among them: "I want the world to realize that Abkhazia is an area of the Empire's sanguinary revenge. . . . It is the explosive used to destroy not only Shevardnadze's Georgia, but Yeltsin's Russia. . . ."

Or, anticipating the rise of Vladimir Zhirinovsky and the Russian far right: "There are people with old scores to settle who want to reconstruct the Russian empire. No one should doubt that the mentality and reflexes of Russian imperialism are still alive. . . ."

In a letter to the United Nations general secretary, written in the style of having a one-sided conversation with an imaginary friend from afar, Shevardnadze poured out his heart on paper: "Amidst the deafening burst of bombs and shells, amidst the distressed cries of people doomed to death, not a single word of protest, not a single promise of help, not a single outcry of resentment and condemnation has reached us. . . . Could it be that the international community is so helpless, so blind and deaf to the universal evil? The world should be aware that the Evil Empire is still thriving, is still sowing the seeds of death, producing and deploying weapons of mass destruction, which are continuously claiming the lives of peaceful, utterly innocent people. . . ."

Vintage Shevardnadze.

But it was all bullshit, copy churned out by someone far away, and sent for his signature. The Silver Fox was trapped, and knew it.

But so long as he was in the city, for the rest of us, there was hope. It seemed impossible that Sukhumi would really become "Shevy's Last Stand," or perhaps "Eduard's Armageddon." Sukhumi was too far from the venues usually associated with the man called the Silver Fox: the Kremlin, the White House, 10 Downing Street, the German Chancellery in Bonn, peopled by Shevardnadze's interlocutors through the years: Mikhail Gorbachev, Margaret Thatcher, Helmut Kohl, George Bush, and James Baker III. The mantra was always the same: Shevy had helped lead the Soviet army out of the morass of Afghanistan; Shevy had negotiated the intermediate missiles agreement; Shevy had given the Soviet nod to the unification of Germany when the Berlin Wall came down; Shevy had let the long-time Soviet client, Saddam Hussein, dangle and then be pounded by the United States in the Gulf War. Even after he left office in December 1990, Shevardnadze had remained engaged in international arms control: that was the subject of the commencement address he made at Harvard in 1991. And now he was about to get blown up himself. The irony was almost intolerable.

For others, however, the idea that Eduard Shevardnadze was risking his life in Sukhumi was regarded as nothing more than a cynical sham. One of these was Nunu. Unlike Shevardnadze, who visited the frontlines, she lived on one. Every time I dodged through the side streets to her house she would take me inside, feed me with whatever food she had, uncork her diminishing supply of homemade brandy, and fill my ear with her pathological hatred of the man whom she blamed for the disaster visited upon her nation, her city, and her home: Shevardnadze.

But with mortars tearing up the very street she lived on, the subject had taken on a certain immediacy that it had lacked before, and the very danger of her position gave her the license to express unconventional ideas.

Nunu's argument was succinct: Shevardnadze was not just a stooge, but also a major active player in the destruction of her country, a process many referred to as "the Georgia Syndrome," the term she used to describe the literal destruction of those former Soviet republics that took the notion of post-Soviet independence seriously. And because Georgia was the most vigorously independence-oriented republic in the late-Soviet era, it was the first on the chopping block when Moscow began to rein in its wayward wards. Next came the "Tajikistan Variant," followed by the "Azerbaijan Example," and finally the "Chechen Conundrum."

According to Nunu, the most salient aspects of this policy were economic subversion (cutting trade as well as energy supplies), creating or encouraging separatist conflicts by local minorities (all conveniently armed with weapons from "outside"), and Kremlin support of opposition groups (Russophile "intellectuals," mainly) against the new, nationalist leadership (itself usually spiked with agent provocateurs and fifth-columnists).

"Can't you see, or don't you want to?" Nunu chided me. "The whole point is making us beg to return to Russia."

* * *

Listening to Nunu's political theories was tough; covering Sukhumi under siege was simple. The best way to do so was by staying alive, and the best way to do that was to play soldier. *Hug* the sides of the buildings between you and the mountains where the Abkhaz were, *zigzag* sprint across intersections rabbit-style, and *make friends* with as many of the trigger-happy Georgian soldiers as possible so that you didn't get shot by mistake.

Unlike other combat zones, you didn't even have to go looking for the war, it came to you—closer and closer every day, and the only way out was by air.

"Where's the front?" a petulant Julian Manon of ITN television demanded of Sheets shortly after his camera crew arrived in city center.

"Just take any street in any direction and you'll run right into it," Larry shot back.

Julian was not amused and probably thought we were trying to lead him astray in order to save all the glory for ourselves. He bundled his team into a taxi and drove away in the direction of the railway station but was back in twenty minutes with the footage that would win the ITN team every international award for foreign war coverage in 1993, culminating with Julian doing a standup in front of a hospital within spitting distance of the Georgian HQ where he had started. The bodies of men not dead five minutes were conveniently scattered all over the street, with their surviving friends wailing and moaning over the corpses. Central Casting could not have staged it better.

"You guys were so right!" Julian positively beamed at us, his standup complete. "The front—it is . . . *so close*!!"

Then he packed up his crew and gear, scrammed back out to the airport, bought, bribed, or bullied his way onto an outgoing flight, and was gone.

"Shevardnadze is a good enough story to risk getting here to cover," said Lee Hockstader of the *Washington Post.* "But it's not good enough to hang around to find out if it is his last."

Like the ITN team, Lee's strategy was get in, get a quote, and get out before he was killed. That was also the strategy of Rory Peck, who swaggered into Sukhumi to shoot his last footage for German ARD TV before getting blasted himself in Moscow a week later. That was the strategy of the guy who wrote a cover story for *Time* with the almost irresistible title of "Shevardnadze's Last Stand," even though the reference to General George Armstrong Custer's disaster at the Little Big Horn River in 1876 seemed to stretch time, space, and content to the limit for the sake of Americanizing the experience for readers. Yes, every visiting crisis correspondent sent to cover the story seemed to have the same idea: get in, get some color, and get back out on one of the few terrifying flights out of the airport. Everyone, that is, except for Lawrence Sheets, myself, and a tiny handful of others. I do not think any of us can adequately explain why we stayed, aside from the idea of spending just one more day in the city on the slim hope that the siege would somehow get lifted, and that we would all be able to walk out because the idea of getting out by air was becoming almost suicidal: a Georgian television team approaching Sukhumi in a fishing boat captured a Yak-40 getting shot down over the Black Sea, from the sudden plunge from the skies into the water to the assorted bloated corpses, bobbing like buoys in the waves. The next jet to get blasted was a Tupolev-154. It had its wheels down, and was maybe even on the ground, when it was hit by a heat-seeking missile and became a rolling incinerator for most aboard—including the devil-may-care correspondent from the *Wall Street Journal,* Alexandra Tuttle and the brother of Alexis Rowell's translator, Nino Ivanishvili. Someone had also told me that another plane, carrying the entire national basketball team, had crashed beforehand, killing all aboard, although I suspect this was the same aircraft bearing Tuttle. The last plane to land in Sukhumi was so riddled by machinegun fire from the ground that people gathered with buckets to collect the aviation fuel dripping from the fuel tanks in the wings. We were finally, really, and totally stuck.

In addition to Sheets and myself, the group of fools included three Reuters cameramen: Serge from Ukraine, Tengiz from Georgia, and Farhad from Azerbaijan (he would later be killed in Chechnya on his first assignment with AP TV); a Russian photographer named Natasha and her Armenian pal, Sasha, who were both associated with *Nezavisimaya Gazeta* in Moscow. Bringing up the rear was a strange English mercenary-cum-war photographer named Ed Parker. Ed had shown up as the bagman for the ITN crew but then elected to stay behind and vie for the honor of being the "last man out" of Sukhumi after his employers left.

Our digs were in the so-called Red Army R & R seaside sanatorium on the southern outskirts of town. Not only was the price right (about a buck a bed) but the complex was regarded as the safest place around because it was run by the Russian army and theoretically the last place the Russian-backed Abkhaz would take potshots at. We were disabused of this notion on the third day when an incoming mortar round blew off part of the facade of the building in which we were staying. Suggesting this was not a random error was the fact that our "observation post" on the roof was then regularly sprayed by tracer and automatic fire from an Abkhaz commando team that had seized the television tower in the middle of town. The incoming fire wasted a couple of the Russian soldiers guarding the gate.

One morning, Sheets and I decided to take a saltwater bath in the sea. We were scarcely back in our clothes on the beach when a barrage of GRAD fire started kicking up huge geysers of water where we had been swimming.

"*Sudba*," said Lawrence, using the Russian word for "fate." How else could you explain why I stopped to tie a shoelace, thus arriving fifteen seconds after an intersection I was to cross was then blown to bits by an incoming 122 mm shell? How else would you explain how we unknowingly walked up "Television Hill" after the Georgians had abandoned it and back down before the Abkhaz took it?

Boom, boom went the shells, exploding exactly where we had been minutes before.

We were incommunicado after the Abkhaz severed the one phone link. This was, after all, in the pre–cell-phone Dark Age of 1993. Out of habit at first and then for entertainment, we would tune in radio broadcasts of the BBC, VOA, Deutsche Welle, and Ekho Moskvy to hear what faraway others had to say about our situation. Ceasefires came and went that never happened. Shevardnadze was trapped in a bunker and presumed captured or dead, even though we had just seen him in his car, followed by his American-trained security detail, moments before. A relief column under the command of now-Defense Minister Karagashvili, whom I had interviewed after his conquest of Zugdidi the year before, had broken through from the south, and was about to cross the Kodori River. Gamsakhurdia had returned from

Chechnya and was uniting his forces with those of Shevardnadze to save the city. It was a real rollercoaster ride of salvation and despair, although the unspoken message was always the same: Sukhumi was about to fall or had fallen, and we were still there, unable to report anything about it.

The following is but one of several stories I wrote during the period that was never filed because either there was no way to do so or it was too late and the story was as dead as many of the people in it:

As the noose of war tightens around the beleaguered Georgian city of Sukhumi and the thud of outgoing and whine of incoming rounds of artillery fire becomes more constant and familiar, bizarre aspects of regular civilian life continue, as residents attempt to cling to some vestige of a normal, pristine past.

On Peace Prospect, a handsome avenue that was formerly named after Stalin, a lanky thirteen-year-old girl named Ira with startling blue eyes takes her prizewinning bulldog out for a stroll.

"He's got papers and he is not for sale," she informs an inquisitive foreigner.

When asked if she and her dog intend to leave Sukhumi like most of the city's other 150,000 residents, her answer was simple.

"No. Where can we go? This is our home."

Her parents were not available to comment, but a neighbor watching the street scene invited the inquisitive foreigner up to the darkened second floor abode he shares with his mother to explain his reasons for remaining in a city under siege that is without electricity, water, or food.

"We are normal people who want to be part of the normal, modern world," said Lado Pochkhia, age twenty-three. "We want to listen to the Beatles, Emerson Lake, and Palmer. I cannot stand the thought of becoming a statistical refugee, someone who has run away from his friends and neighbors due to a senseless war."

Describing himself as a Buddhist, Lado wears a sort of stocking around his right hand that symbolizes his reluctance to fight. He is also an artist, and the walls of the apartment are crowded with his work. Painted over the course of the one-year war that has reduced much of Sukhumi to the level of a slum, most of the paintings are done in a deep, melancholy blue and depict mystical mountain villages, multistory buildings set in botanical gardens inspired by the Sukhumi region's lush tropical foliage, oddly moving still-life drawings, or portraits of friends, real and imaginary. An additional part of the collection are works by Abkhazian artist friends, who deposited their canvases with Lado before fleeing Sukhumi after fighting broke out between the Georgian national guard, the Abkhazian police, and other militia groups in August 1992.

"If there is a leitmotif to my work, it is the avoidance of the subject of war," said Lado, who noted that he had stopped work now not because of the resumed fighting, but because his last tubes of pigment had dried up. "We are at fault, the Abkhazians are at fault, but the real responsibility lies with the Russians, who succeeded in getting us to start fighting each other," he said.

Back out on Peace Prospect, a woman in athletic togs canters by, giving the impression that she was out for a morning jog, while across the street, Elza Prangishili, age fifty, is opening up her bookstore for potential customers.

"I remained open through all the fighting and bombing before and I will remain open now that it has started again," she said. Business was surprisingly brisk, although much of her stock seemed rather outdated: collections of Russian, Georgian, and Abkhazian poets, world atlas hardbacks dating to the Soviet period and even some classic, anti-imperialism tracts detailing American crimes in Africa and Central America. "People need to read in order to relax," said Mrs. Prangishili. "As for me, it gives me something to do and gives a sense of normal times to anyone walking by."

Most of the other stores along Peace Prospect are closed and several burned out, but at the corner of Rustaveli Avenue a Russian couple are selling cheap cigarettes and newspapers that are only two and three days old, while diagonally across the avenue another Georgian woman has taken up her regular hours at a state-owned stand that specializes in jelly-filled cakes. Both ventures would only accept the Georgian coupon, refusing the Russian ruble as legal tender although the coupon is worth almost less than the Monopoly money it so resembles.

"The government says that we must only use the coupon, and we intend to comply," said the jellyroll seller obstinately.

When asked why she was working and not running away, the woman reiterated the standard refrain in Russian: *"Kuda?"*—"To where?"

"I am not a psychologist, so I will not venture to comment on why the others stay when faced with destruction, but for myself I stay because I am a doctor and it is my duty," said Fatima Khonelilia, chief physician at the nearby Sukhumi Second Hospital, one of three venues taking in the rapidly rising number of both civilian and military casualties caused by Abkhazian shelling and Georgian attempts to repulse the creeping advance on the city. While she said that medical supplies delivered by the Red Cross and the Doctors Without Borders organization in Sukhumi were "enough" despite the growing load of patients, her assistant, Dr. Marlin Papava, disagreed.

"We are overwhelmed and are short of almost everything from painkillers to sutures," he said. "I was a physician in the Soviet Army and worked under extreme conditions in a number of areas but never in a hospital literally on the frontlines."

As of this writing, the frontlines are a kilometer north of the railway station, but that says little because Sukhumi is effectively surrounded: the Abkhaz control all the heights around the city, and their patrol boats control access via the sea. Fighting over the past few days has focused on the Abkhaz attempt to force their way down the ravines and cut the city in two, three, or four.

Remarkably, there are still residents in the northern suburbs of Mayak and Novyi Raion beyond the station, who are subjected not only to crossfire between the opposing forces, but also to random violence by the rogue elements from one of the two opposing fighting forces, or both. On Sunday night, for example, a Russian priest who had stayed in his house throughout the most vicious fighting over the past year was beaten, carved up by a bayonet, and left for dead by anonymous robbers operating on the fringes of the virtual no-man's-land, while a neighbor was killed—presumably by the same men. The perpetrators then looted both homes of all valuables, according to two American missionaries who also live and work in the same area.

"They need to believe in Jesus, but they don't," said one of the missionaries in a street-side interview as a jet bomber thundered overhead on a mission to destroy.

Others, such as Mrs. Gala Yudina, sixty-five, say that in addition to the looting committed by elements in the Georgian army, the highest echelons of the government are also "inhumanly" corrupt.

"We, the people who have suffered the most, have not received one gram of the international aid the government says has been sent to help us," Mrs. Yudina said in disgust as she went about her task of drawing a bucket of dubiously clean water from a pond filled with tadpoles that had been created by a bomb blast down the street from her home. "It would be better if the world gave no aid at all, because at least then it would not enrich the national thieves."

Meanwhile, on Peace Prospect, Mrs. Prangishili is closing her bookstore as the evening bombardment in and out of the encircled city intensifies, while young Ira takes her prizewinning boxer out for another stroll. Lado the artist calls down from a window to have a new friend join him for some "minnow soup" his mother is making from tiny fish netted in the shallows of the nearby Black Sea, while another woman in a sort of sports suit and tennis shoes turns the corner to come running by the now-closed jelly-roll and newsstands. She is heading toward Dr. Khonelilia's hospital, and even if jogging in a formal sense, she is crying for reasons known best to her self.

* * *

There were many stories, but few so poignant as that of Dr. Marlin Papava. A small, gnome of a man with bulging eyes in his late forties or early fifties, Dr. Papava was the effective head of the emergency care service of the downtown hospital Lawrence and I visited every day to collect the most recent statistics about dead and wounded even though there was nothing we could do with whatever information was given us. Half Abkhaz and half Mingrelian/Georgian, he was a man who was forced to watch his personal world be torn apart, needed and despised by both sides in the conflict. One day, Marlin invited us into his office for a longer chat.

"I am not a drinking man," he said, closing the door and reaching for an expensive bottle of foreign vodka in his bookcase. "But because it seems likely that we are all going to be killed together we may as well enjoy this special vodka now."

"With pleasure," I said, thinking it an extraordinarily good idea.

"You do not know anything about me aside from that I work at this hospital and that I am the man who gives you numbers about dead and wounded," said Marlin, filling three shot glasses. "I give you what you want because I know the truth and because I know that you are the only ones around to record anything about the tragedy visited upon us at this time."

"It is our job," muttered Lawrence.

"Yes, yes," said Marlin. "And mine is to administer to the wounded and to count the dead in the morgue. But at moments like this we must get beyond that. In this, perhaps the last day of my life, I want to know who you are, and even if you are not willing to share that with me, I want to tell you who I am or at least who I once was."

"Cheers," I said, hoisting my glass and downing it.

"I am a marksman but without my medals to prove that it is so," said Marlin.

"Please explain," asked Lawrence.

"I was a soldier in the Soviet army, a sharpshooter, but my specialty was the pistol. I served in the Soviet army in special places—Vietnam, Africa, Cuba, and elsewhere. I grew tired of it all and asked that I be allowed to become a doctor, to heal wounds, not make them. I do not want to explain details about that. But I was good with guns, with pistols, and I could not leave them. After my . . . special tasks . . . I began entering competitions, first local, and then international. I was good, very good. I won medals. I won medals for the Soviet Union, including a bronze in the 1968 Olympics. I should have received the gold, but I got nervous and was not at my best. . . . Of course, such things happen! But do you understand what this all means? Bronze or gold, I was a hero of the Soviet Union, a medal winner! They showered gifts and praise upon me; I was even allowed to test bullets for capitalist firms and received remittances! I had a house, a dacha, and even a yacht built to specifications only found in the West and of materials only available there! I christened it 'Abkhazia,' and it was at anchor here, in Sukhumi, until last year."

"Where is it now?"

"God knows, gone—stolen like all of my medals, like all of my guns. Gone, now owned by some dope fiend who calls himself a soldier or national guardsman. Gone."

Marlin's frog eyes looked away; then he wiped his white medical sleeve across his face, and turned back to pour us another round of shots.

"I am not a drinking man," he said again.

"It's all right," said Lawrence.

"Tough times," I chirped in.

"Yes . . ." said Marlin, a weird, painful smirk crossing his lips as he topped off the shots. "Difficult times indeed. You have no idea."

We were raising our glasses when a Georgian soldier kicked in the door and started to snarl something at Dr. Marlin. Then he noticed Larry and me. We recognized him from headquarters, and he recognized us. His attitude changed, he tried to smile, excused himself, and departed, closing the door behind him.

"What was that all about?" I asked.

"*Narkoman*," he said softly. "They come every day to raid supplies. They prefer to use drugs while they are on their feet, rather than when they are lying down on stretchers."

We left, and the next time I saw Dr. Marlin was at Moscow's Sheremetyevo International Airport. I was flying in from Istanbul on assignment in Chechnya for ABC television, and standing next to the man sent out to pick me up was a small fellow with a familiar, gnomish face, holding up a sign with some other foreign name on it.

At least he was still alive.

11

Black Sea Refugee

I could empathize with the oblivion-seeking soldiers. Alcohol sure helped pass the time. The problem was there wasn't too much around. I managed to buy some booze from the wife of a Russian soldier living in the building next to ours over at the Red Army Sanatorium compound. She charged me $100 for two bottles of imported vodka, a liter of French Champagne, and a fifth of Armenian cognac. I didn't want to think of what her husband would do when he found his stash was missing, so I just grabbed the bottles and went back to our barracks where I was met as a conquering hero. As might be expected, we got tremendously drunk and then we began to sing.

We made such a ruckus you couldn't even hear the bombs for a while. And in the morning, there were complaints.

"Have you no respect?!" growled the Russian manager of the sanatorium. "People come here to relax!"

He was about to threaten us with expulsion when a mortar shell came singing in down the street. We all dove for cover, and the noise issue was forgotten.

Another time, Larry and I meandered over to where the Metropolitan David had once dwelled, and discovered to our chagrin that someone—presumably Abkhaz, although we could not be sure—was lobbing mortar rounds in our general vicinity from the knob we referred to as "Television Tower Hill." Removing ourselves from the area was trickier than we had originally thought, because it occurred to us that our khaki-colored photojournalist vests might make us look like Russian mercenaries to trigger-happy Georgians, if we continued to slink along the rubble of buildings. It was safer, we decided, to walk shoulder to shoulder down the very middle of the street, singing our new "Siege of Sukhumi Theme Song" at the top of our voices:

> I'd like to roger that little Ruski
> Roger her so sweet
> Take her to the mountains
> Sweep her off her feet

The actual lyrics changed each time we sang it and were considerably more bawdy than that just represented; I have no recollection of how or why we began singing it, other than a vague expression of lust for Natasha, an over-weight (and utterly terrified) Russian correspondent who was also camping out at the Red Army resort.

Our shenanigans came to an end when we espied some folks dusting up their courtyard after a mortar blast. They beckoned us into their basement shelter, and shared the last of their homemade wine with us as we duly took out our notebooks and recorded their hopes, dreams, and fears for the future, knowing perfectly well that it was an utterly useless journalistic exercise, but still expected of us for decorum's sake.

"And how do you spell your family name?" I asked our hosts.

"Bee Eee Are Eye Aye," said the lady of the house, while her husband fetched us a last glass of the rose-colored wine.

"Beria?" I asked, astounded. "Like Lavrenti?"

"Like Lavrenti," smiled the woman forlornly. "We are distant relatives."

"But . . . but the Abkhaz will kill you with a name like that!" I exclaimed. "Why don't you try to get out?"

"This is our home," said the woman. "And besides—if you can't get out, how can we?"

I later heard that they were executed when the Abkhaz overran the neighborhood.

* * *

Then there was Shevardnadze, whose presence always seemed to suggest that not all was yet lost. We saw each other often although there didn't seem to be much point in soliciting an interview every day when the situation was very evident. It was bad and getting worse and you did not need Shevardnadze to say so. One thing soon became abundantly clear. Whoever else Eduard Shevardnadze may have been, he was a man with brass balls and a backbone of steel. He was so casual about his own fate that he almost seemed suicidal—like when he seized the keys of a Zhiguli, or Fiat-style sedan, after his Fort Bragg-trained bodyguards tried to restrain him from making another foray to the front. As things slipped from bad to worse, even his guards became visibly nervous: they were defending a man apparently determined to die in a battle that could not be won, with no way out of the mess he had brought them into.

Then one afternoon, mounting despair was relieved by the miraculous blast and growl of tanks and troops from the south! The Karagashvili relief column had arrived! We rushed down to the edge of town to find two mud-splattered and thoroughly battered T-54 tanks, accompanied by an utterly exhausted column of some 300 men and five armored vehicles that had managed to ford the upper-reaches of the Kodori and make it to Sukhumi. Neither the men nor the vehicles were in any shape to fight for days. The rest of Karagashvili's column, the men reported, had been stopped and then stripped by Loti ("the Drunk") Kubalia and Nunu Chachua's friends in the Eagle Battalion. The Zviadists were helping the Abkhaz block the way in the hopes that Shevardnadze would be killed and Gamsakhurdia seamlessly restored to power.

"We will fight them to the last man, to the last drop of our blood," said Nodar Notadze, nursing a new wound. The old professor and political activist had his thick, stubborn hide slashed by shrapnel in three places. "So long as Shevardnadze is here, we will never submit or surrender!"

"They'll never take him alive," said Sasha, the press officer clutching a pistol in one hand and a signed volume of Shevardnadze's ghostwritten, autobiographical pulp in the other. Sasha was such a devoted admirer of Eduard Shevardnadze that he said he would lay down his life for his leader—or take the leader's life if things got too bad.[1]

Nunu could only laugh when she heard that.

"You still don't understand, do you," she said. "It is all a big, bloody game. The reason that Shevardnadze can travel about so freely is because the Russians know where he is and do not fire on that sector."

"Nunu," I tried. "What you are suggesting is nuts. Unless Shevardnadze is wearing some special locator device that allows every last one of the Abkhaz or Russian gun positions to know exactly where he is, and unless their aim is so good and their weaponry more accurate than the smart bombs the Americans used in the Gulf War, what you are suggesting is physically impossible."

"Really," smiled Nunu. "Then explain this to me. Have you been to Stalin's dacha, up the road from the botanical gardens?"

"Yes, I was there this morning."

"Would you say that it is located in such a way that it is totally exposed to land-based artillery, sea guns, and air power?"

"Yes."

"Then why is it that the attacking forces have not hit it once, while they have concentrated on civilian targets of no military interest whatsoever? Think about it."

More to the point, it was time to think of making an escape.

"I am really starting to dislike this place," said Sheets that night, displaying more worry in that one sentence than he has ever evinced before or since. And he was disliking it for five people. As the Reuters producer, Lawrence was effectively responsible for his three cameramen and their equipment as well as, by default, Natasha, the Russian photographer who was starting to make the inexorable slip into total paranoia and mental breakdown. She would be giggling one moment and then sobbing the next.

Yes, I agreed, it was indeed time to leave. But how? We went over the familiar options: wait out the siege and hope that the Abkhaz would not overrun the Russian base to slit our throats; try to find the truth about a mountain road the Abkhaz had allegedly left open in order to flush the city; or squat at the airport in the vain hope that someone had repaired a plane. We still could not decide.

There was a particularly nasty bout of fighting that night, and when we woke we packed our bags and started making our way along the coast toward—what? Pursuing the rumor about the passage out over the mountains seemed to be the best option: a steady trickle of people were walking down the road carrying their life possessions in beat-up suitcases or bundles made of bed sheets, and seemed to be going somewhere; the airport was in the same direction, anyway.

"I'll stop at Shevy's headquarters to see if there is any news," I said as we passed the turnoff to the so-called Stalin dacha on the hill south of town. Peeling off from the main group, I made my way up through the lush garden, and was dripping sweat and catching my breath near the top when I noticed Gia Janjgava, Shevardnadze's American-educated twenty-eight-year-old chief of protocol on the observation deck. He was staring out at the sea while smoking a Marlboro cigarette.

"Ho, Gia!" I cried. "*Gamarjobat*! Give me a decent smoke!"

"*Madlobt*, Tomas," Gia replied, digging into his pocket and handing me a whole pack, or the sad remnants thereof, meaning a butt or three.

"Any news?" I asked, striking up a cig and sucking deep.

"You mean you have not heard? Our Big Brother has announced a plan to save the innocents," said Gia, his voice dripping with sarcasm. "Boris is sending a flotilla to rescue the women, children, and wounded. I would advise you to join them and go."

"Boats?"

"Warships, actually. The ones shooting at us and knocking down our planes with guided missiles. Look—you can see them at sea, past the point."

I strained my eyes over the expanse of shimmering gray water and saw nothing at first. Then, with a jolt of hope, I thought I could discern several shapes beyond the long swing north of the picturesque bay, pushing south. *Ship ahoy! Salvation! Ho!*

I could barely restrain myself from embracing Gia.

"Where will they . . . dock?" I asked as calmly as possible.

"How should I know?" snorted Gia. "Along the beach somewhere, out by the airport. . . ."

I barely heard his words in my rush to grab my bags and race back down to the main road to try to catch up with Lawrence Sheets and his wards. I found them out at the shattered remains of the airport terminal, hanging around a room with no roof that was filled with corpses on stretchers and wailing wounded.

"Hey, hey!" I crowed. "We're outta here! History, gone!"

"Shut up, you wanna get us shot?" Sheets retorted, cocking his head in the direction of a couple of nasty-looking Mkhedrioni standing guard over a fresh cadaver.

"Boats, baby, boats!" I hissed, sotto voice. "Uncle Ivan has sent in boats to take out the women, children, and international hack-pack who got stuck with them! *We are out!*"

"Gonna take the chicken-run, huh?"

It was Ed Parker, the British mercenary-cum-frontline cameraman, emerging from his lurking space.

"The chicken-run, Goldie, yeah," said Ed, using his own unique bastardization of my name. "The others, yeah—but I didn't think that was like you, Goldie, runnin' and all. Me, I'm here until the bitter end."

"Suit yourself, Ed," I said. "But I'm gone."

"Ditto, Parker," said Larry. He had even less time for Parker than I did.

Then, for reasons I would like to explain but cannot, I left Larry and his wards at the terminal and went looking for the rescue ships with Parker. Our first stop was the closest fishing boat anchorage to the airport—about a ten-minute walk away.

"No boats here, Goldie," sneered Parker, scanning the cove we had been directed to. A half-dozen fishing vessels, swamped or half-sunk, were the only craft to be seen.

"I saw them steaming this way," I said, squinting out over the waves and surf.

"Maybe your salvation is further down the beach."

The idea that the rescue ships would be loading refugees from the docks in downtown Sukhumi was, frankly, insane. But I had seen them steaming in our general direction. That meant they had anchored somewhere along the ten-mile-long beach between the airport and the city docks, or were about to. The problem was that a point of land jutting into the ocean just north of what I will call "airport cove" effectively prevented us from seeing any activity beyond it. Even more problematic was that the road from the airport toward the city skirted inland away from the coast and was lined by groves of citrus trees.

"You're fucked, Goldie," said Parker with weird glee. "You're with me here until the bitter end, whether you like it or not."

What was the greater burden—hanging out in Sukhumi until the bitter end or being obliged to hang out with my new semi-psycho pal Parker? It appeared I was stuck with both.

We walked back to the airport. Sheets and his entourage were gone. An ammunition truck, piled high with Astara cigarettes, lurched around a corner. We flagged it down and got in the back, riding toward town. Then the driver parked in someone's backyard and left with no explanation. After about ten minutes waiting for him to return, I grabbed a carton of the awful cigarettes and jumped down.

"Where are you going?" asked Parker.

"The beach," I said, and started to make my way through the houses, gardens, fences, trash, orange, tangerine, and lemon groves that stood between me, the sea, and rescue.

I knew that I had hit pay dirt when I crossed an irrigation canal and stumbled on a field hospital that was in the process of evacuation. Orderlies were bringing mangled, moaning men out of the hospital and propping them up under the palm trees to wait their turn aboard one of the limited number of stretchers that would carry them to the beach. Parker and I joined the procession and were in turn joined by six, ten, two dozen, and then hundreds of other people emerging from the citrus groves or arriving down paths between houses, all making their way toward the sea. Most of the young women seemed to be wearing their Sunday best, complete with high-heeled shoes, which impeded their progress down the sand and gravel path. Many were wearing makeup and the scent of perfume hung in the air beneath the trees.

Then, emerging from the last garden plot, we saw it. There, not ten feet offshore, lay a huge landing craft flying the flag of the Russian Black Sea Fleet—a red hammer and sickle against a white background. The metal beast was a veritable multistoried, seafaring parking lot for tanks and Russian-made Armored Personnel Carriers called BTRs. It was a beautiful sight to see. So were the two lines of blonde and blue-eyed Ruski marines, backed up by two of the six-wheeled armored fighting vehicles, guarding access to the beast's sea door, which extended like a metal tongue of welcome on the sand in front of me. It looked like a welcome mat to heaven.

"*Bystro! Bystro!*" shouted the captain of the vessel as the orderlies hoisted the wounded men aboard. "Quickly now! We haven't got all day!"

Remarkably, there was some order to the evacuation. The wounded men on stretchers were brought on first, disappearing deep into the bowels of the landing craft. From the screams and moans that followed, I had the image that they were simply being dumped into a heap of ravaged human flesh. Next came the elderly, followed by mothers with infants. It was around this time that order started to break down. A mother with a five-year-old daughter and fourteen-year-old son was denied access on account of the latter; tearing her hair, she threw herself down in the sand—and then got back up to throw her youngest child into the arms of one of the soldiers guarding the sea gate.

"Save her! Save her!" wailed the disconsolate mother. "I beseech you, save her!"

"Mommy! Mommy!" cried the child as she was passed back into the landing craft.

Other mothers then began launching their infants and children aboard in a similar manner while remaining on the sand. I stood near the back of the mob, unable to stomach the idea of fighting with women and children for a berth. I rationalized this by telling myself I was waiting for Larry Sheets and his team. They were nowhere to be seen. About a mile or so further down the beach I could see another warship, a destroyer it looked like; small craft were shuttling out to it from the shore. Perhaps the Reuters crowd was on it? I hoped so. It was every man for himself.

The women, children, and young ladies in their high heels and makeup were now fighting and scratching. Adding to the growing chaos, the Abkhaz let off a new and heavy barrage of artillery fire on the city center, sending shockwaves across the thin curve of beach and water that separated us from hell. The captain was pushing people back from the sea door and screaming at the top of his lungs. Then he was screaming orders to the crew. The engine of the ship rattled to life, and the sea door was cranked up a few feet. I knew it was time to make my move, now or never.

"See you, Goldie," said Ed Parker.[2]

"See you, Parker," I said, shouldering my bags and walking with determination through the mob. I found myself looking at the captain, my face on a level with his feet.

"Sir," I said as formally as possible. "Let me congratulate you on your mission here evacuating the women, children, and wounded. I am an American correspondent working for the *New York Times*, and I must leave Sukhumi in order to report on—"

"Call Moscow," said the captain, a weird smile forming on his lips.

"I beg your pardon?"

"Call Moscow," the captain repeated. "Foreigners like you need permission from the General Staff to get onboard my ship."

He shouted another order to someone inside the craft and the metal tongue of the sea door clanked up higher.

"Please, listen to me!"

But I was only addressing barnacles. The doors had closed and the landing craft was sliding off the sand and out to sea. Still desperately hoping to be saved, I prayed that the captain might change his mind and come back and collect me, a thin hope that flamed into a dream for a brief moment when the huge landing craft turned around and once again opened its gaping loading doors and began to approach the shore. But it was only to collect two amphibious armored personnel carriers that had been stationed on the beach. The APCs swam out to sea, trundled up the steel-tongue elevator, the sea doors closed again, and the landing craft was gone.

I stood on the beach, staring out to sea, as despondent as I have ever remembered being in my life.

Abandoned.

There was nothing else to do other than join the trickle of other failed evacuees who were trudging toward the far end of the bay, where small craft were shuttling people from a pier out to several gunboats in the deeper water. But there was really no hurry or hope. With half a mile left to gain the pier, we started running into countertraffic: would-be refugees who had been turned away from their evacuation point, just as we had been turned away from ours. The escort destroyer and all other vessels in the flotilla, including a flat-bottomed coal barge, were packed to bursting and would take no more.

It was then that despair really began to set in. The sustained heat of the day, the roller-coaster ride of hope and anguish at being rescued, and the sheer physical drudgery involved in hauling luggage across the beach soon conspired into a throbbing migraine that tore at my brain like a saw. I flopped down on the sand, lit an Astara cigarette that only augmented my headache, and watched the flotilla raise anchor and sail away.

"Bastards, Russian swine!"

It could have been me talking, but it wasn't. A young soldier had come up and joined me on the quayside. Actually, he seemed pretty oblivious to my presence. He just stood there looking out to sea, crying.

"First you destroy our city, and then you come to save us!" He babbled, shaking his gun at the departing ships.

"*Tikho*," I said, offering him an Astara. "Be calm, be quiet."

"Who are you?" he demanded, turning with a start and training his gun on me. He was limping. The lower left leg of his trousers was torn and caked in blood. "Russian?"

"No," I said. "Just a stranded American journalist."

"America," said the soldier. "You know, we believed you, but you did not believe. We believed it when you said that the Soviet Union was bad and should be dissolved, but you did not believe us when we said that the Russians would not let that happen. And now . . ."

He burst into sobs again.

"Ah, Russians!" he wailed, shaking his gun at the sea again. "The only thing you know is war, guns, destruction! You know nothing of culture or art or love or food or life! That is why you hate us! That is why you want to destroy us, because we live!"

I waited for a moment, letting him cry, and then asked his name.

"Roman," he said. "Roman Tsanava, from Sukhumi, the once lovely Sukhumi."

We sat smoking in silence again, surveying the destruction from our seats in the beachside amphitheater. The sun had sunk beneath a distant bank of clouds to the west, and evening was coming on; the fires burning around city center to the right and the airport to the left were made more visible by the closing dusk.

"See that fire there, the second one to the left of the parliament building?"

I wasn't sure I could distinguish so closely between distant blazes but said I saw where he was pointing.

"That's where my house is, or was," said Roman, almost giddy now. "Gone!"

I said I had been sleeping at the Russian army sanatorium.

"You will be my guest tonight!"

"But you said your place is ash."

"No, no—not there!" laughed Roman, lurching to his feet. "You will stay at my relatives' place! It is not far from here. There is food, *chacha*, and a clean bed. There is no discussion! I must uphold our Georgian code of hospitality—and you are a guest!"

In fact, there was nothing I wanted to do more than find a bite to eat, a glass to drink, then collapse on a mattress, and forget about where I was. We were soon wandering down the darkened streets of a semirural neighborhood, with Roman asking directions every 100 yards or so. Finally, we entered a fenced compound. A distant flare helped us work our way around mounds of farm equipment and other debris in the yard to the front door. Roman knocked, a head emerged, and a rapid conversation ensued.

"It is settled," announced Roman. "You will stay here tonight as my guest."

"Wonderful."

"Good-bye my friend!" said Roman, limping off into the dark.

"Where are you going?" I shouted after him.

"To die!" his voice came back out of the gloom. "Remember me, my friend! I am Roman Tsanava, a Georgian man who loves his country! Good-bye!"

Then he was gone.

It soon dawned on me what was so strange about the farmhouse. Although a ferocious firefight was under way in the city to the north, and bombs were falling around the airport to the south, everything was quiet here. We were in the eye of the hurricane. I asked my hosts for aspirin and water, and they provided both. Then I lay down on the bed and dozed, letting the aspirin go to my brain. I woke an hour or so later and found the woman of the house standing over the bed with a candle in her hand.

"Come with me," she said. "Your dinner is ready."

I followed her out of the house to the front yard and then around to the back of the building. A couple of chickens squawked and ran into a shed. A pig grunted. A cow stared. Bread, cheese, and pickles had already been placed on the table. A daughter broke free of the family circle to fetch a pot of stew simmering over some coals, and a son busied himself uncorking a bottle of wine.

"Thank you, thank you," I said, and took a step forward. That was the moment the family dog chose to spring forward for a mouthful of my leg.

"*GrrrrrAKHH!*" roared the small mutt monster, and I was twisting and writhing on the ground, trying to force blood out of the wound with my hands. My headache was back with a vengeance. I had not been nipped or bitten; I had been chomped as effectively as if gouged by a fragmentary grenade. And I had a new potential problem to add to the list: rabies. I cleaned the wound with *chacha* before I tried to sleep. I slept badly, cleaned it again in the morning with the remaining booze, and then started back to town, blood from my bizarre wound seeping into my boot.

My destination was Stalin's dacha. There was no real reason for me to go there; it was simply out of habit. I had heard Sheets interviewed on the BBC that morning. He and his wards had managed to get aboard the boats and were gone, safe. I was alone, or nearly. There was still Nunu Chachua, and her nemesis, Eduard Shevardnadze. And Ed Parker.

I trudged up through the garden to the veranda and watched the city get pounded some more. Shevardnadze's headquarters still seemed to be the safest place around, just like Nunu had said. After an hour or so, I heard the sound of tire crunching gravel on the road leading through the botanical garden below and the knock of an accelerating engine using dirty gasoline. Then, with a lurch, the truck carrying Shevardnadze's bodyguards pulled into the drive, followed by a white Zhiguli sedan: Shevardnadze, returning from some part of the front. He looked utterly drained. He saw me and came to say hello.

"Still here?" he asked politely. "How was your night?"

"Pretty tough," I said. "I was wounded."

"Wounded!" Shevardnadze exclaimed with concern.

"Yes," I said, pulling up a filthy trouser leg to show the blood clot. "By a dog."

The Silver Fox pulled up his lips into smile, and began to chuckle.

"*Sobakoi . . .*" he snickered. "By a dog."

Then he turned and walked up the steps to the dacha, laughing.

Gia Janjgava came rushing over to me.

"What did you say?" he demanded. "It is the first time he has smiled in two weeks!"

That is when we smoked his last Marlboro cigarette together, the one he still asks me to replace with a carton of "street" Marlboros from America every time I come to visit.

* * *

The frontlines were now something like 100 yards from Nunu's house, and getting closer by the minute. The entire street appeared to be in flames from the dacha, but when I came clear of the smoke, I discovered her house still standing.

"So he laughed about the dog," she chuckled when I showed her my dog wound and told her about Shevardnadze's response. "He is a Russian dog himself."

I stayed there that last night, first because I was afraid to move through a new and withering rain of Abkhaz heavy machinegun and mortar fire and then, as darkness fell, because I was afraid of getting cut down by Georgians who might take me as an Abkhaz point man in the darkness. We tuned in the BBC and Radio Moscow and both had the same report: Sukhumi had fallen, and Shevardnadze was surrounded in his bunker, suing for peace. I wanted to believe it was true because it meant that it was over, that the frontlines had crossed us and that we might still survive. But we both knew the reports were wrong because there was no BBC or Radio Moscow reporter in the city and no communications out even if there had been. Besides, the mortar shells kept crashing in and the machinegun fire was incessant. There was at least another night to go.

"Scared?" a semi-sleeping Nunu asked when I slithered into a fetal position on the rug beneath the dining room table. I didn't answer, but put my shoes back on and placed my glasses in my shirt pocket just in case I needed to make a quick exit from a burning house. Of course I was sleeping in my clothes.

In the morning, with the house across the street ablaze, I begged Nunu and her mother Lamara to pack a bag and leave with me. Nunu refused for both of them.

"I am staying until the end," she said.

I didn't even bother to ask why. Nunu gave me the penultimate shot off the last bottle of her homemade brandy. I left the last half-inch in the bottom for a "next time" I didn't believe in and said good-bye. She gave me a kiss and I walked to the end of the block, sprinted across the side street in a rabbit pattern, sought smoke for cover down side streets, and dodged bullets, mortars, and GRADs in open places until I was once more on the veranda of the so-called Stalin's dacha, the place where Shevardnadze had allegedly been "surrounded" the night before.

It was silent. No, it was something more than that. The place was empty, abandoned. I hobbled over to the main door to the dacha and let myself in, still hoping against hope that there was someone there, someone who could tell me something else, someone who could tell me what to do. Then I heard a noise in the kitchen area and followed it to its source: an elderly woman, sweeping up the accumulated filth of Shevardnadze's guards.

"Who's here?" I asked.

"No one," she replied.

"Perhaps you didn't understand my question," I suggested with growing unease. "Where is Shevardnadze?"

"I told you he is gone."

We stared at each other for a moment and then the maid went back to her task of cleaning out the dacha before a new tenant arrived.

"Excuse me," I asked the cleaning woman. "Is there anything left to drink?"

I took two bottles of wine and a stale loaf of bread and went out to the veranda. Below me lay the city. Dense plumes of rising ash hung over the center, marking the place where a GRAD missile or 122 mm artillery round had slammed into an apartment block or private home. First came a sudden flash, followed by a small black puff of smoke, then the delayed report of the explosion, rolling upward toward my dacha HQ. It took time for the fires to get going, but soon the only part of the city that seemed to be free of fire was an area to the north of the railway station called "Novyi Raion," or "the New District," that had been shattered and burned by hundreds of rockets over the past week. Now Novyi Raion seemed quiet because the Abkhaz had moved past it, and were now somewhere around the bazaar—that is, Nunu's house. There was nothing I could do for her anymore. There was nothing I could do for anyone, even myself. Except drink.

The warm wine was doing the trick, slurring my mind and blurring my vision. It had to be that, because in the haze, I was seeing things. Boats, rounding the point from the north. I put down the bottle and stared out to sea. It was no hallucination. There were ships out there. First one, then two, then four large vessels were heading toward the bay. I hefted my bags and ran down through Stalin's garden to the coastal road, and began jogging toward the place of my aborted rescue two days before. Once on the beach, I discovered that the ships were collecting people from smaller boats and dinghies that were shuttling from a deepwater pier a half-mile away. The sand, my bags, and the crush of people converging on the place from all directions made it impossible to run, so I slowed to an aggressive walk. I had thought there were maybe 500 civilians left in town, but there were already thousands moving toward the piers, and thousands more clawing at paddleboats, dinghies, rowboats, and anything else that floated in order to get out to the deepwater and clamber aboard a huge, gray cruiser at anchor a half-mile from shore. They were all refugees, or about to become such.

Someone on the deck of the ferry that served as the main shuttle from the beach to the cruiser threw a rope ladder over the stern and instantly a crowd began fighting over who would be first up. There was no contest. Young men pushed old ladies into the surf and clambered up the rope ladder like monkeys. I was tired, really tired, but decided to make some sort of parting gesture of decency. Wading out in the water until it licked at my stomach, I grabbed some kid by the pants from halfway up the ladder, pulled him back down into the sea, and then slapped him hard.

"Women and children first!" I snarled. It felt like the right thing to say, even though I was sorely tempted to line-jump myself, and shimmy up the ladder to the safety of the deck. We stared at each other hard, and then joined forces in helping several old ladies and a few younger women up the ladder before I let him climb up with one of my bags. He dropped another line down to secure my computer bag. Then I climbed up the rope ladder myself and started hauling people onto the deck from above. A signal was given that the ferry was full; the gangplanks to the pier were removed and the rope ladders pulled up. I looked back at the faces of those left behind, and then turned away.

I was a reporter, a foreigner; it wasn't my war. I was here to tell the story; I couldn't tell it if I stayed in Sukhumi, or got killed. I had to get out. I needed to get out. *They* needed me to get out. They *wanted* me to get out. I spun it this way and I spun it that way, but it always came around to the same point: a woman, child, or elder could have been sitting or standing in the place I now occupied on the way to the offshore ship.

We churned out to the cruiser. The name written on the bow and the stern was *Konstantine Olshanski*. I thought it was Russian but have subsequently been told that it was Ukrainian. I do not know. The cruiser dropped its sea door to link with the ferry exit, and everyone vied to be the first off the ferry and the first aboard the cruiser. The only example of bravery or selflessness I can recall was a young man who, after depositing his mother and sisters aboard the cruiser, took a look around, waved, and dove over the side. He was returning to the fight, swimming back to shore. His mother wailed and fainted. Everywhere else there was chaos and confusion, then pushing, shoving, and punching as the crowd of new refugees began to take out their helpless rage against one another. The commander of the *Konstantine Olshanski* tried to restore order first with a megaphone, then by waving a gun, and finally by ordering his men to deal with the situation as they saw fit. There were many bruises and probably quite a few broken bones aboard the *Konstantine Olshanski* that day.

I was disgusted with it all, with myself, with life. There is nothing quite so pathetic as a refugee at the moment he or she becomes one, and by walking across the gangplank from the ferry to the frigate I would become one, too. Maybe I already was. I waited and waited aboard the ferry until I was almost the last refugee aboard, then crossed to the *Konstantine Olshanski*, joining my fate to a mass of sweating, stinking, terrified people, cheek to jowl in the armory bowels of the big ship. I thought of sardines, slaves in the hold, the passage my ancestors from Germany and Ireland made to America—and then I pulled rank.

"Sailor," I said to one of the marines guarding access to the open deck. "I am a foreign journalist and your commander is expecting me for an interview."

I was soon on the open deck, and secured a berth near a rack of depth charges. The anchor weighed and we started out to sea. I was not even sure where we were heading. Sochi? Sevastopol in the Crimea? Batumi? I did not care. I was alive.

* * *

We docked in at the Georgian port of Poti at around four o'clock in the morning. The tourist brochures and press reports usually describe it as the place that Jason and his Argonauts landed, but there was no piquancy to that notion that night. We were all refugee trash, washed up like dirty driftwood on an unwelcoming shore.

I grabbed my bags and stumbled off the ship, stumbled through the port area, stumbled through unmanned security gates to the streets of the sleeping town, stumbling for a place to sleep. By five I had found a filthy hotel, which was already fully booked with the previous batch of refugees. By six I had managed to convince the night clerk to let me sleep on the office sofa for an hour. At seven he woke me and tried to throw me out before the manager arrived. I fought him off and copped another twisting hour's sleep. At eight I was on the streets again, looking for a ride to Tbilisi, by car, bus, or even train. If Lady Luck continued smiling at me, there might even be an airplane. If not, I was even ready to hitchhike across the country again.

I asked someone where a travel agency might be and was directed around a corner. Entering, I asked for the manager, apologized for my filthy appearance, and explained that it was all due to the fact that I was a foreign correspondent and . . .

He asked my name.

"But they announced on the radio that you are dead," he cried, embracing me like a long-lost brother.

"Perhaps I should call some friends in Tbilisi," I suggested.

Within minutes I had Alexis Rowell on the line at the BBC office.

"He's out!!!!" shrieked Rowell in delight, and then began shouting my future obligations at me against the sweet, background thunder of a chorus of voices belonging to friends and rank strangers gathered in his office, apparently there to attend my wake. "Now Dato will pick you up at the airport and then we go live with *News Hour* at three and then you sit down and write 1,000 words for *US News and World Report* they wanted me to do but you can do it better and then Steve LeVine wants you to do another story for *Newsweek* and then Voice of America will call at eight and then . . ."

The manager of the travel agency rushed me to the airport, where a stripped-down Yak-40 was waiting to carry several other VIP survivors of the siege of Sukhumi to the capital. In addition to a couple of wounded sons of eminent citizens who had responded to Shevardnadze's call to arms, the passenger list included the head of the parliamentarian committee that dealt with soldiers' welfare and the shaven-head boss of the Military Police in Sukhumi, who some people said looked like me without a moustache. An additional passenger was the corpse of a Mkhedrioni militiaman who had managed to escape from Sukhumi only to be gunned down by a street vendor in Poti when the militiaman pocketed a pack of L&M cigarettes but refused to pay. There were technical problems with the plane and, rather than sit around and smell the early rot of the Mkhedrioni, I de-boarded and lay down on a cushion of overgrown grass and weeds at the edge of the runway. It was there, staring at the sky, that I noticed something very odd.

I could hear again. I could hear the birds chirping in the trees, hear the wind rustle through the grass. I could hear dogs barking in the parking lot and people talking in the cafeteria. I could hear the backfire of distant cars, the squeal of brakes, the grease splatter of a hot egg on a stove at the airport canteen. I could hear it all through a great absence: there was no more gunfire, no outgoing and no incoming. I lay in the long, uncut grass outside the terminal and listened to the quiet until I apprehended a quite different, muffled sound.

It was me, sobbing.

Notes

1. Eduard Shevardnadze, *The Future Belongs to Freedom* (London: Sinclair-Stevenson, 1991).

2. I never saw Parker again, although he did send me a photo essay on the adventures of the real "last foreign journalist" in the city when it fell, as published in the UK equivalent of *Soldier of Fortune* magazine, a guns and boots rag called *Combat and Survival*. His frontline exclusive, entitled "The Fall of Suhumi" [sic] appeared in the September 1994 issue. I have no idea where he is today.

12

Aftermath in the Mountains

There was still plenty of trauma and human suffering to go around.

Back in Tbilisi, Alexis and our colleagues from the foreign media hack-pack who had descended on the Georgian capital to cover the disaster celebrated my survival by chiding me for having decided to be "the last man out" of Sukhumi, which simply was not true. My putative employers at the *New York Times*, meanwhile, had decided that the story had already changed sufficiently to render obsolete any copy I might offer. I had left when the city was falling, had I not? It had now fallen, ergo, I was not in a position to write about that, now was I? Besides, the *New York Times Magazine* had already commissioned a tear-jerking story about the trials and travails of Eduard Shevardnadze's return to Georgia, his heroic behavior during the siege and fall of Sukhumi, his abject flight from the city, and his arrival in Moscow the next day as a supplicant to Boris Yeltsin, when Shevy was forced to bend knee and kowtow to the Russian president to allow Georgia to join the Kremlin-dominated Commonwealth of Independent States.

I was told that the reporter in question had spent all of a week in Georgia, and no time at all in Sukhumi, but had managed to hitch a ride on the airplane bringing Shevardnadze to Moscow and had used that opportunity to cadge an intimate interview with the Silver Fox in which he poured out his heart and soul.

"We are alone now…" wrote Simon Sebag Montefiore of the moment, which of course filled me with press-envy boarding on psychotic fury when I read it, and subsequently bad-mouthed the writer for years until I discovered— quite recently and quite by accident, in fact—that he had actually been doing research on his future, monumental study of Stalin, and had just sort of stumbled on the most abjectly humiliating moment in the long career of the Silver Fox. Sorry, Simon…

Meanwhile, back at the front, there was there was another story the *Times* agreed to take a look at.

In addition to the boatloads of refugees washing up in Poti, there was word of a mass migration of the terrified Mingrelian-Georgians moving up and over 12,000 foot passes in the mountains of Svanetia after having been ethnically cleansed from Abkhazia. My stubborn friend Nunu might be among them, if she were still alive. Accordingly, within two days of my evacuation from Sukhumi, I joined a small group of foreign journalists aboard a YAK-40 on our way to the refugee relief staging area of Kutaisi. In addition to the human cargo, the plane was packed to the overhead luggage bins with loaves of bread. A quick estimate suggested that the payload weighed 20,000 pounds on a plane designed to carry forty passengers with a combined weight of half that.

"I swore to my wife that I would not do anything like this and certainly not travel with you," joked Hugh Pope, looking at the plane, the load of bread, and then me. "But I am really tired of watching you journey on to the Bridge Too Far while I stay behind."

"Haha," I said, already feeling woozy.

It was not a pleasant ride.

We took off and flew through turbulence that sent the loaves careening around the cabin like projectiles before making an equally bumpy landing at Kutaisi Airport. There we were transferred, along with a good deal of the bread, to an MI-8 helicopter. The craft lifted off in the impossible way that helicopters do and we were soon gliding over the yellowed, autumn fields, then hills covered with neat rows of grapes, and next apple orchards toward the forests and deep ravines that sliced downward from the Greater Caucasus mountain range. It was a wild, pristine, and virgin place where the soul expands and the mind soars to new poetic heights. But the pristine mountains had become an alpine graveyard. Below us, parallel to the blue and white torrent of the upper Inguri River, we could see a long, snaking line of people moving downward toward the timberline after having made the crest. Above them, still trudging through early winter snowfields were thousands more, clawing their way upward along a logging road that was strewn with discarded vehicles. We circled, throwing bread from the doors and portholes, and flew on, landing on a meadow tucked between natural orchards of apple and walnut trees outside a bucolic township called Gentzivshi, a name I noted at the time but have never been able to find on a map. We were instantly swamped by scores of wounded soldiers and civilians.

I asked about Nunu.

"What are they saying?" asked Hugh, keen to start taking down quotes and testimony, with me doing the translation.

"They say they don't know where she is and don't know if she is alive or dead."

"Who is this 'she'?" Hugh asked.

"A mutual friend," I said, finding it difficult to explain all the details just then.

There were plenty of quotes to be collected, however. Whole life stories of personal tragedy and general misery were a dime a dozen.

"We have lost everything, everything!" cried a fifty-four-year-old man named Vitali Turabilitze. He was camping with his family in a school desperately hoping that his son, who stayed behind in Sukhumi to try to secure the family house from marauders, might still arrive in the last trickle of refugees working their way out of the city. The Turabilitze family began their flight in a Fiat-style car, piled high with what were regarded as essential goods. The car broke down after being rammed by a truck on the narrow, muddy road, forcing the family to abandon their remaining goods and walk.

Upon closer inspection, the dirt road from Sukhumi that served as the artery of expulsion looked like an extended junkyard stretching for miles in either direction. Abandoned cars, jeeps, buses, and even a fire engine cluttered the route to such an extent that upward progress was often impeded until a larger vehicle, like a truck, cleared the path by bumping an abandoned vehicle into a ravine. We nearly ended up in one when we tried to return to the Gentzivshi helicopter landing pad and the car we were in slipped off the road and lurched toward a precipice, stopping just short of the ledge when it encountered some fortuitously placed roots and branches.

"Close call," said Hugh, looking down at the remains of three other vehicles below.

It was late afternoon and there was no sign of the "journalist" helicopter that was supposed to have returned for us at Gentzivshi. Even if the chopper returned, there was no way to get back; all traffic (such as it was) was in the other direction, coming up and over the mountain.

So we walked. Then we jogged. Then we ran. Then we walked again. Then we heard the unique *WHOOP-WHOOP* droning of an MI-8 and started to sprint. Fifteen minutes later we arrived at a township I noted in my pad as being called "Senaki," but which cannot possibly be right because Senaki is south of Zugdidi and in the plains, so the township we headed toward was probably Lakhamula, Kveda Marghi, or a village associated with one of those two tiny places in the mountains. Anyway, we got there and followed a steady stream of refugees to a sloping pasture surrounded by thick forest that had been turned into an emergency helipad. A crushed and burned MI-8 chopper lay at the far end of the field, reminding everyone who cared to think about it of the limitations of trying to land a whirlybird in the woods.

We were not alone. Many others had also heard the helicopter and come running to try to get aboard and get out: men and women, young and old, school teachers, nurses, drivers, farmers, "businessmen," and those who found it difficult to define themselves by profession. If there was once a sense of class or caste, it had been erased due to an equal share of defeat, loss, and abject misery. There were weeping grandmothers with bandages on their heads, bearded intellectuals searching for a logical answer to their dilemma, and crying infants with fever in their limbs and dehydration in their eyes. There were also sheepish looking soldiers with full clips of ammunition in their belts, eyeing young girls who, just like those I had seen on the evacuation beaches, seemed to have dressed up for a date in their Sunday best and makeup, oblivious to the national disaster they represented.

"The government has done nothing for us—the army did not defend our homes in Sukhumi, and now it is leaving us to die in the mountains!" wailed a woman named Lana Tzulayia, trying to fend for her shattered daughter-in-law and two children. "We have lost everything but our lives, and now these are to be taken from us due to more neglect. There is no food, no helicopters, no water—nothing. And all due to the criminal lack of organization in Tbilisi."

I told her I was tired of people making speeches. She said she understood, but that the only reason she had spoken to me in such a tone was as a familiar: I had known her son, Vata, and he had been killed during the siege of the city. I said I was sorry, very sorry, and if there was anything I could do . . .

She said there actually was something. I could take down a list of names and telephone numbers of people to call if and when I got back to Tbilisi, to let her relatives know that she was alive but that her son was dead. I promised to do my best. I guess someone overheard our conversation, because soon dozens of other people began flocking around me with requests of their own, some of which were quite elaborate and even excessive, and I guess I told them so.

"Why are you shouting at these poor people?" Hugh asked.

Once again, it was difficult to explain.

Soldiers and guardsmen attempted to establish something akin to priority evacuation lines, but when the helicopter arrived, all semblance of order broke down. Screaming mobs stormed through the lines of gunmen, all determined to be the first aboard.[1]

Happily, I knew from prior experience in war-torn Azerbaijan how to get on an MI-8 in a disaster zone.

Let me tell you how: while the mass of refugees kick, scratch, and jostle with each other in front of the main door, go around to the back of the chopper. Place one foot on the wheel, hoist yourself up on the fuel tank, kick in the portal window and dive through, performing a somersault to clear a path among the bodies inside. Never go in feet first, as it is unlikely that you will make it: someone else who is already inside (myself, for example) will try to force you back out. If you have any girth, it is a good idea to strip down to your shirtsleeves because bulky sweaters, jackets, and dangling objects like a camera may impede your entry. I am a solidly built guy of 5 ft. 10 in. and

185 pounds, and I only just fit through an MI-8 window, so gauge yourself accordingly. Go in head first and roll.

Once inside, try to get people to move toward the back of the chopper to make room at the door and windows for more. Wailing loads of refugees have the collective sense of sheep and tend to gather at the front of the chopper and block the door. Don't be bashful about using force. Climb over the screaming infants and weeping grandmothers to the door to control the numbers of people getting aboard. This, too, may require getting a bit rough, but your life depends on keeping the combined weight aboard the chopper down to a reasonable overload, so do what you have to do. The MI-8 is designed to carry twenty-four people, and luggage, but in a refugee zone this usually goes up to sixty or even eighty people. Although it is difficult to make a head count, never, ever fly aboard an MI-8 with more than a hundred people. If you cannot evict enough folks to bring the total number down to two digits, like ninety-nine, get off because the bird will likely crash and everyone, including yourself, will probably get killed. Once the rotors start and the chopper lurches off the ground, position yourself behind the flight engineer so you can peer into the cockpit. This is actually a pretty useless exercise but it is a good distraction, because the alternative is to stare at the mob behind you in the chopper body, and that is the last thing you need to do to keep your wits. An additional aid to help do exactly that is to regard yourself as dead until you are provably alive again, meaning back on terra firma.

"Nice knowing you!" I shouted at Pope over the motor roar and whine, extending my hand. He grabbed it and looked me in the eye and tried to shout something back. I had not explained my "you are dead until you are alive and on the ground again" theory, but he seemed to intuitively understand the argument.

The rotors swung and the craft grunted and groaned and we began to fly. Squishing myself between the wailing mob in back and the door to the cockpit, I had a perfect view of the treetops ready to skewer us if we dropped more than a foot or two. The snowline was at 10,000 feet and the pass at 12,000, and we chugged right on up and over despite the fact that we were double the weight limit. Then we started down, careening through steep ravines and gullies as the pilot showed off his stuff.

It is a lot easier to show off your prowess as a pilot going down than up, especially if your chopper is overloaded. I wasn't much impressed and neither were most of the other folks onboard. Quite a few got sick. Quite a few started to lose their minds. I had to slap one old codger before he went into shock and collapsed because if he fell a dozen people would collapse on him, and I was at the end of the potential pile. So I slapped him hard and he howled but didn't fall down. Jesus, he was scared. You had to be nuts not to be.

We touched down at a couple of villages forgotten by time to disgorge a dozen passengers here and pick up another dozen there. One village was quite striking: it was studded by stone guard towers, each one looking like a miniature Washington Monument with windows, and was one of those places you would always like to return to and explore, but know you never will.[2]

Finally, at dusk, the MI-8 landed at the Kutaisi airport where we had begun our journey some twelve hours before.

"Well," said Hugh. "I didn't let you go one bridge further than me this time!"

"You're right," I said. "You went the same distance."

"I like traveling with you, but thank God it's over," he said.

"We still have to get back to Tbilisi," I pointed out.

"Nothing can be as frightening as that ride," said Hugh.

Once again, it did feel good to be alive.

Then I noticed a YAK-40 behind us that seemed to be loading passengers. We ran across the tarmac and arrived at the rear stairs just as the hostess was closing the door.

"Tbilisi!" we shouted.

"*Billety!*" she shouted back over the YAK-40's whining motors.

"What?!" I shouted, still wearing the earplugs I had shoved in the ol' auditory canal to cut the rotor noise of the MI-8. I was probably overdoing it on the volume a bit, but it really didn't matter to me where the plane was going. *Billety*, fine. It was probably close enough to get a taxi to the capital. Then it occurred to me. *Billety*—tickets! *Tickets!* Hahaha! What a gal! Gotta ticket? Gotta gun? Tickets! *Ha! Ha! Ha!* . . .

"Come on up, boys!" cackled the buxom stewardess at her own joke, and we clambered up the stairs, avoiding the drops of hot oil seeping down from somewhere in the fuselage, and got onboard, laughing like old friends.

There were no seats left anyway, even if she really wanted tickets for them. All had been taken either by military policemen on furlough from the civil war or by their mates who would never enjoy anything but the cold ground: corpses on stretchers, slung between the seats, and crowding the narrow corridor. That was one of the perks of having friends killed. Entire units would pull themselves off the line to bury one man, even if the graveyard was 300 miles away. While a nice gesture, it certainly wasn't a very efficient way to fight a war, especially a civil one. The men on the plane (allegedly Shevardnadze's personal jet) had all been in action that morning against the Position forces of Zviad Gamsakhurdia, led by Commander Loti "the Drunk" Kubalia, and had taken a beating. Kutaisi, it was said, was about to fall. This was a matter of indifference to us, however, perched in the only available space on the plane—the floor between the luggage rack and the toilet. The good-natured stewardess, whose name was Nana, sat on my boot even though my foot was still in it. I guess it was more comfortable than the steel floor, which was pretty muddy.

So there we were, camped on the floor between the toilet and the hand-luggage rack, the former reeking of old urine and unflushed feces and the latter filled with the MP's collection of Kalashnikovs, sniper rifles, and the odd RPG. A couple of assault rifles fell down at takeoff and Nana removed her butt from my boot to pick one up.

"Watch this," she said, and began to disassemble the gun. She got the magazine clip off, but had more trouble with the firing mechanism and springs. Black grease was soon smeared all over her hands, blouse, and dress. The head of the MPs then came back and gave her a few tips and bounced her on his knee while she tried to reassemble the weapon. When she had succeeded, she turned, and pointed the barrel at my head.

"You like our country?" she asked me.

I assured her this was so.

"It's a crazy place, isn't it?"

Then she pulled the trigger.

Click . . .

The head of the MPs chortled, and bounced Nana with gusto. She threw the gun back in the luggage rack and reached her greasy hand into her bra, extracting the equivalent of a nickel bag of marijuana.

"Try this," she said, trying to make up and be friends.

I opened the bag, took a taste and pronounced it as excellent.

"Give me that," said the MP boss.

"Sure," said Nana, and rolled him a joint.

"No one will ever believe this if you tell them," said Hugh.

* * *

When we landed in Tbilisi, I sought out and found a man flying up to Moscow on another flight that night, and prevailed upon him to take the six rolls of print film I had shot in Sukhumi and the mountains to the bureau of the *New York Times*. He was as good as his word and the film arrived safely in Moscow. Then the *Times* bureau sent the film to New York for processing and use, where my entire Sukhumi collection was promptly lost by a photo editor who claimed it had never arrived, which was quite simply an ass-covering lie.[3] Next, we taxied over to the Metechi Palace Hotel to have a cold beer and a house-special hamburger and fries. However incongruous, we felt we deserved it.

It had been a long day.

Sitting in the lobby like a Londonderry lord was my old friend Rory Peck, who called me over for a couple of drinks and a chat about having survived Sukhumi and the mission in the mountains. If it had been anyone else, I might have punched him, but Rory was that swashbuckling kind of cameraman and war aficionado who made it impossible not to giggle along with him about the absurdity of this Vale of Tears.

"We just have to do our job," chortled Rory. "No one else seems to want to."

He flew up to Moscow the next day and was killed the day after that while filming for German ARD TV when Boris Yeltsin turned his guns first on parliament and then on protestors marching on the Ostankino Television tower.

The first report I heard was that Rory had been wounded; then wounded badly in the head. I was already giddy with relief that it would all be okay, when someone from the Moscow BBC called to tell me Rory was already in a morgue.

I hit the streets of Tbilisi in as bleak and black a mood as I could recall ever having owned, which soon magnified a thousandfold when I found myself staring into a familiar face smack dab in the middle of the Rustaveli Avenue sidewalk.

It was Nunu Chachua's sister, Nana.

"*Tomas?*" she said, looking at me as if she had just seen an apparition. The rest of the world disappeared and the enormity of the catastrophe washed over me like a new tsunami of death, destruction, and destroyed dreams. "Where are they?"

I waited in silence for what I knew had to come.

"You don't know?"

I tried to explain that Nunu would not leave, and that her mother Lamara would not go without Nunu.

"You left them there?"

Then Nana collapsed on the street, wailing and punching and clawing and screaming at me in Georgian as I tried to help her up, help her, and help myself.

"YOU LEFT THEM THERE?"

There was nothing to be done but receive her blows and try to hold her.

But she would not be held by the likes of me.

Notes

1. Ghia Tarkhan-Mouravi, a descendant of the last Georgian queen, friend of Georgi Derluguian, and an acquaintance of mine, was at this exact time organizing a group of mountain climbers to lead the fleeing civilians out of danger, and expressed astonishment at how many people were dying from exposure simply due to a lack of organization and leadership. Accordingly, he and his mountaineers decided to impose what discipline they

could on the exodus, selecting campsites for the night, starting fires, and forcing the refugees to cook and take care of each other. One day a white cargo plane appeared over their heads and began dropping containers with American humanitarian aid. It turned out to be some sort of Weight Watchers dietary shake similar in concept to the infamous (or just ridiculous) Slim-Fast noodles I had seen being distributed in Sukhumi. Ghia was very bitter. Not only was much of the food aid past its last date of recommended use, but in the mountains, it takes twice the regular amount of calories to keep people healthy and moving and the last thing needed was low-cal powder to mix with dirty water from streams.

2. I later learned that it was the venue for a famous Soviet-era film called *Mimino* about a Georgian helicopter pilot with delusions of grandeur who somehow ends up sharing a room in a Moscow hotel with an Armenian truck driver, and which was quite a popular ethno-art movie among the late-Soviet-era Caucasian student crowd.

3. A year later, when visiting the *Times*'s offices in New York on another matter, I convinced an assistant photo editor to look under "G" for Goltz, "G" for Georgia, "T" for Thomas, "S" for Sukhumi, and "A" for Abkhazia, under which letter I discovered one of the developed rolls, but with no photographer I.D. attached. Having proven that the pictures were actually there, I wanted to search for the others, but was not allowed to do so because it would have meant tearing the entire archive apart. I was tempted to do so on my own, because by that time, my relationship with the *New York Times* had been reduced to almost zero, and getting kicked out of the Grey Old Lady by security might have actually been kind of fun. But I did not want the assistant photo editor to lose his job, so I just took the one roll I had found and swore never to send the pictures department another image.

Georgia—Land of ancient churches tucked in hidden, wooded valleys. *Courtesy of Abkhazia Information Center in Exile, Tbilisi.*

The "Red Riviera"— The Black Sea coast of Abkhazia/Georgia was the fun-in-the-sun playground for Soviet citizens from Murmansk to Kamchatka, with revenues to go along with the trade. *Courtesy of Abkhazia Information Center in Exile, Tbilisi.*

Tbilisi is bisected by the gently flowing Mtkvari (Kura) River. The city's name means "warm waters," after its natural hot springs. It has been everybody's favorite town in the Caucasus for over 1,500 years. *Courtesy of Abkhazia Information Center in Exile, Tbilisi.*

Modern gargoyles greet the passersby on Tbilisi's Rustaveli Avenue.
Yola Monakhov, Photographer.

Young Georgian women pray to Saint Nino at Kakheti church and tomb-shrine. The fourth-century saint brought Christianity to the Georgians. *Yola Monakhov, Photographer.*

An Ahiska Turk (Meskhetian Turk/Georgian Muslim) at prayer. *Giorgi Tsagareli, Photographer.*

The cult of the gun starts young in Georgia. *Giorgi Tsagareli, Photographer.*

The Georgian Orthodox church has always been an essential part of Georgian national identity, in history and today. *Giorgi Tsagareli, Photographer.*

VE-Day in Georgia—Veterans of the Great Patriotic War against Hitler celebrate the 50th anniversary of victory with a shot of state-supplied vodka, honoring their heroism. *Giorgi Tsagareli, Photographer.*

Georgia's native son, Joseph Stalin, still beloved by many for turning an agrarian state into a superpower. *Giorgi Tsagareli, Photographer.*

Last meeting of Komsomol (Young Communist League) members in Lavrenti Beria's former residence in Tbilisi before dissolution of the Communist Party in Georgia, April 1991. *Giorgi Tsagareli, Photographer.*

Georgian citizens mourn victims of the April 9, 1989 crackdown in Tbilisi. *Giorgi Tsagareli, Photographer.*

Zviad Gamsakhurdia, leader of the Georgian independence movement in 1989–1990, ousted from power in 1991 and succeeded by Eduard Shevardnadze. *Courtesy of Abkhazia Information Center in Exile, Tbilisi.*

Battered apartment block in South Ossetia. Breaking free of Georgia in 1991, the region has become a "black hole" in international affairs, although tacitly controlled by Russia. *Giorgi Tsagareli, Photographer.*

All quiet on the western side of the street: Anti-Gamsakhurdia forces survey the scene during the Hundred Meters War in downtown Tbilisi, December 1991. *Giorgi Tsagareli, Photographer.*

"Tekhnika" in front of shattered ruins of Tbilisi's Intourist Hotel on Rustaveli Avenue, ground zero of the Hundred Meters War of December 1992. After a decade of neglect, the hotel was restored and reopened by the Marriott group in 2002. *Courtesy of Abkhazia Information Center in Exile, Tbilisi.*

On the front in South
Ossetia, a fighter's girlfriend
ponders the future of a land
filled with weapons.
Giorgi Tsagareli, Photographer.

Ground zero, Tbilisi, post-putsch January 1992. At center is the burnt shell of the historic "Gymnasium Number One" and to its right (viewer's left) the shattered remains of the Parliament. *Courtesy of Abkhazia Information Center in Exile, Tbilisi.*

The return of the Silver Fox: Former Soviet foreign minister and Mikhail Gorbachev's confidant Eduard Shevardnadze returns to Tbilisi from Moscow in March 1992 at the behest of the triumvirate that drove Zviad Gamsakhurdia from power in December 1991. *Giorgi Tsagareli, Photographer.*

Georgian volunteer militia redeploys in Abkhazia. *Courtesy of Abkhazia Information Center in Exile, Tbilisi.*

Georgian refugees flee Abkhazia into the towering Caucasus Mountains in Svaneti following the fall of Sukhumi. *Courtesy of Abkhazia Information Center in Exile, Tbilisi.*

Inhabitants of Tagiloni, an ethnic Georgian village inside Gali province of Abkhazia, watch their homes burning from a destroyed railway bridge over the Inguri River on May 25, 1998. *Dima Chikvaidze, photographer, Courtesy of Abkhazia Information Center in Exile, Tbilisi.*

Smoke billows from the Abkhazian Government House/Parliament building a day after the chaotic retreat of the Georgian "army" from Sukhumi, leaving their dead behind, on September 30, 1993. *Courtesy of Abkhazia Information Center in Exile, Tbilisi.*

Zviad Gamsakhurdia's funeral on February 25, 1994, in front of his residence-in-exile in Grozny, Chechnya. Note Gamaskhurdia's host, Chechen president Djohar Dudayev, standing against the wall at upper right. Manana Gamsakhurdia, regarded as "Lady Macbeth" by opponents, stands over coffin. *Courtesy of Abkhazia Information Center in Exile, Tbilisi.*

Mothers mourn their fallen sons years after their heavy loss in 1993.
Stanley Greene, Photographer.

Vladislav Ardzimba (l) and Eduard Shevardnadze (r) appear on state television to negotiate the status of Abkhazia in 1993. *Courtesy of Abkhazia Information Center in Exile, Tbilisi.*

Heartbreak Hotel—The Iveria, in downtown Tbilisi, home to hundreds of refugees from Abkhazia. The refugee residents, who had lived there for more than a decade, often five to a room, were bought out for a reported $7,000 per hotel unit in late 2005 by developers who intend to either restore or raze it. *JoAnne Beringer, Photographer.*

The Silver Fox—Eduard Shevardnadze, shortly before his forced resignation, after almost four decades of power. *Stanley Greene, Photographer.*

Georgians celebrate the first anniversary of Mikheil (Misha) Saakashvili's Rose Revolution in November 2004. *Giorgi Tsagareli, Photographer.*

The mercurial Mikheil Saakashvili at his swearing-in ceremony as third president of Georgia on January 25, 2004. Note the new national flag, that of Saint George, which was previously his party's banner. *David Mdzinarishvili, photographer, Courtesy of Abkhazia Information Center in Exile, Tbilisi.*

Vardzia—the 11th century "Hidden Monastery" carved into the cliffs above the upper Mtkvari River. Once a major tourist destination in Soviet times, the stunning cave-complex attracts only a handful of hardy travelers a year, down a good road gone bad.
Thomas Goltz, Photographer.

PROGRAM

MODERATOR
Mr. Hugh E. Price
Associate Deputy Director for Operations

PRESENTATION OF COLORS
Central Intelligence Agency Color Guard

NATIONAL ANTHEM
The Keynotes

REMARKS
Mr. R. James Woolsey
Director of Central Intelligence

AMERICA THE BEAUTIFUL
The Keynotes

EULOGIES
N. John MacGaffin, III
Chief, Central Eurasia Division
Colleagues
Allyson Woodruff, daughter

GOD BLESS AMERICA
The Keynotes

TAPS

I bequeath myself to the dirt
to grow from the grass I love,
If you want me again
look for me under your boot soles.

You will hardly know who I am or what I mean,
But I shall be good health to you nevertheless,
And filter and fibre your blood.

Failing to fetch me at first keep encouraged,
Missing me one place search another,
I stop somewhere waiting for you.

Walt Whitman

Freddie Woodruff funeral program. *Special thanks to Georgia Woodruff Alexander.*

IV
THERE DWELL DRAGONS

Shattered tombstone of the second grave of Zviad Gamsakhurdia, amid the general ruins of Grozny, Chechnya, circa March 1995. Credit: Thomas Goltz.

13

Chaos in the Caucasus

The white horse, draped with a Georgian flag, walked gingerly, its hoofs slipping on the thin layer of ice covering the streets. Behind it came an APC, towing the casket on a gun caisson. It was followed by a wall of women, all dressed in black. They wept as they walked, clenching their fists above their heads. The man they were mourning was Zviad Gamsakhurdia, who had died, was killed, or committed suicide in the mountains of western Georgia two months before, but was now about to be reburied in the courtyard of his residence-in-exile in Grozny, the dreary capital city of the breakaway Chechen Republic in the Russian North Caucasus. My quest for Gamsakhurdia was finally over: I was within three feet of him but had never met the man.

It was February 24, 1994, less than five months after the fall of Sukhumi and the chaotic march of misery in the mountains, and the world had lurched on. Specifically, while I and a couple of other foreign hacks had been charting the aftermath of the Georgia collapse in Abkhazia, Eduard Shevardnadze had been up in Moscow, negotiating with Boris Yeltsin on the matter of how Georgia might immediately be brought into the Commonwealth of Independent States.[1] While the public issues were diverse, the essential, unspoken question was how the extant Russian military bases in Georgia might be legally reestablished, or achieve legality. The answer was that in exchange for maintaining the status quo (and perhaps in remembrance of the fact that Shevardnadze was one of the few Politburo members not known to have publicly mocked and abused Yeltsin when he left the Communist Party in 1990), Yeltsin would deliver a little Russian military muscle to help Shevardnadze put down the new rebellion sweeping western Georgia.

And the new rebellion did not involve the hated Abkhaz. Taking advantage of Georgian military (and moral) collapse in Sukhumi, Zviad Gamsakhurdia had returned from exile in Chechnya and landed in Zugdidi, to declare himself restored to power. Shevardnadze, by definition, was nothing other than a foul usurper.

Events passed quickly.

Zugdidi, Poti, Kutaisi!

With Zviad's men marching on Tbilisi, Shevardnadze agreed to the Russian conditions (subject to ratification by the Georgian parliament) of Georgia joining the mutual security pact of the Commonwealth of Independent States. Yeltsin, meanwhile, freed up enough Russian armor to add spine to Shevardnadze's battered forces. The tide soon turned, the Zviadist revolt collapsed and Gamsakhurdia fled into the mountains where he died in mysterious circumstances on December 31, 1993, to be buried secretly in an unmarked grave. Then, in an effort to heal wounds and bury the recent bitter past (and to confirm that Gamsakhurdia was indeed really dead), Shevardnadze agreed to allow Zviad's widow Manana to bring the body to Grozny, Chechnya, for reburial and a state funeral. The Georgian state forensic authorities would be satisfied with a visual confirmation that the corpse in question was indeed Gamsakhurdia; no autopsy would be performed.

Standing at the graveside, with Georgian dirges playing on the speaker system, Chechen President Djohar Dudayev spoke of his deep friendship with Zviad, a "true son of the Caucasus," and their common effort to make a "Caucasus Home" free of Russia that would include all the small nations of the area.

"I begged him not to return to Georgia," intoned Dudayev. "I knew that only disaster would ensue. But he would not listen. . . ."

All of the eulogizers condemned Eduard Shevardnadze as a stooge of Russia.

"I am ashamed that I am a Russian," said a woman who identified herself as the representative of something called the "St. Petersburg Decolonization Movement." "Forgive me, people of Georgia, for the support my government gave to the putschist junta and its leader, Shevardnadze!"

As for the question of just how Zviad had really met his end—disease, assassination from within his movement, suicide—there was silence, speculation, and smoke screen.

"Zviad Gamsakhurdia may not have been the most intelligent man in Georgia, but he was the bravest—and did what a brave man had to do," said my old friend Merab Kiknadze from those early Sukhumi days, standing with me at the edge of the mourners as the speeches went on and on that cold February day.

"What do you mean by that?" I asked Merab, who had been living in exile at times in Grozny and at other times in Sweden.

"Don't ask me anymore," he said elliptically. "I don't speak to the press anymore after the way your profession maligned, lied about, and then crucified him."

"But you are talking to me."

"You are different, sort of," said Merab. "But I still want to know why you let Shevardnadze off so lightly in that *Foreign Policy* piece of yours."[2]

"You read it?"

"We read everything," snarled Merab.

"I couldn't get it published any other way."

"Oh."

We stood together and listened to the speeches and eulogies for hours, it seemed. And it was bitterly cold. Finally, mercifully, Gamsakhurdia's wife Manana was pulled off the casket while pallbearers, led by an incense-sprinkling priest, lifted Zviad and placed him in the earth of Muslim Chechnya.

The Gamsakhurdia-Shevardnadze rivalry was over, at last.

"Remember that night in Sukhumi when I told you that you could see Zviad?" Merab mused as we walked away from the single-entry graveyard, referring to the Gamsakhurdia video night way back when in Sukhumi, circa February 1992. "We actually hoped we might be able to win, that the West would support us. We miscalculated badly."

"I'll say."

"Georgia has now entered a long dark period," he sighed. "I can only hope that future generations appreciate what they have lost, but I doubt they will."

"Do you remember Nunu Chachua?" I asked.

"Sure, the woman who ran the theater."

"That's the one. Any word about her?"

"Dead, probably," said Merab. "But then again I thought you were, too."

"Yeah," I replied. "I heard the same about you, but here you are, alive."

* * *

The next morning, Alexis Rowell offered to smuggle me out of Chechnya to Georgia via the Russian subrepublics of Ingushetia and North Ossetia and its capital city, Vladikavkaz. Both sides of the road into town were lined with burnt-out buildings and empty streets, the result of yet another short and nasty war that had never made it onto the international radar screen but continued to simmer until exploding onto the world stage with the horrible slaughter of school children in the town of Beslan in 2004.

My understanding with Alexis was that if I got caught trying to sneak out of Russia it was my own problem, and that I would not hold it against him if he left me in the lurch. I said fine. At the frontier post, I found myself chatting with the chief duty officer, an Ossetian guy who had a pen pal in Chicago, USA.

"I'm from Montana," I said.

"That is still the USA, right?"

He waved us on without even bothering to ask for my exit visa from the Russian Federation. Alexis was furious.

"The most rigidly controlled border in all of Russia and you just walk through it!"

"Just lucky, I guess."

* * *

In preparation for the rigors of life in cold and dark Tbilisi, Alexis and I dropped in at the Marco Polo ski resort at Gudauri for a couple days on the slopes. The contrast between life at the resort for those who could afford it and the grinding existence of ordinary mortals in the capital who could not was acute, starting with dress code. In Tbilisi, professor-paupers such as my friend Alexander Rondeli went to bed in the greatcoats they had been wearing all day to stay warm, while on the slopes of Gudauri, the standard uniform was spandex jumpers and matching Gortex parkas by day, and Marks and Spencer (or Italian) après-ski evening togs for dinner and disco by night.

Built in 1988 as an extension of the Metechi Palace Hotel in downtown Tbilisi, the Marco Polo resort was designed to attract foreign skiers to the towering mountains that define the frontier between Soviet Georgia and Russia, and thus serving as a cash cow for hard currency. The list price for a week in the resort was $2,000 per person, with food and lift tickets (but not helicopter service to high altitude powder) included in the bill. For those interested in other sports, there was an indoor tennis court, a weight-room/sauna complex, and even kegel ball bowling. The sex trade was also discretely represented.

"The conditions here are excellent and the staff is very friendly," said one of the few foreign guests at Gudauri, who confessed that one reason he was there was for adventure's sake. "There aren't too many giant slalom enthusiasts who want to ski a country that is sliding into social chaos."

Faced with financial ruin, the resort had initiated discounts for locals in order to keep Gudauri afloat. The price for a single was $50 a night, although drinks were no longer included. That may sound pretty steep for citizens of a country where the monthly wage of a professor equaled about that much, when paid. But cost was not of much concern for most of the guests, and there was no real mystery about who the skiers were: gentlemen (and their ladies) connected with the murky Georgia underground, and specifically with the much-feared *Mkhedrioni*, or "Knight-Horsemen" paramilitary organization.

Confronted with all too frequent power outages and attendant lack of running water in the capital, Tbilisi, the Mkhedrioni, being more equal than anyone else in the country, chose a unique way to wait out the cold and dreary winter weather. Rather than shuffle through deserted shops by day and shiver through the long dark nights in Tbilisi, they checked into the Marco Polo.

"I come up every weekend to escape from Tbilisi," said a young "boogie board" enthusiast named Irakli Toradze, who said he had an interest in "construction." "It is in our nature to try and enjoy life, even in the face of adversity."

After a surreal weekend at Gudauri, Lex and I pushed on down the Great Military Highway toward Tbilisi, only learning a few days later that we had missed a good piece of theater at the ski resort. A Svanetian cook, insulted by a visiting Mkhedrioni boss whose comments on the quality of the dinner buffet went just a little too far, threatened the guest with a butcher knife. The knight responded by pulling his gun and shooting the cook in the legs. The cook, in turn, vowed revenge by bringing up relatives from a nearby Svanetian village renown for its mean streak, whereupon the Knight called up armed reinforcements from Tbilisi. A showdown in the lobby between the two groups was only narrowly averted by last minute negotiations initiated by other guests.

"It was almost like Tbilisi," said one witness.

* * *

No, there was nothing quite like Tbilisi that late winter/early spring of 1994. A few lucky folks like Lawrence Sheets had fireplaces in their apartments, but most homes depended on gas and there was none, or too little to talk about. Or electricity, aside from little spurts of juice after midnight, when televisions and radios would suddenly blare, waking up their owners—which was good, because the sudden surge in power also announced that city water would soon be gushing out of bathroom and kitchen spigots, and it was not uncommon to forget when a faucet was on or off.

Yes, Georgia had hit rock bottom. It was beyond grim—and far worse than the exaggerated (and well-advertised) "winter from hell" in Armenia the year before. The difference between the two might have been that in Yerevan, people seemed to delight in suffering—and in displaying their real but self-created discomforts as if they were holy wounds.

In Tbilisi, most folks bore up under the cross of adversity by remaining furiously silent behind their frosty lips.

Their stoic mien was tested on all fronts. The Tbilisi metro was usually out of service, forcing those who actually went to work to walk or try to flag down cars driven by people who were reluctant to pick up strangers due to endemic car-jackings. Gasoline was of poor quality, when available at all, and engine repair almost impossible due to a general lack of spare parts. Half the city's telephone lines were out of service at any given time, and the university had to postpone commencing its winter semester due to a lack of heat in the classrooms. Breadlines formed every morning at subsidized government outlets, and the Salvation Army opened up a soup kitchen that soon proved itself to be too small for demand.

The motif of misery, however, remained electricity. The only district that enjoyed consistent power was that immediately around the parliamentary building, where Georgian head of state Eduard Shevardnadze had his office. Even there, however, voltage was low. A live broadcast of the discussion and voting about Georgia's entry into the Russian-dominated CIS was effectively censored not because the government was afraid of what the opposition would say—the session was carried on radio—but because the transmitter could only send an audio-visual signal that appeared on working television sets as a wash of color and static.

If the situation in Tbilisi was bad, the state of affairs in the rest of the country was chaotic. In the south, home to an eclectic mixture of ethnic Azeris, Armenians, and displaced Svanetian tribesmen, the frequent sabotaging of the railway and gas lines leading to Armenia attracted periodic attention and alarm. Suspicion usually fell on the ethnic Azeris of the region, although all my interlocutors among that group maintained that it was all a government plot designed to give security officials the excuse to displace them. In the southwest, meanwhile, Moscow had managed to pressure Tbilisi to accept, in principle, the return of the Meskhetian (Ahiska) Turks to their ancestral lands in Akhaltsikhe and Akhalkhala, the latter now inhabited mainly by ethnic Armenians who were allegedly being armed by the local Russian army base in order to resist (and possibly to pursue a Karabakh-style move toward autonomy or independence). The only place or province in Georgia that seemed reasonably stable was Adjaria, run almost as a separate fiefdom under the iron hand of "Batono" Aslan Abashidze, the old communist-cum-mafia lord, whom many both in and out of the country were starting to consider as a replacement for Shevardnadze. And Abkhazia, of course, had become a depopulated wasteland, a land of burnt houses, barren fields, and banal violence. Of the 500,000 people living there during my first visit in 1992 less than a third remained.

"What do they want from us?" howled Alex Rondeli over a long, liquid lunch one day, referring to the continued efforts by Moscow to dismember Georgia. "At every meeting we have with the Russians, they demand more and more and more. It seems to me that Georgia is to be sacrificed on the altar of Russia's revenge against Shevardnadze for being the man who dismembered the USSR!"

"Alex," I said. "You have to admit that each and every one of Zviad's paranoid predictions have come true—the rape of Sukhumi by the Mkhedrioni . . ."

"Yes, yes . . ."

" . . . followed by the loss of the province . . ."

"Yes, yes . . ."

" . . . and finally by Shevardnadze's bringing Georgia into the CIS . . ."

"Yes, yes . . ."

" . . . and the stationing of Russian troops here."

"Yes, yes . . . a thousand times yes!"

"Well?"

"Your arguments are all correct and are all based in experience and objective fact but still lack the essential subjective element."

"Which is?"

"This is *Georgia*, Soviet Georgia. Not 'post-Soviet' or 'independent' or any of the other constructions you journalists and researchers from the West come up with but *Soviet Georgia*, the place subjected to the game of smoke and mirrors for the past seventy years. . . . It is not your American state by the same name where one and one equals two, or maybe three. Here it equals five, or maybe six. I cannot prove it to you logically. But if you live here long enough you will know it *does* equal five or six or seven, too."

"Alex, you are drunk . . ."

"Yes, of course I am—because I am *Georgian*. But while we are drunk, why not consider this as an alternative to your Shevardnadze scenario? *A catastrophe!* You have seen what has happened with all the nationalist leaders and parties in the Caucasus—unmitigated disaster and human suffering! *A catastrophe!* Look at Azerbaijan! Look at Chechnya! Have you ever considered that those very same *lumpen-nationalist* leaders, all of whom spent enough time in KGB jails or in the security services to be 'turned,' are not the real agents of destruction in their native lands? *A catastrophe!* Think about that, I beg you!"

* * *

I did think about just that when I applied for an interview with Eduard Shevardnadze. Access was easy. I called Gia Janjgava and was immediately whisked into Shevardnadze's office in the parliamentary building on Rustaveli Avenue. The Silver Fox greeted me as some sort of comrade in arms—or at least the man wounded by a maybe-rabid dog in Sukhumi.

Goltz:	Sir, it is good to see you again, certainly better than the last time . . .
Shevy:	By God, it's true—I thought you were dead!
Goltz:	No, it got a little scary—but in comparison with your escape, mine was banal. I only got bit by that dog.

Shevy:	Yes! *Haha!* The dog! *Haha!* How is the bite?
Goltz:	I was worried because the doctors say that dogs in war zones are more apt to have rabies than others, you know, all the corpses and fetid stuff, but here I am, six months later and still alive! Rabies kicks in after two or three months, they tell me . . .
Shevy:	Ah, but that is American rabies!! Here in the Caucasus, the incubation period is much longer. . . . You still might die!!
Together:	*Hahahahaha!*
Goltz:	But how did you get out? I have heard so many different versions—ship, helicopter, plane . . .
Shevy:	It was fantastic, I still cannot believe it myself. We thought we had made an arrangement with the Russians for a helicopter, but that fell through. Then we were resolved to taking a ship out, but word came that gun-ships were waiting to sink us, and that became impossible, too. So we went out to the airport and discovered there one plane that had been blasted by machinegun fire through its wings and had lost most of its aviation fuel but that could still fly. We took that plane, although there was only enough fuel left in it to take off and land. Basically, we glided to Batumi, after which we got another plane and came here.

Then we sat down, turned on the tape and camera, and began our "formal" interview in Georgian with a translator.

The date was February 28, 1994, just before Shevy's first official visit to the United States, on the occasion of the forty-ninth meeting of the General Assembly of the United Nations.

Goltz:	What is your assessment of the situation in Georgia after the death of Zviad Gamsakhurdia and the likelihood of national reconciliation?
Shevardnadze:	I pitied him; and his death was a sad thing for me because Gamsakhurdia was already dead as a political figure, and his movement did not represent a political threat to the country. There are remnants, but his followers do not represent a serious threat. I call this phenomenon "provincial fascism" and now we can say that this fascism is defeated.
Goltz:	But in October, you had to ask Moscow for Russian aid against Gamsakhurdia's followers—can you really minimize the support they enjoy?

Shevardnadze: We lost Sukhumi and Abkhazia because of Gamsakhurdia's treachery, and the following threat was great indeed because they managed to disarm the Georgian army of its heavy weapons. After taking western Georgia they were threatening Tbilisi because some powers supported them. But as for Russian aid, it was mainly symbolic. They did not participate in military actions. But I do not deny that they had a huge psychological importance for us, because without their involvement there would have been many more casualties.

Goltz: Could you identify those outside supporters?

Shevardnadze: When Gamsakhurdia was in Zugdidi, Abkhaz, Chechens, and Cossacks were fighting on his side.

Goltz: Tomorrow is the parliamentary session on ratification of Georgia's inclusion in the Commonwealth of Independent States—are you not worried that you will lose Western support if it passes and Russia continues to expand its influence in the region, including setting up military bases?

Shevardnadze: The deputies might ratify the treaty and then again they might not. Most Georgians are for joining—70 or 80 percent. As for the second issue, we have not signed the agreement on Russian bases, but we must start negotiations about this issue. If it is seen as mutually beneficial, we will sign. Our main aim is to form our own army. We do not have all the necessary material, and I think this is understood in the West. When we talk about the assessment by the West, the West must consider the situation here and whether we have any alternative.

Goltz: Is what you term "support" for joining the CIS really little more than exhaustion on the part of the Georgian people? Two years ago a similar percentage of Georgians were opposed to joining the CIS.

Shevardnadze: It is true, it is a matter of exhaustion. The population is now persuaded that the isolation of Georgia must end. We overcame political isolation and must now overcome economic isolation. That is why joining the CIS will accelerate the process of reestablishing traditional economic links.

Goltz: Do you foresee a danger of Georgia being absorbed into a larger Russia, as suggested by Vladimir Zhirinovsky?

Shevardnadze: If Russia decides to reinvade the ex-colonies, it will succeed. Georgia cannot go to war with Russia. But I think this will not happen.

Goltz: You travel to the United States soon. What do you expect from the trip and do you feel at all disappointed by the lack of Western support both for Georgia as well as for yourself personally?

Shevardnadze: The program of the visit is huge. I have great expectations. The most important thing is meeting with President Clinton. It will be our first contact. It will be interesting for him and for me it is absolutely vital. I hope that the USA will continue to assist Georgia within the framework of its possibilities. The second most important factor are my connections with the IMF and World Bank because these organizations have not had contact with the Georgian economy yet. If we do not receive aid, at least we might get some promises.

I also have several meetings planned. One with various business leaders because I think that Georgia is an interesting place for American business. Another key appointment is with Congress, then one with my connection with the Security Council. I also think that President Clinton and I will be speaking about the series of meetings in Geneva about Abkhazia. The result of that conversation might have a certain influence on the decision of the Security Council. The Security Council meeting is of vital importance in solving the Abkhazia conflict.

Goltz: Could you be more specific?

Shevardnadze: We hope to solve the question of the return of refugees as well as the status of the region within the context of a unitary state of Georgia. The most important thing is guaranteeing security through the deployment of peacekeeping forces in the region. As you can see, it will be a busy three days.

(Translator jokes about the lack of shopping opportunities in New York.)

Goltz: I have a personal interest in Abkhazia. We were there together and we saw that there was no serious deployment of peacekeepers in September. How can you be sure that deeds will match words now?

Shevardnadze: I think that the UN can play a vital role in this matter, and must. This is extremely important for the standing and authority of the United Nations. I think the UN does not have the right to *NOT* play a crucial role in this instance. If this does not happen then I will say that whatever I did to help establish the New World Order was not understood by the world, and was in vain.

Goltz: When we were together in Sukhumi, you made direct accusations that the "highest echelons of the Russian military" were involved in a "well-coordinated, synchronized attack" on Sukhumi. Has the Russian military changed?

Shevardnadze: I don't think that the highest echelons have changed. But one and the same persons can perform different policies. Our decision to join the CIS and visit President Yeltsin and establish friendly relations plays a role in this.

Goltz: Your career, too, might be an example of change and transformation. You began as an officer in state security [KGB], became a general in the MVD [Ministry of Internal Affairs, or police], were first secretary of the Georgian Communist Party and then a member of the politburo. How and why did you change?

Shevardnadze: Life itself and reality guided me to change. I do not respect those who conceive of the world as immutable, and themselves incapable of change. It so happened that I realized the reality that I was living in and was aware it had no future. I was not willing to remain on the communist side of it.

Goltz: Perhaps, the most delicate question of all: The opposition in Georgia and other parts of the former Soviet Union speak of the "Georgia Syndrome"—the election of a nationalist leader, the slow slide into war and destruction, a putsch, and then the return to power of a communist leader with Moscow's blessing. According to this theory, the process began here, was followed by the Azerbaijan example, and the Tajik variant. Could you comment on your own role in this?

Shevardnadze: [after a long pause] There are those who suggest that Gamsakhurdia was placed here by Moscow—that is another theory. As for my being brought here by Moscow, the idea is an obscenity. It was the will of the people, as declared and shown by the people of Georgia. As for Azerbaijan, I do not regard them as inspired by Moscow. [Heydar] Aliyev won the presidential election, and it was an impressive victory. As for Aliyev returning to power in Azerbaijan and Shevardnadze in Georgia, it was not a return to the communist regime—it was merely an expression of the disappointment of the people in those that followed the communists. It is impossible to govern and rule with the experience of the streets—provincial fascism. It was the psychology of the streets that destroyed Georgia. A great amount of time will be needed to rebuild, it was not democracy—and it was not an accident that I used the term "provincial fascism" wrapped in the flag of democracy. And I do not regard this as a delicate question.

Goltz: Thank you.
Shevardnadze: I thank you.
Translator: Let's go.

The next day was devoted to the parliamentary ratification of Shevardnadze's promise to join Georgia to the Commonwealth of Independent States, and emotions ran high.

"You returned from Moscow as part of an agenda to bring our nation into the CIS by any means," blustered my old friend Nodar Notadze, addressing the assembled deputies in the freezing hall. "We have been utterly duped by this communist stooge of Moscow!"

During the siege of Sukhumi, Nodar had been wounded three times—and had held to his gun due to his belief that Shevardnadze would never try to bring Georgia into the CIS, much less invite Russian soldiers into the country.

"There are times in the lives of all small countries when it is better to fight than to bow one's neck," he intoned. "Shevardnadze's effort to deliver Georgia to Russia is nothing less than treason."

Shevardnadze's supporters countered with their own epithets, labeling Notadze and his ilk "demagogues" and "political necrophiles."

"They are all political dwarves who are afraid of their own political deaths," hissed Alex Rondeli during a break in the action. "It is easy to get up and cry 'treason' but it is another thing entirely to look reality in the eye, and that reality is Russia!"

The floor-fight went on throughout the day, and it was not pretty. Shevardnadze supporters leapt to their man's defense and pelted Nodar with glasses of water and then their fists; those who believed in the old man's words returned the favor in kind.

"This man has brought Georgia nothing but war, humiliation, capitulation, and destruction," wailed the leader of the National Independence Party.

"Shut up, you cowardly scum, or you'll get what you deserve," threatened Jaba Ioseliani, referring to his Mkhedrioni men.

Perhaps, the former theater director, movie critic, novelist, convicted bank robber, and Mkhedrioni warlord said nothing of the sort. All he did was enter the assembly hall, silently survey the melee, and almost regally walk to his parliamentary chair. The hall fell silent in his wake; the chill in the air was not due to the cold, but to naked fear.

"Alex," I whispered. "I am your friend. Don't spin-doctor me. You don't have to repeat the official line all the time. What is really going on?"

"The self-destruction of our country," said Rondeli quietly.

I walked outside, shouldering my way through the crowd gathered in front of parliament and headed over to a large square overlooking the Mtkvari (Kura) River defined by two very Soviet structures—a curious series of cement arches-within-arches referred to by locals as "Andropov's Ears," and the fifteen- or sixteen-story Hotel Iveria. The Ears are only ugly and have no architectural interest or practical use. The Iveria Hotel, in contrast, was both ugly and functional: over the past five months, it had lost its functions as a Soviet-style hotel and become home to several thousand refugees from Abkhazia. Laundry and bicycles hung from the balconies, and children played on the roof and in the foyer. I began taking pictures of some of the more mundane aspects of refugee-hood in downtown Tbilisi, but was soon surrounded by an irate crowd of refugees/residents who were quite specific in their request that I cease and desist from recording their misery. I was about to go into a harangue about "only doing my job" when a man sporting a five-day beard and wearing a brown, Svani-style skull cap stepped forward and took control of the situation, first ordering the assaulting refugees to leave me alone and then turning to me.

"Please stop, Thomas," he said. "It is too painful for us."

"How do you know my name?" I asked, baffled.

"Because you ate at my table and slept in my house in Sukhumi," said the man.

It was Zorab, my host the night Merab and Nika took me to "see" Gamsakhurdia on videotape two years before. He had fled his lovely house and was now living with his family, six to a room, in the Iveria.

We stood there, looking at each other, a couple of miserable survivors from a place everyone wanted to forget but couldn't.

Notes

1. Interestingly, there were two other supplicants from the South Caucasus at the Moscow meeting—newly elected president of Azerbaijan Heydar Aliyev and Armenian president Levon Ter-Petrossian, whose presence at the Kremlin table seemed to indicate a formal confirmation of the return of Russia's sphere of influence in the region, and the declaration of a sort of modern-day *Monrovski Doktrin (Monroe Doctrine)*. One good description of the day placed a gloating Yeltsin in the role of a Roman emperor, accepting the crowns of defeated eastern kings who had been brought in chains before him.

2. See Thomas Goltz, "Russia's Hidden Hand," *Foreign Policy* (Autumn 1993), a piece about the wars in Karabakh and Abkhazia that fingered the Russian secret services' efforts to destabilize Azerbaijan and Georgia on the basis of massive circumstantial evidence. It soon became one of the most cited works of political journalism I have ever written, and I stand by it, with one exception: *I had to go light on Shevardnadze*, lest the piece get spiked. It was almost refreshing that Kiknadze caught me out on this issue.

14

Bridge Across the Inguri

"I wonder if he'll recognize me," mused the Divine Miss K, better known as the actor Margot Kidder, who played Lois Lane to Christopher Reeve's Superman in the series of films by that name. "I think I sat next to him at a state banquet in Ottowa when I was dating Pierre."

It was ten o'clock on a bitterly cold and wood-stove polluted night in mid-January, 1998, and Kidder was setting up the tripod and checking sound levels for our interview with Eduard Shevardnadze. But if the Silver Fox could actually recall the distinctive voice and face of Canadian Premier Trudeau's companion that glasnost evening back in the late 1980s, he did not let on during our one-hour taped conversation, and Margot did not feel it appropriate to remind him of her temporary First Lady (or Mistress) of Canada status. In fact, she was making every effort to maintain the lowest profile she could, that of second camera operator for a BBC television documentary I was shooting about conflict resolution in Georgia and Abkhazia.[1]

The late-evening interview was held on an upper story of the former Communist Party *Apparatchik* building that served as the Georgian equivalent of the White House. Located just uphill from the historic (and now restored) parliament flanking Rustaveli Avenue, the presidential building oozed some sort of post-Soviet sleaze. Perhaps it was my eyes. Tbilisi was suffering yet another midwinter brownout and the ten-story structure seemed to be the only building downtown that had electricity. Whatever positive social and economic factors I had sensed to be on the move the last time I had been in Georgia now seemed to have fallen back to the cold, dark, and drab Tbilisi that I remembered from 1992, 1993, and 1994.

Shevardnadze, too, looked older, grayer, and generally more rumpled.

He had survived an assassination attempt in 1995, as well as several other downturns of fortune, most of which had to do with the growing level of corruption in the country, and much of that had to do with oil. Chevron might have signed a transit-revenue generating deal to transport its Caspian crude through

Georgia by rail, but the end terminal was Batumi and thus outside of Tbilisi's direct control. British Petroleum and the Azerbaijan International Operating Company were building a new terminal at Supsa on the Black Sea coast to transport so-called early oil via a refurbished small-gauge pipeline from Baku, but the existing pipeline was not only discovered to be made of substandard steel as part of some Soviet-era corruption kickback scheme (therefore needing replacing and not mere refurbishing), but even where the pipe itself was of the proper quality, it had been so riddled with holes from people tapping into the line to siphon off fuel for their own use that it had to be replaced and put underground. The problem would continue even after the Baku–Supsa line was commissioned, despite public warnings that tapping into the high-pressure line would result in explosions and almost certain death for the illegal oil collectors. The clever drillers managed to find unique ways of getting at the pipeline, presumably with insider support. In 2000, acting on a tip, police busted an entire underground "cracking" station with direct links into the main line.

But Miss Kidder and I were not in Tbilisi to talk about oil; our focus was on Abkhazia, and Shevy did not seem to want to share too many insights into how to resolve the continuing, festering problem other than muttering clichés about how grateful he was to the "international community and particularly the United Nations" for its "continued support for the concept of the territorial integrity of the Georgian state." Still, the situation remained "potentially explosive" because the "patience of the population" was running out and he was unsure how much longer he could "restrain rogue elements from taking the matter into their own hands," this last being a reference to the White Legion and Forest Brethren who operated along the ceasefire line along the Inguri River and the sub-Abkhazian province of Gali. As for the internal situation in Georgia, Shevardnadze claimed that things were much improved. The interior minister Tengiz Kitovani had been dismissed, and Mkhedrioni leader Jaba Ioseliani arrested on charges of racketeering and attempting to overturn the state. In fact, Ioseliani and his henchmen were currently on trial. We could bring our camera into the courtroom, should we so choose.

* * *

The Jaba Ioseliani trail was a fascinating moment of retro theater, and one perhaps demanding the imaginative pen of Bertolt Brecht. Here was the former and much-feared leader of the Knight Horsemen militia group that had so terrorized the country, sitting in the dock with perhaps a dozen others, at least half of whom seemed to be so-called Zviadisti, or militant supporters of Zviad Gamsakhurdia, the man and movement Ioseliani had putsched from power back in late 1991.

The pen holding the accused in the High Court across from Lawrence Sheet's abode looked like nothing so much as a large monkey cage: floor-to-ceiling bars around a twenty- by five-foot enclosure that contained a single bench. Maybe it was larger; at any size, it was utterly humiliating and designed to be just so.

This is not to say that the defendants so penned up accepted the judgment of society with appropriate stoicism. On the contrary, without waiting for the judge (or prosecutor) to read the charges against them, they rattled spoon on bar, spat at anyone near by, and generally made themselves extremely unpleasant. Perhaps I would have done the same, if in their shoes.

"Citizen XYZ," intones the judge, "You are accused of terrorism this and terrorism that . . . how do you plead?"

"GUILTY OF BEING MAN ENOUGH TO MAKE MY COUNTRY FREE!" screams the plaintiff, revealing himself as a nonbeliever in the Georgian court system.

In the United States, perhaps, such an outburst might have resulted in court deputies removing the offending plaintiff from the scene. But not in Tbilisi State Crimes Court, where the security guard took an active disinterest in bringing the putative criminal to order. The cops were reluctant—meaning they were afraid—of entering the monkey pen. This was understood by the men inside, who continued to howl, shout, and generally make spectacles of themselves. And in the near corner of the monkey pen sat Jaba, smirking at the entire spectacle, head shoved into a woolen ski cap, chatting with his fellow defendants as if they were talking about today's headlines, which Jaba and his incarcerated pals literally would have been if yesterday's news were today's.

I have never seen an incarcerated *anyone* as confident as Jaba Ioseliani was that everything would turn out okay.

"The defendant Jaba Ioseliani, accused of using his influence to undermine the authority of the state . . ."

Jaba hitches his spine up a mini-notch or two upon hearing his name, then turns to another jailed monkey-man sitting next to him and says something.

They chuckle, and then something is said to the guard that is then passed to the judge. Silence sweeps the court.

The boss has spoken.

A plea? A threat? A promise?

Somewhere in that ten-second action/reaction, Jaba rolls his eyes over the court, and for a liquid moment, they freeze on Miss Kidder and myself. He stares in what seems to be confusion that then turns to disbelief, and then recognition. *He smiles.* Am I imagining things? Or has Mkhedrioni-leader Jaba Ioseliani just realized that fellow thespian Margot Kidder is covering his trial?[2]

"He is staring at you," I say.

"I know," says Margie.

"And smiling," I add.

"Shut up," says Kidder. "I am shooting."

Then the sheriffs or the Georgian equivalent thereof arrive and drag the defendants, including Jaba Ioseliani, back to jail in chains.

* * *

Kidder and I shot a lot of film in Tbilisi, from the Shevardnadze interview to on-camera conversations about the Russian policy of promoting ethnic strife in the Caucasus with local "wise man" Alexander Rondeli to a half-hour chat with the United Nation's Special Envoy, Liviu Bota, on the international community's concern for promoting the territorial integrity of member states. The result, if truth be told, was a mind-numbing litany of dates and venues of negotiations that stumbled or failed when Georgia refused to allow Abkhazia "equal partnership" in a federated state, or when Abkhazia refused to accept Tbilisi's idea of an "asymmetrical sovereignty" between the two sides, meaning that Georgia was Georgia with a somewhat special but absolutely *not* independent place called Abkhazia inside it. While all very informative—and arguably the very nub of the issue—none of this was very good television. What we needed was a tight focus on the failed campaign to return Abkhazia to Georgian control, personified by the knots of refugees huddled around street-side stands, or passing through the doors of sanatoria and hotels that had been converted into "temporary" housing until Shevardnadze fulfilled his promise to get them home again.

The physical symbol of despair was the Hotel Iveria, the fifteen-story high "modern" Soviet-style cement monstrosity at the end of Rustaveli Avenue, where all rooms were filled with refugees. Their laundry flapped from a hundred balconies like so many flags of failure.

Marina Davidadze was but one of the special "guests" to have taken up residence in the Hotel Iveria after the fall of Sukhumi. Like the rest, she had assumed that her stay at the Iveria would only be temporary. But in January 1998, Marina and her two children, Nana and Okry, were entering their fifth year in room 614. Her husband, a man named Kela, had been killed in the fighting around Sukhumi, and they existed on his pension of 15 lari, or about 8 dollars a month, plus some international aid.

"What are we to do?" she asked rhetorically. "At least in Sukhumi, we had a vegetable garden."

There were similar stories up and down the dim hallways and on every floor. One woman from the town of Gagra drew a map of her house and asked me to see if the pear tree she had planted in her yard just before the war was still there, and whether there was any fruit.

Indeed, it was now time to take a look at the far side of the lines, inside Abkhazia, by crossing the Inguri. To get there, I called on an old friend to secure clearance for Kidder and myself as the special guests of the United Nations Observer Mission in Georgia, or UNOMIG, which maintained joint headquarters in Zugdidi and Sukhumi and another base in the almost lawless no-man's-land subprovince of Gali. We claimed to be working on a BBC documentary about international conflict resolution, but at least I was working for more; I was looking for personal conflict resolution between me and my demons.

* * *

We did not have to wear our UN-issued flak jackets until we crossed the Inguri, and our UNOMIG minders did not insist that we wear the helmets we had been given even when outside the protective half-inch-thick metal walls and bullet-proof window slits of the Mamba that was to be our transportation while inside the "red" area of the ceasefire zone. We had received a briefing on the technical points of the agreement signed between the Georgians and Abkhaz under the supervision of the Russians back in 1994 at the UNOMIG headquarters in Zugdidi, where we were also asked to sign away any and all potential claims for liability should we be injured or killed while in UNOMIG hands. Essentially, the "zone of conflict" was divided into three distinct circles: the red zone along both banks of the Inguri and expanding back ten kilometers, in which Georgian and Abkhaz police with side-arms were allowed; the purple area abutting the red, which had a depth of about ten kilometers, and where uniformed soldiers might stand guard, but only with light weapons; and then the blue zone beyond the purple, in which the Georgian and Abkhaz forces could maintain artillery, tanks, and other "heavy" weapons, because they were in effect out of range should they want to shoot at the other side. For the UNOMIG and its guests such as Miss Kidder and myself, what this translated into was a series of dos and don'ts that could become confusing or downright irritating: the red zone required us to wear flak jackets and travel in the incredibly uncomfortable Mambas; while once in the purple zone, we could travel around by normal, armor-plated land cruisers and jeeps, but still had to wear the flak jackets until we entered the blue zone, where we could dispense with the thirty pounds of Kevlar and shock-plate survival gear. Whatever the colors, Abkhazia had ceased being a chaotic war zone of multiple fronts, and been converted into a bureaucratized map of post-conflict rules and regulations administered and monitored (theoretically, anyway) by a crazy-quilt cross-section of international military observers (who were really spies), Russian "peacekeepers" (who were actually allied with the Abkhaz), who were in turn supported by a staff of local translators and drivers (who were suspected of partisanship on both sides of the lines) along with a bevy of mainly third world administration assistants who had been appointed through UN nepotism and who often seemed to want the conflict to continue because at least then they kept their jobs at "hardship posting" salary rates. That is harsh, I know, but after listening to some guy from Barbados or Trinidad complaining/bragging on his satellite telephone to a relative on the other side of the world about having to spend another two weeks at triple overtime pay on Abkhaz duty, and what he intended to do with extra loot in Paris as soon as his duty-related additional trials and tribulations were over, I was not left with a particularly good impression.

* * *

Our first UN security transfer happened on the far side of the bridge over the Inguri River that separated Georgia from the subprovince of Gali inside Abkhazia. That is where we were obliged to put on the flak jackets and get inside the Mambas, which were designed to be more or less resistant to mines. The shadowy White Legion and Forest Brethren Georgian partisan groups had infiltrated the Gali region and were increasingly engaged in planting the odd roadside bomb against the Abkhaz administration as well as the Russian patrols, but the UNOMIG was obliged to use the same roads, and once a mine was planted it did not distinguish between drivers. Soon they would up the ante by kidnapping the odd UN observer, although less for ransom than to draw attention to their cause.

Along the main road, the visual memory of the war of five years before was stark from the moment we boarded our Mamba at the Inguri crossing, all the way into Sukhumi town, where we arrived several hours later. Almost every house and building to the right and left of the road was partially or wholly burnt out. Sweeping balconies hung at wrong angles and stairways led upward into nowhere, while all manner of other wild greenery protruded through the spaces once covered up by roofing destroyed by bombs or subsequent arson. Tangerine and other citrus orchards stood untended and often marked by warning signs bearing a black death skull and red cross that indicated the plot was a suspected or proven mine field that had not yet been cleared.

For those of us inured to such random, casual, and useless violence in places like Grozny, Aghdam, al-Quneitra, Sarajevo, Kabul, or Fallujah (to name but a few of the more famous systematically destroyed cities over the past couple of dozen years), it may have been a familiar scene. For pacifists like Miss Kidder, who had never been in a war zone before, it was baffling and massively depressing.

Our host that first night in Abkhazia was Colonel John Bunne, a big, lanky, honey-tongued PsyOps or "Psychological Warfare" man who served as the senior officer of the four-man American military team, and temporary commander of the UNOMIG base at Gali. His previous career had included deep penetrations in Kuwait during the first Gulf War and an extended stint at Guantanamo Bay in Cuba before it became known as the Gitmo Gulag.

"It took me a lot of time and thought to put on the blue and white of the UN instead of the stars and stripes," said Bunne in his light Texas twang, referring to his getting seconded to the UNOMIG and thus theoretically to serve a master other than the American People. "The problem is that Washington won't let me do my job."

That job, according to Bunne, was to monitor the peace and ensure that violations of the 1994 ceasefire agreement (such as the sighting of an Abkhaz tank inside the purple zone or a uniformed Georgian soldier with a Kalashnikov inside the red zone) be recorded and formally protested. But beyond the fact that the UNOMIG had no authority (or even weapons) to do anything more than verbally chastise an offender, they rarely had the opportunity to actually see a violation to record and then protest.

"The Abkhaz are not going to be pulling an artillery piece behind a tank on the main road into a no-go zone," said Bunne. "They will put it on a donkey cart and hide it in the trees—and we are not allowed to travel the back roads to see the donkey cart."

On our way to the bridge over the Inguri, we had actually busted a Georgian soldier in uniform entering the red zone on the Georgian side of the lines; he was going to visit relatives, and had no other clothes. The breach of the ceasefire regulations was duly noted, however, including the man's alleged name, rank, and unit number, which we had to take on trust because he was not carrying any I.D.

Even more demeaning was the "buddy" system imposed on the Americans by the Department of Defense in DC, which insisted that members of Bunne's team always have another American at hand in order to somehow ensure that the other not be kidnapped. Then, after a spate of kidnappings of UNOMIG monitors, came new orders: the Americans under Bunne were to remove themselves from the Abkhaz conflict sector entirely, and do their monitoring from the safety of Tbilisi. Miss Kidder later told me that she was up all night, first because she was nervous (the fact that Bunne had assigned one of his teammates to sleep outside her door made her worry even more) and then because she was trying to eavesdrop on an hour-long conversation between Colonel Bunne and the Pentagon, in which his side of the dialogue consisted in cursing whoever was on the far end of the phone and shouting "just let me do my job!"

A rather different approach was taken by our next UNOMIG hosts, who belonged to the German Bundeswehr contingent and were responsible for patrolling the purple-colored security area of the upper Inguri River between the town of Taglioni and a Soviet-era mega-mega hydroelectric power plant, where the turbines were located on the Georgian side of the lines and the generator part of the plant on the Abkhazian. Somehow, the plant had survived the war and was actually transmitting power to both sides, albeit on an intermittent basis due to a general lack of repair, spare parts, and salaries for the personnel. A descent down into the bowels of the plant was like a "save the world mission" in a bad Hollywood movie: sparks leapt off naked cables and wires, rats scurried here and there, and manhole covers were missing over man-size holes into the roaring torrent feeding the one operational turbine in the place.

"Let's get out of here, *now*," said Kidder, apparently not believing me capable of saving her, Superman style, if the dam burst beneath us.

Actually, I am not sure if we were even supposed to be in the plant, which was under the lethargic guard of Russian troops, but our host Captain Siegfried (Cap'n Ziggy, as we took to calling him) understood his mission in Abkhazia to project a friendly presence at all times and all places, and the power plant was as good a place as any to show the blue and white of the UN flag.

"As a German, as a European, as a soldier, I believe in the mission of the United Nations," he explained. "And for me, Georgia is something very special: my father worked as a prisoner of war laborer here on roads and bridges after World War II."

Not content to just patrol the roads in a Mamba or armored land rover, Cap'n Ziggy had gone so far as to order in a number of mountain bikes from Germany so he and his men could get closer yet to the local population and show them that they, the Germans, had no fear—and that thus the locals should not have any, either. After the most recent kidnappings, his superiors had cracked down on the bike patrols, but Cap'n Ziggy regarded them more as temporarily suspended rather than formally banned.

We spent our evening with Cap'n Ziggy and his merry crew by sneaking out of the UNOMIG HQ after curfew and going over to the house of a local notable to have dinner with a middle-aged or at least prematurely gray nurse named Nana, who had stayed in her hospital during the darkest days of the conflict, giving medicine and succor to the wounded on both sides.

Was this the beginning of some thread of hope for reconciliation?

Cap'n Ziggy thought so, which was why he had arranged the feast for us in the first place.

"The world needs to know about people like Nana," he said. "She is Georgia."

In the morning we were deposited in yet another task force, this time headed by the British contingent to the UNOMIG, who patrolled the most problematic part of Gali, known as Sita. A tropical lowlands, it was defined by the Inguri River and also abutted the Black Sea, and was thus a smuggler's (and partisan guerrilla's) paradise. If there were a fourth color to the security zone scheme, Sita would have been crimson or even black. Several bridges had once crossed the river here, but had been blown up during the course of the war. Rickety planks tied together with wire, rope, and steel cables over, around, and under the cement bridge abutments now served as pedestrian walkways across the river, thereby creating a means of entering Gali without bothering to notify the Abkhaz authorities (or the UN) and, as a result, traffic was heavy. Unlike other parts of Abkhazia where the population had at least been mixed, in the Sita part of Gali the population had always been almost 100 percent Georgian (or at least the Mingrelian variety of Georgian), and their attitude toward the Abkhazian authorities (and the Russian peacekeepers) was bad at best and often a lot worse. This was White Legion and Forest Brethren country, and I had the sense that everyone we spoke with was less interested in reconciliation than revenge.

"We are the real Abkhazians!" declared a lean and mean looking man named Artvandil. "I was born here, my father born here, his father born and buried here, and I intend to be buried here myself. Let the so-called Abkhazians come and drive us out . . ."

* * *

We exchanged our Mamba for a Land Rover and our flak jackets and soaking undergarments for dry shirts and jackets at the edge of the purple and blue security zones (or perhaps on the border of the blue zone and the rest of the county) and continued down the monotonously violence-scarred main highway to Sukhumi, arriving at the Aitar Hotel and Spa Complex, where I had crashed in February 1992. Everything else about the Aitar was the same as the last time I had been there—the scalding hot water from the tap, but no cold; the screeching peacocks in the yard; the price (about a buck a bed) and even the sullen service of the *dezhurnaia*, or floor supervisor, a hotel-spy position during the bad old days of the USSR, which had disappeared from history as totally and absolutely as the job of chimney-sweep in the West, with the exception of post-Soviet holdout places such as Sukhumi, where the *dezhurnaia* remained queen of her floor.

There had been one major change at the Aitar, however. It was manifest in the rows and rows of blue and white UN vehicles lined up in the hotel's parking lot, all nicely protected behind walls of concertina wire, with a deacon's

list of other vehicles bearing the emblems of the new international missionaries in the post-Soviet age. These were the nongovernmental organizations
(NGOs) such as World Vision, CARE, Oxfam, United Methodists for Peace,
Mothers Without Borders, and a host of other like-minded NGOs, all determined to save the world from its present, ugly self because—well, it needed
saving. All were camping at the Aitar because it had become, in effect, a UN
compound, and was thus regarded as "safe," unlike the rest of Abkhazia.
The result was that with few exceptions, the NGO community had created
a ghetto for itself that remained utterly cut off from the traumatized society
the well-meaning merchants of peace were allegedly there to understand,
protect, and nurture.

* * *

The UN may have had an American-style blueprint for the future of Abkhazia, but there was another reality at the Aitar bar. In addition to delegates
from diverse NGOs, it was filled with an international group of soldiers
from Turkey and Greece, Pakistan and India, Serbia and Albania as well
as other member states of the United Nations almost at war with themselves. The international military men were friendly enough, if guarded by
training. But unlike Colonel Bunne and Cap'n Ziggy in the Gali district,
the UNOMIG boys in Sukhumi really did not have much to say. There
was a Brit known at the bar as "Lawrence of Kodori" due to his periodic
forays up the Kodori Gorge in the nasty highlands above Abkhazia to
inspect what the mean and generally nasty Svanetians were up to, but that
song only played well among people who had never been there, did not
know the Svans, and did not know the Kodori Gorge. To anyone who had
actually been there, the idea of a British officer, beholden to an Armenian
translator arriving in an APC filled with Pakistani and Columbian fellow
officers in a UN vehicle backed by Russian firepower in a wartime limbo
zone between the failed state of Georgia and the nonstate of Abkhazia,
designed or promoted somehow to suggest that anything resembling *the
truth* had come out of that five- or six- or seven-hour forced meeting
over tea (or *chacha*) was so utterly ridiculous that it was—well, utterly
ridiculous. The stories related by Kodori Lawrence of his adventures in
the mountains of Abkhazia were ultimately only one-day affairs, with the
unspoken reality being that the majority of Kodori Lawrence's time had
been spent negotiating the monotonous five-hour drive up and then the
monotonous four-hour drive back down the mountain, with only a minimal
amount of time spent with his target audience (and the claim to his fame),
the notorious Svans. "*Hohoho*," chortled Kodori's Bengali, Malaysian,

Czech, and Zimbabwean fellow officers on the Sukhumi-based UNOMIG staff, listening to the Brit's most recent antics and adventures in the Abkhazian highlands. *"Hohoho!"*

* * *

Indeed, the only soldiers with any direct contact with legal or illegal ordnance seemed to be former sappers associated with the British de-mining charity called the HALO Trust. I had had contact with the group in Chechnya, and knew they were active everywhere from Cambodia to Afghanistan to Karabakh. Thus, I was not very surprised to find them in Abkhazia, where once again these strange sappers were teaching local youths the delicate art of removing hidden death from beneath the nation's feet.

"Mines are traditionally laid to force the enemy into a killing zone," explained a HALO man named Perce, who sported a stiff upper lip and vaguely aristocratic mien. "But in this war, both sides just planted them anywhere as preventive bombs, especially along the rivers."

He was referring to the Gumista, which had defined the northern front during the war, and the Inguri, which now defined Abkhazia's southern front with Georgia. In fact, we were standing in a suspected mine field along the former stream; the HALO Trust will conduct interviews with the press only inside a danger zone, which is a rather effective means of cutting down media requests to a bare minimum.

Nor was danger of stepping on a mine limited to former frontline contact points. Annual floods and erosion had washed certain areas almost clean of mines, only to deposit them in a helter-skelter manner elsewhere. As we stood chatting with some local Armenians in the area where I had once bunked down with the Rustavi Battalion back in March 1993, a couple of kids pulled up on their skateboards, holding an antipersonnel mine they had just found in the garden between their house and the river.

"It is a live one," muttered Perce, gingerly removing the lethal device from the kid's hands and expertly removing the detonator.

Nearby, the HALO lads had discovered a more problematic project: an unexploded rocket projectile that was three-quarters buried in the cement substructure of what seemed to be the house where I had stayed with the Rustavi militia the night of that aerial attack on Novyi Raion. Perce and his cohort insisted that the area be cleared of everyone, including Kidder and myself, until they managed to safely dislodge the ordnance.

"Our policy is zero risk after we have cleared an area," Perce explained with a wry smile. After all I had lived through in this tortured land, all the horror and treachery I had personally witnessed, it was all I could do to prevent myself from cynically wondering what sort of crimes Perce and his mates had committed during their military past that they were trying to atone for in embracing this most dangerous form of international philanthropy.

* * *

Back in 1996, and during the darkest days of the "first" Chechen war with Russia, a group of desperate "Circassian" diaspora Turks hijacked a Black Sea ferry outside the Turkish city of Trabzon and held hundreds of Russian "suitcase" tourists hostage as a show of support. The assumption therefore, was that the hijackers were ethnic Chechens. While investigating the incident, I had sought contact with the family of the group's leader, a man named Muhammad Tokcan (pronounced 'Tok-jan'), and learned that the ringleader was in fact an ethnic Abkhaz, who had fought with Chechen warlord Shamil Basayev's "Abkhaz Battalion" in the 1992–93 war. Contact with Tokcan was impossible, as he had recently "escaped" from a maximum-security prison in Turkey (more likely "released" by rightwing ultranationalist Turkish police who shared his views on Russia) and was either deep underground or had fled the country. But my interlocutors told me that contact with his father might be possible if and when I should ever return to Abkhazia, where the elder Tokcan had emigrated at the end of the 1993 war. Details were fuzzy, but I thought I might find him through the association of diaspora Abkhaz who had returned to the ancestral homeland in Sukhumi. The head of the association was a gentleman named Oktay Chtizia, and I could find him either in his office at the Ministry for Diaspora Affairs, or down at a coffee shop off Peace Prospect that was known locally as the Turkish Café.

Breaking free of our UN minders, Kidder and I set forth to find Oktay, locating him among a knot of fellow diaspora Abkhaz returnees over at the aforementioned Turkish café. And in doing so, not only did we find new friends and excellent guides, but also unique access to a quite different perspective to the Georgian–Abkhaz conflict—that of the descendants of the survivors of the great nineteenth-century exodus from Abkhazia, in which some half of the entire population perished due to battle wounds, famine, or disease before washing up on the shores of Ottoman Turkey.

"In Turkey, we retained Abkhaz culture and customs but lost the language, whereas in Abkhazia, they retained the language but lost Abkhaz culture and customs," Oktay explained over a round of Turkish tea, sipped from the tulip-shaped glasses all visitors to Istanbul are familiar with. It sounded like a good way to describe the mutuality between the two Abkhaz communities, but I had to wonder about its accuracy. The language of the coffee shop was certainly Turkish and not Abkhaz, and everything from the posters of the

"Yellow Canary" Galatasaray football team, the obligatory heroic portrait of Mustafa Kemal Atatürk framed by the red flag and white star and crescent of the Turkish national banner, and even a photograph calendar of the Ka'aba in Mecca during the Muslim pilgrimage all seemed to be more a part of Turkey than Abkhazia. Football loyalties aside, inside Turkey there was an ongoing movement to somehow rehabilitate an Abkhaz commander who had turned on Mustafa Kemal and gone over to fight on the (losing) side of the Greeks in the Turkish War of Independence of the early 1920s, and as for religion, while the diaspora Abkhaz (and Chechens and other Circassians) were known as conservative Muslims throughout Turkey and the Middle East, the Abkhaz in Abkhazia were essentially pagans, worshipping everything from ancient trees to bears.

"There are differences," intoned Oktay carefully. "But we are one people."

Oktay himself was no Johnny-come-lately Abkhaz. As a kid in the Turkish town of Adapazar, he had insisted that his grandparents explain the non-Turkish language they spoke among themselves. He had then taught himself the Cyrillic script used for modern Abkhazian, acquired the odd textbook or novel to improve his vocabulary, and made his first trip to Sukhumi back in the late 1980s, when there was still a Soviet Union. With the outbreak of war in 1992, he had managed to get himself dropped offshore north of the Gumista, and then joined the resistance to the Georgian forces, but as a logistical coordinator and expert smuggler, not as a fighter per se.

"I could not kill a fly," he smiled. "But I know how to get things done."

He was referring, obliquely, to the arrival of a sanctions-busting junk freighter now docked at the quay about 100 meters from where we sat. It was flying the Turkish flag, and offloading goods from Turkey as fast as it was on-loading tons of twisted, rusted scrap metal for export.

That was the moment that Miss Kidder decided to catch an intimate moment between Oktay and myself at the Turkish café on camera, which resulted in a diaspora Abkhaz from Turkey pulling out his pistol and shooting it a couple of feet over Margie's head. It was not clear whether this was in celebration of some unannounced event, or merely an act of posttraumatic stress expiation.

"He just shot at me!" screamed Kidder, which was true.

The next day, Oktay took us by smoke-belching car on a journey north to the Russian frontier to show us his adopted country's only semilegal export point, called Psou. I must have crossed through it during my first trip to Georgia, but I could hardly recognize the wide-open frontier of January 1992 now in January 1998: a sea of hundreds, maybe thousands of elderly and middle-aged women, wrapped in shawls, scarves, and greatcoats against the cold, slowly shuffled forward three and four abreast through a narrow pedestrian walkway framed by metal bars, lugging huge plastic bags filled with tangerines toward a police checkpoint on the border. They looked like cattle, being forced through a chute for branding.

"Animals are treated better than this," said Oktay in disgust. "Perhaps that woman over there is a professor; maybe that one is a doctor—but all have been reduced to this semilegal smuggling of our fruit into Russia to sell for a fraction of its value. And all because the so-called international community says we do not exist."

Returning toward Sukhumi via the empty former tourist towns of Pitsunda and Gagra, I was suddenly struck by an odd thought: the mass of women at the Psou crossing was the first and only group of people that could be described as anything like "a crowd" that we had seen in Abkhazia. The official population might be half of the 500,000 registered in the last Soviet census of 1989 due to the expulsion/flight of the Georgians, but it *felt* like there were a lot fewer than that. There were more cows on the road than people; the place was empty. Accordingly, I asked Oktay how many ethnic Abkhaz from Turkey and the larger diaspora in the Middle East had actually returned to settle, but he merely smiled.

"I could lie and give you a number that you might think as large or small," he said. "The truth of the matter is that this is a state secret, and for obvious reasons."

The diaspora Abkhaz had played a role in the war, however, and quite a few had been killed, many uselessly or stupidly. Seemingly every bend in the road (and thus potential ambush sites) was marked by strange and sad lithographic stone portraits where the diaspora heroes had fallen, along with their local Abkhaz cousins, pushing forward straight into the crosshairs of a hidden Georgian machinegun nest. By definition, there were no such markers denoting Georgian sacrifice or heroism. They were mere ghosts. And as for the living, it was increasingly clear that neither Oktay and his diaspora friends nor the local Abkhaz ever wanted the Georgians to come back and live among them again. While both sides agreed that refugees should be allowed to return "home," and that borders should be opened and the economy rejuvenated, the Abkhaz were merely mouthing the words.

"We say 'let all innocent refugees return to their houses,'" said Oktay. "But the important word is 'innocent.' We will not allow any one back who has blood on his hands, and the list of Georgian murderers is long."

Did that mean any Georgian from Abkhazia who picked up a gun to defend his home?

"And their families," said Oktay with finality. That meant people like Marina Davidava and her two kids in room 614 at the Hotel Iveria.

"We want peace, but it will take generations," added an Armenian neighbor of Oktay's who had dropped in for tea. "There are people here who lost their entire families. How can you expect them to forgive?"

* * *

Dropping Miss Kidder off with the camera at her new fan club among the UNOMIG soldiers at the Aitar Hotel, I returned to town to find a few ghosts of my own. It had been nearly five years, and with so much destruction most familiar landmarks were long gone. That park was over *there*, right? And the burnt-out ruins of *this* building could have been that fine, whitewashed house where you *turned left* before heading down *that* street to the market. . . .

Another fragment of a house, a second and third burned structure on the left, and then I was standing in front of a wrought-iron gate, looking into a small yard on the right. The yard contained a stone fountain framed by two benches and shaded by a grape arbor. There was an arc of bullet holes across the brown stucco of the house beneath the living-room window, but the pane of glass was intact and the fact that there were curtains suggested someone was living there. I saw a trace of movement near where I knew the door to be, and then heard a trickle of water splash in a sink, from where I remembered the outside well.

"Excuse me," I said in Russian, calling gently lest I frighten whoever was there, washing their hands or the dishes or preparing tea. "How long have you lived here?"

The figure of an older woman emerged from the shadows, took one look at me behind the gate, and almost fainted.

So did I.

It was Lamara, Nunu Chachua's mother.

"*Tomas?*" she cried, rushing to the gate. "We heard you were dead!"

"We?" I asked, hoping against hope.

A babble of words, things such as "She's okay, in Moscow, she is fine."

What I heard was one thing: *Nunu Chachua was alive.*

And contactable.

"Here is her address in Tbilisi, where Nana lives," she said. "Tell her I am fine, and not to worry. *I am fine!*"

She was pouring that last dram of homemade brandy for me, the prodigal son who had once tried to save them from themselves so long ago, but could not, need not do so, mainly because he was not prodigal and not a son at all, but merely a very odd and time-sensitive friend.

Notes

1. For the sake of clarity, in addition to being an extraordinarily gifted actor on stage and screen, Margie is also my neighbor in Livingston, Montana, and has always been politically active. She now runs an organization called "Montana Women For—" with the "for" being conceptually open to any project she and her many friends think deserves attention.

2. This is not farfetched. Whatever else he was (or became) Jaba Ioseliani was a Soviet-style state artist, and thus obliged to be aware of who won what prize at the Hollywood Oscars, Cannes, and other film festivals, as well as what diverse scandals were at play in the global movie industry, such as Miss Kidder's famous 1991 Los Angeles flip-out, which ultimately positioned her to become the poster-child for manic depression for the next decade and obligatory guest whenever the subject came up on such shows as CNN's *Larry King Live*.

Rough road to the future. *Giorgi Tsagareli, Photographer.*

15

Trying to Square a Chalk Circle

What good is a road if it does not lead to a church?

—the last spoken line in Tengiz Abuladze's
1985 film about Beria/Stalin, *Repentance*

"They are kids, my dear Thomas, kids!" said Gia, banging his fist on the table. "Okay—we were once kids, too—but not like these! The mayor of Tbilisi is thirty-four years old and our new president? Thirty six!"

It was March 2004, and my old friend Gia Janjgava, last seen giving me a cigarette in Sukhumi in 1993, but now consul general of the Republic of Georgia's representational office in the Turkish Black Sea commercial hub of Trabzon, was incensed—and not because I had quit smoking, and thus had "forgotten" my usual tribute of a carton of American "street" Marlboros to His Excellency in exchange for a free visa. No, Gia was peeved for other reasons. At the ripe old age of thirty-eight, he was feeling himself to be an old and crumpled veteran of the political and military hurly-burly that had rocked his native land at the time of the collapse of the USSR in 1991 and was now being shunted off to the side as younger compatriots seized control of the levers of power, prestige, and authority in the "new" Georgia ushered in by the Rose Revolution—the George Soros/Open Society Institute-funded vehicle of social and political change that was led by the dashing, six-foot-four, thirty-six-year-old Mikheil ("Misha") Saakashvili.

The previous November, Saakashvili and his followers had taken to the streets of Tbilisi following the most recent in a long series of corrupt elections —this time for parliament. Sticking symbolic roses in the gun barrels of the security forces called on to squelch the nonviolent rebellion, the assembled and deeply frustrated masses had stormed the parliament building, forcing Eduard Shevardnadze to first flee and then resign the office he had held for more than a decade, removing himself from all positions of power he had held in Georgia for thirty or forty years.[1]

225

Almost overnight, Georgia was declared transformed. No longer was *Sakartvelo* to be regarded as the very symbol of post-Soviet corruption, intrigue, and separatism; henceforth, the country was to be a beacon and model of democratic pluralism, commercial transparency, and interethnic cooperation for other post-Soviet societies to emulate, throwing off the legacy of the communist past as well as the political, economic, and social poverty associated with the post-Soviet present. Firmly entrenched in the presidential administration building in Tbilisi since January, when Saakashvili had garnered something on the order of 90 percent of the vote in snap elections (which were deemed both free and fair by everyone aside from a couple of pathological grumblers), the American-trained lawyer and former minister of justice was now overseeing new parliamentary elections that seemed sure to legally sweep away the last vestiges of the long Shevardnadze legacy and give Saakashvili and his brash, young coterie of Western-oriented allies a mandate to ram through real reforms, root out endemic corruption, and put paid to the pretensions of several-decades-long separatist movements. But the real cause to celebrate the Rose Revolution, in Western circles, anyway, was the potential impact it might have on other foundering post-Soviet states.

The first ripple effect would be the bitterly contested presidential elections in Ukraine in November and December 2004, where the "Orange Revolution" would employ many of the same "Rose Revolution" techniques of mass, nonviolent protest to oust the old and replace it with the new. Next came the "Tulip Revolution" in the spring of 2005 in Kyrgyzstan. Although not as pretty as the popular uprisings in Georgia and Ukraine, it managed to depose the Akayev family "democratic dictatorship" that had held power in Bishkek since the collapse of the USSR in 1991. But the wilt was on the tulip almost as soon as the flower opened (or the smoke cleared), and by the time the Rose Revolution formula arrived in Azerbaijan for parliamentary elections in November 2005, the would-be democratizing revolutionaries could not even decide on an appropriate symbolic color, and ended up using used orange tents and orange T-shirts imported from Kiev. (The most natural color for the Azerbaijani oppositionists might have been green, as it is part of the tricolor on the flag. But the would-be revolutionary leadership thought that foreign television teams might confuse that color with radical Islam, and thus opted for orange, even though it was a color more intimately associated with enemy Armenia.) Yerevan, meanwhile, had been somehow exempted from the need for democratic revolution for the time being, or until its voting population returned from self-imposed exile as guest-workers in Russia, Europe, and (perhaps most shocking) Turkey. And as for Belarus and Uzbekistan . . .

But all that was later.

In the immediate aftermath of the Rose Revolution of late 2003, all the authoritarian regimes of the former USSR were said to be looking over their shoulders as the promise of democracy, a truly free market economy, and the rule of law took root in Saakashvili's New Georgia, almost as a reverse Bolshevik Revolution of 1917. Even Vladimir Putin's Russia was starting to get edgy, where aides to the former KGB colonel and avowed George W. friend were muttering that "forced" democratization of countries that were not yet ready for truly popular government was merely an invitation to chaos. . . .

Democracy as chaos?

Well, that seemed to be the attitude of my old friend Gia, too, and he had every right to feel that way. A child (teenager, actually) of perestroika in the mid-1980s, he was twenty-three at the time of the April 1989 crackdown on nationalists in Tbilisi, twenty-five at the time of the abortive putsch against Soviet President Mikhail Gorbachev in August 1991, and serving as Eduard Shevardnadze's chief of protocol when we first met and bonded over a last Marlboro cigarette in Sukhumi in September 1993. Subsequently, Gia had been elevated to the post of Georgian consul general to Trabzon and tasked with everything from monitoring the sentiments of Turkey's large and influential Circassian émigré population and illegal ship traffic to Abkhazia, fetching or rescuing Georgian prostitutes from the clutches of Turkish sex-slave mafia groups, and issuing or denying visas to everyone from naive Euro-tourists on bicycles off to discover the wonders of the Caucasus to Wahhabi-type Arabs on their way to perform holy war in Chechnya. On top of all of this, Gia had to deal with the most recent crisis in Batumi and the activities and antics of "Batono" Aslan Abashidze, the self-styled "Lord Protector" of harmony, stability, and economic happiness in the sub-Georgian entity known as the Autonomous Republic of Adjaria, which had been threatening to secede from the rest of Georgia as had Abkhazia and South Ossetia before it. A week before my arrival in Trabzon, militiamen loyal to Abashidze had blocked all roads into Adjaria to keep representatives of the Tax, Port Authority, and other central government ministries out. The situation was rapidly ratcheting up to the rhetoric of secessionist war before several Abashidze friends, private business associates, and corporate investors in the Batumi oil terminal showed up to counsel caution. The several delegations included the Lord Mayor of Moscow, Yuri Luzhkov and the Danish high-risk investor, Jan Bonde Nielsen, whose Greenoak company had picked up the rust-bucket oil terminal for a proverbial song in the dangerous early 1990s, and had no intention of letting something like national consolidation get in the way of business-as-business. The Rose Revolution promise of clean and democratically elected government and an attendant anticorruption campaign would not extend as far as Adjaria, the businessmen made it clear. They, too, were players.[2]

This did not sit well with Saakashvili, or with Gia, for that matter.

"The whole point of the Rose Revolution is to extend the rule of law throughout all of Georgia," said Gia. "You can't have little pieces of real estate like Adjaria going around doing their own thing, refusing to put a *tetri* (a nickel, as it were) into the national exchequer. You either are a government or you are not."

To keep his little part of the Georgian state afloat (and his staff from hitch-hiking back to Tbilisi to get jobs cleaning expatriate apartments or guarding the extraordinary dachas of their newly and mysteriously wealthy compatriots), Gia had recently hawked part of his prize personal possession of Georgian gold and silver coins dating back to the tenth century. Open Society creator George Soros—reputedly the man who financed the Rose Revolution—had agreed to pay all governmental salaries for one year in a unique frontal assault on endemic corruption. (Saakashvili, as president, was reportedly receiving an executive salary of $1,500 per month, with a sliding scale downward from him to something like $200 a month for traffic cops, who previously had to buy their place on the road and then augment their meager official salaries of perhaps $20 per month with casual income based on harassment.) But the gravy train had not yet arrived in Trabzon, and Gia was obliged to look after his own. It was the Georgian way.

"The problem is how to survive in this new environment," breathed Gia, inking up his official seal to whack my passport with the annual, multi-entry, one-year visa he had been giving me since assuming his post in 1996. "At least in the old days, I knew who was who in Tbilisi. Now I am clueless. And because the government is now made up of inexperienced kids, they are capable of letting the whole thing blow sky high. The problem, as I say, is to figure out how to survive."

* * *

The Shevardnadze era in Georgia might have seemed over, but there were still a few lingering, last loose ends to be tied, and the most immediate and specific was the question of Adjaria, or more specifically, how Misha Saakashvili intended to get rid of "Batono" Aslan Abashidze, the Lord Protector of the oil-soaked Black Sea port of Batumi. In the smoggy, pot-holed streets of the provincial capital, independent printing presses were springing up, and folks were actively calling "Misha" to depose Aslan, preferably through demo-cratic means, but through force if necessary. The former had jumped aboard a Georgian patrol boat to survey the Batumi beaches for the best landing place for U.S.-trained Special Forces troops, while the latter had blown up several approach bridges between Adjaria and neighboring Guria province. The prospect of inter-Georgian violence loomed over all.

Why could I never come to Georgia in summer, and have some non–war-related fun?

My last few trips had all been rather disheartening, if truth be told. In 1997, Alexis Rowell and I had taken a jaunt down the "early oil" Baku-Supsa pipeline from Azerbaijan to a loading station on the Georgian Black Sea in order to film the impact of promised oil wealth on locals. What we found were dozens of holes drilled into the pressurized pipe to siphon off raw petroleum to "crack" in secret, homemade refineries.

In 1998 came the trip to Abkhazia with Miss Kidder, followed by the ugly business of the May 26, 1998, Independence Day celebration debacle in Gali. Then, in 1999, came an autumn visit to "Gorby's dacha" in Abkhazia with Lawrence Sheets and some other pals to observe and report on the one-candidate presidential elections in Sukhumi. Vladislav Ardzinba won with a handy 99.9 percent landslide. This was followed by a trip up to the Khevsureti town of Shatili to watch urban Chechens from Grozny and elsewhere in that blighted piece of modern hell stumble over the insanely rugged mountainous frontier with Russia to become refugees in Georgia (and, according to Moscow, then create a suspected al-Qaeda terrorist training camp in the Pankisi Gorge, which quickly became a no-go zone for Georgians and foreigners alike). In early 2000 came a turn-of-the-millennium midwinter trip up from Baku with my eighty-year-old father to tour ice-cold Kakhetian monasteries. One was that of Saint Nino, but we also visited a number of others so that my Catholic dad could explore the mysteries of Orthodoxy, all frozen over with no gas or electricity, all once-good places gone bad, with sullen and listless men smoking endless cigarettes along every roadside. Then there were the multiple reconnaissance journeys to Tbilisi to organize the political aspects of a bizarre, 2,000-kilometer-long, symbolic sidecar motorcycle circus I had created down the future Baku–Tbilisi–Ceyhan crude-oil pipeline, which started in Azerbaijan and ended in Turkey, but stretched across very rough parts of south-central Georgia, and thus required permissions, protection, and patience in dealings with road police, customs inspectors, and other elements of Georgian bureaucracy.

"This is the most corrupt country in the world," said my old friend, weightlifter, father of Alexis Rowell's godchild and Hemingway buff, Petra Mamradze, during a meeting we had in 2000. He repeated this remark in our next meeting in 2001 and then again in 2002. The comment might not have been notable save for the fact that Mamradze was the chief of staff in Shevardnadze's administration, and he made it while we were sitting in his office in the presidential building in downtown Tbilisi.

"Ministers and mafia men are heating their outdoor swimming pools in winter, while 80 percent of the population does not have electricity for more than a few hours a day," noted my new friend Mike Scholey, country manager of the Telasi electrical concern, then owned by the AES Corporation.[3]

Someone had opened a blackjack casino built next to the sordid Iveria Hotel, where refugee girls had turned to prostitution and refugee boys into junkies after a ten-year wait for the promise of return to Sukhumi. I remember watching a "biznessman" listlessly losing $10,000 in the hour I played next to him, and then stopped seeing the painted girls lined up like so many different bottles of beer to choose from at a sauna-bar on the banks of the Mtkvari.

"So many people are dying of disease and despair that life expectancy is crashing," said Nunu Chachua. She had no statistical evidence to submit to prove her point, but we were standing at her mother Lamara's grave, which was basically a pauper's plot wedged between trees in a new cemetery on the edge of Tbilisi. All around were other new burial sites, none of which displayed anything remotely fancy or frivolous and thus did not correspond to the traditional funeral exuberance (or waste of expenditure) one associated with the Georgian cult of bereavement. I doubt many people attended Lamara's funeral; she was just a refugee lady from Sukhumi.

The same was not true for the last rites of the hugely popular star investigative reporter for the Rustavi II television station, Giorgi Sanaya, who was assassinated at his home on July 26, 2001, presumably for getting a little too close to all manner of corruption at the highest levels of government and general sleaze in the street. His funeral was attended by a sea of furious mourners, and almost ended in a plunge into insurrection.

Still, Shevardnadze managed to hold on, and continued to be praised as a political genius by the crush of foreign oil-pipeline contractors associated with the Baku–Tbilisi–Ceyhan export line from Azerbaijan and the legions of international aid workers, conflict-resolution specialists, and media development experts. All of them, of course, absolutely loved and adored Georgia and everything about it. Sometimes it seemed that the Georgian economy existed off little more than services associated with conventions: drivers and translators and rented hotel rooms and banquets catered by armies of out-of-work professors of physics or philology and stage or plastic artists and computer programmers and electronics engineers. Maybe it had also been so in Soviet times, and before that in tsarist Russian times, and before that in Qadjar Persian times sometimes overlapping with Ottoman Turkish times and Byzantine and Sassanid times before that (save for the telecom experts, of course). But now the new overlords whose language and ways one had to learn to get ahead were the New Romans, better known as the Americans, who often seemed to be about as sensitive about local issues as Sherman during his Civil War slash and burn March to Savannah, so long as they could chomp down on their imported hamburgers and quaff their imported Budweiser beer in bars catering to expatriates.

* * *

The very incarnation of Americanism in Georgia in the mind of Nunu and her friends was my old friend Dick Miles, former U.S. ambassador to Azerbaijan, Serbia, and then Georgia. There had been a coup in each of the countries he had been posted to during his tenure as ambassador, so it was actually not so unreasonable that many local folks had begun to regard him as the very prototype of the putsch-making diplomat extraordinaire. I did not get that impression when he made room in his busy, preelection schedule for a little chat in his super-security-conscious embassy. I cannot share any elements of our conversation due to State Department ground rules of attribution, but I don't think I will have crossed the line if I note that I was received with a kiss on both cheeks, and that the most profound thing Dick asked me for was to deliver, if possible, a specific type of Azerbaijani rose for his Tbilisi garden before he retired.

Others were more emphatic about the lack of an official American embassy role in the November 2003 events that forced Eduard Shevardnadze to resign.

"What did Miles say about Misha?" demanded Daniel Kunin, the former country-delegate of the U.S. Democratic Party's international outreach organization known as the NDI and current "advisor-on-loan" to the presidential apparatus of "Misha" Saakashvili. "It is my job to try and figure out what is wrong and why and how to fix it, if possible," said Kunin.

There was no love lost between the ambassador and the president, Kunin explained, precisely because Miles had done so little to assist the Rose Revolution in its infancy, and that "higher powers" in the Washington establishment had to be called on to convince Shevardnadze that the jig was up and that it was time for him to go.

"It is my job to try and figure out what is wrong and why and how to fix it, if possible," said Kunin.

"Can't help," I told Kunin, due to my vow.

Daniel Kunin did not hold it against me, and was friendly enough to get me two meetings with his boss. The first took the form of sneaking me into a briefing the president was giving the heads of the various international delegations that had arrived in Tbilisi to monitor the parliamentary elections to be held in a few days, in which Saakashvili acted as his own translator in English, Russian, Ukrainian, and Dutch (I believe). The second was a private interview a few days after the elections, which, as expected (with the exception of a few congenital believers in the Grand Conspiracy), had resulted in a sweeping majority of pro-Saakashvili MPs, thus giving the young president an even greater, and now a parliamentary mandate to continue his anticorruption campaign. This took the effective if ironically extralegal form of rounding up "known" graft-takers associated with the former regime, and subjecting them to public humiliation. Roving teams of television cameraman accompanied the newly formed anticorruption squads as they literally kicked in the doors of the rich reprobates, dragging them off to prison until their friends or families could come up with major donations to the public exchequer to buy the freedom of the suspect. Extorted bail by any other name. Shevardnadze's daughter was obliged to fork over some $15 million to get her spouse out of prison after he had been accused of benefiting a little too directly from a successful telecommunications tender; the actual charge that presidential son-in-law Gia Jokhtaberidze had bilked the state for some $350,000 in back taxes owed by MagtiCom, a cell-service provider, was never legally filed.

"How the stolen money gets back into the state bank account is of less interest to me than the fact that its gets taken back," chuckled Misha. He was curled up like a huge cat on one of the sofas in his office during the course of our second meeting a couple of days after the elections, and visibly relaxed with the power of success. "The main thing is that the individual respects the state."

I had informed his chief of staff that while it was of interest to me to see the president, I feared it would be a waste of his time, press-wise, as I had already filed my "election" story to the *Wall Street Journal*'s Opinion page, and no longer needed a representative presidential quote. She informed me that the president wanted to see me anyway, and so I went—albeit without notebook, tape recorder, or camera. Accordingly, the following is merely a paraphrased representation of what Saakashvili had to say about life, liberty, the Rose Revolution, and even rats.

"This place was full of them when we took over," Misha snorted, referring to Shevardnadze's former office in the presidential apparatus building. "They had chewed through the telephone wires, run around the inside of the walls with impunity—and the only thing Shevardnadze did to stop them was bring in a cat! It was unbelievable. . . ."

He asked me about my trip to Batumi and Adjaria, and I told him that even people who might be described as fundamentalist Muslims were sick and tired of Aslan Abashidze and supported change, even secretly, but demanded their right to autonomy, whatever that meant.

"It is a sensitive subject, and a holdover from the Soviet period," said Misha. Within a month, he would launch a bloodless coup against Abashidze and force the Adjarian "Lord Protector" to flee to Moscow, leaving a kennel of trophy dogs (and cars) behind to be auctioned off for charity. Adjarian autonomy remained. About Abkhazia and South Ossetia, Saakashvili was less forgiving.

"My primary duty is to restore and preserve the territorial integrity of the Georgian state," he said with finality.

We bounced around various subjects, ranging from Saakashvili's relations with Ilham Aliyev, son of the late leader (and, like Shevardnadze, former Politburo member) Heydar Aliyev in neighboring Azerbaijan, Russian President Vladimir Putin, and of course George W. Bush, who was even then starting to use Georgia and Saakashvili as the very incarnation of Washington's model of "democratization" in the post–9/11 world.

But the main subject I wanted to talk about was Eduard Shevardnadze, and just what had gone wrong—or rather, why nothing had ever seemed to go right.

"It was not just the corruption—every country must cope with that," Misha mused. "It was the seeming permanence of Shevardnadze as self-declared 'leader' of Georgia. Perhaps you need to be Georgian to understand this. We Georgians had lived with Shevardnadze as our 'leader' most of our lifetimes— from the time he was Party Secretary, through the Politburo period and then of course throughout the entire Independence period, with the exception of the Gamsakhurdia interlude. We were just sick of him and his style of politics, his need to be the leader because it was the only thing he knew how to do. It was leadership in the old Soviet sense: allow underlings to grow fat and corrupt on the system to the point where you have them under your control because they know they are criminals who are completely dependent on your manipulative mercy. . . ."

At the end of our hour-long chat, I gave Misha a signed copy of my book on Chechnya, and he escorted me to the door.

"Thanks for your time," I said.

"And thank you for yours," replied the president. "By the way, I really liked your lectures when I was a student in the U.S."

The rusty cogs in my brain whirled and then clicked in on that panel at Georgetown University a full decade ago, when a voice at the back of the room had howled out approval to my politically incorrect remark that Eduard Shevardnadze had come to power as the result of a military putsch. But so had Misha, in a sense. Even if the Rose Revolution had been nonviolent, it had not been "democratic" in the formal sense of the word. And where it would lead to was still very much in question. Still, I felt exonerated and just a little bit old.

Dinner that night was with Nunu and a friend, whom I picked up over at the Red Partisan Street abode, and just down the street from a huge equestrian statue and square named after that dubious sixteenth-century Georgian national hero, Giorgi Saakadze. In all my years of coming and going through Tbilisi, I had not known this before. My reference point to Nunu's pad was still the Hotel Adjaria, where I had once attended a mind-blowing concert by that jazz-piano playing miracle, the dwarf Frenchman, Michel Petrucciani. I guess we choose our references and ways of looking at the world in private, and cleave to them. At least that certainly seemed the case with Nunu.

"The Rose Revolution, so-called?" scoffed my seemingly perennially antigovernment agitator friend, who was looking a lot more attractive in leather pants and white blouse than the last time I had seen her, when she had been draped in mourning black. "It is all part and parcel of the Jewish-Armenian-Masonic conspiracy."

Some things never seemed to change with Nunu . . .

"But Zviad Gamsakhurdia's son Konstantine is the head of an opposition party contesting parliamentary seats," I noted. "He seems to have embraced the system."

"It is all a show," spat Nunu. "America wants to make sure Georgia stays deindustrialized and a client state to Turkey. . . ."

She had renovated the place from top to bottom but still insisted that she was an unemployed refugee. Rather than burden her kitchen, I suggested dinner out for once, and so we wandered over to a new Georgian version of a fast-food joint, a link on a recently opened chain of restaurants based on the McDonald's concept but serving the whole range of Georgian traditional quick cuisine: greens called weeds in the rest of the world, chicken and walnut soup, gut-fat drizzled burgers, sausages large and small, *khatchapuri* and *khingali* dumplings, along with *tkhemali* plum sauce instead of ketchup and mustard.

"Can your friends in Baku supply me with discount oil?" asked Nunu, out of the blue. "I am making a trip up to Moscow to meet with some Israelis and . . ."

Nunu.

How well did I really know her?

* * *

As ever when in Tbilisi, I was somehow Baku-bound. For those who today extol the democratic joys of Georgia and somehow disparage the despotic evils of Azerbaijan, I can only say that if pressed, I have to confess that I am a Baku boy.

Accordingly, it was with great reluctance that I canceled my departure from the city aboard the new, luxury night train from Tbilisi to the Azerbaijani capital. The ride was pricey compared to the old days, but worth it: for around two hundred legal dollars, payable by credit card in a travel agency, you could ride at speed and in comfort and style: included in the ticket price were hot meals, all the drink you wanted, clean sheets, private toilets, respectful customs officers to inspect your passport and bags with no three-hour shakedown wait on the Azerbaijani-Georgian frontier, and a rock-solid guarantee that the conductor would not allow wandering bag women to board at obscure station stops to distract you by hawking warm cola and stale crackers in the hallway while their kids pilfered your room. The growing traffic in foreign oil men traveling on business between Baku and Tbilisi and back had made that journey positively civilized, and I had been looking forward to the ride when I chanced upon the owner of Prospero's, a newly opened and mainly foreign bookstore on Rustaveli Avenue, where I had stopped off in hopes of picking up some light reading for the train. Actually, I was dawdling in the bookstore because I had just run into myself, at least in rather distorted form: a modern femme fatale and writer named Wendy had decided to include me as a character rather unkindly called "Kurz" in the most recent addition to journalistic books on the Caucasus, hers, and in a literary style that seemed to consist of half-seducing her subject matter, and then writing highly imaginative essays about the experience.[4]

"Don't worry," chuckled a familiar looking face from behind a stack. "We are all in there. I am the guy who wears 'execrable shoes'."

It was Peter Nasmyth, a British photographer and naturalist/hiker of distinction, who had taken the author under his wing only to find himself moderately maligned for his taste in footwear in the kiss-and-tell epic. We had a few good laughs, and then got serious.

"There is another story for you to work on, you know," said Nasmyth. "Fred Woodruff. They are talking about reopening the case."

Freddie. He had been in his grave for over a decade, but every time I came back to Georgia, the subject of his obscure killing seemed to come up, and usually in the context of a new wrinkle in The Grand Conspiracy.

"Freddie was killed in the course of a stupid accident," I said. "The rest is speculative junk."

"No, there is more," says Nasmyth. "An American lawyer is trying to get the case reopened because the Woodruff family thinks the guy sitting in jail for killing him is innocent. You are the guy to take a fresh look."

"Why me?"

"Because you were his friend."

I feel suddenly very old, ancient, and responsible for everything I have ever done or written about in my writer's life, warts and all. There is never, ever a clean-cut walk-away from a subject, even decades on.

"I'll take a squint," said I. "But it will take some real convincing."

* * *

I would like to end this convoluted story of post-Soviet Georgia on a high note, a closing of a Brechtian *Chalk Circle* marked by a nice dash to the finish line with the deposal of Eduard Shevardnadze, the rise of Mikheil Saakashvili, and the triumph of the Rose Revolution as a beacon of hope and democracy for all post-Soviet societies.

Alas, thanks to my new research on the Freddie Woodruff case, all I can offer is a plaintive, parting wail that is less a conclusion than a never-ending aftermath, and the creation of a double helix of unanswered questions spinning into infinity.

Indeed, it seems increasingly clear to me that the still unexplained killing of my old pal Freddie more than a decade ago is so central to an understanding of the general dysfunction of Georgia, whether under Shevardnadze *or* Saakashvili, that without an adequate accounting of the Woodruff killing I have to worry about the validity and worthiness of anything else in this book.

That is a mouthful, I know. But if a small, expendable human being can be left to rot in a series of hideous prisons after having been convicted of a crime that everyone knows he did not commit, then there is a lot to worry about. Specifically, if the convicted killer did not kill Freddie Woodruff, the implications of identifying who actually did do so are very, very dire. In essence, the case serves as a mirror in which to see the real dynamic at play between that old, imperial power in the Caucasus, Russia, and the new kid on the block with hegemonic pretensions, the United States of America.

The fall guy in this geopolitical scenario is Anzor Sharmaidze, and his story is pretty straightforward. A twenty-year-old village kid from the mountains, in 1993 Anzor got caught up in the nationalistic euphoria of the times and became one of the many ill-trained gunmen who made up the Georgian "army" of the day. Like all the others in that rag-tag entity, he was tasked with bringing the wayward region of Abkhazia back under the control of a central government that was not in control of itself, which basically meant acquiring a license to loot in exchange for putting himself in harm's way.

During a lull in the fighting around Sukhumi, Anzor and two pals-in-arms decided it was time for a little R&R, and so on August 5, they took a "war trophy" Kalashnikov for self-protection and started hitchhiking home. Sometime around eleven o'clock on the night of August 8, they found themselves on a road outside Tbilisi when the random injustice of a lawless land descended on them. Or at least that has been Anzor's story for the past twelve horrible years of incarceration.

Others, specifically the Georgian state, thought otherwise and arrested, tried, and convicted Sharmaidze of shooting at a car driven by Shevardnadze's chief of security, Eldar Gogoladze, and killing a passenger in the backseat: my old friend and "alleged" CIA officer, Freddie Woodruff.

The FBI was on the scene the next day, the corpse picked up by then-CIA director James Woolsey, the day after that, and a Star of Honor soon placed on the entrance wall to the agency's Old Headquarters in Langley, Virginia.

End of story? Hardly.

For starters, Gogoladze and Woodruff were not alone in the car. The former had some floozy at his side, and, as previously noted, in the backseat next to Woodruff sat Metechi Palace barmaid Marina Kapenadze. Along with Anzor's two fellow militiamen (who were later given jobs in the police force), Freddie's three companions testified before a Tbilisi tribunal that it had indeed been an inebriated Anzor Sharmaidze who had fired the fatal shot. The court hardly needed to deliberate before finding Sharmaidze guilty of unpremeditated manslaughter, sentencing him to ten years in prison for his crime. A sigh of relief could almost be heard reaching from Tbilisi to Moscow to Washington.

Case Woodruff was officially solved, sealed, and closed.

Not.

Enter Michael Pullara, a Houston-based lawyer who describes his regular law practice as mainly involving "complex commercial litigation" that requires "an obsession for detail."

"I was reading a news report about an American diplomat named Woodruff who was shot and killed in Georgia," Pullara told me later. "I had gone to Bible school with some girls named Woodruff in Searcy, Arkansas, and later attended a little religious college where their father was on the faculty, and I remembered something about an older brother who was in the foreign service."

This led him to find Georgia Woodruff Alexander, the eldest Woodruff sister, who was now living in Oklahoma, and Michal Woodruff, Freddie's daughter by a first, failed marriage, in Florida. Both had their own doubts about the guilt or innocence of the man accused of having killed their brother/father. Pressure from Woodruff's second wife, Meredith, "just to accept" Freddie's death as officially reported only added fuel to the fire.

Thus began a tortured odyssey into the intricacies of the legal system of a foreign country where the strict adherence to accepted norms of jurisprudence was far more the exception than the rule. And this is not to suggest that obscure Georgia was to blame. Michael Pullara's legal journey would soon involve the collection and decipherment of thousands of pages of documentation concerning the Woodruff case, most of it collected through the Freedom of Information Act from reluctant archivists at the FBI, National Security Agency, and State Department, and then in heavily redacted form.[5]

* * *

My first real contact with Michael Pullara came in the guise of an extended interview with Lale Kereselidze, a Shakespearean scholar who acted as Pullara's translator (and previously served Shevardnadze in that same capacity). It did not take long for Lale to put a big dent in my ten-year-long attitude of doubting that the killing was anything more than an accident.

"Everyone knew Anzor was innocent from the time he was picked up," said Lale. "But the truly remarkable thing is that he is still alive."

She detailed the last ten years of the no-longer-young man's life in a series of prisons that made Billy's story of survival of Turkish jail time from the film *Midnight Express* seem like the proverbial cakewalk.

"He was dying of self-inflicted gangrene after having smashed his arm into pieces in order to gain admittance into another prison hospital when we first met him," Lale told me. "Michael paid for the ambulance transfer to hospital because the prison infirmary did not have money for gas. . . ."

Intrigued, I asked Lale for Pullara's contacts, and fired off an e-mail explaining who I was, and that I wanted to interview him for a story.

"Sir," Pullara responded to my first e-mail, "Do not talk to anyone, write to anyone, or address this subject in any way. If you reveal anything you know about this case to the media at this time you may be responsible for Anzor's death."

My first instinctive response was to tell Pullara to go to hell; that he had no idea how the media worked, and that if I had learned about the case so casually when in Tbilisi, others certainly would as well, and at the very least he might count his blessings that I, an old pal of the victim, Freddie Woodruff, might at the very least be counted on to not do a slapdash, sensationalist job on the reopening of the Woodruff Case.

Actually, Pullara did not refer to the issue by that term at all, but rather as the "Case of Anzor Sharmaidze." Freddie Woodruff, after all, had been dead for more than a decade. Recognizing that, I reluctantly kept my mouth shut—in a furious journalistic silence, I might add—until the lawyer chose to tell me that the time was right to broadcast talk.

He called about a fortnight later, apologizing for our initial communication.

"This is Michael Pullara," came a Texarkana twang on the other end of the phone. "Ask me anything you want."

I had about 5,444 specifics to ask, but settled for a reasonable, hour-long conversation to establish the basics. A host of subsequent e-mails determined a joint strategy of how I might be of assistance in getting Anzor's case reviewed by the Georgian Court of Appeals in the speediest manner possible. Although not a condition of our cooperation, I nonetheless was happy to allow Pullara to comment on and correct anything I wrote or proposed to write and was glad he chose to do so.

And thus began one of the most extended, infuriating, and finally disillusioning encounters with the American media that I have experienced in a quarter of a century. Nothing that I attempted to write or file on *Case Anzor* ever saw the light of day. The attitude of all editors I contacted could have been reduced to this: running the risk of getting killed was part of the job description when Freddie Woodruff joined the CIA.

"But it is not about Freddie Woodruff!" I tried to counter. "The story is about a kid from post-Soviet Georgia wasting away his one-and-only, dear-and-precious life in a series of prisons because for over ten years, Washington, Tbilisi, and maybe Moscow find it a lot more convenient to have the wrong guy imprisoned than to investigate the question: if not Anzor, who did kill Freddie Woodruff, and why?"

But no one was interested, with the exception of Michael Pullara.

Based on new (or neglected) evidence he had obtained, in the summer of 2004, Pullara submitted three petitions to the Georgian State Prosecutor's Office: one from the Woodruff family, a second by Sharmaidze, and the third from the ombudsman of the Office of the Georgian State Public Defender. All claimed to refute the case of the prosecution at the time of Sharmaidze's trial, on grounds ranging from the reliability of eyewitness accounts, contradictory forensic results conducted by the FBI and American pathologists on the one hand and their Georgian counterparts on the other, and admissions from government officials regarding the fabrication of evidence at the time of Anzor's arrest, to a formal retraction of Sharmaidze's torture-induced confession.

In the first category, that of calling into question the reliability of the eyewitness accounts used by the prosecution, Pullara pointed to major contradictions between verifiable facts and the testimony of Eldar Gogoladze, then head of Shevardnadze's security detail and a self-proclaimed "good friend" of Woodruff. According to Gogoladze's sworn testimony, he, Woodruff and two women were returning from an all-day excursion outside Tbilisi. It was allegedly nighttime and "very dark" thus necessitating the use of the vehicle's bright lights. According to Gogoladze's testimony, at around nine o'clock, the car passed three uniformed men who were attempting to flag down the car, either to buy or possibly steal gasoline. Gogoladze declined to stop, and suddenly Woodruff began to flop about convulsively in the back seat. Realizing he had been shot, Gogoladze first sped to the nearest hospital, arriving before 9:30 P.M., where doctors determined that Woodruff still had a pulse, but would not admit him because the hospital had no electricity. Even the initial emergency survey of Woodruff's wound was carried out by candlelight. According to Gogoladze, he drove to a second and then a third hospital in Tbilisi itself, arriving at 10:00 P.M., by which time Woodruff was already dead. He then led security men back to the scene of the shooting and Anzor Sharmaidze, who later confessed to the crime.

"There are many problems with this testimony," Pullara said. "First, the sun did not set until 9:06 P.M. on the evening of August 8, 1993, thus calling into question not only the need to use candles at the first hospital, but also removing the nondimming of the car headlights as 'the source of pique" on Anzor's part."

Second, there is the problem of the state of Woodruff's body when it arrived at the Tbilisi hospital. According to a contemporaneous report by an FBI special agent, the body was in a state of advanced rigor mortis when it was delivered to the Tbilisi hospital at 10:00 P.M. According to Pullara, it would have been impossible for Woodruff's body to obtain this state of rigor between 9:30 P.M. (when the first doctors said he was alive) and 10:00 P.M. when he was pronounced dead.

"It was not even dark at 9:30 that night," noted Pullara. "And given the other contradictions (in Gogoladze's testimony), it is my contention that Freddie Woodruff was killed well before the claimed two-hour period between sunset and Anzor's arrest at 11:00 P.M.—and all this seriously calls into question the reliability of the witness's account of all events that evening."

Third, Gogoladze claimed that he was in shock and therefore failed to follow standard police procedure. He did not shoot back. He did not instruct the police officers on duty a mere 300 meters from the alleged shooting to arrest the young man who had allegedly shot the American. He did not correctly identify the time or place of the shooting. He did not surrender his weapon for ballistic testing. He did not preserve his clothing or that of the women passengers for forensic analysis. According to Pullara, all of this is inconsistent with his training and experience as a homicide investigator, a professional in the Intelligence Service, and the head of the president's protection force.

Even more problematic was the physical evidence used to convict Sharmaidze. First, at trial the prosecutor claimed that a brass shell casing found at the crime scene was from the fatal bullet. A former minister of internal security revealed that this evidence was fabricated by the police—several days after the shooting the police took Sharmaidze's weapon to the alleged crime scene, fired it, "recovered" the spent shell, and subsequently testified that this shell had been ejected when Sharmaidze fired the fatal shot.

In addition, there was the more basic question of how the lethal bullet entered the car. Gogoladze initially stated his belief that the bullet had come through an open front window, killing Woodruff as he sat in the backseat—despite his in-court testimony that Sharmaidze was fifteen to twenty meters behind the car when the shot was fired. An FBI forensic expert sent to Tbilisi to inspect the car the day after the shooting found no trace of bullet entry. But at Sharmaidze's trial, the Georgian ballistics expert described the bullet hole as being "obvious" to the naked eye, basing his claim on a subsequent inspection of the Niva conducted several days after the killing, when a bullet hole was discovered in the upper-right corner of the hatchback. The prosecutor argued that the bullet had been shot from behind the moving vehicle and had somehow entered the car by passing through the rubber mounting of the back window without breaking the glass.

Equally controversial are the completely contradictory reports of the autopsies conducted on Woodruff. The one conducted in Tbilisi by Georgian pathologists concluded that the bullet had entered his head above the right eyebrow and caused a massive exit wound on the right upper-back quadrant of his skull. Pathologists at Walter Reed Hospital in Washington, DC, reached a completely opposite opinion regarding the entry and exit points. They found "with 100 percent certainty" that Woodruff was shot from behind and that a fragment of the bullet exited above the right eye.

Whatever the disagreement between the two reports, however, the Georgian and U.S. pathologists agree that there was no powder burn or "stippling" on the skin, and that the fatal shot was thus fired from at least six feet away. This finding would seem to dispose of speculation by some circles that Woodruff was the victim of a shot fired from inside the car—including the possibility that the death was just a stupid accident that needed a quick cover-up.

"It was no accident," Pullara told me. "The murder was professional; the cover-up, an act of panic."

Without going into unnecessary speculation as to why someone would want Woodruff dead, Pullara pointed out that the FBI investigation not only continued after Sharmaidze's conviction, but was officially reopened twice—once after the arrest of Aldrich Ames in 1994, and again after an attempted assassination of Eduard Shevardnadze in 1998. The case remains officially "unsolved" to this day.

"This lack of conviction on the part of the FBI calls into question the airtight and speedy conviction of Anzor by the Georgian authorities at the time," says Pullara. "[The conviction] . . . was an expedient and perhaps necessary political decision needed to protect the integrity of the Republic of Georgia (in 1993). But perhaps now the time is ripe for Georgia to deal with these questions in a more direct fashion, to assure its citizens and interested outsiders in the primacy of the rule of law."

* * *

But it all went nowhere.

Michael Pullara chased the case all the way to the Georgian Supreme Court and even confronted "Misha" Saakashvili at a special Rose Revolution anniversary meeting at Tbilisi University in November 2004, only to be subjected to a nationalist browbeating about having the audacity, as a foreigner, to question the impartiality of Georgian justice.

"Your intervention here, in Tbilisi, is the equivalent of a Georgian national demanding an opinion of some old court case in the United States of my good friend George Bush!" exclaimed Saakashvili, as applause erupted through the hall.

So much for the idea of a presidential pardon and monastery retreat for soul-damaged Anzor Sharmaidze. One could also argue: so much for the idea of a new, humane and self-critical government of Georgia. As for Freddie's friend Eldar Gogoladze, he was last seen running the security department for the Kartli ("Georgia") Bank. As for the femme fatale Marina Kapenadze, she is variously described as having disappeared to "go fight" in Abkhazia, having become the victim of a KGB snuff-job, or as currently living very nicely in Tbilisi under a new name. Her attractive face, some say, graces a new series of toothpaste advertisements on billboards throughout the city.[6]

* * *

What else might a reader want to know as this wandering opus wends its way to press?

In early 2005, the Abkhaz elected Sergei Bagapsh to replace the Hittite-scholar/separatist president Vladislav Ardzinba as president after the latter had stepped aside for reasons of ill health. In one of his first public pronouncements, Bagapsh announced that some 84 percent of the citizens of "independent" Abkhazia had applied for and received dual Russian passports, that the country was open to Russian investment of all types, and that the Abkhaz army and navy were conducting joint exercises with their Russian counterparts, thus opening up the "final" stage of Abkhazia's departure from Georgia and "merger" with Russia, and in violation of all manner of international law. Some call this the "Texas Solution," referring to the mid-nineteenth-century history of the Lone Star State, which famously ripped itself away from Mexico in the 1840s for the holy sake of "independence," only to soon merge with the United States in an act that many regard as the spark that ignited the U.S. Civil War.

Then a self-styled Texan himself arrived in Tbilisi. This was none other than George W. Bush, who descended on the Georgian capital on June 10, 2005, following VE-Day (Victory in Europe) celebrations in Moscow. In preparation for the visit, Saakashvili ordered that all buildings—apartment balconies, independent houses, factories, and even sheds—lining the road in from the airport to Freedom Square in downtown Tbilisi be bunted out with a rainbow of new paint, making the route into a modern Potemkin village. Following Bush's stopover, billboard-size photographs of the two leaders standing side by side began appearing all over the country as a reminder to the populace of who their new foreign friends were supposed to be. To certain jaded observers, the resemblance to the Soviet-era, pictorial hagiography of leadership was way too close. *Sakartvelo*—Georgia—had just found a new official sponsor, and all official (and nonofficial) rhetoric was turning in the direction of fawning, client-state-style praise: the sun no longer rose in the North, in Russia, as Eduard Shevardnadze had once famously said to his eternal chagrin, but in the West, in George W. Bush's America.

Meanwhile, in Moscow, officials from President Vladimir Putin's administration hosted a forum on "Democracy and Multiculturalism in the Euro-East," which was attended not only by representatives from the major, recognized states that had emerged from the rubble of the USSR, but also the unrecognized post-Soviet statelets such as Abkhazia, South Ossetia, Transnistria, and Karabakh. During the course of the conference, delegates called for Georgia to become a federation, that the Russian language become an official language alongside Georgian, and that Georgia's constitution be amended to assign Russia the role of guarantor of the minority rights.

In addition to talk about the so-called Kosovo Gambit, one presenter recommended a sort of "Louisiana Purchase" solution to the frozen ethnic conflicts in the Caucasus, namely, that Russia use its windfall oil profits to purchase Abkhazia and South Ossetia from Georgia, or lease them for 150 to 200 years, based on the fact that the populations in the two territories had legally become citizens of Russia.

Georgian delegates at the conference took advantage of the forum to announce the creation of an "Anti-Soros Foundation," to combat the globalizing tendencies of the Saakashvili government, and urged participants to set up similar "anti-Soros foundations" in Abkhazia, South Ossetia, Armenia, Azerbaijan, and other countries where American-sponsored NGOs are active in the destruction of "national values."

More ominous was the fact that while Russian troops had completed their long-overdue withdrawal from Batumi and Adjaria in the summer of 2005, said forces remained entrenched not only in South Ossetia and Abkhazia but were warming to the request issued by the Armenian population in the area known as Javakheti, where locals were insisting that the Russian troops remain in their bases and that the entire region be given autonomy status along the lines of Adjaria, Abkhazia, and South Ossetia.

My last trip to Georgia prior to the publication of this book was right after New Year's Day, 2006, to collect the pictures used as art in this volume. Lawrence Sheets was back in town working for National Public Radio. Uncle

Larry was settling down at long last, while a new generation of reporters and analysts had started to stake out turf and cultivate relations with newly arrived American diplomats, now tucked away in the new, high-security American embassy, which was about as drop-in friendly as a high-security prison. The ghastly Hotel Iveria, meanwhile, was empty: along with all the other resident refugees from Abkhazia who had called the place home for over a decade, Marina Davidava and her two kids had been bought out by investors who wanted to convert the dump into a luxury apartment complex.

A sea change was at hand, and I wanted nothing to do with it.

But I still had old friends. There was Nunu and her diehard Zviadisti restorationists, Nana and the rest of the Reuters crew, and my motorcycle pals from the Oil Odyssey, such as the insane stuntman, Valerian Gelashvili, now recovering from his most recent high-speed crash. I stopped in to see Professor Alexander Rondeli's fancy new office at the fancy new Georgian Foundation for Strategic and International Studies, financed by Temuri Yakobashvili, a man with excellent connections in Israel. The good professor's digs were a very long way from the pair of rooms on the cold and dark third floor of the Foreign Ministry building he had once shared with refugees from Abkhazia. I found the Leslie Nielsen look-alike hobbling up and down stairs with the aid of two walking sticks due to crippling pain in his knees, but still singing the same song about regional security, with verses devoted to the evils of Russian imperialism and the beauties of the American president, George W. Bush. The United States had sent in some 200 military trainers for the Georgian national army, sort of in exchange for the same number of Georgian troops in Bush's so-called Coalition of the Willing in the so-called War on Terror. Both numbers would grow.

"Our contribution of 200 symbolic soldiers to the American antiterror effort in Iraq is a small price to pay for the protection we have thus achieved from the Russian menace," extolled Rondeli. "*Gaumarjos Amerika!*"

Next came Petra Mamradze, Shevardnadze's chief of staff, who had managed to survive the Soros-funded soft-putsch/Rose Revolution and maintain his place in the presidential apparatus despite his intimate connection to the deposed president. The most recent addition to his growing book collection in Georgian, Russian, Spanish, German, and English was my contribution to his obsession with Papa Hemingway: a signed copy of Valerie Hemingway's *Running with the Bulls*, the Old Man's daughter-in-law's correct-all-other kiss-and-tell-all book on the master storyteller, and Petra was showing the thing around to one and all as proof positive of the Hemingway family's appreciation of his singular devotion to Papa.[7]

"The seeds of our moral degeneration started with the influx of easy money from Soviet-style tourism in the 1960s, the purchase of titles and positions, and the creation of the cult of the Georgian man," intoned Petra after we had gone through our literary greetings and gotten down to the subject of Georgia. "That cult led to the rise and celebration of people like Jaba Ioseliani and the destruction of education, or respect for the academy."

The leader of the Mkhedrioni was dead; but his last rites had reached almost state-funeral proportions—a scandal, in Mamradze's eyes.

"And Shevardnadze lauded him as a patriot at the funeral!" cried Petra.

As for the man he had loyally served for some twenty years, Mamradze was surprisingly forgiving: Shevy had become "understandably unstable" after the second assassination attempt against him in 1998, then drifted into a paranoid state that verged on "insanity" for the last five years of his reign.

For Petra, the breaking point had come during the murky events of the so-called Gelayev Incident of 2001, which nearly resulted in war between Russia and Georgia. The essence was this: due to Tbilisi's alleged tolerance of (or lack of control over) Chechen rebel forces based in the ethnic Chechen exclave in Georgia called the Pankisi Gorge, the Chechen warlord Ruslan Gelayev had set up shop in the regional capital, Akhmeti. The area soon became a virtual no-go zone for any one aside from Wahhabites on the run, as ethnic Chechens and their alleged al-Qaeda-connected allies sallied forth over the mountainous frontier to launch attacks on Russian occupational forces inside Chechnya. Russia threatened cross-border operations, but was always restrained by the United States and other Friends of Georgia, who backed up Tbilisi's claim that there were no Chechen fighters in Pankisi, only destitute refugees. Then one fine day, a different sort of report filtered in over Petra's desk. It came from Reuters, and said that Ruslan Gelayev and his gang of bearded fighting men had been spotted buying honey and meat in the western Georgian town of Zugdidi while preparing to launch a mercenary attack on Russian forces in Abkhazia.

"I almost laughed when I heard the report," sighed Petra. "Gelayev, in Zugdidi, getting ready to fight in Abkhazia, for us?"

But the Reuters people were insistent that it was true, and that the Chechens had been transported all the way across the country by Georgian security people, and were being paid to go fight the Abkhaz, which really meant fighting the Russians, too.

"So I called Nugzar Sajaia (the head of National Security), and asked him to check it out," breathed Petra. "He laughed as well. Then he called back in fifteen minutes, confirmed the report, and demanded a meeting with me to talk about what to do about the fact that Shevardnadze had lost his mind."

The price tag for this little misadventure that suddenly (if temporarily) seemed to put Georgia on the side of the likes of Osama bin Laden was reportedly a cool $7 million. Given Georgia's dependency on American aid, this translated to an indirect subsidy of the Chechen rebels by the American taxpayer. True, half true, or fantasy? Who knew?

* * *

We had antelope steaks smuggled in from Montana via Istanbul and Baku that night, grilled over the coals at the Old House restaurant on the Mtkvari River embankment by special, presidential intervention (Petra's) and washed down with Georgian wine and *chacha*. It was supposed to be a truth-talk meeting between old friends, but the moment I got up to tend the barbeque pit, Petra, Alex Rondeli, and Gia Janjgava (formerly consul to Trabzon but still-not-ratified ambassador to Egypt and Syria) would switch from the English they were speaking for my benefit to a mixture of highly nuanced Russian to Georgian, shouting at one another about a host of deep, dark subjects, names, and places so far over my head and beyond my ken that I began to wonder if I ever really knew anything about this place at all, this country called *Sakartvelo*.

"O, thou fifteen-year-old foreigner," I said to myself. "Thou hast seen but not observed; thou hast heard but never understood."

It was a relief when the discussion turned back to familiar issues (at least from my perspective) such as the obscure death of Prime Minister Zurab Zhvania in a secret sex flat with his male lover (the official cause of death was asphyxiation when a gas heater malfunctioned; the family demanded a second investigation to uncover a much darker scenario, but in vain), or why the confirmation of Gia's appointment as Georgian ambassador to Egypt and Syria had been held up by the new parliament.

Some of the gossip was decidedly salacious, such as a tip-off by the British Foreign Office to the London tabloid press of the post-midnight abuse of the Visiting Dignitaries Emergency Medical Hotline when, during a state visit to the United Kingdom, a "certain leader of a certain post-Soviet country in the Caucasus" dialed the hotline because his female companion had apparently overdosed on Viagra.

All agreed on one thing: that while it was certainly possible to seek an interview with Eduard Shevardnadze, it might not be worthwhile, and might in fact just be pathetic.

"He is drinking, and he never used to," Petra remarked. "His mind wanders, and the only thing he seems to want to talk about is how his friends deserted him, James Baker and the Bushes, and how George Soros paid for his downfall in order to insert Mikheil Saakashvili into the presidency for ease of manipulation."

And all my friends agreed on one more thing: Misha was mad. Crazy, that is.

"Of course, Misha is insane," chortled Rondeli in all seriousness. "You have to be nuts to want to be president of this country."

If not yet wilting, the shine was coming off the Rose in a hurry.

First came the changing of the national flag from the subdued, purple background banner of the Mensheviks to the stark red and white Cross of Saint George of Saakashvili's party; then the creation of a new national anthem (the fourth in a century); next arrived the billboard-size pictures of Misha and George W. Bush slapped up around the country; and finally the public use of concepts such as "Cultural Revolution" and the creation of "Patriot Camps" for disadvantaged youths, where said kids, in exchange for vows of fealty to the state, were being taught how to lock and load Kalashnikov machine guns and scamper between trenches by drill sergeants in anticipation of a new round of war—but with whom? Breaches of the public peace between Svans and Armenians over logging and land use rights in the region around the former Greek town of Tsalka in south-central Georgia caught my attention, as did reports of Saakashvili's brinksmanship in South Ossetia. While the ethnic Azerbaijanis were high-tailing it to Baku to open up Georgian-style restaurants to make economic ends meet, reports from Abkhazia suggested that the local authorities were well on their way to reopening the touristic Sun and Sand resort business for swarms of lower-middle-class New Russians who could not afford Antalya or Cannes, and thus stitching themselves ever closer into the giant to the north, while the Georgian economy remained as precarious as ever.

In the winter of 2005–6, Saakashvili publicly accused Russia of sabotaging primary gas and electrical power lines into Georgia, plunging the country into cold and dark during the height of the "worst winter in a decade" (meaning that my very cold and dark winters of 1992, 1993, and 1994 were excluded from the list). Russian President Vladimir Putin quickly countered with several devious measures designed to let Georgia know who ran what in the region. The most humiliating was the sudden import-ban on Georgian wines and the famous mineral water called Bojormi, and on hygienic grounds. Jennifer Lopez soon offered to come to Tbilisi to help . . .

The last stop before boarding my Baku-bound train was a last lunch of *kingali* dumplings and pig-on-a-stick better known as *shashlik*. My companions were His (new) Excellency, Ambassador and Plenipotentiary Representative of the Republic of Georgia to Egypt, Jordan, and Syria, Giorgi Janjgava and a mutual friend from France who shall remain nameless, possibly for his own good. Gia had finally received his marching orders, and was packing his bags for Cairo, and was being reflective.

"Our friends should not have bad-mouthed Shevardnadze the last time we were together," said Gia. "At the very least, we must continue to respect him because he is our elder."

The researcher from France was not so much interested in this as encouraging me to delve into a ten-year-old scandal in Azerbaijan involving the defunct company he had once worked for, called Minaret. The founder and CEO was the notorious "Pirate of Prague" (others called him the "Bouncing Czech") Viktor Kozeny, and in the mid- to late-1990s, he had managed to dupe investors from Aspen, Colorado to the Bahamas (including former Senator George Mitchell, who was on his board of directors) into shelling out millions of dollars for future shares in the State Oil Company of Azerbaijan (SOCAR), on the promise that it would soon be privatized and worth billions. The pyramid scheme had come crashing down a few years before, and Kozeny had closed up his multi-mansions and hit the road with lots of coin jingling in his pocket and names in high places to name until he was finally picked up and tossed in jail in the Bahamas, pending extradition to the United States to stand trial for financial flimflammery, fraud, and general malfeasance. And now the Frenchman wanted to spill the beans on his former boss, and give me an "exclusive" exposé of abuse of power in high places.

"Why don't you write the story yourself?" I asked. "There is only one trial I am interested in right now."

"What's that?" asked the Frenchman, amazed at my disinterest in the scoop he was offering me.

"Anzor Sharmaidze and the question of who really killed Freddie Woodruff," I replied.

Silence around the table for a moment, and then Gia spoke.

"I can tell you exactly who killed Freddie Woodruff; we all know who set it up and why, but no one can talk about it."

"Why?"

"Because it is too early."

"Too early for what?" I countered. "So we just let the kid rot in jail for crimes he did not commit?"

"There are plenty of people rotting in jail for crimes they did not commit," said the Frenchman carefully. "Georgia is not ready to look into this aspect of its recent past. We have to first get our house in order and secure relations with the United States."

It was a little odd that he was including himself in the Georgian nation, but I let that pass. It was also more than a little disturbing that he wanted me to blacken the name of his former boss on information he could have provided years before, while counseling caution in getting Sharmaidze up for a retrial.

I wanted to quote Veriko, the Audrey Hepburn of Soviet Georgian cinema, and her parting line in the classic film *Repentance* about the pitfalls involved in ducking moral responsibility over years, decades, and generations: *"What good is a road if it does not lead to a church?"* But I kept silent.

I guess I had been looking for that road for almost fifteen years of association with Georgia, and perhaps I still am and always will.

But the Baku-bound train beckoned, and thus, rather like that unqualified judge extraordinaire, Azdakh, who scrambled from the scene as soon as he had issued his Judgment of Solomon in Brecht's rambling *Chalk Circle*, I will also duck out from between the covers of this opus before it closes, even while wishing the citizens of *Sakartvelo* well.

> *Take note of what the men of old concluded:*
> *That what there is shall go to those who are good for it,*
> *The children to the motherly, that they prosper*
> *The carts to good drivers, that they are driven well*
> *And the Valley to the waterers, that it bring forth fruit.*

Notes

1. See the remarkable footage shot by Georgian videographer Valery Odikadze, which shows Saakashvili and his supporters literally busting into the Georgian parliament in November 2003, and Shevardnadze's bodyguards hustling him away from the dais to safety and then eventual resignation. The material is a mini-documentary included in the supplemental material package to Paul Devlin's award-winning PowerTrip documentary about the corruption-driven collapse of the Georgian electrical grid, despite the best efforts of the Virginia-based AES power company. The movie's Web site is www.powertripthemovie.com

2. I have it on very good authority that Greenoak also saw the merits of betting on the future rather than the past and managed to convince Saakashvili not to use force if and when push came to shove in Batumi. "The ice-cream will continue to flow," chuckled an oil-man pal I shall refer to simply as "sharkie." It did and it does.

3. Scholey was later to "star" in Devlin's PowerTrip.

4. See Wendell Steavenson, *Stories I Stole* (New York: Grove Press, 2004)

5. The CIA refused to cooperate on the basis of "national security," although Pullara was granted an interview with CIA former director James Woolsey.

6. The bad news, however, is spiked with some good. As of this writing, while Anzor Sharmaidze has not yet been released or exonerated, local press exposure to his plight (including, apparently, the rumor that I was bringing in a team from *60 Minutes* to Georgia) resulted in the kid's transfer from a hell-hole jail for rats to a more modern prison facility, as well as a pen-pal communication with a certain young lady who had heard of his case. This, in turn, resulted in prison visitations by the young lady that ultimately resulted in a marriage proposal and subsequent consummation inside the prison's walls.

7. Valerie Hemingway, *Running with the Bulls* (New York: Random House, 2004).

Epilogue: The Olympics War

"Thread the needle."

That was Uncle Larry's challenge, issued on the evening of August 13, 2008, addressing how I might cross newly Russian-occupied Georgia in the wake of the Kremlin's invasion of its tiny neighbor.

"Uncle Larry," of course, is Lawrence Sheets, former Reuters/NPR correspondent but now South Caucasus representative of the International Crisis Group, the Brussels-based NGO specializing in conflict resolution. He was just starting his new peacemaking gig when the Russians invaded on August 8, and was bound to his desk on the third floor of the Soros Center in downtown Tbilisi—which was sort of like being locked into the first bunker the Russians might bomb in a widened war, given the personal animosity toward George Soros and his Open Society Institute and all it represented to the leadership of Vladimir Putin in Moscow.

That was international geopolitics.

My worries were a little different, such as getting to Tbilisi. On the face of things, this was going to be problematic.

On August 8, 2008, I was in Turkey, preparing to return home for a new job at Montana State University, when I punched into my e-mail and collected a message that stated that Georgian President Mikheil Saakashvili had effectively declared war against Russia. He had done this by invading the breakaway Georgian region known as South Ossetia, thus initiating what some folks perhaps hyperbolically were describing as the preliminaries to World War III.

A mouthful, I know.

The narrative was very fluid that first day of the Russia–Georgia war, and remains extremely contentious even now. The contemporary press reports coming out of Tbilisi and Moscow were diametrically opposed, and shared only one thing: the accusation that the other side was doing nothing more than spewing out raw propaganda.

On the Russian side, this might be best summed up as the accusation that Saakashvili, emboldened by his relationship with the West, had taken advantage of the opening ceremonies for the Beijing Olympics to launch a blitzkrieg into South Ossetia under the banner of "restoring constitutional order" and was engaged in a "genocide" against the local population, thus forcing Russia to intervene to avert a humanitarian catastrophe.

From the Georgian perspective, the picture looked quite different.

Despite repeated warnings from Saakashvili to his friends in the West that Russia was intent on reversing the Rose Revolution by force, no one wanted to listen to the Cassandra in the Caucasus as he cried *The Russians are coming! The Russians are coming!*

Alas, this time, on August 8 (or August 7), 2008, it happened to be true, and there was no way I could return to the United States and be forced to answer the question *"What is happening in Georgia?"* with a pathetic *"I don't know."*

The reason for this is terribly obvious to friends of mine who have led a somewhat similar life, and seems completely insane to those who have not. In sum, you cannot write a book about a place sunk in war and brutality at one time, and then remain aloof or indifferent when that place descends into war and brutality again, especially if you happen to be in the country next door. You have to see how your predictions play out. You have to touch base with old friends and compare your thinking about the pending or immediate catastrophe with theirs. You have to own what that first thing was, and sometimes risk something, and perhaps, weirdly or horribly, feel as adrenaline-spiked and alive as your old self once felt—or perhaps discover a new you.

I had to go see for myself.

But not as a reporter.

Tbilisi was already awash in journalists from all over the world; and a similar hack-pack of "embedded" correspondents had descended from Moscow to the South Ossetian capital of Tskhinvali via Vladikavkaz. Thus, my self-appointed mission was to return to Georgia and send dispatches to friends as a sort of "blog" while collecting material for what I imagined might be a new epilogue to this book. The fact that you are reading these lines in the new edition strongly suggests I made the right call, although at the time, it seemed to be one of the more irresponsible things I had done (at least for awhile).

Canceling my return ticket to the United States, I headed off to the Turkish-Georgian border town of Sarp/Sarpi on the Black Sea coast, crossed over, and then crashed in someone's living room in Batumi. In the morning, I took a look around. The city was weirdly calm. I noticed that the train oil tankers were moving in and out of the loading zone, and people were walking around in swimsuits, heading off to the Black Sea beaches. The only soldier I saw was a bearded young man in camouflage who got on my mini-bus somewhere outside of Batumi and got off somewhere near Poti. Other than that, there was no trace whatsoever of war.

My destination was the main western Georgian city of Kutaisi. I arrived around noon, found a phone, and called Lawrence to tell him I was in the country. Though swamped with International Crisis Group work, he filled me in on developments. After quick, vicious fighting in the "autonomous district" of South Ossetia on August 8 (that the Russian Foreign Ministry claimed had left up to 2,000 dead), the Russian forces had overwhelmed the Georgians and were expanding their objectives. These included pushing out of Abkhazia to roll to the airport and military base of Senaki, which they had destroyed, and demanding that Georgian soldiers and civilians evacuate the last chunk of territory under Georgian control in Abkhazia, the Upper Kodori Gorge. They had also reportedly occupied the main Georgian port town of Poti on the Black Sea coast, where the Russian navy had sunk the Georgian "navy," such as it was. There were also reports that they were lobbing the occasional missile as far as the resort town of Borjomi, where the national forest was on fire. They were also allegedly threatening the security of the Baku–Tbilisi–Ceyhan (BTC) pipeline, which had been shut down.

The most recent reports were the most disturbing, however.

After forcing the shattered Georgian military and some 60,000 refugees from the administrative district of South Ossetia, Russian tanks and troops were rolling on the city of Gori, which straddles the main east–west highway and railway lines, and thus threatening to divide the country in two. As a show of support for the beleaguered president (who had just announced a declaration of war that theoretically mobilized the entire country to face the Russian challenge, but then almost simultaneously declared a unilateral ceasefire), international diplomats ranging from French foreign minister Bernard Kouchner to U.S. Secretary of State Condoleezza Rice were on their way to Tbilisi to read Russia the riot act. Meanwhile, the leaders of the new NATO member states of Latvia, Lithuania, Estonia, and Poland, along with President Viktor Yushchenko of NATO-wannabe (and putative next Russian target) Ukraine, were on their way to Tbilisi (via car from Azerbaijan) to demand that Russia cease and desist and immediately withdraw from all conquered territories.

The Russians, for their part, from Prime Minister Vladimir Putin (and his stalking horse, President Dmitry Medvedev) on down to Foreign Minister Sergey Lavrov, were having none of it, and even seemed to relish the helplessness of the West in the face of their "humanitarian" action. Indeed, the terms used by the Russians to justify their aggression seemed tailored to evoke the familiar formulas conveniently developed by Washington as justifications for intervening to prevent "ethnic cleansing" and "genocide" in countries such as Serbia and Sudan. Especially interesting was Prime Minister Putin's invocation of the so-called Bush Doctrine allowing for preemptive war-making with no regard for international institutions (such as the United Nations), as in the case of Iraq. Should any observer doubt the impact of these and other unilateral American actions on Russian thinking, one need look no further than Putin's reference to Iraqi dictator Saddam Hussein, and his eventual hanging for having crushed a local rebellion in southern Iraq, when speaking of Saakashvili's "crushing" of local Ossetians.

What?

Saddam the Beast of Baghdad equals Misha Saakashvili the democratic darling in the political panoply of the post-Soviet space?

Well, yes—that is exactly what Vladimir Putin was saying.

* * *

At Lawrence's urging, I decided to make a quick jaunt to Zugdidi on the border of Abkhazia. The reason for this was my suspicion that whatever had happened in the backwater dump of South Ossetia was merely the bait, and that the real Russian prize to come out of the lop-sided conflict would be the absolute control and likely annexation of exquisite Abkhazia—and just in time for the upcoming 2014 Olympics to be held right across the Russian frontier in Sochi. Accordingly, I boarded a mini-bus in the Kutaisi bus station, and was immediately confronted by a young man with a slightly insane gleam in his eye who was escorting his twelve- and thirteen-year-old niece and nephew to a refugee camp outside Zugdidi, on the banks of the Inguri River that separated Abkhazia from "mainland" Georgia. My new friend, who called himself "Fred," demanded to know whether I was afraid of traveling toward a war. If not, Fred would make sure that I would feel fear by accepting his invitation to be his guest for the night at his hovel on Shamgoni Island in the middle of the Inguri, in other words, smack dab in the zero-zone. I spent that night drinking *chacha* with shady characters associated with the White Legion/Forest Brethren guerrilla groups often engaged in cross-Inguri sabotage operations, such as the abortive operation of May 26, 1998, described in the introduction to this book. In fact, I was not quite sure whether I had accidentally passed into Abkhazia or not until the next morning, when, searching for the outhouse behind a chicken shed, I discovered that there was still one more channel in the river separating Shamgoni from Taglioni. Then Fred and I jumped on a rattletrap local bus and returned to Zugdidi across a rickety bridge, which is when we were buzzed by Russian fighter-bomber jets.

Wrooosh!!! went the air all around us, and I suspect all aboard waited, like me, for the attendant "boom."

It never came.

The pair of raptors took another roar over our heads, and then drifted away to the east, presumably looking for better prey.

We are buzzing (and bombing) you, Georgia. And neither you nor your American friends can do anything about it. This is our airspace, now.

We left Zugdidi at the very moment that the Russian ground forces moved in. They were on the road, moving toward the city—and they were not all in vehicles emblazoned with the blue "M.C." that designated units belonging to the "peacekeeping" force of the Commonwealth of Independent States (the rump Soviet Union set up by Moscow after the collapse of the USSR). It was the dozens of other military vehicles moving down the road that caught my attention, because while the CIS peacekeepers had been given a mandate to patrol South Ossetia and Abkhazia by the UN, and thus had some claim to be in the 1993 ceasefire zone along with the United Nations Observation Mission in Georgia (UNOMIG), there was nothing even quasi-legal about all the other non-CIS Russian armor. Lolling about and completely casual, and even parked under the "Welcome to Khobi" sign outside that town, these forces of the Russian Army had been brought in for the event from Russia proper, and were all part of an illegal invasion force that was not making the least effort to disguise its mission.

The strangest thing, perhaps, was the seeming apathy among the western Georgians aboard my mini-bus. We drove by scores of troops, lounging around the side of the road, spiking tents, washing dishes under the shade of a tree, and not one person on the bus jeered or grumbled darkly beneath their breath, much less tossed out a grenade. Apparently my fellow passengers understood the futility of such gestures or were simply resigned to the inevitable, having been hammered into an eerie and utter indifference about their own national fate. But what else could they do?

* * *

Back in Kutaisi, Fred urged me to stay at his place for safety's sake, which I found a little odd after his having dragged me to the zero-zone the night before. But I was determined to get to Tbilisi, and took my leave. Other people at the bus station looked at me as if I were insane when I asked for any transportation going east. The only way to Tbilisi, they maintained, was a nine- or ten-hour bone-crunching ride via Tsalka, the little town in the upland pastures above the Bakuriani ski resort.

That is when I called Lawrence to ask his advice about my next step, and when he suggested that I try to "thread the needle," which really meant challenging me to talk my way through the Georgian, then Russian, and then Georgian lines currently blocking the main road at Gori. Well, it had been some time since I had done anything really foolish as I used to do all the time, so I took up Uncle Larry's dare and started to hitchhike down the nearly empty road going east, toward war.

My first lift was with a Georgian man named Guram, who worked for the World Food Program. He was going home to a place called Zestaponi to get his family out and back to the relative safety of Kutaisi. "South Ossetia is the bait, but Abkhazia is the fish," I opined, giving this concept first breath, at least on my lips.

"No, Georgia is the fish," Guram observed.

The second ride was with an Orthodox priest heading to the diocese at Borjomi. He had a completely normal name in Georgian but one that translated into something ridiculously funny in Russian, along the lines of (in Georgian) "Son of the Red Wine Maker" to (in Russian) "Meanest SOB in Town." I wanted to write this all down but could not because the priest's belief in God was profound, and this took expression in his combining the concepts of "infinity" and "car" into one transcendent whole. In real terms, this meant that he took complete advantage of the fact that there was no other traffic on the totally empty road, and screamed around blind, up-hill corners at outrageous speeds. Happily, we were finally flagged down at a Georgian police roadblock outside the western mouth of the highway tunnel located at the confluence of the Greater and Lesser Caucasus ranges. What the cops were trying to interdict at that point was unclear, but the priest managed to talk our way through the roadblock with the aid of his crucifix and the promise that we were not interested in the tunnel, but were happy to roar up and over the pass the old-fashioned way, which he promptly did.

And it was there that I saw the first real signs of the 08.08.08 Olympics War.

Big chunks of the road were missing. It was not difficult to maneuver around the outsized potholes, but knowing the origin had been aerial ordinance exploding on impact made the war and the danger real nonetheless.

"*Haha,*" said the priest, swerving.

"*Hoho,*" said I, wondering if we were now a target.

On a certain level, I was not exactly sure what represented the greater danger to my future health and well-being: Russian planes smacking the highway with their bombs, or my life in the hands of Father *Schumacher*-ishvili, now careening down the switchbacks, trusting in God to get him into the lead in the *Sakartvelos*-500. To my great relief, the priest did eventually drop me safely at Khashuri, the railway junction town on the east flank of the mountains, which now served as a very serious Georgian police checkpoint blocking all traffic from going down the road to Gori.

"What's up?" I asked casually, sauntering up to the cop cars, cool as cake.

"No one goes beyond this point," said one very serious cop.

We were both speaking Russian, the language of the new or contemporary or perhaps eternal enemy, depending on how one looks at the sweep of Georgian history.

"But I am a journalist, and . . ."

"I don't give a shit who you say you are," said the cop. "I think you're Russian."

"American," I replied, perhaps nervously, flipping out my passport.

"There are a lot of fake passports around here lately," said the cop, leafing through my battered travel document. "Prove you're not a Russian saboteur."

With all eyes glued on me, I pulled out my *real* passport: the hardback version of *Georgia Diary*.

The cop could not read English, so I showed him the picture selection—Sukhumi, Gali, Zugdidi, Batumi, just as I had shown the folks of Shamgoni Island the night before, and with the same effect, when they started wondering who I really was. Looking at the photographs in my book about his country, the top-cop started finding friends' faces, some dead, some alive.

"How far do you want to go?" he asked, friendly now.

"I told you Gori, but I really meant Tbilisi," I said.

"Then what you want to do is take the train," said the cop.

"The train?" I asked incredulously.

Ten minutes later I was at the station, ticket in hand.

Woo-woo! sounded the whistle, as we pulled out of the station and into the inky dark, toward Stalin's hometown of Gori. The conductor killed the lights ten miles out of the station, as if doing so meant the Russian spies-in-the-sky would not know where we were should they choose to interdict. Minutes later we pulled into the Gori station, a place all the news media in the world said we could not possibly be. But there we were, and there we lingered for about ten tense minutes, faces glued to the windows looking north, staring into the almost dark.

What were we looking for? Burning buildings? Pillaging Russian soldiers? Raping and looting Cossacks?

While potentially real, none of that was evident in our view from the Gori train station. We were merely passing through, and could, because the Russians had let us. Then the lights-out train pulled out of the station, and my fellow passengers started dialing cell-phone numbers to relate their death-defying experience in tense, hushed voices that turned into a dim roar as we approached Tbilisi, letting everyone aboard know they were now safe. We pulled into capital around midnight. Debarking quickly, I jumped in a cab and called Lawrence on the driver's phone.

"I just threaded the needle," I said.

"Knew you would," cackled Larry.

The Russians bombed the train bridge outside Kaspi the next day, cutting off the last east–west connection across Georgia.

But I was back in "Tib," the beleaguered "beacon" of democracy and freedom in the post-Soviet Caucasus, and exactly where I felt I needed to be.

* * *

For the new Russian leadership under the thumb of Vladimir Putin, Saakashvili's "democratic" experiment in Georgia was more than a thorn in Russia's side, it was a geopolitical nightmare come true. Right there, running for almost 400 miles along its restive southern border, was a country that was seeking to join not only the European Union, but the North Atlantic Treaty Organization as well. While these ideas had actually been initiated in a half-hearted way by Eduard Shevardnadze back in the late 1990s, it was Saakashivili who made them central to his internal and external policies—and it drove the Russians crazy.

I vaguely remember the first time I heard of the Georgia-in-NATO application. I believe it was at a conference on the Caucasus at Harvard, in 1997 or 1998, and everyone in the room chuckled because the idea was so ludicrous. *Georgia, in NATO?* What could the economic basket case and semi-occupied mini-state in the Caucasus offer in exchange for the NATO Article Five promise of Common Security, meaning an attack on one member is an attack on all? Of course the experts also thought about Moscow's potential response to this most recent affront, but Russia under Boris Yeltsin was itself an economic basket case at the time, and still reeling from its humiliating defeat in Chechnya. In retrospect, it is precisely because of Russia's perceived weakness that certain parties in Brussels (and Washington) actually allowed the seed of Georgia's hope to join the alliance to germinate.

And Georgia began to push at this possibility every chance it got. Usually, these chances came in the form of participation in U.S.-led international military peacekeeping operations, first in Kosovo (1999), then in Afghanistan (2001), and then, most significantly, in Iraq (2003), where the Georgian contingent in the so-called Coalition of the Willing grew from a symbolic 200 soldiers to 2,000, eventually making it the third largest contingent of foreign troops in the field after the United States and Britain, until Saakashvili pulled them out and had them flown home aboard U.S. Air Force transport planes at the height of the Olympics War crisis. In addition to currying favor with George W. Bush and his advisors, the Georgian mission was also clearly designed so that Georgian grunts could receive specialized training in a real-time combat zone—and then bring that newly acquired knowledge back to Georgia and apply it when and where needed, such as the breakaway territories of Abkhazia and South Ossetia.

It is necessary to note that Georgia was not alone among the south Caucasus states to dabble in this realm. Azerbaijan, too, sent troops to Kosovo, Afghanistan, and Iraq with the same aim of currying favor with and acquiring training from the United States. So did Armenia, although its decision to join the American-led coalition always seemed to have been made more out of a sense of not wanting to be left out than because of any sort of strategic enthusiasm (or possibly because Moscow wanted to keep a pair of Russia-friendly Armenian eyes and ears in the multinational operations). What is instructive is a comparison between Baku's policies toward Moscow and those of Tbilisi, particularly after the arrival of Saakashvili to power in 2004. While Tbilisi embraced an openly anti-Russian policy in virtually all spheres—"baiting the bear" is one way to describe it—Baku was going out of its way to reassure Moscow of the long history that had bound the two fraternal peoples together, as part of a great tactical schmooze-job, and one that apparently has worked (at least so far). Although participating in diverse NATO-related events and even exercises, Azerbaijan made no attempt to "standardize" its military equipment with that of NATO, and made sure that its large purchases of machines and ordinance in recent years had "Made in Russia" stamped on a healthy proportion of all incoming lethal orders. Baku even offered to lease the giant Russian radar station at Gabala to the United States as an alternative to the missile shield Washington wants to build in Poland and the Czech Republic to "protect" western Europe from a sneak Iranian nuclear attack. That offer, no doubt made sincerely by the Azerbaijanis to enhance their status with Washington and get some legal American boots on the ground, could not possibly have been made without explicit acquiescence (or direction) from Moscow. In the event, the United States declined the Azerbaijani offer of the missile shield and radar site, citing "technical reasons," and went on pursuing the Polish/Czech site deal, which Russia for obvious reasons regarded as being directed not against Iran, but against Russia itself. This became another irritant in the growing pile of (sometimes paranoid) complaints against NATO, adding still more fuel to the fire of Moscow's growing ire toward upstart Tbilisi.

The Kremlin's response to all this was to make life in Georgia as miserable as possible, presumably to incite discontent and eventual revolt against Misha's Rose Revolution government. These efforts included Moscow's slapping a visa regime on Georgian nationals wanting to work in Russia (and thus repatriate money), first restricting and then banning the import of traditional Georgian products (such as wine), shutting off gas supplies, terminating all banking and postal connections, and then cutting off all transportation links between the two adjacent states, thus forcing all travelers to get from Moscow to Tbilisi via Baku or Yerevan or Trabzon, and vice versa.

All this only made Saakashvili push ever harder to get under the NATO security umbrella, and as a full member. This program included the purchase of NATO-standard boots and bullets, and even the attempt to prove Georgia's value for NATO training by building a "NATO-spec" Special Mountain Forces school at a place called Sachkhere on the southern flanks of the Caucasus Mountains—within spitting distance of the Russian frontier. This was opened to great fanfare in the summer of 2007.

While very heartening to Washington and certainly infuriating to Moscow (James Baker III had allegedly "promised" Mikhail Gorbachev that NATO would not expand eastward beyond a unified Germany if Gorby would let the Berlin Wall come down), the idea of having a feisty new member on Russia's southern flank—and one that had two smoldering conflicts ready to spark into war with Moscow—gave other NATO members pause. This became only too apparent when Georgia formally notified NATO that it meant to follow other former Warsaw Pact states into the Atlantic alliance and wanted a MAP, or "Membership Action Plan."

The meeting that would decide the issue was held in Bucharest, Romania, in April 2008, and it turned out to be a disappointment for Georgia (and its fellow applicant, Ukraine). Although there may have been others feeling a similar reluctance, it was Germany and France, over the protests of the United States, that scuttled both applications, declaring them to be "premature." Not surprisingly, Saakashvili warned that unless Georgia were to be locked into NATO's collective security arrangements immediately, Russia would attack his country.

And indeed, while Misha's words might have sounded like impatient howling from a distant upstart, Moscow had in fact gone beyond the fulcrum point, having decided that the time to destroy Georgia's irritating inability to understand its place in the "world system" had come. Contingency plans dating back to at least 2004 were activated and the gears of Moscow's war machine began to turn.

Hindsight allows 20/20 vision that makes a number of things now seem totally obvious. Arguably, the most important of these was Moscow's unilateral decision to grant Russian citizenship to the citizens of the breakaway Georgian regions of Abkhazia and South Ossetia, allegedly to ease the burden of isolation felt by the people living in those unrecognized entities. Thus, when the conflict exploded, new Russian president Dmitry Medvedev was able to look the camera in the eye and announce to the world that Russia was merely protecting its citizens. The fact that these new "citizens" happened to live outside the legal frontiers of the Russian Federation contained a truly ominous element—namely, that Russia was claiming the right to intervene anywhere in the world where its citizens, new or old, might reside, such as eastern Ukraine and the Crimean Peninsula.

The second obvious signal of nefarious intent was the decision to send railway workers to Abkhazia in early 2008, allegedly to upgrade the line leading from the Russian border crossing point at Ptsou down to the port of Ochamchira near the Georgian frontier. This, too, was announced as a humanitarian gesture designed to help end the plight of the isolated Abkhaz. As it turned out, those upgraded railway tracks served the Russian military very nicely to transport tanks and other equipment to "the front" in a speedy manner once war broke out.

The third step, observers suggest, was to hold military exercises in July in and around North Ossetia, an autonomous republic inside the Russian Federation that flanks South Ossetia in Georgia—and then keep those forces there in pre-position before the order to "counterattack" after sufficient provocations had goaded Georgia into a police action against South Ossetian separatists.

The day selected was 08.08.08—the Grand Opening of the Beijing Olympics, presumably because the entire world would be distracted by the fanfare surrounding the games, which would then provide a suitable backdrop for a "shocked" Vladimir Putin, wagging his finger at George W. Bush for allowing his hotheaded "client," Misha Saakashvili, to destroy the peace in the tinderbox of the Caucasus on such an auspicious occasion.

So, why South Ossetia?

Quite frankly, because it was so easy.

Ever since breaking away from the rest of the country in 1990/91 after the government of Zviad Gamsakhurdia declared a policy of "Georgia for the Georgians," the erstwhile Autonomous District of South Ossetia was effectively divided into three minuscule parts: the area of the administrative capital city of Tskhinvali ("Skin Valley" to some wags) and north, populated by some 40,000 or so ethnic Ossets; another third, populated by ethnic Georgians, and which remained under de facto Georgian control; and the remaining third, which was more or less uninhabited mountain. But because the territory had been legally defined as "the Autonomous District of South Ossetia" during Soviet times, the totality of the territory was claimed by both sides, demographics be damned (and despite the odd fact that almost the same number of ethnic Ossetians were resident in "mainland" Georgia outside the autonomous district).

In any case, the "Ossetian" third of the blighted territory sought and received protection from Russia back in 1990, and soon devolved into a "black hole" criminal state famous throughout the region for smuggling, thanks to the porous nature of the "border" between "mainland" Georgia and the Ossetian entity, and the proximity of the Roki Tunnel leading north under the Caucasus Mountains and into the friendly Autonomous Republic of North Ossetia inside the Russian Federation. Most of the northbound traffic in contraband took the form of stolen cars, while women, fake high-end booze, and drugs made their way south into Georgia, and from there to Azerbaijan, Armenia, Turkey, and elsewhere.[1]

Tension only increased with the emergence of Eduard Kokoity as the new honcho of the quasi-state. Kokoity, born in 1964, was a champion freestyle wrestler, a member of the national wrestling team of the late USSR, and leader of the Tskhinvali chapter of the Komsomol, or Young Communist Youth League, until the collapse of the USSR and the outbreak of hostilities in South Ossetia in 1990/91. In the code-studded world of the former USSR, "wrestler" is usually equated with the concept of "enforcer," and all indications are that the burly Kokoity spent time in the thug trade after becoming involved in *"biznes"* in Moscow and St. Petersburg. (I often wonder whether I used him as my driver during the Sakhalin Island earthquake in the Russian Far East in 1996, but cannot be sure.) Eventually, he moved back to Tskhinvali, got involved in what passed for local politics (basically, clan rivalry concerning who would control lucrative smuggling operations in the area), and was elected president in 2001. The ousting of Shevardnadze in Tbilisi in 2003 and the attendant clean-up campaign initiated by Saakashvili almost inevitably put the two men and all they represented on a collision course.

As part of his post-Shevardnadze promise of restoring a Georgia that was in control of all its territory, Saakashvili's first move was to put paid to Adjarian leader "Batono" Aslan Abashidze's pretensions to independent action, forcing the Lord Protector to flee from Batumi to Moscow in the spring of 2004. Leaving for later the more problematic issue of how to bring secessionist Abkhazia back into the happy family fold, Saakashvili next turned to South Ossetia, where he initiated a carrot-and-stick approach. The carrot was the appointment of a special Minister for Reintegration, in the person of Timuri Yakobashvili, to deal with all aspects of the Georgian–Ossetian standoff, ranging from the construction of schools and even swimming pools to conflict management among hotheads on both sides, as well as setting up a "loyalist" government-in-exile with offices in downtown Tbilisi, led by one Dmitri Sanakoyev. The stick was the upgrading of Georgian military forces with the help of U.S. and Israeli trainers (although the government-in-exile might be regarded as part of the stick, too). Tension ebbed and flowed, peace initiatives launched and died as Saakashvili's Georgia embarked on a remarkable economic boom and lifted itself ever further away from Russia, even while Kokoity's South Ossetia slid ever deeper into the post-Soviet morass.

Then came the year 2008. Although there had been "incidents" prior to the (failed) Georgian effort to be granted NATO MAP status at the April Bucharest summit, there was a decided spike in intercommunal violence afterward. Georgian police patrols were ambushed, and villages in the "Georgian" sector of South Ossetia came under attack under cover of darkness, resulting in retaliations against Ossetians. Russian "peacekeepers" stationed in the area as part of the OSCE's reconciliation agreement did little or nothing to stem the growing violence in the early and mid summer of 2008, and were accused by the Georgian side of tacitly aiding and abetting Ossetian militia forces.

Minister for Reintegration Yakobishvili later told me that he was perhaps the first Georgian to learn of the impending war, albeit without actually being aware of that fact at the moment. The revelation came when he traveled to the outskirts of Tskhinvali on the early afternoon of August 7 in hopes of defusing the growing tension by meeting with one Yuri Popov, the Russian point man in crisis talks, only to discover that he had been stood up. Calling Popov on his cell phone, Yakobishvili was informed that the Russian was delayed because of a flat tire. "Well, put on the spare," Timuri suggested. "The spare is flat, too," was Popov's response. "Let me send my car to get you," Timuri tried. *"Nyet,"* said the Russian. "Let's postpone it all until tomorrow."

Little known to Yakobishvili (or if he knew, he did not bother to share this information with me), his government was already in possession of the recordings of two cell-phone conversations intercepted by Georgian intelligence during the predawn hours of August 7. The conversations were between an Ossetian guard named "Gassiev" at the South Ossetia end of the Roki Tunnel that links the territory to the Russian Federation, and someone in the Tskhinvali military HQ.

"Listen, has the armor arrived, or what?" the voice on the cell phone traced to the HQ asks at 03:41 in the morning.

"I'll check," says Gassiev.

He calls back with an affirmative at 03:52. The column had arrived and trundled on under the command of one Colonel Kazachenko, presumably to the Russian base outside a town called Java. (Kazachenko was later identified as Colonel Andrey Kazachenko of the 135th Motorized Rifle Regiment of the Russian Army's 158th Division, which had no business being in South Ossetia at all.) When the story finally broke over a month after the event, the Russian leadership first declared all of the above to be complete nonsense; it later shifted its explanation of the deployment as being merely a routine "rotation" of CIS peacekeeping troops and transport—although according to the OSCE-brokered agreement that officially allowed Russia to station 500 armed peacekeepers in the region, all such "rotations" require prenotification and must occur during the day, not in the dead of night.

Why was none of this printed in bold newspaper headlines throughout the world? Sadly, the individuals responsible for archiving the intercepts had apparently somehow lost track of them, and they were not retrieved until long after the short war was over—but not before the intercepts had convinced Saakashvili and other members of his security council that the country was under imminent attack, and that the only thing to be done was to make a desperate bid to interdict *further* Russian reinforcements from coming through the tunnel to join the units already in country.

And that is what Georgia did on August 8, thus allowing Russia to claim that CIS forces were under Georgian assault, and that its response was merely to mount a "counterattack," to dominate the finger-pointing debate about who shot first. But a central fact remains: If the "Olympics War" between Georgia and Russia began on August 8, the Russian *invasion* of Georgia began early in the morning of August 7. Indeed, there is evidence to suggest that the United States warned Saakashvili that Russia was planning to use ongoing provocations to lure Georgia into a so-called R-2-P trap, and urged him to resist the temptation to engage the Russians on any level because the larger Russian plan was the destruction of the infant Georgian military, major infrastructural projects, economic development, social cohesion, and ultimately, political stability, if Saakashvili should rise to the R-2-P bait.* But Saakashvili decided that even if he ducked and dodged on August 8, there would be another provocation on August 9, and then another on August 10, and so forth and so on. The only thing to do was make a stand, allow the conflict to escalate, and then hope for some sort of international intervention.

In a word: brinksmanship, in true Caucasian style.

"We had to," he told me during a 3 A.M. meeting over at the new presidential apparatus building some days after my arrival in Tbilisi, of which I will share details presently.

In the event, the fighting was fast and furious and over almost as soon as it began, with Russian forces dispatching the newly trained Georgian forces with unsurprising ease. Although Saakashvili later claimed that his army had remained disciplined in retreat, and thus somehow managed to extract some sort of victory out of the debacle, other observers begged to differ and offered searing critiques of the Georgians' performance in the field. Many losses reportedly were due to units using cell phones to communicate with

---

*R-2-P was a new acronym for me, and one I like so much that I have used it here twice: it means "Right to Protect," as in "Send in the Marines."

one another; the Russians easily detected these, and then honed in on the positions as revealed.

Intercepting cell-phone conversations was just the tip of the iceberg. Supplementing their tanks and aircraft, the Russians also mounted what some observers describe as the world's first real "cyber war," launching wave after wave of hacker attacks on Georgian government Web sites and Internet servers, which then had to be "mirrored" in safer areas such as the United States before becoming functional again.[2]

* * *

Lawrence was up all night collecting data for the ICG timeline, and asked me to come by in the morning to make him coffee and proofread his copy and wait for U.S. Secretary of State Condoleezza Rice to fly in and demand that Russia immediately withdraw from all of Georgia, or . . .

Or what?

Threaten to not buy Russian oil and gas?

Threaten to exclude Russia from discussions concerning Iran?

Threaten war with Russia over the gross mistakes made by Americaphile Saakashvili—who even calls himself hotheaded and emotional?

Fat chance.

While waiting for Condi, I logged on to one of the ICG computers and scanned the growing mass of diatribe drivel, sound-byte-smooth news articles, general information (and disinformation), and hardheaded analysis being churned out by pundits around the world on *What the Russian Invasion of Georgia Really Means.*

Briefly, and leaving out the parachute hack-pack's cliches, the analysts I was reading can be broken down into several categories: neocon polemical, retired spook, and independent/impassioned. The neocon cheerleader stuff from the folks who brought us Iraq evoked historical "errors of appeasement," such as not standing up to the Bolsheviks in 1918–20, not standing up to Hitler in 1938, not standing up to the Soviets in 1968 (Prague), with occasional references to 1956 (Budapest) and even 1973, as in Vietnam, if I recall correctly. On the other side of the ledger were quite a few Op-Eds by knee-jerk America-bashers, whose basic argument was that Georgia deserved to get smacked down because Saakashvili had had a Tbilisi street named after George W. Bush.

The most consistently lucid analysis however, came from the indomitable Paul Goble, the former CIA analyst–turned Radio Free Europe analyst–turned academic in Estonia–turned head of research at the newly founded Azerbaijan Diplomatic Academy, who was churning out an average of four articulate and often anguished articles per day from his recovery bed in the DC area after undergoing heart surgery. His main theme was calling for an urgent narrowing of the "gap" between what the United States (or "West") appears to promise its new geopolitical friends, and their understanding of same. In an August 10 dispatch posted on his "Window on Eurasia" Web site entitled "What the Georgian Events Demonstrate" he wrote the following:

The war that has broken out between the Republic of Georgia and the Russian Federation calls attention to two features of that region which Western governments have been loathe to recognize and which, having failed to acknowledge, have led those governments to make statements that help explain and are compounding a looming tragedy.

On the one hand, the conflict over South Ossetia shows that Russia is not the status quo power the United States and the Europeans have wanted to believe that it had somehow become and that it cannot be transformed into one simply by constantly suggesting that it is and including it in various institutions intended for countries who want to make the current system work.

Instead, Moscow in recent years thanks in large measure to the rise of Vladimir Putin has emerged as a revisionist power ready, willing and increasingly able to challenge the 1991 settlement, especially when any of the governments of the former Soviet republics such as Georgia has just done act in ways that open the door to Russian aggression.

And on the other hand, precisely because the U.S. and its allies take their wishes about Russia for facts, Washington and to a lesser extent the European capitals routinely have made statements to the non-Russian governments that suggest the West will back them up in any dust up with the Russians.

Sometimes that has taken the form of the reiteration of the notion that the U.S. supports "the territorial integrity" of this or that country, a statement with meaning only if someone is challenging that but one that leads the non-Russian governments to conclude that the West will back them if they seek to defend that principle, something the West will not do beyond rhetoric.

And sometimes, the American notion that Washington can include all or almost all of the post-Soviet states in NATO if it so chooses and that it can actively promote "color" revolutions in one place or another again sends a message different than intended: it suggests that the U.S. can and will intervene decisively to support its friends, something it will not do against Moscow.

In short, the yawning gap between the rhetorical excesses of the West regarding Russia as a status quo power and the non-Russian countries as the West's "strategic partners" and what the West is actually prepared to do in the event of a crunch between these countries and Russia is creating an ever-widening series of disasters.

In the first instance, it is encouraging non-Russian leaders like Georgia's Mikheil Saakashvili to adopt a more forward leaning approach than any country in the West will support, thus setting the stage for a retreat that will leave Georgia not only worse off than it was before in terms of control over its own destiny but also disillusioned with the West as such.

(Snip)

And finally—and this is a danger that cannot be ruled out—such a disorderly recession of Western and especially American power and influence in the region means that the Russians, never all that sophisticated in gauging just where the lines are, may finally cross a red line and provoke an explosion in East-West relations that could rapidly get out of hand.

No one—and I mean no one—would have been happier than the author of these lines if American and Western actions had matched American and Western rhetoric in support of the non-Russian nations who escaped the evil empire 17 years ago, but again no one can be less happy than I that the emerging gap is leading to a disaster for both these nations and the West . . .

(Snip)

It is, of course, very late for this in the Georgian crisis, but it is not too soon to start thinking carefully about bringing words and actions into line so that the tragedy now visiting the people of the Republic of Georgia will not soon extend to other nations in the region and to the broader world as well.

I wrote Goble thanking him for the piece, adding an anecdote regarding the (possibly apocryphal) response of Chinese foreign minister Zhou Enlai to an urgent query from Beijing's new ally in the 1950s Balkans, the Albanian Communist leader Enver Hoxha, about whether China would come to Albania's aid in the event of a Yugoslav invasion.

"Distant water does not extinguish local fire," Zhou replied, quoting Confucius, or someone like him. Translation: "You are on your own."

Goble chuckled cynically as well as one can do, e-mail-wise.[3]

* * *

Meanwhile, we waited for Condi Rice and Misha to emerge from their meeting about exactly this subject—narrowing the gap between Misha's understanding of Washington's commitment to his government in its hour of need—and then tell the world about it at a press conference, scheduled for around noon. And when the two finally strode out in front of their respective microphones some five hours later than expected, both looked beat and not particularly happy.

Misha appeared haggard, spoke first, and was nearly bellicose. His preamble to announcing that he had signed the French-"negotiated" ceasefire agreement was basically a declaration of continued war when he was good and ready. For a guy needing his friends to help him achieve a ceasefire, his language was foul, insulting, and volatile. The Russians were "barbarian killers," and their target was not just Georgia, but "democratic movements throughout the world." They hated progress and happiness, rock concerts, kindergartens, and peace in general, he suggested.

Condi, for her part, seemed to tolerate Misha's rambling diatribe with a grim smile, and then came forward with pro forma cold-war rhetoric that was all ultimately toothless. President Bush had stated unequivocally that Abkhazia and South Ossetia were fundamental parts of Georgia and the United States recognizes them as such and thus they must be immediately returned and Georgia's territorial integrity acknowledged, she said, leaving unanswered the question about what the United States would do if Russia did not fulfill this or that element of the ceasefire accord.

Indeed, nothing that Condi or Misha said changed anything in the message delivered by the material I was culling for Lawrence from my list groups and other Internet sources. In sum, these all stated that Russia had achieved an enormous victory on multiple levels that would be very difficult or impossible to reverse. Moscow had shown the world in the most basic terms that (a) its military works; (b) it will not tolerate Western meddling in its backyard; (c) Europe is certainly not ready to go without Russian gas for a U.S. puppet who named a street after George W. Bush; and (d) the United States could no longer be called the world's only "hyperpower," after having been reduced to saber-rattling as the Russians laughed and savored their return to the world stage.

Additional gallows humor was supplied by Republican Party presidential candidate John McCain's policy statements about Georgia, which were all cut and pasted from the online encyclopedia Wikipedia. Future American foreign policy based on a changeable Web site favored by plagiarizing students? But the most delicious tidbit to emerge from the entire sordid affair was provided by Angela Merkel, whose Gazprom-dependent country, along with France, had been the main obstacle to Georgia's desire to become a full-fledged NATO member at the Bucharest summit. "Shocked, shocked!" said the German chancellor during her brief stop in Tbilisi to express Germany's "outrage" at the Russian invasion. Then, at Saakashvili's state dinner in her honor, Frau Merkel reportedly confided that, as an East German youth, unable to travel to the West, she had joined up with a couple of friends to explore the exotic Caucasus. They were hitchhiking across Soviet Georgia, camping along roadsides, when they were busted by the local KGB (in Batumi, I believe). It was looking bad until then-Fraulein Angela charmed her captors into releasing her and her companions without charge by drinking *chacha* with them through the night . . . or so related a deep, dark source who happened to be at Saakashvili's table.

* * *

I did not have the chance to meet with Condi or Angela, but I did benefit from the wisdom and analytical insights of several senior European ambassadors who turned out to be members of my unofficial fan club. One was a Swedish gentleman by the name of Peter Semneby, EU Special Representative for the South Caucasus, who invited me to dinner. (Being the esteemed author of a book about a formerly obscure but suddenly important part of the world has certain perks.) Another was Jon Ramberg, the Norwegian ambassador to Azerbaijan and Georgia, up from Baku to crisis-squint. While the former must be praised for initiating the event, the latter should be identified as an exceptional diplomat by dint of the fact that he can actually cite pages of all three of my books on the Caucasus. His take on the West's best response to the crisis in the way of providing a security umbrella for Georgia underlined his acute insight into international affairs as well as his mordant humor.

"As a Norwegian, I think that Georgia should immediately be brought into the European Union," Ramberg deadpanned. "And as for my Swedish colleague's views on the matter, I am fairly certain that Ambassador Semneby would advocate Georgia's immediate accession as a full NATO member."

NATO-member Norway, of course, does not belong to the EU, while EU-member Sweden is not in NATO.

Throughout the wide-ranging conversation, I noticed that all of us were starting to slide into "post–08.08.08-speak" by adding qualifying adjectives when referring to Georgia, such as "rump" or "mainland" or "core." This may have been accurate on a certain level, but it was also a tacit acceptance of the sad fact that the best Georgia could hope for would be the withdrawal of Russian forces from those areas it was occupying *outside* the legally defined borders of South Ossetia and Abkhazia, and not a return to the status quo ante of August 7, 2008, much less a complete and total Russian withdrawal from the two secessionist entities.

Indeed, thanks to the loose wording of the poison-chalice ceasefire agreement prepared by the French president Nicolas Sarkozy and signed by Saakashvili at the behest of Condi Rice, the Russians were saying that they needed to defang the Georgian military a little more before departing, and were still engaged in searching out and destroying weapons depots around the country, not to mention loading up all Georgian coast guard Zodiac boats at the port of Poti and hauling them off as trophies of war to Abkhazia. How long would this clean-up take? Russian foreign minister Sergey Lavrov had just answered this question at a press conference in Moscow, stating succinctly, "As long as it takes."

As for Abkhazia and South Ossetia, the general consensus was that those two territories had been permanently removed from Georgian control, and that Georgia had better get used to joining the family of nations with "phantom limb" syndrome, including (to cite just a few, in no historical order) Indonesia (East Timor), Pakistan (Bangladesh/East Pakistan), Ethiopia (Eritrea), Syria

(Alexandretta/Hatay), Germany (Koenigsberg/Kaliningrad), and Denmark (Schleswig-Holstein).

Readers can come up with their own examples, I am sure, but my own favorite paradigm remains the so-called Texas Solution, better known as President James K. Polk's Mexican War back in the 1840s. There are so many obvious parallels to the 08.08.08 Russian-Georgian Olympics War that I am still surprised no one else has used it to explain the dynamic at play, starting with the initial provocation (the 1836 siege of the Alamo). If we remove the romance of the John Wayne movie, we are left with a central fact: the American heroes at the Alamo were the secessionists, while the Mexicans, were merely defending their own territory. Ah, well.[4]

Given the Nordic presence at the table, a related example of national yearning for obscure pieces of lost territory came up that I had never heard of before, and which I immediately seized on. This concerned the burning question of Jamtland and Harjedalen, forcibly ceded by Norway/Denmark to Sweden following the Peace of Bromsebro of 1645. To this day, someone at the table noted, all Norwegian naval officers keep two buttons on their dress togs undone, in memory of those two lost chunks of turf and in hope for their eventual return. When I mentioned this to a Norwegian correspondent in Tbilisi at the time, he supplemented the naval officers' loose button story by adding King Harald to the mix: While helping Harald climb into his naval commander's uniform for some national affair, the king's valet noticed that two buttons had not been fastened on his tunic, and informed His Majesty of this omission. *"Youth!"* thundered the King. *"It is not I who has forgotten my buttons, but you who has forgotten the ancient Norwegian lands of Jamtland and Harjedalen!"*

I sent a draft file on this to my new friend Ambassador Ramberg, who immediately demanded assurances that I not cite him as the source because he had never heard of the story. Putting another nail in the yarn was Per Egil Hegge, former cultural editor of the Norwegian *Aftenpost* and author of a recent authorized biography of HM King Harald, who sent me the following message through a mutual friend:

"The myth about the buttons is a good story, but it is a myth. It is possible that the Danish kings from 1645 till whenever—but hardly longer than 1814—marked the loss in this way, but for them it was much harder to lose Skaane, Halland and Blekinge in the peace treaty of Roskilde in 1658 . . ."

The final spike came from Robert Rinehart, who teaches Nordic history at the Foreign Service Institute outside Washington, DC, and which I include here as a lesson (to myself) underlining how a little history can be a dangerous thing.

"Regarding the paragraph in question, I don't know how the king and his officers button their tunics. I've never met the king in uniform and can't recall having paid that much attention to Norwegian naval uniforms . . . except that ratings wear broad caps that could do double-duty as umbrellas. I doubt if the four kings of Norway 1814–1905 wore their tunics unbuttoned. They were also the kings of Sweden. And Norway didn't have a navy. Jamtland and Harjedalen were not forcibly ceded by Norway to Sweden in 1645. Denmark ceded the two provinces [because] 'Norway' didn't exist as a political entity . . ."

Sometimes it is a downright pity and shame to get confused by the facts.

Still, I would like to believe that the story of King Harald's buttons is true, because it gives hope that over the course of the next 300 years, the Georgians, Abkhazians, and Ossetians might be able to bury their historic enmities and only trot them out on ceremonial occasions, acting like Scandinavians the rest of the year.

* * *

One could only run down the fifty-odd kilometers from the Marriott bar in central Tbilisi to the last Russian checkpoint outside of Stalin's hometown of Gori so many times before the journey became boring.

My first such dash occurred with a couple of casual companions, Terry Friel and the international affairs blogger Michael Totten, who had just come up from Baku. They both wanted to conduct an interview with me in the Marriott bar, but I forced them into a taxi with the announcement that we were going to Gori or as close as we could get, even though they had sworn to their wives that they would not do anything crazy. The roadshow made sense to me because it sort of mirrored the attitude of the HALO-Trust folks, who only hold media meetings in the fields where they are removing landmines.

Racing down the empty four-lane highway, and driving beneath a huge (and thus hugely ironic) sign announcing that we were only some 400 kilometers away from Sokhumi (now the official spelling of the place I had always known as "Sukhumi"), we hit the last place where Georgian journalists felt comfortable waiting for news to occur, and then pushed on to the last place where foreign journalists felt comfortable hanging around, waiting for news of a Russian pullback or push forward, or something. Weirdly, someone had run an American flag up a telephone pole, and locals were doing a brisk business hawking cold drinks and snacks from several beat-up kiosks. Announcing ourselves to be foreign press, we drove through a quasi barricade set up by a knot of depressed Georgian police, and pushed on until, after a kilometer or so, we came up to the first Russian post, manned by a gaggle of Russian grunts backed by a BMP-2, or light tank, lurking in a ditch, the Russian tricolor fluttering above it. Leaving the car at a safe distance, I sauntered up and asked for the commander and found myself chatting with a baby-faced fellow of maybe half my age who identified himself as coming from Dagestan. I made a joke about the fact that I was from Dagestan, too—which is sort of how "Montana" translates, if you want it to.

"Mind if we take some pictures?" I asked.

"No problem," said my new friend from Russia's Montana.

I passed the permission to Michael, who started photographing the grunts and their gear. It was bizarre. The normally photophobic Russian soldiers were acting, for all the world, as if they were under orders to be as nice as possible, and even pose for pictures.

"Any problem with taking a look further down the road?" I asked.

"No problem at all," said the baby-faced *nachalnik,* or post commander.

So we pushed on, despite the growing concern of our Georgian taxi driver. His name was Paata, the same as the son of that famous multiple apostate and ambivalent seventeenth-century Georgian hero, Georgi Saakadze, and he liked the fact that I knew the story, including the part where the Persian Shah Abbas sent Paata's head to Saakadze as punishment for his treason. Then we came up to a second Russian roadblock, talked our way through it, and drove on. Silence sort of fell over the car and my gut started to tighten in the way it does when you start to wonder if maybe you have gone too far. I have to admit, though, that the old dog of war in me kind of liked that sickish adrenaline tingle, and I suspect that Terry and Michael kind of liked it, too.

The only other traffic was the occasional Russian troop carrier, moving from one field position to another; the yellow fields on either side of the road, upon closer if still casual inspection, were blotted green with dug-in Russian military encampments.

Finally, just before dusk and exactly sixty-four kilometers from Tbilisi, we came up against a third Russian barricade across the road, some two miles from Gori, and here we were turned back. Perhaps in another context, I might have pushed the issue and tried to talk my way through. But at the moment, doing so seemed pointless. Our driver, Paata, was starting to express concern about getting back to the Georgian side of the lines before nightfall, lest someone decide to kill us and commandeer his car, and call it a provocation. So we turned around and drove straight back down the empty road, looking at entrenched Russian armor to the right and left of the road and collecting all sorts of other impressionistic data until we got to the first Russian checkpoint where I had made the joke about being from Dagestan, meaning Montana, and I leaned out the window and started doing it again. Paata the driver wanted to go and so did Michael and Terry, but I let them know I wanted to talk, and kept on jabbering at the small knot of Russki grunts, and particularly the two bearded guys wearing bandoleers and quasi-civilian clothes and nasty looks on their faces. The point of the idiot's exercise was to get a much closer look and maybe even throw my best Chechen at them, because that is who they most clearly were: Chechens. What in God's name were they doing here, shoulder to shoulder with Russians? I later learned that the Chechens at the post belonged to the *Vostok*, or "Eastern" brigade, who had the reputation of being the most merciless killers in Chechnya (on the side of the pro-Moscow government of Ramzan Kadyrov), who had been seconded to the main Russian army to instill fear among the Georgian civilian population and create blood feuds between my two favorite indigenous Caucasus peoples that will spin out over generations.

Then I gave Paata the nod, and we shot down the road and back into "Free Georgia" until we got to the first roadblock in that direction. It was swarming with media. It seemed that Alexandre Lomaia, the secretary of the National Security Council in Saakashvili's government (and, at age fifty, the oldest member of Misha's team), was on his way back from negotiations with the Russians, and would be giving a roadside briefing. We bought some warm beer and waited, and within about five minutes Lomaia's small convoy appeared down the road we had just come from, and so we three joined the gaggle of camera and notebook brigade crowding around the minister, who was talking about his having reached agreement with the Russians to remove their most forward post. This would most likely be broadcast as a Georgian victory on the evening news, but anyone with eyes to see knew otherwise. If the Russians withdrew a step (or even a kilometer or two), it was because they felt like it, and not because they were caving in to European or U.S. pressure.

The Georgians, and with them, their backers in the West, had been utterly humiliated, and looking at it in any other way was self-delusion.

We drove back to Tbilisi very depressed, the adrenaline war-jag long gone. Michael later wrote up our little junket and posted it on his blog.

One thing, at least, was certain: Moscow had pulled out all the stops in its operation to destabilize Georgia, from blitzkrieg to PsyOps to disinformation to false-flag to bait and switch to cyber war, and then just good old raw provocation.

The blitzkrieg element was self-evident, as was the disinformation campaign. As for provocations, these took the form of the nightly, languid overflights of Tbilisi undertaken by Russian military aviation. They seemed designed as a sneer at Saakashvili, as well as an invitation for someone on the Georgian side to respond with a Stinger and thus violate the French-brokered ceasefire. I am not sure who else among the newly arrived foreigner crowd in Tbilisi really understood what the overflights were all about, because you needed to know where the airport was and what the relief-plane flight routes were, as well what the (night) profile of civilian and military aircraft happened to be. I suspect that most of the international hack-pack, bedded down in the Marriott and other downtown hotels, remained completely clueless about the taunting, nightly overflights. But from my perch above the city, in Lawrence's house hanging on the precipice beneath the national television tower, it was all too evident—particularly when someone hit the switch on the lights on said tower, to make it less attractive a target.

"Ah, here they come again!" we would sigh while sitting on his balcony and pouring another round of local wine at 3 A.M., listening to the neighborhood guard dogs go berserk as the raptors approached, lights on. If a fighter jet can fly on go-slow mode, that is what the jets did. I was almost tempted to throw a stone, but my aim and arm were not up to the task—and that was exactly what the Russkis wanted in any case: a response, and thus an excuse to bomb.

Another and very disturbing form of provocations to trigger renewed violence involved the truly devious use of false-flag "volunteers" to the Georgian cause from Blackwater-type "private security companies." A best nameless friend of mine who works in that curious corner of the international security sector had sent me a query about the costs of renting armored SUVs and English-speaking armed guards for a couple of weeks. I thought the first place to ask would be my new friend Patrick Worms, a German national and Georgiaphile working as a PR consultant to the government over at the Marriott.

"The last thing Georgia needs at this moment are guys with guns wandering around the countryside outside of the direct control of the central government," said Patrick, aghast, when I brought up the subject. Subsequent efforts to nail down just who the clients seeking the armored rigs were and why they wanted them led to a sudden and very silent dead-end, with my initial, nameless contact backing off from the security project as quickly as he had gotten involved. Worms also noted that the arrival in Tbilisi of a group of some dozens of Estonian humanitarian relief specialists had nearly resulted in a diplomatic rupture between the tiny Baltic state and behemoth Russia. Among other concerns was the big one that Moscow might use the "saving its citizens" pretext in another area on its long frontier.

Patrick shared quite a bit of other data with me that perhaps was regarded as too "rich" or unverifiable for use in the mainstream press, or was never picked up because he was working as a self-admitted "spin doctor" for the Georgian side. A pity, because what he was purveying all seemed very hard news to me, and ranged from before-and-after satellite images of unpronounceable Georgia towns and villages in South Ossetia that had been razed to the ground *after* the ceasefire, to the names, ranks, and serial numbers of dozens of Russian security personnel (mainly FSB/KGB) who had been seconded to Tskhinvali and Sukhumi in the months *before* the August war.

For the record, these included (former) Russian Army Major General Vasily Lunev, previously stationed in Perm District but now Minister of Defense for South Ossetia; Colonel Anatoly Barankevich, formerly deputy military commissioner in Stavropol but now head of the South Ossetian National Security Council; and Colonel Mikhail M. Mindzaev, apparently a North Ossetian police officer who had been the commander of the "Alpha" attack group during the September 2004 Beslan school siege and slaughter, but who now serves as the Minister of Interior for South Ossetia.

Yes, there were fascinating details and new wrinkles to the "Georgia story" being added every day. But the essential thing was this: the ancient, delightful, and exaggeratedly pro-Western post-Soviet state of Georgia had been raped and pillaged, albeit in a postmodern manner, and "The West" (whatever that means anymore) could do nothing more than finger-wag, and in a very postmodern way.

God, I hate that word.

Postmodern, that is.

* * *

There was a plane crash in Madrid on August 16 that killed 154 people aboard, which was almost as many as those who died due to violence during the five-day Russian–Georgian war. Many of the Marriott hacks were happy about this in the standard, cynical way because it allowed them to stop covering the "yesterday" Georgia/Russia war story and move on to the next tale of meaningless death and destruction. Others at the Marriott bar thought of traveling to Pakistan to cover the impact of General Musharraf's resignation, and some to cover Barack Obama's anointment at the Democratic Party convention in Denver. The Olympics War, which had been the news of the day from August 9 through August 12 or thereabouts, was rapidly dropping off international news bulletins, soon to disappear entirely for the very good reason that it had become an "old" story.

There were still some flashes of interest, however.

Sitting in the Marriott lobby, trying to get online, I watched valets bring in a ton of luggage, and then listened to a huddle of American-accented voices pass by my table. It was the "support Misha" delegation of Indiana Senator Richard Lugar, whom I had last seen at a fancy DC-do in honor of Azerbaijani first lady Mehriban Aliyeva. He looked at me for a nanosecond and I at him, wondering if there was any recognition on his part. I got his famous smile, anyway. Then he and his well-fed delegation were gone, pushing world-class luggage into the nearby elevator while discussing a dinner date with Misha and the logistics of flying out the next day to the Adjarian port of Batumi to welcome incoming American aid.

After Senator Lugar, Misha's next high-profile American guests would be Joe Biden (just before his nomination as the Democrats' VP candidate), Cindy McCain, and then Vice-President Dick Cheney. According to a *Newsweek* report, Misha had had daily telephone conversations with his old friend John McCain, then the Republican Party nominee for president, as well as periodic chats with Barack Obama and of course George W. Bush himself. All went out of their rhetorical way to stress their support for Misha and Georgia, as if the two were identical.

The strangest moment came when the Americans announced that U.S. aid to Georgia would be delivered by U.S. Navy vessels, presumably to convey some sort of symbolic military message to the Russian General Staff. If so, the implementation exposed the "Goble Gap" between the promised commitments of the United States of America, the understanding of the meaning of same on the local level, and the slough of unexpected consequences that can result. In this instance, the biggest unintended consequence was kicking out another brick of the fifty-year-old Turkish-American alliance through arrogance mixed with sheerest ignorance. Specifically, what the Bush administration planned to do would stomp all over the Treaty of Montreaux, which Turkey holds very dear.

Signed in 1936 with the shadow of war looming over Europe, the treaty allowed Ankara to re-establish military bases along the Bosphorus strait connecting the Black and Marmara seas—all of which are legally international waters—in exchange for specific limitations to the total tonnage of "foreign" warships allowed into the Black Sea (as well as a fifteen-day prior notification requirement so that Turkey could alert other interested parties in the region, which really meant notifying the USSR then and means notifying Russia today).[5] When the Bush administration announced it was dispatching the hospital ships USNS Mercy and USNS Comfort, it neither notified the Turks nor seemed to notice that either ship alone was far beyond the 45,000 ton total limit allowed any outside power in accordance with Montreaux. Making things worse was the Russian suggestion that the U.S. ships were possibly carrying more than just bottled water, blankets, and SlimFast noodles to Georgian refugees. Russia then warned Turkey to abide by the treaty terms, even while the U.S. media were accusing Ankara of having denied the ships' passage, adding further fuel to the fire of almost pathological anti-Americanism in Turkey these days.

The Turks did allow passage of two smaller ships, the USS McFaul and the Coast Guard cutter Dallas. Then, after Washington announced that the ships were steaming to the deepwater (and Russian-occupied) Georgian port of Poti, the boats were ordered to offload from anchorage about a mile or two offshore from Batumi. This probably scaled down the potential of a direct confrontation between the U.S./NATO naval forces and the Russian fleet sent down from the Black Sea naval base of Sevastopol in the Crimea (which happens to be in Ukraine, but that's another story); it also served to underline just how little the United States was willing to risk for Georgia in real terms.

It was all so humiliating, and the eventual arrival of the U.S. Mount Whitney, flagship of the U.S. Sixth fleet, from its Italian base to Poti on September 5, some three weeks after the original Bush announcement of showing some symbolic muscle, only reinforced the fact that short of going to war with Russia, there was little the United States could do for Georgia aside from contributing to a massive reconstruction package.

The Russians, for their part, were already doing exactly that in their recently conquered territories—rebuilding, that is. In addition to hundreds of millions of rubles already sunk into the fun spots of Abkhazia, Moscow mayor Yuri Luzhkov (a man with his own foreign policy, it seems; previous sister-city aid from Moscow to Tskhinvali had prompted the Osset authorities to name a street after Luzhkov in a weird mirror image of "Bush Avenue" in Tbilisi) had announced plans to bulldoze the Tskhinvali suburb of Tamarasheni and spend some $100 million constructing apartment blocks, schools, and a shopping mall on the rubble, which would then be renamed "Moscow District." Its erstwhile ethnic-Georgian inhabitants were not part of the jubilant committee welcoming Luzhkov; Ossetian authorities had previously announced that the Georgian owners would never be allowed to return.

* * *

I was warned to arrive sober some hours before, but it was already too late for that. Having asked Misha's advisor Daniel Kunin for a Misha-meeting in order to hand deliver my book on his country before I boarded a train to Baku, I was instructed to wait. And wait and wait. With no word forthcoming, I packed my bags and departed from Lawrence's place underneath the television tower and started out toward the train station, only to be waylaid by my new friends, Larry's neighbors. Sadly for me, they were celebrating a birthday—an alcohol-soaked event that custom and tradition demanded I attend. Sitting at the table in the heights above Tbilisi with a Russian-speaking knot of Georgians, Azerbaijanis, and Assyrians, we toasted Peace and Georgia and Friendship and the Ladies and the Birthday Girl and then more Peace and Georgia and Friendship for good measure. We toasted many profound things, such as building Bridges of Peace, and many less than profound things, such as building Bridges of Peace. Eventually, we were just toasting because the bottle (or bottles) of homemade apricot hootch was (were) not yet empty, and one could never leave a half-drunk bottle on a Georgian table, now could one?

In other words, I had just been subjected to a "*chacha* ambush."

Making things worse, Lawrence pulled up in his Michigan-plated convertible and announced that I could not go to Baku on the train that night because we had a dinner date in town with a couple of media pals, which included still more imbibing of fermented grape. Then, around midnight, Lawrence's cell phone rang.

I knew who had called without having to ask. I had just been summoned by the President of Georgia for an exclusive personal meeting, and I was plastered.

We pulled up in front of a security gate of the newly constructed Presidential Apparatus building on the far side of the Mtkvari River, and then were directed to another gate and then another, until finally, around 2 A.M., we arrived at the right one.

"Leave me here," I begged Lawrence, regretting every beer I had ever drunk in my life, not to speak of the super home-brewed hard stuff I had imbibed all day at the birthday party and then into the night.

"No way," sneered Larry. "You are the guest of honor."

He seemed to take malicious glee at my misery, and I hated him for the first time in my life.

We entered the building and went through metal detector after metal detector, cell phones out of pockets and then back in, loose change setting off alarms, beltless pants sliding from hips and boots removed from stinky socks, again and again as we progressed deeper and deeper into the maze. It felt like a modern American airport, until you remembered that this was the presidential bunker of Mikheil Saakashvili, who had summoned me to see him in the middle of the night so that I could deliver a signed copy of my damned book on his damned country, and at 3 A.M.

* * *

A last goon-job electronic walk-through device; a last pat-down by security bulls. An individual who is clearly an aide is lurking on the far side of the screener and looking at me oddly. Lawrence takes my elbow, and suddenly we are walking down a long corridor toward a door that opens and now we are inside and Misha gets up from behind his desk to say "Hello, Thomas—please sit down!"

How many presidents do you know on a first-name basis?

So the president of Georgia tells me to sit down and I do so, *clump*. And then he starts to talk and talk and all I can do is try to sit upright and try try try to remember every single last word and hope that Lawrence will be doing so too.

Misha is almost giddy, which seems very strange. Is this because he has managed to survive this national disaster, because he is punch-drunk, or because he actually believes that he has fashioned some sort of success out of this disaster? He has scabs on his right hand from scratching the skin to raw meat. There is fine white wine on table, and I am obliged to drink it. I see no traces of the alleged gallons of Red Bull energy drink he reportedly consumes every day.

Lawrence uses the occasion to tell Misha what the ICG is recommending and to try and nail down other essential who/what/where/when/why data about the early days of the war, while I try hard not to slide further back into the deep sofa after that last sip of fine, crisp, dry, white, Georgian presidential wine. I also realize that I have to say something, anything, and if that is the case I have to ask the most obvious question of all.

"Mister President," I mutter, interrupting some super-detailed discussion about terms of engagement and withdrawal that Larry wants for the record. "I am assaulted daily by largely ignorant foreign journalists who want an answer from the alleged Georgia Expert, me, as to why you reacted to the provocations of August 7 and engaged the Russian military on August 8. Please let me help you by helping them by supplying them with a succinct answer."

Given the circumstances, this is a paraphrase.

Misha looks at me for a moment, and then begins to explain. I am not sure if it was the standard explanation that he gave everyone else who asked this obvious "who started the war?" question, because I cut him off in the middle.

"Sir," I say, interrupting. "I know all that. What I need is a nugget."

"I don't understand," says Misha, president of Georgia and the center of the world's media attention, at least recently.

"A nugget," I repeat, remembering every rambling television appearance he had made to explain the crisis. "An informational nugget. Give me one."

"I still don't understand," said Saakashvili.

"A nugget, nugget, nugget," I repeated, worried I was slurring.

"Like a nugget of gold."

It was the voice of Uncle Larry, now serving as my Montana English translator to the Columbia-educated Georgian president.

"Oh," says Misha.

"Tell me something I can tell anyone else who ever asks me why you did it."

There was silence in the presidential office for a nanosecond.

"Because we had to," said Saakashvili. "We are Georgians, and have our honor."

"Thanks," said I.

On the way out the door, I turned and related the Norwegian admiralty's button "phantom lost limb" story in its unqualified form, with the implication that Misha and his Georgian nation should get used to the fact that South Ossetia and Abkhazia were now gone forever.

Misha seemed to smile bitterly.

"'Nugget,' ha!" chortled Uncle Larry as I plunked myself into the back seat of his Michigan-plated BMW convertible for the ride back home at four in the morning. "Looks like Misha has learned a new word."

* * *

The next day, with a world-class hangover and feeling like gunk for having been drunk during my personal meeting with the president of a country at the center of the world's attention, I decided to take a last look down the "Sokhumi Highway," hitching a ride with a small knot of Georgian journalists led by my old pal (and Rob Parsons mate), the videographer Nino Kiknadze. I do not know what she will do with the material shot in her ancestral homeland, but if it is anything like her searingly powerful documentary *Chechen Lullaby*, it will soar. Weirdly, Nino and the two other Georgians in the cramped car seemed almost as giddily happy as Saakashvili the night before. Their Warholean fifteen minutes of fame, world attention-wise, perhaps.

The drive down the open road was the same as before—a fast cruise down an empty world-class highway, with speed checked only by periodic "idiot roadblocks" designed less to interdict further passage as to warn motorists that they might get shot by Russians, Ossetians or Chechens if they went beyond certain mile markers or tried to return to their abandoned homes via certain back roads.

Oddly and ironically, the only place we got hung up was near the junction where Freddie Woodruff had been (allegedly) killed by Anzor Sharmaidze almost exactly sixteen years before, and where the cops were quite serious about checking out my I.D. Now lacking the *Georgia Diary* "passport" that I had given to their president and commander-in-chief the night before, I tried to pass off my Montana State University faculty card to the cops as a press pass, but the lads with the guns and badges would have none of it. It was the most serious impediment to travel and research I had experienced during the course of the Olympics War, and utterly ridiculous. Finally, Nino talked me through, and we joined the crowd of cars and local and foreign press corps already massed at the last Russian checkpoint. Word had it that the Russkis were going to make a symbolic withdrawal. This would be declared a "Russian retreat" in newspapers around the world, but seemed much more like a smirking walkaway by all who witnessed it. The following is an adapted version of what I wrote about it at the time in a blog titled "The Creeping Caucasus Catastrophe," partially inspired by a brief meeting with Alex ("You Are a Catastrophe") Rondeli a few days before.

Outside Gori, "Free" Georgia, August 23, 2008: Russian troops and tanks may have completed a partial pull-out from Georgian territory seized during its August 8, 2008, blitz of this tiny post-Soviet country, but that should be little reason for friends of Georgia to celebrate, as the real (if creeping) catastrophe has just begun.

In addition to smashing the Georgian army and generally reducing any Georgian military installations to rubble, the Russian blitz has humiliated the EU, the United States, and NATO by exposing just how little "friends of Georgia" could do in the country's hour of need. Even after Russia announced that it regards itself in "full compliance" with all points of the emergency ceasefire plan negotiated by France, Russian troops continue to occupy numerous locations in western Georgia, and are in the process of setting up a self-declared "security zone" well outside the legally defined geographic limits of the two contested autonomous areas of Georgia that sparked the week-long conflict. As of this writing, Moscow effectively keeps one hand throttling Georgia's economic throat, and the other ready as a mailed fist to smash this proud, ancient nation of poets and artists to pulp again, should the need arise.

At the last checkpoint outside the hub-city of Gori, yesterday, hundreds of Russian tanks and armored personnel carriers poured out of feeder roads and fields as part of the well-ordered pullback, but there was absolutely no sense that the Kremlin was somehow bending to any outside pressure in doing so. Rather, the Russian military seemed to be flaunting its success, and was quite content with allowing a damaged Georgia to come to understand the enormity of the disaster that had just washed over it, and tacitly encourage a spirit of revolt to fester against the government of the young, brash Mikheil Saakashvili, whom many blame for igniting the conflict in the first place.

The scale of projected problems directly associated with the disaster is ominous. According to European Union experts, the country suffered some $1 billion in direct infrastructural losses, and will lose a projected $1 billion more in direct foreign investment over the next year or so, as foreign capital shies away or decides to cut losses and walk away—and just when Georgia, with a population of about five million, seemed to have turned the economic corner and was starting to look and feel like a prosperous place.

One small example is the fate of Karl Griffin, an old motorcyclist friend of mine from the Oil Odyssey days who has been running the Caucasus Construction Ltd. firm in Tbilisi for the past couple of years.

"We had contracts worth $7.5 million, were employing 152 workers, and looking to grow," said Karl when I bumped into him on Rustaveli Avenue the other day, both of us suffering from severe crisis-induced hangovers. "But now the government has frozen our accounts and we cannot even pay our value-added tax. I paid my workers during the week of war because most are reservists who got called up. But now I have been forced to serve them all notice that at the end of the month, they are all officially unemployed."

Laying off 152 men might not seem like much, but Karl says the situation is mirrored across the economy, and will result in the sort of knots of sullen, unemployed men that used to people roadsides from Tbilisi to Batumi not so many years ago, joining the estimated 120,000 displaced people from the current conflict as the lush and productive Georgian countryside turns from green to gray with the coming of winter.

"We are looking at a creeping catastrophe," said my new friend Peter Semneby, EU Special Representative to the three Caucasus countries of Georgia, Azerbaijan, and Armenia. "The only silver linings I can see are the level of international political support expressed to Georgia as a result of this crisis."

International political (and financial) support may indeed be forthcoming, but the big-ticket items that might never be recovered are obvious to all with eyes to see.

The first to come to mind is the Baku–Tbilisi–Ceyhan (BTC) pipeline linking Azerbaijani oil and gas fields to an eastern Mediterranean terminal in Turkey. The BP-run line was shut some weeks before the conflict due to alleged Kurdish sabotage in Turkey, and everyone associated with that project continues to publicly insist that there was no connection to the brief Georgian-Russian war, and that the line will be functional again in the nearest future. Perhaps. But the idea of building other oil and gas lines through a country that might get bombed again will be met with extreme caution by Caspian hydrocarbon producers; Azerbaijan has now started to export its crude via a smaller-gauge line that passes through Russia, even though the $4 billion BTC was specifically built as a Russia bypass. Longtime observers in the region can only chuckle at the idea of the rapid completion of a new railway line, the Kars–Tbilisi–Baku (KTB), initiated with such fanfare in the Turkish city of Kars on July 14 of this year.

This so-called "Steel Silk Road" project was to spur trade from Central Asia all the way to Europe when completed in 2014. Azerbaijan had advanced credits to Georgia to pay for its portion of the line, but will soon be looking at a credit crunch itself until the BTC (and another cross-Georgia line that ends at the Black Sea terminal of Supsa) come back online. Rumor has it that Baku is now entertaining "oil swaps" with Iran as well, further removing it from the preferred Washington-dominated orbit that existed until early August of this year.

Which brings up the question of where all this leads.

At this point, aside from issuing empty threats such as "reconsidering" the choice of Sochi for the 2014 Winter Olympics or "re-evaluating" Moscow's bid for membership in the World Trade Organization or somehow "devaluing" Russian participation in the G-8 group, the West has few pressure points on Putin.

Weirdly, the best might be oil.

If the West (and now China and India) could wean themselves of their hydrocarbon addiction and cause the collapse of Russia's main stream of income (and control over much of western Europe), its behavior might be modified.

Fat chance.

Get ready for a long, cold winter in Georgia, with social chaos around the corner.[6]

* * *

It was time to move on, but before doing so I had to make my traditional stop at Red Partisan Street and have a deep-dark-conspiracy conversation with my refugee sister pals Nunu and Nana Chachua.

Their attitude toward the conflict was not surprising.

"Let the Russians come and bomb Tbilisi a bit so that the people here understand what we had to get used to in 1993 in Sukhumi, and then let the Russians occupy the country, demilitarize it, and turn us into a neutralized satellite state. At least we will know where to sell our wine," said Nunu, or something to that effect.

Nothing new in that regard; the only question was how many other Georgians shared Nunu's deeply cynical attitude toward almost everything having to do with Mikheil Saakashvili. Following a November 7, 2007, crackdown on opposition groups (including several key former allies) protesting what they called his increasingly authoritarian rule, Saakashvili's response was to assert that many opposition groups were actually financed by multimillionaire Arkadi ("Badri") Patarkatsishvili, a Moscow- and London-based Georgian "financier," who had previously been Saakashvili's pick to head the Georgian Olympic Committee, and owner of the main nonstate television station, Imedi ("Hope"). Badri had made his fortune back in the wild and woolly, anything-goes mid-1990s in Boris Yeltsin's Moscow, but was allegedly run out of town with the rise of Vladimir Putin due to Badri's connections to self-exiled Russian media tycoon and oligarch Boris Berezovsky. Badri was also connected to Andrey Lugovoi—the (former) FSB/KGB man suspected by Scotland Yard to have been the sinister hand behind the bizarre death in 2006 of defector Aleksandr Litvinenko, but who was spared extradition to London or trial by Russian courts by dint of his immunity status as a newly elected member of the Russian Duma. Litvinenko, too, was a former FSB (KGB) operative, but one who had flip-flopped and fled to London and become part of Berezovsky's security entourage. He supposedly was about to blow the whistle on Putin for some nefarious crime when Litvinenko (allegedly) tried to recruit Lugovoi to the cause, whereupon Putin (allegedly) ordered his slow, excruciating murder by means of Polonium-210 poisoning at the hands of Lugovoi. What Badri may have had to do with any of this is unknown, aside from running in the same émigré circles in London, and also dying a mysterious death. After Saakashvili had closed down Imedi on some legal pretext, Badri announced that he was running for president against Misha, and put his personal fortune behind the opposition. Then he thought better of it, and withdrew from the race even while offering a $100 million bribe to a Saakashvili loyalist to claim massive fraud in the January 5, 2008, polls.

This was caught by a hidden camera and broadcast throughout the land. In the event, Misha won the election and claimed a renewed mandate from the people; international election monitors slapped him on the wrist a bit, but declined to join opposition leaders in claiming that the polls had been rigged. Patarkatsishvili died soon afterward in London, with cries and rumors of foul play almost immediately trumping the announcement that he had suffered a fatal heart attack.

A real-life made-for-Hollywood grand conspiracy, or a series of coincidences bouncing around in Nunu's creative political mind?

The only constant seemed to be that association with Misha often seemed to bring people low.

Meanwhile, as Misha and his ministers desperately tried to keep the Georgia story alive, media-wise, by evoking the litany of Western cave-ins to fascists like Hitler and communists like Stalin, an increasing number of erstwhile Saakashvili allies-turned-opponents were trying to get their nuanced voices heard, but were failing for the very good reason that Misha had largely succeeded in making himself synonymous with the cause of "Georgia," at least outside the frontiers of that state. Former foreign minister Nino Burjanadze could demand a parliamentary inquiry into the actual number of dead resulting from the Olympics War, along with the causes and circumstances, and even accuse Saakashvili of blatant lying about the disaster, but the president's response (or lack thereof) never translated into a "story" that could play in the foreign press. The lede of "Russia Invaded Georgia One Fine Day Because Russians Do Things Like That" was so much easier to comprehend than (and this is no joke) the analysis of the findings of Misha's "Temporary Committee to Study Russia's Military Aggression and Other Actions Undertaken with the Aim to Infringe [on] Georgia's Territorial Integrity."

Whew . . .

For the record, depending on how one counts, casualties accruing from the "hot" period of the war turned out to be surprisingly low. Discounting the original Russian disinformation number of South Ossetians killed by rampaging Georgians (2,000—a figure repeated so often that many foreigners came to accept it, while the Russian human rights group Memorial could only come up with around 100 confirmed dead), according to most statistic-keepers the Russian deaths were in the upper two digits—71—with a composite number of 200 Georgian military and police killed in action (and a whopping 1,964 wounded). The most painful number for Georgia was the initial 158,000 displaced from South Ossetia and neighboring "pure" Georgian regions such as Gori (56,000; many of whom would return home by October) and the Gali region of Abkhazia, plus the Svans of the Upper Kodori Gorge.

Tragic and sad, yes—but a drop in the bucket compared to the wars that rocked Georgia between 1990 and 1993, when some 25,000 were killed and 250,000 made homeless. What was most notable about the events of August 2008 was their apparent permanence, and how the brief conflict had so changed the post-Soviet Caucasus (and indeed, the world). I figured that the next best place to take a look at the new seismic fault line was my home-away-from-home in the region, the neighboring republic of Azerbaijan.

* * *

I missed the Tbilisi–Baku Iron Horse at Tbilisi station, but caught up with the beast during its three-hour wait at the Georgian–Azerbaijani frontier, thanks to some very good driving by my new pal Paata, the taxi driver named after the son of Giorgi Saakadze.

Getting to that station, on the far side of the industrial wasteland town of Rustavi and the prison-land outside it, was nothing new for me; I had shown up without a ticket a half-dozen times before, handed the conductor a couple of bucks, and *presto*, gone on my way to the Land of Fire.

But this time it was different.

For starters, the conductor and other stewards working the passenger wagons were all Azerbaijani women, and they would have none of this "let me slip you a bill and give me a berth" business that I used to get away with all the time when the train was staffed with males. It took real convincing (speaking Azerbaijani of course helped) as well as the real promise that I would allow myself to get kicked off the train if there were no ticket to be had at the first station on the Azerbaijani side of the border.

In the morning, my friend Yusuf Agayev picked me up at the Baku station and we went through our standard *realpolitik* evaluation of the situation.

As a military man and historian (wounded in action three times during the Armenian–Azerbaijan war over Karabakh of 1991–94), Yusuf now works for Transparency International, and could only chortle about reports that the Russians had merely made an emergency (if disproportionate) response to Saakashvili's "invasion" of South Ossetia.

"In war, all wars, there is an order of battle, and an order of command," Yusuf snickered. "The general orders the colonel to order the major to order the captain to order the lieutenant to order the sergeant to order the corporal to order the private to drive the tank to the right or left to attack or defend points A, B, or C in association with infantry group M, N, or O and to refuel at depot X or Y or Z. You do not get that organization done in a day without pre-existing plans."

We scooted back to his place in a nondescript Baku suburb for me to wash the week of road-filth out of my clothes, have a quick breakfast, and watch and compare Russian TV with the BBC reports on the decision of the Russian Duma's upper house to ask for recognition of South Ossetia and Abkhazia as independent states. What was so extraordinary about this largely pro forma process was the almost desperate belief of Western leaders that their words held any sway over Russia at all. George W. Bush, Gordon Brown, and Nicolas Sarkozy had all "warned" Russia not to recognize the two wayward entities lest the West impose diverse meaningless sanctions, and the words of warning were picked up and paraphrased by the diverse expert talking-heads on Russian affairs at the BBC, CNN, and Fox, who advised viewers why Moscow needed to take seriously the toothless threats (changing the venue of the 2014 Olympics, nonadmittance to the WTO, go-slow on the G-8, and so on), even while Russian television stations were devoting live, exclusive coverage to the thundering, standing ovation afforded South Ossetian leader Eduard Kokoity and Abkhaz leader Sergei Bagapsh when they approached the Duma dais to thank the Russian Federation for recognizing them as independent statelets. The disconnect between the West's perception of its ability to influence much less govern events in the lands of the former USSR and the real situation could not have been greater, but became even more profound with the prediction by the same "expert" commentators that Russian President Medvedev would of course take the West's reaction into account before signing the Duma's recommendation into law in accordance with the Russian constitution.

But Medvedev did no such thing.

Within twenty-four hours, the former Gazprom boss and Putin acolyte not only inked his signature on the Duma recognition document, but invited the international hack-pack to his luxurious dacha outside the Russian Black Sea resort city of Sochi to celebrate the fact of his presidential imprimatur on the Abkhaz/South Ossetian recognition business in a series of oh-so-exclusive and oh-so-respectful interviews. Ironically, one invited guest was none other than the BBC's Bridget Kendall, my media colleague of "Quest for Gamsakhurdia" fame from January 1992. CNN, Al-Jazeera, and other mass-media outlets soon followed suit in their obsequious homage and de facto (and almost breathless) sanction of the Russian invasion of Georgia and subsequent recognition of the two entities.

For balance, the BBC and all the others generally rolled live, rambling interviews with Saakashvili, who usually appeared unkempt, distracted, and scratching his scabby wrists. Unlike Medvedev, Misha was repeatedly subjected to unregal interruptions by the interviewers, along the lines of *"Excuse me Mister President, but you told our listeners the same thing last week . . ."*

* * *

The next three days in Baku were a bit of a blur, but all infused with a sense that, thanks to the Russian–Georgian 08.08.08 Olympics War, Azerbaijan had, as I suspected, become an international cul de sac, and knew it all too well.

I had meetings with former and new friends ranging from government to opposition types among locals to progovernment and antigovernment types among the internationals. It was all very interesting and I suspect that most conversations were under Chatham House rules of no attribution, but I will cut and paste from an article written by (former) U.S. ambassador to Azerbaijan, Stanley Escudero, who set up a lunch with me and the board of directors of the U.S.–Azerbaijan Chamber of Commerce. Our rather pessimistic views on the "creeping catastrophe" in Georgia coincided closely and Escudero wanted the AzCham folks to hear my "from the front" report because it mirrored his own take.

In my view this affair is an exercise in nineteenth-century balance of power politics in which it continues to be the case that the strong do what they can while the weak suffer what they must. And brilliantly played by Moscow so far.

In the short term the Russians are going to win this one. The question is, "What exactly do they want to win?" If what they seek is to institutionalize the separation of South Ossetia and Abkhazia from Georgia proper, I believe that the West will reluctantly acquiesce, in fact if not in name. There is no choice. The present Georgian government insists that it will never accept separation but, in the end, what can it do about it? Public acceptance would doubtless prove politically fatal to Saakashvili but the ceasefire itself was built on the time-honored diplomatic tactic of constructive uncertainty and it is the essence of good diplomacy to devise those polite fictions which enable even the reluctant to disguise the inevitable. . . .

There are any number of hypothetical scenarios which could produce regime change in Georgia but, fortunately, the Kremlin seems to have decided not to follow the most direct one—simply conquering the country and replacing the government by main force. One likely scenario for coming days has the Russians insisting on maintaining substantial armed force within Georgia until the arrival and emplacement of the international peacekeepers envisaged by the ceasefire agreement on grounds that internal Georgian security cannot otherwise be assured. Afterwards it seems probable that Moscow will permanently re-enforce the numbers and military capacities of its peacekeepers within South Ossetia and Abkhazia and conduct occasional armed probes into Georgian territory on one security ground or another.

These and other measures could be intended to increase internal Georgian dissatisfaction with Saakashvili's regime, creating conditions in which a Russian-backed but publicly deniable movement to replace him could succeed. Stranger things have happened. But any scenario which involves regime change in Georgia, and thus dramatically increased Russian influence over the east-west flow of oil and gas, significantly raises the stakes for the West, Russia, Georgia and the South Caucasus. And that leads one to ask what, questions of payback for Kosovo and national prestige aside, would Russia hope to gain by having a government in Tbilisi more responsive to its wishes?

The risks to the West stemming from regime change in Georgia would virtually ensure western counter measures to damage Russian interests. The French, Germans, Poles, Ukrainians and the Baltic nations have demonstrated their support for the Tbilisi government. But the more severe the counter measures under consideration, the less likely it is that the Europeans (well aware of their energy dependence) will be unified in supporting their imposition or their implementation. NATO, for example, has so far shown itself incapable of anything more than a relatively mild statement of disapproval on the invasion.

The West will try to keep its response proportional to Russian actions so, if Russia can be satisfied with the gains in regional prestige it has already achieved along with the separation of South Ossetia and Abkhazia, as opposed to regime change or something more, the chill in the Russo-Western relationship will be less deep and of shorter duration. At some point, before the process of action and counter action sets too many teeth a-grind, Russia, the United States, and, one hopes, a unified Europe need to sit down for a no-holds-barred discussion of their respective interests and how they can be mutually accommodated.

More immediately the whole crisis and the possibilities that flow from it suggest that Azerbaijan and those of us who live and work here are entering a very delicate period in which Azerbaijani oil and gas passing through Georgia will be as secure as Russia wants it to be. No matter how it turns out, Russia has made a compelling statement regarding its perception of the scope of its interests, its willingness to act on that perception and the limits of Western opposition to such action. None of this will be lost on regional governments.

This period will call for extremely deft management of Azerbaijan's role within what I call the Quadrilateral Balance. Think of Azerbaijan as a point within a square defined at its four corners by Russia, Iran, Turkey and the West (the US and Europe). The Azeri point can never move too close or too far away from any of the four corners but must periodically adjust its position within the square in response to developments at the four corners. Easy to describe but very hard to do. Fortunately, President Ilham Aliyev is very, very good at this. We can be sure that he is paying the closest attention to events and should have confidence in his sure-handed ability to guide Azerbaijan through this suddenly troubled period. The Azeri government has already issued a statement supporting Georgia's territorial integrity. This was a courageous step in view of the obvious risks but Baku could do no less, as territorial integrity is the very heart of its position demanding the freedom of Nagorno Karabakh and the other seven provinces from Armenian aggression and occupation.

As for those of us who conduct business in Azerbaijan, we need to recognize that in this process we, even the largest among us, are not actors but are acted upon. This is a time for careful observation, for assessment and adaptation, for hedging our bets while advancing our business plans and continuing our businesses in ways which help both our bottom lines and the future of Azerbaijan.

Finally, I cannot state too unequivocally that the views expressed here are entirely my own. They do not reflect the opinions of the American Chamber of Commerce in Azerbaijan, the Government of the United States or those of any other government, institution or entity.

Thanks, Stan.

* * *

On several occasions during the August war, I posited something along the lines of my belief that if South Ossetia was the "bait" used by the Russians, then Abkhazia was the "fish" they meant to catch. Several of my interlocutors tried to correct this assessment by suggesting that while South Ossetia was clearly the bait, the fish was Georgia itself. I, in turn, would now like to correct that notion, and posit that if South Ossetia was the worm and Abkhazia a rather attractive acquisition, Georgia was less the fish itself than the net, and that the actual prize catch was (or is) oil- and gas-rich Azerbaijan.

But, as suggested by Stan Escudero in other words ("quadrilateral balance"), Azerbaijan is as slippery as a Yellowstone trout. While it is true that, in addition to restarting oil shipments via Russia, Baku has started "swaps" with Iran, thus giving itself other export options outside the much-vaunted BTC line, this is only part of the story, and one that seems to change day by day. (The irony about this be-friendly-with-everyone policy is that it is the mirror image of the mantra that drove the BTC to completion: "Happiness is multiple pipelines," which really meant "Avoid Russia and Iran.") What the brief Georgia–Russia war so clearly exposed was the embarrassing fact that the BTC itself was a solo (and vulnerable) oil artery, and that Baku's economic and geopolitical future might be better served not by pumping all its crude to Western markets via Georgia and Turkey, but by giving a nod of respect (and transit fees) to both Moscow and Tehran. But as a new friend in Baku (who claims he did not coin the phrase) remarked, "Oil is money but gas is power"; and that is where Moscow's real focus would appear to be: establishing itself as a global power by exploiting its hammerlock on gas-based energy reserves.

Europe, of course, is famously overexposed to Russian energy blackmail, as evidenced by the brownouts during the winters of 2006 and 2007 when the Russian Gazprom decided to remind Ukraine whose hand was on the gas spigot. The real weak link in the chain, however, is Turkey, which was made all too evident at various points during the August crisis, ranging from Ankara's application of the spirit and letter of the 1936 Montreaux convention to the announcement of the new "Caucasus Stability Platform," with Moscow in the cat-bird seat. All were a function of Turkey's extraordinary dependency on Russian natural gas to provide heat and light: more than half of all energy produced in Turkey comes from natural gas, and two-thirds of that gas comes from Russia.

How strange, then, that Azerbaijan's President Ilham Aliyev, while paying lip-service to Moscow's resurgence as a major player in the region, should decline Moscow's offer to buy all of Azerbaijan's natural gas at the European market price, and recommit the country to its role as the "cork in the bottle"

(Zbig Brzezinski's phrase) in an alternative Caspian-gas-to-Europe scheme known as Nabucco, which, like the BTC, would avoid passing through Russian territory.

At an energy summit in Baku in November 2008, which was attended by presidents and other senior officials from fourteen countries in the Caspian, Black Sea, Central European, and Baltic regions, as well as U.S. and EU delegations, President Aliyev was quoted as telling Lithuania's President Valdas Adamkus that: "From a business point of view, the [Russian-proposed] agreement should be signed and everything given to Russia. But there are other values and goals that override a good business proposal."

Even more extraordinary was the signing of a five-year contract for Azerbaijani gas supplies to Georgia, which effectively frees Georgia from dependence on Gazprom, as well as the signing of (yet another) deal designed to route significant amounts of Kazakh oil—after its transit across the Caspian via barge—into the BTC.

The question that remains is what form Russia's inevitable response to this Azerbaijani waltz-on-the-high-wire act might take. Stirring the embers of the Karabakh conflict would be the most obvious means of letting Baku feel the Kremlin's disproval of an overly independent line. If there is one thing the Azerbaijani leadership learned from the South Ossetian conflict (and the de facto secession of Abkhazia, too), it is that no Western power is going to come to Baku's rescue if push comes to shove.

* * *

So, as this updated version of *Georgia Diary* goes to press in late 2008, what is the status of Georgia's two breakaway territories?

Aside from Russia, at last count only Belarus and Nicaragua have recognized the independence of South Ossetia and Abkhazia. This is nothing like the almost instant recognition of Kosovo's declaration of sovereignty by much of the world in early 2008; but it is still a step closer to the general dissolution of the Old World Order put in place following World War II, and raises the energizing idea of the right of self-determination for every imaginable national group in world history. How deny the Abkhaz or the South Ossetians their own state when the Kosovar Albanians get theirs?

In the context of Georgia, the same national self-determination/deconstruction program now seems set for areas as different as the northwestern region known as Mingrelia, inhabited by the descendants of Medea of the Golden Fleece fame, and Marnauli, where Georgian passport holders of the Muslim/Azerbaijani persuasion dwell. The Ahiska (or Meskhetian Turks) are a little more problematic, with Moscow insisting that these far-flung folks be repatriated to Georgia no matter what the result, such as a confrontation between Ahiskas and Armenians in the area known as Javakheti.

The same problem pertains outside of Georgia. Neighboring states—notably multinational Azerbaijan and to a lesser degree Turkey, Ukraine, and of course Russia itself—are all blessed or cursed with a plethora of ethnic minorities (Adygei, Balkars, Chechens, Dargins, et al.) who could theoretically make a play for ethnic self-determination based on the Abkhaz/Osset/Kosovar precedent.

Yes, the world has indeed turned, and many were blaming it all on Misha for having taken the Russian-cast bait—that is, if you could find any mainstream media attention to the "Georgia story" at all after, say, September 11, 2008, and the seven-year anniversary of another seismic event that just won't seem to go away.

By that date, a mere month after it went bang, the Olympics War had slid far off the front or even middle pages of the newspapers, due to the odd mixture of Wall Street meltdown and U.S. presidential election mud-slinging between Barack Obama and John McCain (not to mention Sarah "I understand Russia because I can see it from Alaska" Palin). Around the same time, Vladimir Putin was seen saving a TV team by snap-shooting a Siberian tiger with a dope-dart before tagging the beast and then kissing it on its way back into the taiga (while checking out a new natural gas line east to China and Japan). Misha Saakashvili took a break from the woes of his homeland to late-night it in Manhattan during the annual United Nations General Assembly meeting, showing up as the surprise guest at my pal Owen Matthews's book-bash, a Greenwich Village soirée for his family memoir, *Stalin's Children*, and there to watch the first Obama/McCain debate (which included an emotional salute from Senator McCain to Georgia's "great young president").[7]

The question, of course, is whether Misha can survive the events of August 2008. The disaster of the Russian–Georgian war makes him a target for external and internal enemies, and not only a heroic figure for those who need one. Neither assassination nor a berth as an adjunct professor-in-exile nor maturation as an international statesman who "baited the bear" and lived to tell the tale should be excluded from the range of future possibilities.

As for Georgia itself, whether geographically reduced as it has been today, or somehow expanded into someone's idea of ideal form or even obliterated from the map for some period of time as has happened before, thanks to its location and turbulent history, *Sakartvelo*—Georgia—will continue to exist, because its lovely yet lethargic, problematic yet poetic people insist that it do so, blood vendettas, *chacha*-ambushes, political chaos, and all.

I would dearly like to invoke Bertolt Brecht and his *Caucasian Chalk Circle* to close this epilogue in a fancy, literary manner, but the words fail me or seem too faint to create a corresponding echo.

Accordingly, let me end this opus with a deeply felt apology to anyone and everyone associated with this book:

Bodish vikhdi, Sakartvelo: Sorry that I never knew you well enough.

Thanks to all who taught me, thanks to all who sheltered me, and thanks to all who both taught and sheltered me, sometimes at once.

Cheers, and thank you.

Gaumarjos, Gmadlopt.

Notes

1. The most interesting item to come to the light of day, however, was a 100-gram sample of weapons grade uranium, as part of a sting operation mounted in January 2006. Saakashvili's security people managed to infiltrate a smuggling network and lured a North Ossetian by the name of Oleg Khintsagov to sell his "sample" for a million bucks to a cop posing as a Turkish bad-guy. Uncle Larry stumbled into a world exclusive on that story, which gave new meaning to the concept of "loose nukes," and revealed "Skin Valley" as a potential transit point thanks to the casual attitude of the local government toward crime of all sorts.

2. Even I got caught up in the ether attack: A day after I had arrived in Tbilisi, my primary e-mail address went dead. I later learned that someone had hacked into it and used it to send thousands of pieces of spam into the World Wide Web, forcing my U.S.-based server to pull the account and temporarily leave me in Internet hell, as I desperately set up new accounts on different servers in order to continue to file my 08.08.08 blog to the waiting world. Although I have no proof that I was specifically targeted by Russian hackers to disrupt my acting as an independent information source during the crisis, friends try to flatter me that it cannot have been a coincidence, particularly as I was filing out of the so-called Soros Building in downtown Tbilisi, where Lawrence's International Crisis Group office is located. Apparently, my Georgia Crisis "blogs" were getting quite a bit of play, and it was rather flattering when old friends and new fans checked in to ask if they could be included on the growing list, or pass the material on to others. One such message was from former U.S. ambassador to Georgia Richard Miles, who was a well-known if terse critic of Misha. I asked Lawrence if he wanted to say hello, and he took the occasion to ask Dick if he had "thought it might turn out like this." The response was typical Miles-speak: "Yes, I did."

3. Among his four-a-day articles, the indomitable Goble churned out what I think was one lemon, but one worth investigating. The thrust of the article (written long before the August 7 cell-phone interceptions revealed a Russian invasion launched before the first shots were fired on August 8) concerned how Vladimir Putin was bestowing medals of honor on diverse security personnel for their outstanding intelligence work that predicted the Georgian thrust into South Ossetia, and thus allowed Russia to counter that thrust in a timely manner. Citing discreet sources in Moscow, Goble posited that all the medals were undeserved, and that Moscow had been caught completely unawares by Saakashvili's nefarious plans: generals had been dismissed or were on vacation; Putin himself was in Beijing attending the Olympics when informed of the brewing trouble, and so on. All this, based on Moscow sources, is completely contradicted by the play of events, and suggests that an exceptionally nuance-sensitive observer got taken in by the finely tooled Russian press and propaganda machine on some level. Some weeks later, Goble posted a correction to another story he picked up from the Russian media, concerning the visit Dick Cheney made to Baku in early September to stiffen Azerbaijan's spine in the wake of the Georgia crisis. A source "inside the presidential apparatus" of Ilham Aliyev had been cited as saying that the U.S. vice president's meetings had been so sour that he had refused to show up for the grand dinner Aliyev was giving in his honor. It turned out that this "story" was

nothing more than a trial balloon—and only serves to illustrate how the Russian media had been enlisted in the war effort, including the aftermath.

4. The best guide to that subject is none other than the man whose visage appears on the fifty-dollar bill, namely, U.S. Grant, and as expressed in the first part of his *Personal Memoirs*. Grant, who served in President Polk's Mexican campaign, was an eyewitness to all the martial provocations that would force Mexico to retaliate against the U.S. army, and thus start the war that would end for him literally at the Halls of Montezuma. He was against it all from the start, declaring it to be just one big imperial set-up. "The occupation, separation and annexation were, from the inception of the movement until its consummation, a conspiracy to acquire territory out of which slave states might be formed for the American Union," he wrote. And more: "The Southern Rebellion was largely the outgrowth of the Mexican War. . . . Nations, like individuals, are punished for their transgressions. We got our punishment in the most sanguinary and expensive war of modern times."

5. For those with a historical turn of mind, all the arcane provisions were echoes of the event that dragged the Ottoman Empire into World War I on the side of Germany against England, France, and tsarist Russia. Two German cruisers, the Goeben and the Breslau, were fleeing the English fleet in the eastern Mediterranean and managed to get to Istanbul/Constantinople and deliver themselves as "gifts" from the Kaiser to the Sultan, whereupon they got reflagged and had all the officers and crew seconded to the Ottoman Turkish navy. They steamed up the Bosphorus and into the Black Sea to start bombing Russian coastal positions in the Crimea and elsewhere—and the heretofore quasi-neutral Ottomans suddenly found themselves at war on the side of the Germans, and bound for future partition.

6. Less than two months later, and thanks to the Wall Street meltdown, the price of a barrel of oil crashed from around $150 a barrel to well below the magic barrier of $70 that Russia needs to balance its budget. Whether this will deter Moscow from further mucking around in its backyard is another question.

7. For all my carping about a lack of media interest in the "Georgia story," it would appear that I myself was blind to what might be considered the most important and gratifying story to come out of Georgia in years: the release from prison of Anzor Sharmaidze, the alleged killer of Freddie Woodruff. It happened when my friend and Wall Street Journal correspondent Andrew Higgins, whom I had just seen in Turkey (where he was grousing about the meaninglessness of so many of his stories), arrived in Georgia after the events of August had almost gone cold. Looking for something to write about, he contacted me to ask what I thought about the Woodruff killing in light of the August war, and whether I thought it worthwhile taking a look at the (arguably) "first" Russian red line in the Caucasus. "Go boy, go," I urged him.

And go he did, dredging through the evidence collected by Anzor's angel, the American lawyer Michael Pullara, double checking with security types, and finally getting his long, meticulous story into print on October 18 2008, replete with a mug shot he had taken of an utterly emaciated Anzor in his prison cell. (http://online.wsj.com/article/SB122428609504746507.html). The article link was sent to me by several friends who knew of my interest in the story. What I did not learn until late December was that on October 27, 2008, Andrew was able to write a much shorter story—this one about the Georgian government's sudden decision to release Anzor into the custody of his family, apparently to take pressure off the government to launch a full-scale re-investigation into Freddie's murder (http://online.wsj.com/article/SB122506571169670511.html). Alas, the conviction still stands—but at least Anzor is out.

I would like to think that I had a little piece of rectifying this 15 year injustice by periodically trying to keep the story alive, but Mister Tenacity in this saga was Michael Pullara, and the journalist who actually got to make a difference was Andy Higgins.

Congratulations—you both have removed a small portion of the dead weight of cynicism from my jaded soul, and provided perhaps the only uplifting means of ending this book. Thanks.

Bibliography

The following list is less a bibliography than a rough guide to books on Georgia that are readily available in English. I have omitted all foreign language material, starting with Sevket Aydemir's *Suyu Arayan Adam* (Man Seeking Water), because even with the publisher's name (Remzi Kitabevi), most readers would be hard pressed to find a copy unless they happened to be in Istanbul, and could read Turkish. Likewise, Georgian, Russian, French, German, and Persian sources have been left out of the list, as have journal articles. The motivated reader will find abundant citations to this literature in the bibliographies of several of the more academic works listed below, such as those by Jones, Suny, and Derluguian. The bibliography does, however, include a few important works that are not about the Caucasus, such as the two books by Ernest Gellner, whose writings on nations and nationalism have *everything* to do with Georgia today.

Bird, Chris. *To Catch a Tartar*. John Murray Publishers, 2002.

Braund, David. *Georgian Antiquity*. Oxford University Press, 1994.

Conquest, Robert. *Stalin: Breaker of Nations*. Penguin, 1992.

Coppieters, Bruno and Robert Legvold, eds. *Statehood and Security: Georgia and the Rose Revolution*. MIT Press, 2005.

Coppieters, Bruno, David Darchiashvili, and Natella Akaba, eds. *Federal Practice: Exploring Alternatives for Georgia and Abkhazia*. VUB Brussels University Press, 2001.

Derluguian, Giorgi M. *Bourdieu's Secret Admirer in the Caucasus*. University of Chicago Press, 2005.

Gellner, Ernest. *Nationalism*. New York University Press, 1998.

———. *Nations and Nationalism*. Cornell University Press, 1983.

Goltz, Thomas. *Azerbaijan Diary*. M.E. Sharpe, 1998.

———. *Chechnya Diary*. St. Martin's Press/Thomas Dunne, 2003.

Hewitt, George. *The Abkhazians*. Curzon, 1999.

Hobsbawm, Eric. *The Age of Extremes*. Vintage, 1996.

———. *Nations and Nationalism Since 1780*. Cambridge University Press, 1990.

Jones, Stephen F. *Socialism in Georgian Colors*. Harvard University Press, 2005.

Karumidze, Zurab, and James V. Wertsch. *Enough! The Rose Revolution in the Republic of Georgia*. Nova Science, 2005.

Karny, Yo'av. *Highlanders*. Farrar, Straus and Giroux, 2000.

Kelly, Laurence. *Diplomacy and Murder in Tehran*. I.B. Tauris, 2006.

King, Charles. *The Black Sea: A History*. Oxford University Press, 2004.

Knight, Amy. *Beria: Stalin's First Lieutenant*. Princeton University Press, 1993.

Koestler, Arthur. *Darkness at Noon*. Vintage, 1994.

———. *The Thirteenth Tribe*. Random House, 1976.

Lang, David Marshall. *A Modern History of Soviet Georgia*. Greenwood, 1975.

Lermontov, Mikhail. *A Hero of Our Time* (many editions).

Maier, Frith, ed. *Vagabond Life: The Caucasus Journals of George Kennan*. University of Washington Press, 2003.

Martin, Terry. *The Affirmative Action Empire*. Cornell University Press, 2001.

Montefiore, Simon Sebag. *Stalin: The Court of the Red Tsar*. Randon House, 2004.

Nasmyth, Peter. *Georgia: In the Mountains of Poetry*. Routledge 2001.

———. *Walking in the Caucasus: Georgia*. Mta Publications (distributed by IB Tauris), 2006.

Ouspensky, P.D. *In Search of the Miraculous*. Harcourt, 1949.

Pope, Hugh. *Sons of the Conquerors*. Overlook, 2005.

Potier, Tim. *Conflict in Nagorno-Karabakh, Abkhazia and South Ossetia*. Springer, 2000.

Rayfield, Donald. *Stalin and His Hangmen*. Random House, 2004.

Rosen, Roger. *Georgia: Sovereign Country of the Caucasus*. Odyssey, 1999.

Said, Kurban. *Ali and Nino*. Random House, 2000.

Service, Robert. *Stalin*. Macmillan, 2004.

Shevardnadze, Eduard. *The Future Belongs to Freedom*. Sinclair-Stevenson, 1991.

Smith, Sebastian. *Allah's Mountains*. IB Tauris, 2005.

Steavenson, Wendell. *Stories I Stole from Georgia*. Atlantic Books, 2002.

Suny, Ronald Grigor. *The Baku Commune*. Princeton University Press, 1972.

———. *The Making of the Georgian Nation*. Second edition. Indiana University Press, 1994.

Tieke, W. *The German-Soviet War in the Caucasus, 1942–43*. J.J. Fedorowicz, 1995.

Tishkov, Valery. *Ethnicity, Nationalism and Conflict In and After the Soviet Union*. Sage, 1997.

Tolstoy, Leo. *Hadji Murad* (many editions).

Wheatley, Jonathan. *Georgia from National Awakening to Rose Revolution*. Ashgate, 2005.

Yagan, Murat. *I Come from Behind Kaf Mountain*. Threshold, 1984.

Index

British Petroleum (BP), x, 209, 229, 230, 244. *See also* Oil
Brown, Gordon, 285
Brown, Kenneth, 87, 131. *See also* U.S. State Department
Bucharest summit, 259, 262, 267
Bukharin, Nikolai, 36. *See also* Beria; Bolsheviks; Stalin
Bunne, John (U.S. Colonel), 214, 217
Bush, George H.W., xiii, xix, 52, 87, 159, 246
Bush, George W., xiii, xv, 233, 244, 246, 247, 258, 260, 275, 285
Tbilisi street named for, 264, 267, 276
Tbilisi visit of, 242–243
"Bush Doctrine", 253
Byzantine Empire, 20, 21, 22, 29, 56, 95

C

Campbell, Matthew, 3, 7
Carter, Billy, xiii
Caspian Sea, 25, 27, 31, 87
Catherine the Great, 24
Caucasian Chalk Circle (Brecht), 236, 249, 290–291
Caucasus Mountains, xxxi, 6, 25, 26, 27, 50, 57, 72, 81, 184, 190, 196, 198
Ceasefire agreement, in Russia-Georgia war, 266, 268, 273, 286
Central Intelligence Agency (CIA), xxxi, 85, 147
Chacha (Georgian moonshine), xxvi, 15, 16, 19, 56, 66, 70, 93, 104, 176–177, 246
Chachavadze, Ilya, 99
Chachua, Nana, 244, 282
Chachua, Nunu, xxx, 17, 18, 58, 64, 68, 72, 133, 136, 137, 141, 142, 153, 159, 160, 170, 177, 178, 184, 190, 197, 222, 230, 233–234, 244, 282
Chechen Lullaby, 279
Chechnya, xi, xxviii, 18, 71, 89, 91, 122, 123, 134, 135, 157, 162, 195–197, 227, 229, 245–246, 272
Cheney, Dick, 275, 292n3
Chorokhi (Choruh) River, 22, 108, 109, 116
Chtizia, Oktay, 219–222. *See also* Abkhaz Diaspora

Circassians, 26, 60, 61, 62, 63, 134, 148, 157, 219, 220, 227
CIA. *See* Central Intelligence Agency
CIS. *See* Commonwealth of Independent States
Clinton, President William, xiii, xv, 51,87, 131–132, 204
CNN News, 13, 52, 81, 285
Coalition of the Willing, 244, 257
Colchis, 19, 105
Commonwealth of Independent States (CIS), xxi, 6, 65, 183, 195, 196, 200, 203, 205, 206, 207
Peace-Keeping Force (CISPKF), xxi, 212, 254, 262–263
See also Russia
Communism. *See* Bolsheviks; Mensheviks; Union of Soviet Socialist Republics (USSR)
Confederation of the Mountain Peoples of the Caucasus, 60, 62, 134. *See also* Circassians
Constantinople, 20, 29
Cossacks, 135, 157
Council of Europe, xiv
Crimea, 26, 181
Crimean Tatars, 122
Custer, George Armstrong, 50, 161
Czechoslovakia, 93

D

Davidadze, Marina, 211, 221, 244
David the Builder, 22
Derluguian, Georgi, 40, 43, 53, 54
Dmanisi, ancient Georgian archeological site of, 95
Dragadze, Tamara, 44, 54
Dudayev, General Djohar, 18, 89, 196. *See also* Chechnya
Dzerzhinskii, Felix, 35, 40
Dzhugashvili, Iosif, xi, 28. *See also* Stalin

E

Elbrus, 152. *See also* Caucasus Mountains
Elchibey Abulfaz (Aliyev), 89
Engels, Friedrich, 28
Escudero, Stanley, 286–287

Thomas Goltz has written news, features and Op-Eds for most leading U.S. publications, ranging from the *New York Times, Los Angeles Times, Wall Street Journal,* and *Washington Post* to *The Nation* on the Left and *Soldier of Fortune* on the Right. His *Azerbaijan Diary* (M.E. Sharpe 1998) has been hailed as "essential reading for all post-Sovietologists." The second book in his post-Soviet triptych on the Caucasus was *Chechnya Diary,* published by St. Martin's Press/Thomas Dunne in September 2003. The third and last book in the series is *Georgia Diary.* A memoir about his days as an itinerant actor in Africa in the late 1970s, *Assassinating Shakespeare*, was issued by Saqi Books, London, in 2006. Born in Japan in 1954, Goltz grew up in North Dakota, and has been a Montana resident since 1978. In 2005 he was appointed Visiting Scholar in the newly created Central and Southwest Asia Studies Program at the University of Montana in Missoula. He currently teaches at Montana State University in Bozeman.